WRITING IN ORGANIZATIONS

WRITING IN ORGANIZATIONS

PURPOSES, STRATEGIES, AND PROCESSES

PEGGY MAKI
Beaver College

CAROL SCHILLING
University of Pennsylvania

McGraw-Hill Book Company

New York   St. Louis   San Francisco   Auckland   Bogotá   Hamburg
Johannesburg   London   Madrid   Mexico   Milan   Montreal   New Delhi
Panama   Paris   São Paulo   Singapore   Sydney   Tokyo   Toronto

Library of Congress Cataloging-in-Publication Data

Maki, Peggy.
  Writing in organizations.

  Bibliography: p.
  1. English language—Rhetoric. 2. English language—
Business English. 3. Communication in organizations.
I. Schilling, Carol. II. Title.
PE1479.B87M34 1987   808′.066651   86-10277
ISBN 0-07-030361-4

WRITING IN ORGANIZATIONS: PURPOSES, STRATEGIES, AND PROCESSES

1 2 3 4 5 6 7 8 9 0 DOC DOC 8 9 8 7 6

ISBN 0-07-030361-4

This book was set in Times Roman by Automated Composition Service, Inc.
The editors were Emily G. Barrosse and Barry Benjamin; the designer
was Scott Chelius; the production supervisor was Joe Campanella.
The drawings were done by Volt Information Sciences, Inc.
R. R. Donnelley & Sons Company was printer and binder.

About the Author

PEGGY MAKI is Assistant Professor and Chair of the English, Theatre Arts, and Communications Department at Beaver College where she teaches writing courses in the Writing Across the Curriculum program, undergraduate and graduate courses in professional writing, and in theories of written communication, the teaching of writing, and linguistics. She has also directed the College's Writing Center. Since 1981 she has been on the faculty of NEH summer institutes in the teaching of writing and has consulted with colleges, universities, and elementary and secondary schools as they developed writing programs. She has served on the faculty of several colleges and universities and developed workshops on professional writing for government, business, industry, and health organizations. In 1983 she was Chair of the Eastern Regional ABCA Conference. She has delivered papers at CCCC, national and international ABCA Conferences, the Penn State Conference on Rhetoric and Composition, NEMLA, the International Conference on Computers in the Humanities, the Mid-American Linguistics Conference, and the Penn Linguistics Colloquium. In 1984 she received the Lindback Award for Distinguished Teaching.

CAROL SCHILLING served as Assistant Professor of English at Beaver College while teaching the writing course from which this text grew. She worked with the Beaver College faculty to create its Writing Across the Curriculum program and taught graduate and undergraduate courses in cross-disciplinary and professional writing, literature, and theories of written communication. She is currently teaching courses in writing, the humanities, and literature at the University of Pennsylvania in the College of Arts and Sciences and the School of Engineering and Applied Sciences. At Penn, she has been designated a Senior Fellow and a Research Fellow in the Writing Across the University Program, for which she has researched and designed writing courses and worked with faculty, TAs, and students in the Wharton, Engineering, and Arts and Sciences schools. She has studied literature and rhetoric and has a diverse background in teaching, which has included appointments in several colleges and universities. She has served as a consultant to NEH summer institutes in writing, and she has presented papers at MLA, CCCC, the International ABCA Conference, and the Penn State Conference on Rhetoric and Composition.

TO OUR FAMILIES
WITH EVERLASTING THANKS
FOR THEIR SUSTAINED
AND CHEERFUL SUPPORT

CONTENTS

CHAPTER 7
WRITING CORRESPONDENCE 148

CHAPTER 8
A WRITER AT WORK: A CASE STUDY OF COMPOSING A LETTER 176

SECTION FOUR
STRATEGIES FOR WRITING INSTRUCTIONS, DIRECTIVES, AND OTHER PROCEDURAL DOCUMENTS

"It would be easy to describe the courses of lectures that have been read to classes, and methods of conducting the critical exercises in composition. But how insufficient do all these appear to account for what we see [students] do when [they pass] from the rudiments at school to responsible writing in the real work of life."

Edward Tyrell Channing

Lectures Read to the Seniors
in Harvard College (1856)

PREFACE

Background: Principles and Practices

This book has grown out of our experiences teaching an advanced writing course at Beaver College. Our goal for this course has been to prepare juniors and seniors to make the transition from writing as students to writing as professionals. Our aim is to challenge students to transfer their growing expertise in their chosen disciplines to the kinds of problems and issues they will encounter during their professional lives. We emphasize that writing enables students to translate their understanding *of* the world into what we hope will be useful and responsible actions *in* the world, where words and actions are linked.

Like our course, this book focuses on principles of rhetoric, problem solving, and critical thinking that apply to composing various organizational documents. As we developed the course, we were immensely fortunate to be able to participate in cross-disciplinary faculty seminars in teaching writing which the National Endowment for the Humanities sponsored at Beaver College. These seminars introduced us to a remarkable array of scholars and writers from several disciplines who taught us recent theories of language, discourse, composing, and critical thinking, as well as ancient and modern theories of rhetoric.

As we applied these theories, which were rapidly being absorbed by freshman composition courses and texts, to our professional writing course, we conducted our own first-hand investigation of writing that occurs in organizational settings. As we taught and shaped our courses over the years, we discovered we had accumulated the makings of a book that could enable others to put current research into practice. The first five chapters of this book introduce the principles that inform our teaching of writing; the remaining ten chapters apply those principles to particular kinds of writing.

Collaborative Writing

As we surveyed organizational writing, we quickly discovered that documents composed in organizations are frequently the products of two or more writers—often from different disciplines—working together. Such collaborative efforts are more successful when participants can listen to and accommodate different points of view. As a result, we guide students through various strategies for working and writing together. For example, throughout this book, we teach students how to review each other's work in progress. We also introduce them to some principles of working together to produce a single document with a multiple authorship. Although Chapter 15—''Writing Collaboratively''—is the final chapter, the principles in it can be applied to any genre of writing at any point in the course.

Classifying Organizational Writing

Our readers may wonder why we have included genres of professional writing under the rubric of organizational writing. One reason is our discovery that no matter what careers our students choose, the common shaper of their writing will be the organizational setting in which they work. Although it is difficult to replicate the context of organizational writing in classrooms, we can recreate some of its essential features. For example, we have found two useful ways to simulate work-sponsored writing. First, we have directed students to work on problems and issues within their own fields or on their own campuses. Second, we have emphasized the rhetorical principles of writing *to various readers, for various purposes*, and *within various situational contexts*.

We have further classified organizational writing according to both its rhetorical purposes and its conventional genres. The latter include letters, memos, instructions, directives, reports, and proposals. We found that the conventional genres of workplace writing frequently overlap. For example, a ''report'' may follow the format for long, formal reports or it may be more like a memo.

We also discovered that documents classified under different genres, or even covered in different courses, can share some important rhetorical principles. For example, directives are considered a form of ''business'' writing carried out by executives, while instructions are usually considered a form of ''technical'' writing carried out by engineers. Yet both kinds of writing follow the rhetorical principles of writing that instructs. In addition, engineers work within organizational contexts and often carry out executive functions—such as writing directives.

For these reasons, we have initially classified the documents considered in Chapters 6 through 14 according to four commonly accepted genres—correspondence, directions, reports, and proposals—and we have then classified the documents within each genre according to their primary and secondary purposes—to express, inform, explore, document, instruct, and persuade).

Processes of Writing

In addition to emphasizing the organizational context that both generates and shapes career writing, we pay careful attention to the *processes of composing* documents intended to fulfill a particular purpose. We frequently show a composing process in slow motion and pause to consider both large and small steps, often recursive ones, along the way. We also stop to suggest an array of strategies for managing the complexities of that process. As a result, we often make these "steps" look more discrete than they often are in practice.

Our readers may wonder if the models of composing we present, workable though they are for classroom writing, are realistic for career writing. After all, deadlines, a mainstay of life in organizations, shorten and simplify any writer's process. Our own observations support the research that concludes that writers in an organization frequently write only one draft. Yet many documents go through numerous drafts, including several reviews and extensive revisions, before being sent.

Furthermore, we have learned that when writers tackle a new genre of writing or write about a new problem or issue, they compose more slowly than when they write in familiar modes about familiar subjects. Since we introduce students to new genres and new problems to solve, we find that slowing down the process is pedagogically wise. We tell our students, however, that as they become more experienced, they will collapse the detailed process that we outline.

An overview of processes of composing and problem solving is introduced in the first five chapters of this book. Chapters 7, 8, 10, 11, 13, and 14 show individual writers shaping their own composing processes in accordance with their experiences, talents, and intuitions as they write within the constraints of deadlines, policies, and the vagaries of life in organizations.

Acknowledgments

Transferring our actual classroom interactions onto paper and making our principles and practices accessible to others has been a lengthy and challenging process. Along the way, we discovered that we couldn't have managed without extensive collaboration—first of all, with each other. We have also benefited from the compelling responses of our students and the generosity of our colleagues, reviewers, and publisher.

We have borrowed from the thinking and research of many teachers and scholars. Their work has reached us through the media of printed pages, university and faculty seminars (including ones sponsored by the National Endowment for the Humanities in 1979, 1980, and 1981 and by the Fund for the Improvement of Post-Secondary Education in 1982 and 1983), lectures, conference presentations, and conversations. Many of those we name already know how indebted we are to them; others may be surprised to find their names listed here. Those whose work has been particularly helpful include Kenneth Bruffee, Edward P. J. Corbett, Peter Elbow, Linda Flower, M. A. K. Halliday and Rugaiya Hasan, Maxine Hairston, John R. Hayes, E. D. Hirsch, James Kinneavy, Richard Lanham, Walter Ong, Joseph Williams, and Richard Young. Our colleagues at Beaver College have been a sustained source of ideas and expertise. We thank Elaine Maimon for encouraging us in our triple endeavors of teaching, researching, and writing. We have benefited from her leadership in the teaching of writing, especially her exploration of relationships between writing and thinking. We would also like to thank our resident philosopher, Barry O'Connor, social scientists Elizabeth Clark, Edith Gross, Norman Johnston, and Barbara Nodine for sharing their expertise when we called on them. Suzanne Kinard of the Atwood Library also contributed her informed assistance. We are especially grateful to Maryanne Bowers of the English Department for reading a draft of our manuscript thoughtfully and critically and for testing it in her classes.

In addition, our publisher provided us with several rounds of reviews from the time we began generating ideas until we had a finished manuscript. We continue to appreciate the efforts and suggestions of all our reviewers: Vivian Davis, Joseph Dunne, Larry Fiber, Robert Gieselman, Earl Harbert, Dennis Kawaharada, Gloria Lewis, Robin Bell Markels, Elaine Palm, Thomas Reigstad, Philip Rubins, Kathryn Seidel, Jack Selzer, Annette Shelby, and Michele Souda. Their range of responses enlightened us as we worked.

Several organizations opened their doors to us, allowing us to observe, question, and sometimes work with their managers and staff. We appreciate their cooperation and trust. In particular, we thank AMP Incorporated, especially Yvonne Walko; Leeds & Northrup Systems, especially Robert Manne, Joe Peca, Kenneth Creech, and Sumner Peirce; Nashua Corporation; McNeil Consumer Products Co., especially Johanna Jones; Pacer Systems, Inc., especially Dee McCornac; the Pennsylvania Department of Consumer Affairs, especially Mary Saylor; and RCA-Americom, especially Charles Church and Rodney Stevens.

Over the years our students in Writing for Careers (EN/BA 215) have illuminated our work more than they may realize. A number of them, currently successful writers in organizations, have kept in touch and shared their work with us. We offer a special thanks to Gayle Assetto, Wanda Burke, Michele DiCarlo, Suzanne Eckert, Marie Lawrence, Andrew Leschak, Gena Recigno, Lynn Rogers, and Mimi Seyfert for allowing us to include their classroom and work-sponsored writing in this text.

Carol Lynn Daly and Gale Trusky have our thanks for relieving us of some of the typing chores.

The editorial staff at McGraw-Hill remained committed to what turned out to be a complex project. Phillip Butcher, editor-in-chief for social science and humanities texts in the College Division, got our project under way. Emily Barrosse, our sponsoring editor, and Barry Benjamin, the area editing supervisor, made thoughtful suggestions and practiced extraordinary patience as we moved from drafts to final copy. Mel Haber, art director, initiated novices into the *art* of textbook production. We are grateful to the entire McGraw-Hill staff for their sensitivity and professionalism.

Finally, we thank our extended and combined families for their remarkable good humor and generous spirits. Above all, Elizabeth, Carl, Ron, Andrew, David, and Lee provided delightful distractions, necessary support, occasional free labor and advice, and constant cooperation during the course of this project.

Peggy Maki
Carol Schilling

PRINCIPLES
SECTION ONE

PURPOSES, STRATEGIES, AND PROCESSES

CHAPTER

1

AN INTRODUCTION TO WRITING IN ORGANIZATIONS

THE COMMUNICATION PROCESS AT WORK

The director of a county-sponsored recreation program for teenage girls needs to evaluate its success and determine the budget request for the following year. The director asks her staff assistant, a recent college graduate, to assess the community sports programs and report her findings and recommendations. The assistant reviews all the available records. She notes enrollments, attendance, and payment of dues. She interviews the adult leaders and coaches, observes an after-school session, and talks to some of the girls. She calls neighborhood schools to discover whether they offer competing programs. The assistant reviews her notes and summarizes both her findings and recommendations in a memo report to her boss. Later, the program director will incorporate information from her assistant's memo into an annual report on community programs, a report she submits to the county commissioners.

An accountant for a commercial construction firm receives a memo from his organization's comptroller asking him to investigate a financial problem. Present costs for constructing an office complex have exceeded the estimates. Why, the comptroller wants to know, have costs risen? The accountant reviews internal records regarding the project. After checking current costs of building materials and labor, he reviews the status of the project. His investigation reveals several probable causes of the problem, including the rising costs of materials and the delays caused by changes in the original design. With this information in hand, the accountant plans, drafts, and revises an inter-office memo informing the comptroller about the causes of the rising costs. He documents each cause with supporting data. Following company policy, he also sends copies of the memo to the corporate treasurer and president.

The administrative systems analyst for a manufacturer of communications equipment is troubled by an organizational problem he has observed. His company is composed of a baffling number of departments, many of which do not communicate directly with each other; nor do they always understand each other's functions. The systems analyst has discovered that when a problem occurs within one department, its members seldom know what organizational resources they can turn to. In addition, the company is so large that its employees do not always know where to find basic information about personnel and procedures. As a result, the analyst decides that the company needs an organizational directory that not only lists personnel, departments, and resources, but also outlines policies and procedures.

He writes a memo proposing his idea to the appropriate manager. The manager supports the idea but asks how the systems analyst plans to proceed. The analyst and manager write a series of memos to one another until they agree on a procedural strategy. Once they do, the systems analyst writes memos to department heads to solicit their help and assembles a team of writers from a cross section of the organizational hierarchy. This team collates and verifies information it receives from each department. The team then decides how to organize and present this information in a useful guide. Each member of the group is assigned to write certain sections of the directory, which the team reviews and revises together. As the systems analyst directs this enormous collaborative writing project, he manages both people and the words they write.

The writers in these three scenarios wrote with a purpose in mind. Each one made an effort to solve a problem occurring within an organization. The purposes of their writing and the problems they were solving differed somewhat in each case. The first writer primarily needed to inform the directors of her organization about its routine operations. The second writer aimed at exploring the causes of a problem. The third writer first had to persuade his reader that a problem existed, and then had to write a directory that both informed employees about the organizational structure and instructed them on ways to use it. Yet the documents that everyone wrote share a larger common purpose: to further some specific organizational goals.

The Situational Context

The writing that people compose daily in organizations, whether it is directed to readers within the organization or those on the outside, is shaped primarily by its *situational context.* This term refers largely to the *setting* in which communication takes place. But the word also indicates the *timing* of an act of communication and its *background.* The background can include the history of the issue under consideration, the relationship between the reader and the writer, and the experiences they have previously had in addressing one another. You saw the influences of the situational context in the three scenarios you read. It affected the three writers' purposes for writing, the content of their writing, the kinds of documents they wrote, and their processes of composing those documents.

The setting

The kinds of writing that you will explore in this book are defined by the organizational setting in which they are composed or to which they are being sent. While organizations take various forms, they always consist of people who coordinate their activities and exchange resources to reach a goal. Some organizations, such as partnerships, may consist of only two or three people, while other organizations contain hundreds of thousands of employees. Their specific goals also vary. These organizations can produce products, such as computers, pharmaceuticals, books, or toys; or they can provide services, such as legal assistance, health care, or counseling. Organizations can be as complex as multinational corporations and government agencies or as simple as a barber shop. The college or university you are attending is itself a highly complex organization.

Once you graduate, most of the career writing you do will be defined by its particular organizational setting. The organization might be public or private, profit or nonprofit, large or small. You are even likely to find yourself working, as an employee or volunteer, in several organizations at once. All of them will depend on your verbal expertise to help them accomplish their goals.

As a college student moving closer to graduation, you can use this book to help you make the transition from writing in a classroom setting to writing outside a classroom. Begin by thinking about how the academic setting you are now a part of affects the writing you compose. Academic writing serves the goals of higher education: to create and exchange knowledge. As students, you write primarily to learn and to prove that you have learned information and skills pertaining to special areas of knowledge. Examinations, biology laboratory reports, psychology case studies, essays of literary criticism, and economic market analyses exemplify some of the kinds of writing that meet those goals. Sometimes you make your own discoveries and inform others about them.

Like academic writing, workplace writing can help you clarify your ideas and allow others to judge your abilities. Organizational writing also aims at informing readers. However, its primary purpose is to motivate people and, thereby, accomplish work. To meet this goal, a large portion of organizational writing is sent to keep channels of communication open. These channels are needed between individuals, between divisions within an organization, and between representatives of an organization and outsiders.

A striking difference between academic writing and work-sponsored writing exists between you and your readers. Your professors are obligated to read your

A Sequence of Replies

First letter: Your letter of January 19 alerted us to the error in your
                       December bill.

Second letter: We were disappointed to learn that, in spite of our efforts,
                       your December bill is still in error.

Third letter: The observation that "To err is human" may be no comfort
                       to you at this time, but it is all we have to keep us going.

Figure 1-1   The situational context.
The replies above are the first sentences in three separate letters of apology to a customer.
Explain how the situational context influenced each reply.

writing. They are captive, if not always captivated, readers. However, readers at
work can lack the time or motivation to read your writing, unless your message
and presentation compel them.

Timing and background

Although its setting primarily defines the writing in this book, other aspects of the
situational context also shape organizational writing. Timing and timeliness are
foremost. For example, they lead to the practice of sending short memos. Some
issues demand a quick response; some kinds of information rapidly become obsolete and need regular updating.

   Timing and background also influence the way to respond to particular readers. Figure 1-1 illustrates this influence with a series of replies to a disgruntled
customer. Notice how the timing of each reply and the background—of both the
issue and the previous communications between the reader and the writer—affected
the way the writer composed the first sentence in each new response letter to the
customer.

Elements of the Communication
Process

Whatever the circumstances, communicating with others is risky. The process is
charged with complexities that can cause misunderstandings. However, envisioning how the communication process works, along with practicing how to use it,
can reduce our risks.

   Acts of communication begin with a primary purpose, take place within a
particular context, and engage four main elements:

THE WRITER
THE READER
THE SUBJECT OR ISSUE
THE MEDIUM, SUCH AS A WRITTEN DOCUMENT

The writer

We project a part of ourselves as we write; readers draw inferences about us as they read. For example, readers can infer that we are authoritative, submissive, serious, careless, objective, confident, contrite, enthusiastic, indifferent. As a result, we need to think about the way we want to project ourselves in a piece of writing. We quickly need to establish who we are and what our relationship is to our readers, or what relationship we are trying to establish.

Answering questions about the "self" you want to project can help you decide how to present your message, especially how to create an appropriate tone of voice. For example, a request worded, "I want your report on Wednesday morning" or "Bring me the results by 3 o'clock" indicates that the writer has authority over the reader. The verbs give clear commands; the tone is direct, matter-of-fact, and unapologetic. Adding "please" or a conditional verb, such as "would" or "could," tones down the request and indicates that the writer does not have authority over the reader. Developing sensitivity to the connotations of words will help you project the "self" you need to project in a particular message (see Figure 1-2).

The reader

The art of writing begins with finding the words to represent what is in your head. But effective writers don't stop there. They also think about *how to convey* their message to particular readers. For that reason, thoughtful writers try to imagine their readers. These writers speculate about what readers already know, what their motivation is for reading or acting on a message, and what use they will make of a particular document. The following chart includes many of the important questions writers keep in mind as they write to others:

Questions writers ask about their readers

What is my reader's *knowledge* of this issue?

- Does my reader understand why I am writing to him or her?
- Do I need to explain my purpose first?
- Do I need to remind my reader that I am responding to a previous communication?
- How familiar is my reader with the facts and the issues?

Dear Professor Keyes,

In our conference on October 27th we discussed the required speech course, Speech Communications 201. Specifically, I spoke to you about challenging the course and receiving credit for it based on my extensive professional experience as a public speaker.

I have enclosed several letters documenting some of the occasions when I have spoken publicly. These include conducting training sessions for groups ranging from twelve to several hundred people. Please feel free to call the individuals who have provided these letters.

This speech course is the only course I have challenged in my four years at this university. I hope you will give my request careful consideration.

Thank you for taking the time to talk with me last week and for reviewing this issue.

Sincerely yours,

Figure 1-2   Request letter.
List three or four adjectives that describe the ''self'' the writer projects in this letter. Locate the specific words and phrases that lead you to describe the writer as you do. What kind of relationship between the writer and reader does the letter suggest? What words or other elements of the writing, such as content and organization, suggest that relationship?

- Is my reader inside the organization and knowledgeable about its goals, or do I first have to represent my organization and its goals?

What is my reader's *motivation* for reading this document?

- Can I assume that because I am interested in this issue my reader is also?
- How important will my reader think this document is?
- How much time is my reader likely to spend reading it?
- Has my reader been waiting to hear from me or about this issue? How long?
- Is my reader expecting favorable or unfavorable news?
- What is my reader's preconception of my organization or me? How is that preconception likely to affect the way my reader will respond to a message from me or the organization I represent?

What *use* will my reader make of this document?

- Will my reader read it once and throw it away?
- Will my reader discuss it with others? With whom?
- Will this document assist my reader and others in making a decision?
- Will my reader file this document for future reference?
- Will this document be used frequently as a ready reference to help readers carry out a procedure?
- Will my reader refer to it while writing another document?
- Will it be used to evaluate my job performance?

Some readers are difficult to write to, especially ones who don't know about the issue or subject at hand, who are unmotivated to learn more about it, and who don't know what use they'll make of the information you give them. However, you can anticipate writing to these readers frequently. In fact, once you leave college, you will usually write to readers who are less knowledgeable than you are about the subject or issue you're writing about.

When you write mostly about what concerns your reader, you send a "you" message. Such messages focus on why *you*—the reader—want to read them rather than on why *I*—the writer—want to send them. Such writing motivates readers to read. It anticipates readers' questions, presents information in the order that readers need to see it, and either uses words that readers understand or defines the unfamiliar words.

Linda Flower, who researches the processes people use when they compose, calls writing a "you" message "reader-based" writing. Read the apology in Figure 1-3 and determine whether it conveys more information about why the reader wants to read it or about why the writer wants to write it.

Dear Ms. Stevens,

Last month we changed the procedures for recording the payments of our credit card customers. Making this change taxed our small office, but we now have a computerized system which promises to be more convenient and accurate. Your payment notice arrived as we were changing the system and, unfortunately, was not recorded. That explains why you received a payment due notice from us even though you did indeed pay your bill.

I apologize for this error. We have now credited your account with your payment of $145.00.

I hope you will give us an opportunity to be of better service to you in the future.

Sincerely,

Figure 1-3   An apology.
Discuss how effectively this apology focuses on the reader's concerns. Underline the information the reader wants to know first. Is the order of information primarily "reader-based" or "writer-based"? Is there any information that is likely to concern the writer more than the reader? Should you rewrite the letter to make it more "reader-based"? If you think so, rewrite it.

The subject or issue

The first two elements of the communication process, the writer and the reader, concern people. The third element pertains to things: the material, observable world and the issues it engenders. Sometimes, as in the case of a biography or a personnel report, the subject of a message *is* a person. But in those cases writers are not communicating *with*, but *about*, the person. The subject of a message is, quite simply, what it is about.

In the scenarios that opened this chapter, you read about writers dealing with different subjects: an after-school sports program, the cost overruns on a construction site, and an idea for improving intra-organizational communications. Writers in workplaces, unlike many student writers, seldom search for a subject to write about. Like the assistant to the director of the recreation program and the accountant described in the beginning of this chapter, organizational writers are often told what to write about. Like the systems analyst, other writers in organizations discover the subjects they *need* to write about as problems occur. In Chapter 2 you will read more about how the subjects of organizational communications are generated.

The medium or the written document

The medium refers to the means a writer uses to present a message. Written and spoken media depend on language—which writers arrange and style in appropriate ways to serve a document's purpose. Visual media include photographs, illustrations, graphs, films, television broadcasts, and the plastic arts. The medium of communication you will explore in this book is the written document. However, even written documents often include visual media. The media, or types, of organizational documents include memos, letters, instructions, directives, reports, and proposals.

Each of these documents follows a general format. Later chapters will show you the formats followed in specific kinds of organizational writing. However, these formats vary somewhat from organization to organization. Some organizations have even developed their own guide books for writing organizational documents. When you write on the job, you are likely to see why the prescribed formats serve the goals and procedures of your place of work. However, if you find the customary formats unwieldy or counterproductive, you can recommend changes.

THE PURPOSES OF WRITING AT WORK

You can recall these four elements of the communication process to help you define and focus on your primary purpose as you write. Of course, whenever you write, you engage all four of these elements—yourself, your reader, the subject matter, and the language and media you are using. However, writers usually *emphasize* one of these elements more than the others in any particular piece of writing. The element the writer emphasizes, or aims at, and the purpose the writing serves are linked. For example, when you focus on yourself, the writer, your writing serves the purpose of self-expression. When you emphasize your reader, your writing has a persuasive aim. When you highlight the subject matter, rather than your own or your readers' responses to it, you can aim to instruct or inform about, explore, or document some aspect of that subject. Such writing is often called *expository* or *explanatory*. When you emphasize the medium, itself, such as language, you can create artistic or entertaining writing, such as a poem, a play, a story.

Organizational writing tends to emphasize the reader and the subject matter. As a result, you will find that most organizational communications serve persuasive and expository aims more than the others. The following table summarizes the primary purposes and kinds of organizational writing.

PRIMARY EMPHASIS	PRIMARY PURPOSE	KIND OF WRITING
Writer	To Express	Expressive
Reader	To Persuade	Persuasive
Subject	To Instruct	Instructive
	To Inform	Informative
	To Explore	Exploratory
	To Document, or prove	Documentary

Of course, many pieces of writing share multiple purposes. For example, a letter of application aims primarily to persuade a reader to call the applicant for an interview. However, the letter also informs the reader about the writer's background and experiences while expressing the writer's goals, interests, and personality. These latter two aims—to inform and to express—are important, but subordinate.

Once you rank your purposes for writing, you can ask yourself questions about how to accomplish your purposes. In the application letter, for example, you can ask yourself, "What would best convince the reader to call me for an interview?" Chances are that a chronological narration of your background would not be convincing. Instead, you could begin by selecting the specific skills you have that best match the ones needed for the job you are applying for. Writing a narrative of your experiences without highlighting the ones that would interest your reader has an expressive aim rather than a persuasive one.

Similarly, venting your emotions or deluging your readers with your opinions can be psychologically satisfying for you, but not necessarily persuasive to your readers.

General Features of Organizational Writing

If you know what your main purpose is, you will be more able to stay on track as you compose. That is, the purpose of a document tends to shape its focus, content, organization, and style. The table that appears below outlines the general features that are characteristic of the kinds of writing introduced in this book. Naturally, when a document shares more than one purpose, the writing can exhibit features from more than one aim. Generally speaking, however, the features of the primary aim will dominate. In later chapters, you will observe writers applying the rough guidelines in the following table as they write specific documents.

GENERAL FEATURES OF WRITING FOR EACH PURPOSE

Purpose: To *Express*

Focus:	the response of the *writer* or the *writer's organization* to the subject or issue under discussion (the "I" or "we" in the writing)
Content:	feelings, opinions, beliefs, values, goals, ideologies, personal experiences
Strategies for Arrangement:	narrating, listing, free associating, developing chronologies and analogies
Vocabulary and Style:	connotative, personal, exclamatory
Example:	An Expressive Sentence I'm disappointed that the committee tabled our report until the next meeting.

Purpose: To *Persuade*

Focus:	the *reader's responses* to the issue or subject under discussion (the "you" in the writing)
Content:	appeals to the reader's logic facts, lists, numerical data, verifiable observations and testimonials appeals to the reader's emotions shared beliefs and opinions, conventional wisdom, maxims, proverbs, stereotypes, sympathetic expressions, emotive testimonials

Strategies for
Arrangement: vary greatly depending on whether the writer appeals primarily to the reader's logic or emotions

Vocabulary
and Style: appeals to the reader's emotions
    connotative, exclamatory, frequently superlative, can feature word play, grammatical flexibility, rhymes, and rhythmic phrases and sentences
  appeals to the reader's logic
    denotative, objective

Example: A Persuasive Sentence
If you wish to avoid meeting during the summer months, prepare to vote on the subcommittee's report during our April meeting.

Purpose: To *Instruct*

Focus: directions that help the *reader* understand how the *subject* works (both the "it" and the "you" in the writing)

Content: concrete operations, abstract concepts

Strategies for
Arrangement: sequencing, analyzing, describing, making analogies

Vocabulary
and Style: denotative, objective, highly reader-based (thus, sometimes familiar, sometimes technical)

Example: An Instructive Sentence
To prepare for the next meeting of the Curriculum Committee, please take the following steps:
- Review the enclosed report.
- Speak to your departments about it.
- Write down suggested revisions.
- Bring them to the next committee meeting on April 25.

Purpose: To *Inform*

Focus: the *subject* or *issue* under discussion (the "it" in the writing)

Content: facts, data, new information, comprehensive coverage

Strategies for
Arrangement: classifying, defining, supporting claims and generalizations

with specific information, comparing, analyzing, describing, synthesizing

Vocabulary
and Style: denotative, objective

Example: An Informative Sentence
On March 23, the Curriculum Committee tabled the report from the subcommittee on Majors in the Humanities.

Purpose: To *Explore*

Focus: questions and speculations about the *subject* or *issue* (the ''it'' in the writing)

Content: questions, speculations, observations, facts

Strategies for
Arrangement: asking questions then suggesting answers, indentifying problems then surveying solutions, identifying problems then seeking causes, proposing solutions then anticipating effects

Vocabulary
and Style: denotative, objective, often conditional constructions, such as ''if . . . then . . .''

Example: An Exploratory Sentence
Perhaps the Curriculum Committee voted to table the subcommittee's report because members needed more time to discuss it in their departments.

Purpose: To *Document*

Focus: the verification of facts concerning the *subject* or *issue* (the ''it'' in the writing)

Content: facts, numerical data, verifiable observations

Strategies for
Arrangement: categorizing, listing, sequencing, enumerating, alphabetizing, describing procedures, defining, proceeding inductively

Vocabulary
and Style: denotative, objective, especially appropriate for readers with expertise in the subject or issue

Example: A Documentary Sentence
According to the minutes of the March 23d meeting, the Curriculum Committee tabled the report prepared by the subcommittee on Majors in the Humanities by a vote of 7 to 4.

EXPLORING THREE CASES OF THE COMMUNICATION PROCESS AT WORK

This chapter has presented writing as a process of communication that the writer shapes by taking the context, the reader, the subject, and the purpose of a document into consideration.

We have especially stressed the need for writers to keep their readers and purposes in mind. One way to practice this skill is to role-play the reader—that is, to imagine how you would respond to a particular message if you were the reader in the set of circumstances that prompted the message. You can practice on the letters printed in the three cases below. As you read the following letters, put yourself in the place of their readers. Judge whether the writers asked all the questions they needed to about the purpose of their letters, their relationship to their readers, and their readers' motivations for reading the messages. A checklist of all these questions appears at the end of this chapter.

Case One: A Request

A college junior wrote the inquiry letter printed below to the personnel director in a state agency. As you read the student's letter, identify the following elements: her primary purpose; her way of representing herself to her reader; and the assumptions she makes about her reader's knowledge, authority, and motivations to read and reply to the message.

Last summer I worked as a laboratory assistant for the State Department of Agriculture. I would like to work there again this summer. But after asking my former supervisor about returning to the same job, I was told that I must first take an examination for laboratory assistants.

I knew nothing about this test until now, and no one from the office where I worked told me about it. I was away at college and no one tried to get in touch with me.

Will you please let me know if this test really is necessary for me to take since I am an experienced laboratory assistant? Also, how I can arrange to take it if I have to?

It is extremely important for me to work during the summer so that I can pay my tuition in the fall. Without a summer job, I will not be able to finish my senior year.

Your help is greatly appreciated.

If your friend wrote this letter and asked you for your advice, what suggestions would you give her? Would you advise her to send it as it is? What exactly was her purpose? What did she want to motivate her reader to do? Did she? Where or where not? Look at the "Checklist of Questions Writers Need to Ask" on pages 19–20 and determine whether the writer asked herself all the questions she needed to.

Case Two: A Reply Letter

Someone in a personnel office in the state capital had the unfortunate task of telling the college junior in Case One that she missed the examination and was not eligible to reapply for the job she held the previous summer. Understandably, the personnel office employee who had to write the reply wanted to finish the letter as quickly as possible.

Imagine that the hurried personnel officer drafted the reply printed below. As you read the draft of his letter, decide how well the writer understood the communication process and the aim of the reply letter. For instance, what kind of relationship did he establish between himself and the reader? What words or phrases convey that relationship? Did the writer take the context or circumstances of the letter into account? How? How is the reader likely to respond to this reply? What particular words or phrases are likely to trigger the response you imagine? The personnel officer's reply was as follows:

> This is in reply to your letter of April 13 with regard to your failure to learn of the Science Assistant Examination and your subsequent inability to qualify for a summer job with the State Department of Agriculture.
>
> Examinations are now being given to screen applicants and ensure fairness in hiring procedures. These examinations were publicized on a statewide basis through such media as newspapers, the radio, and notices in state offices. The last chance to take the examination was January 15. Since it was widely publicized, it was unfortunate that you were not aware of it sooner.
>
> We are unable at this time to accept any applications for this examination. In fairness to all our applicants, we are bound by the specified terms of competition for summer jobs.

Look at the "Checklist of Questions Writers Need to Ask" and answer them in regard to this reply to the college junior. Considering that the writer of the reply letter doesn't know the reader, will probably never communicate with her again, and is providing a service to the reader simply by answering her question, can you think of any reasons why he should write a reader-based message? How would you feel if you received this letter? Why?

Case Three: An Alternative Reply Letter

Writers in organizations are frequently constrained by policies, deadlines, limitations on their authority, and other circumstances that they cannot change. However, writers can make a range of choices within the limitations imposed on them. No matter how much the writer in Case Two sympathized with the student's need for a summer job, he could not give a favorable reply. He had to send a "bad news" letter. Nonetheless, that writer had a multitude of choices to make regarding *how* to write that negative reply. Those choices will reveal whether the writer considered the *person* he was writing to or simply addressed the *problem* at hand.

To understand this distinction, imagine that the personnel officer used another strategy to reply to the college student's request. That strategy appears in the reply letter printed below. Compare the first reply you read with this second version:

        Thank you for writing to us to convey your interest in
    returning to a summer job with the State Department of Agri-
    culture. We value the services of experienced laboratory
    assistants and understand how important summer employment is
    for college students.

        I regret that you did not learn about the January exam
    you referred to because it is now an essential part of the
    hiring procedures. Since the deadline has passed and the
    office is now reviewing applications and test scores, we
    cannot administer any more tests. Realizing how important
    summer employment is for you, I suggest that you investigate
    possible openings in other state departments. Many do not
    require a test, and some might still be accepting student's
    applications for summer work.

        Jobs that require science backgrounds pay well and are
    always in demand. If you are interested in working for the
    State Department of Agriculture next summer, write to my
    office in September for a listing of test dates and locations.

```
        I hope you will find summer employment this year to help
   you finance your schooling.
```

Observe how the two reply letters differ in the (1) way the writer presents his "self" to the reader and (2) role the writer casts the student in. Identify the different word choices and content choices the writer made in each letter to create the "self" and the relationship to the reader that you observed. Compare the writer's purposes for writing each letter.

As these cases suggest, we can be more effective writers when we try to imagine what our messages will sound like to our readers. By thinking about the whole process of communication as we write, we can develop "second ears" and "second eyes" to enable us to write with our point of view and our reader's simultaneously in mind.

To guide your thinking about the communication process, you can refer to the checklist that follows. It summarizes the major issues introduced in this chapter. Of course, you can concentrate on one group of questions at a time. After a while, the questions will occur to you so automatically that you won't need to refer to them as you write.

A CHECKLIST OF QUESTIONS WRITERS NEED TO ASK

1 Who is my READER?
   - ☐ Am I writing to the appropriate person?
   - ☐ What is my relationship to this reader?
   - ☐ What is my reader's previous knowledge of this subject?
   - ☐ What motivates the reader to read this document?
   - ☐ What use will the reader make of this document?
   - ☐ Who are my secondary readers? What must I do to include their knowledge, motivation, and purpose for reading this document?
2 What is my primary PURPOSE for writing this document? What goal do I hope to accomplish?
   - ☐ To express my feelings or opinions or my organization's goals or values?
   - ☐ To persuade my reader?
   - ☐ To instruct my reader?
   - ☐ To inform my reader?
   - ☐ To explore an issue or a problem?
   - ☐ To document events or decisions for future reference?
3 What is the CONTEXT of this writing?
   - ☐ What is the appropriate way to write this document in this setting and for the setting it is being sent to?
   - ☐ Will it reach the reader sooner or later than expected?
   - ☐ What are my previous experiences with this reader?

□   Have I communicated with the reader previously about this matter? What should I keep in mind about the previous communications?

□   What is the background of this issue?

4   What type of DOCUMENT should I send?

□   Would a letter, a memo, a long or short proposal, or a formal or informal report be suitable?

□   Is writing preferable to speaking on the phone or in person? Why?

□   Is there a standard format to follow?

5   How do I want to REPRESENT MYSELF and my RELATIONSHIP to my reader?

□   Do I want to indicate my authority or acknowledge my reader's?

□   Do I want to present myself as an objective observer or recorder, or to emphasize my personal involvement in this matter?

□   Do I need to introduce myself, my organization, or my reason for writing?

1. Observe the kinds of written communications composed during the course of a day or a week by someone who has a position in a field you are preparing for. If you can, collect representative samples of this writing. Then classify the writing according to its purpose and its readers. Did you find writing that primarily expresses, instructs, informs, explores, documents, or persuades? Were readers inside or outside the writer's organization? Were they more or less informed about the subject of the documents than the writers? Also note how much of the writing is self-sponsored, how much is written in response to someone else's writing, and how much is written at someone's specific request. What generalizations can you make about the writing you observed? How does it illustrate the aspects of the communication process described in Chapter 1? Discuss your findings with the class.

2. Rewrite one of the pieces of writing you found as you were working on the project described above. Make the writing more effective in at least one of the following ways:

   • Change the projected "self" by changing the tone of voice
   • Change an "I" message to a "you" message
   • Make the writing more suitable for the situational context and the writer's purpose

3. Imagine that you are a faculty member who *receives* the memo on page 22. First read the memo. Then rewrite it to make it more reader-based. However, before you begin, write out answers to the following questions about the memo's intended purpose and readers:

   1 What is the writer's primary purpose?
   2 Which sentences seem to help the writer accomplish that purpose?
   3 Who are the readers?
   4 What is the writer's relationship to them?
   5 What is their knowledge of the subject?
   6 What is their motivation for reading this memo?
   7 How much attention are they likely to give it?
   8 What has the writer done to motivate the readers to read and respond to the message?
   9 How does the writer help readers act on the request?

   As you plan your version of the memo, decide what you can do to motivate readers to respond to the request. When you finish, compare your memo with others written by members of your class. What strategies did the class discover to accomplish the purpose of the memo?

21

September 8, 1986

TO: All Faculty

FROM: F. Newton, Director of the Computer Center

RE: <u>Your Files</u>

    I want to inform you that there have been some changes in our computer operations. We have added a new ZDP 11/60 computer system including 20 new CT101 terminals and eight new graphic terminals to supplement the ZDP 11/45. The new system will be operational early next month. These two systems will not be linked, so each user will be assigned accounts on either the 11/45 (which runs BASIC, FORTRAN, or Assembler programs) or the 11/60 (for Pascal, COBOL, and SPSS). The main memory in these systems is equal. Also, we will operate under a new version of the ABC/3R operating system, 7.2 as opposed to the present 7.0, so obviously some restructuring of the disk files will be needed.

    If you have files on the present ZDP, please identify each account. If you have further computer needs, please let me know immediately. A quick reply will ensure the availability of necessary files for your use. Thank you for helping me as we make this change in our systems.

CHAPTER 2

STRATEGIES FOR SOLVING PROBLEMS

INTRODUCTION: USING WRITING TO SOLVE PROBLEMS IN ORGANIZATIONS

Problems exist when we have to reach a goal but don't know how to get there. Cognitive psychologist John R. Hayes suggests that we picture the process of solving a problem as a search for ways to cross a gap between where we are and where we want to be.

Writers in organizations use writing as one way to solve problems pertaining to their place of work or to their professional concerns. As you recall from the three scenarios that opened the previous chapter, one writer, the administrative systems analyst, identified a problem within his organization: employees and entire departments seldom knew where to find important information. The analyst had to figure out how to cross the gap between the uninformed employees and the information they needed to know. The analyst solved that problem, or crossed the gap, by developing a policies and procedures manual and a corporate directory.

If you are searching for a job, you are also trying to solve a problem. The

23

gap you are trying to cross is between your present unemployed state and a job offer. To cross that gap, you will research employment opportunities, identify the ones that look promising to you, draft and revise a résumé, and send the résumé with an informative and persuasive letter of application.

We frequently rely on writing in the process of solving a problem. Writing assists us in two ways. We can use it both to think through the solution to a problem and to record and present the results of our thinking to others. In the process of choosing words and ways of organizing documents, writers engage some complicated processes of thinking about meaning and about relationships among ideas. Because writing engages a process of systematic thinking, writing is a powerful way to figure out the solution to a problem. In addition, the finished document, such as the systems analyst's manual or a résumé, records the writer's solution to the problem and, therefore, accomplishes work.

Individual documents, however, seldom stand alone. Instead, each document represents one small link in a series of events that move toward the resolution of a problem. Thus memos, meetings, discussions, and reports generate even more memos, meetings, discussions, and reports.

Throughout this book you will see examples of problems that were solved with written documents. Of course, this book can't cover all the problems people work on or all the kinds of documents people write in organizations. But it will introduce you to some frequently written documents and some useful strategies for systematically thinking about and writing those documents. You can practice those various strategies in this course so that you can apply them to the writing you do later. We agree with those who propose that recognizing and rehearsing patterns of problem-solving is one way to become a better problem-solver.

HEURISTICS FOR PROBLEM-SOLVING

The strategies that we use to search for solutions are called *heuristics*. The word "heuristic" is related to a Greek word that you might be familiar with: "eureka," meaning "I found it." Experienced problem-solvers carry a repertory of heuristics in their heads and use these strategies to solve problems more effectively.

Heuristics are not the same as rules which, if followed exactly, lead us to correct answers. Such rules, called *algorithms*, guarantee correct solutions. The procedures that you learned in order to add, subtract, multiply, and divide are examples of algorithms. Heuristics, on the other hand, are not guarantees, but they increase your chances of finding a good solution. You will find some heuristics for problem-solving in general on the next few pages. Later in this chapter, in the section entitled "Using Problem-Solving Strategies to Help You Compose," you will see heuristics that have been adapted for solving the problem of writing various documents. As you write, you can choose the heuristics that work best for you.

Define the Problem

One way to begin solving a problem is to define the issue at hand and find a way to represent it. Often problems are already defined when they are given to us to solve. The size of the organization we work in and our particular responsibilities within that organization often determine the kinds of problems we are likely to solve. Regardless of the circumstances, however, we increase our chances of finding a useful solution if we stop at the beginning of a project and ask, ''Now, what do I have to do here?''

One useful way to answer that question is to think about the four components of a problem:

THE GOAL: the point where you want to be
THE INITIAL STATE: the point where you are now
THE OPERATORS: the specific actions you take to move you from where you are now to where you want to be
THE RESTRICTIONS: the constraints that impede your progress toward your goal

If you are looking for a job, you can represent your problem this way:

YOUR GOAL is to persuade employers to invite you to a job interview.
YOUR INITIAL STATE is not having any interviews.
YOUR OPERATORS include (1) the books, journals, and newspapers you use to locate information about jobs and the organizations you would like to work for; (2) the network of people you know; (3) the career services office on campus; and (4) the résumés and letters of application you write.
YOUR RESTRICTIONS include time, your competition, and your lack of previous experience.

The following scenario illustrates how two writers defined a problem by asking questions about each of its four components.

A university librarian received a growing number of students' requests to keep the campus library open additional hours during exam week. Specifically, most of the students making requests wanted the library open until midnight before and during exam week. As a result, the chairwoman of the Library Committee asked the student delegates to that committee to draft a feasibility study that explored the issue of extending library hours. The chairwoman wanted the study submitted to the com-

What is our goal?

      To explore the possibility of keeping the library open longer, possibly until midnight on the week-end before exams and during the five days of the week we are taking exams.

Where are we now? [the Initial State]

      (1) The library is open every Saturday night until 8:00 P.M., Sundays until 10:00 P.M., and week nights until 11:00 P.M. (2) The committee seems sympathetic to the students' requests, but needs more information before making a decision.

What will we do to meet our goal? [the Operators]

      We will draft a feasibility study after we (1) survey 500 students on their study habits and study needs during exam week; (2) investigate library hours and library use in past years; (3) elicit support and suggestions from the dean of students; and (4) anticipate additional costs to the library operations and inconvenience to the staff.

What might keep us from meeting our goal? [the Restrictions]

      (1) Students might not return our surveys in sufficient enough numbers to draw useful conclusions from. (2) We might not be able to get an appointment with the dean as soon as we'd like. (3) We might not be able to get the information we need to investigate past use during exam weeks or to estimate additional expenses and staffing involved in extending the library hours. (4) Our coursework might interfere with writing and revising our study in time for the next meeting.

Figure 2-1   Representing the problem of keeping the library open.

mittee for a first reading at the committee's next monthly meeting. Refer to Figure 2-1 to see how the students represented the problem they had to solve.

Understanding the problem you have to solve and the conditions you are working under can keep you from pursuing counterproductive solutions. Representing the problem sets it out in front of you so that you can see how simple or complex it is. You can also anticipate how much time to allow for each step. The care you take in thinking about your problem will ultimately show up in the final document you submit.

Of course, analyzing the problem is no guarantee that you will meet your goal. Sometimes, while working toward your goal, you discover it is not worthwhile. Other times, you discover that your operators are unworkable. Problem-solving invites flexibility.

Similarly, defining the problem can be a problem in itself. Some problems require long periods of investigation simply to locate them. What may seem like a problem on the surface—excessive absenteeism, for example—can be the symptom of a larger problem: some aspect of working conditions, health care policies, or broader social issues, such as drug and alcohol abuse or changing family structures.

Divide and Conquer

When a problem seems too big or complex to solve all at once, you can think of ways to subdivide it. For example, writing a feasibility study, such as the one on extending library hours, is a complex activity. You know you will have a better chance of doing well if you use a divide-and-conquer strategy of setting subgoals. In the case of the library study, these subgoals include:

- Writing a survey
- Talking to the dean
- Interviewing the director of the library
- Preparing a cost analysis
- Drafting, revising, typing, and proofreading the proposal

Once you have divided the problem into smaller parts, or subgoals, you can make a work plan to help you anticipate the amount of time you will realistically need to accomplish each of the subgoals. Write in a target date next to each subgoal and try your best to finish the job by that date. You will find that complex problems become less overwhelming when you use such a divide-and-conquer strategy. The work plan for the library proposal is illustrated in Figure 2-2.

Generate a Variety of Solutions

By generating a variety of solutions, you increase your chances of actually solving the problem. First, you increase your chances of finding an excellent solution when you have several to choose from. Second, you can pursue one or two of the discarded solutions in case something goes wrong with your first choice. Finally, you can create a hybrid solution, one which combines features from several of your ideas.

One useful strategy for generating a variety of solutions is to write or dictate as quickly as you can, using your powers of free association as you go. As you come up with ideas, avoid judging them. Simply record them. Judging or crossing out as you go sometimes inhibits your creative processes. Once a fair number of ideas are on paper or tape, you can sit back and evaluate them, anticipating their consequences and matching each solution against criteria.

Generating ideas with other people can frequently lead to more and better solutions than individual problem-solvers can come up with on their own. You can find strategies for collaborative problem-solving in Chapter 15.

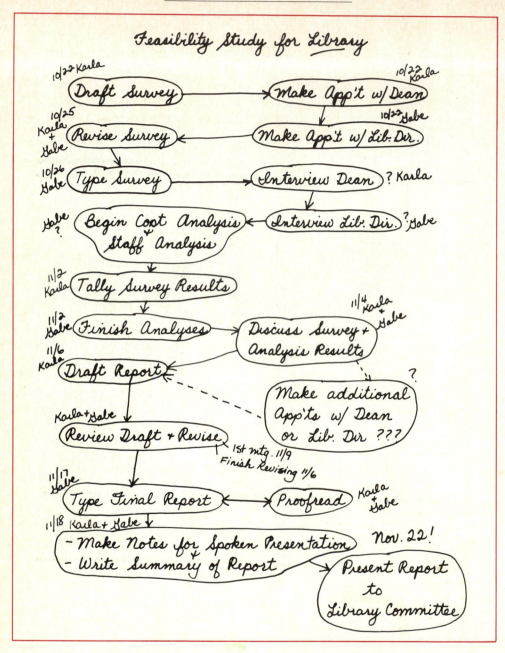

Figure 2-2   A work plan.
The two students working on the feasibility study first projected the steps they would take to complete their report. Then they divided the responsibility for carrying out each step by a particular date. To decide how much time to allow for each step, they worked backwards from their due date.

Rest Your Mind

Sometimes when we concentrate on solving a problem, we feel so bogged down that we think a solution will never come. These are the moments when we can benefit from turning our attention away from the problem and resting our minds. Some cognitive psychologists propose that during these moments of rest, a process they call *incubation* takes place. During this process, the mind silently works on solving a problem even though we are not aware this process is going on.

Of course, you want to refuse to rest your mind too soon. Stopping before you have made a concentrated effort to find a solution will not give your mind enough material to work on during moments of rest.

USING PROBLEM-SOLVING STRATEGIES TO HELP YOU COMPOSE

Writing a document can solve a problem for an organization. Yet figuring out *how* to write that document presents still another problem to solve. In this case, however, the problem to be solved, or the gap to be crossed, is the one between the blank page and the finished document ready for a reader's attention. To cross that gap, writers can use problem-solving strategies to help with the process of composing.

For example, during the years you have spent in school, you have devised strategies for completing writing assignments. Some of these strategies may have been consciously and carefully thought out, while others may have happened simply by default. That is, throwing up your hands and saying, ''Well, here goes!'' is one way to solve the problem of composing a piece of writing by default.

The following section shows you ways to apply problem-solving strategies as you compose.

Divide and Conquer

When you write, your challenge is to find a strategy that allows you to solve all the problems that the complex process of composing involves. To simplify this complex process, you can divide it into three important and interrelated parts:

THE CONTENT PROBLEM
(what to say in your message)
THE PRESENTATION PROBLEM
(how to present your message to particular readers)
THE COMPOSING PROCESS PROBLEM
(how to proceed with the process of writing)

You can manage the complexity of writing if you begin by thinking about only one of these problems at a time.

Solving the content problem

Solving the content problem involves generating or collecting relevant information and then selecting what is significant and appropriate. Sometimes we derive the content for our writing from what we already know. In that case, we need strategies for recovering, or teasing, information from our heads. Other times, we need to search for information in the external world. In those cases, we turn to our observations, other people, organizational documents, and references of all kinds to locate the content of our writing. For these occasions, we need strategies for observing, surveying, interviewing, conversing, using statistical and other data, and searching for books and articles.

Of course, the search for information continues even as we write. In the process of drafting an argument, for example, we can discover that to be convincing we need more information. Nevertheless, it is useful to *concentrate* on finding the content first and shaping it for readers next.

Specific strategies for generating and recording information are given in Chapter 3. You can practice using them as you write in this course. In later chapters, you will see how writers use research techniques to help them collect information before they write. You will also watch writers evaluate content from their readers' points of view.

Developing an effective presentation

Part of the art of writing is knowing *how* to convey your message to your readers. To figure out how to cross the gap between how you want your message to affect your readers and how to achieve that effect, you need to solve the presentation problem. That is, you need to decide how to arrange your information, what style and tone to use, and how to format the finished document.

Analyzing your audience's thinking and assumptions is a large part of deciding how to write your message. For instance, when you write to someone who has as much expertise as you do, you write quite differently than you would to someone who has less. As a result, there may be no such thing as clear writing. What is clear to one person under certain circumstances might not be clear to someone else. The writer's challenge is to figure out what is clear to whom.

When you enter a profession, you can expect to write more frequently to readers with less expertise than you have. Therefore, you will need to translate writing that may be clear to experts into more accessible language for uninformed readers. Figures 2-3 and 2-4 illustrate two different ways information about the same product is written for different readers—ones with technical expertise and ones without—and for different purposes—one to inform and one to persuade. Notice that the company representative had to make catalog information that was clear to her, similarly clear to her potential customer.

**Semi-Automatic
Bench Equipment**

**Basic AMP-O-LECTRIC
Model "K" Terminating
Machine**

This device is the most commonly used terminating machine for bench-top operation as a power source for operating standard and quick-change applicators because it is easily adapted to either mechanical or air feed systems. It is also easily adapted to serve as the basic component of many special machines by modification and/or installing available accessories and kits.

Rates of up to 1800 per hour are attainable with the mini or standard applicator depending on item being terminated, work flow, layout and operator dexterity.

Dimensioning:
Values in brackets are metric equivalents.

Specifications
Weight: Approximately 230 lbs. [104.3 kg].
Height: 24" [61 cm] (without reel)
Width: 21" [53.3 cm]
Depth: 20" [50.8 cm]
Air Supply: 80-120 psi [5.52-8.27 bars] when necessary
Power Required: 115 vac, 60 Hz, 6.0 amp (¼ hp motor)

CSA certified
File No. LR 7189

Application	Part Number
Std. applicators & basic terminating machine	1-471273-2
Std. applicators with mechanical feed	1-471273-3
Miniature quick-change applicators	565435-5
30° Mtd. miniature quick-change applicator	1-565435-7

Copyrighted and reprinted with the permission of AMP Incorporated; AMP is a trademark of AMP Incorporated.

Figure 2.3   A catalog description of a wire crimper.
The catalogue this description appears in serves as a ready reference for sales representatives when they talk to customers and write orders. The catalog also provides a reference for customers who want to compare exact specifications. That is, the description aims more to inform than to persuade. Discuss the differences between the way information about the crimper is presented in this figure and in Figure 2-4.

Forecasting the process of composing

Writers further need to puzzle over the procedures and schedules they will follow to finish writing a document on time. These procedures are the operators for solving the third problem, the composing process problem. Writers can ask the following questions about how to proceed:

"When is my deadline?"
"Will my first draft be my finished writing, or can I take time to revise?"
"Should I begin by writing the first sentence or first paragraph? Or should I write down the heart of the matter and figure out how to introduce it later?"
"How much time for researching and planning should I allow before I begin writing my draft?"
"Will anyone assist me as I write?"
"Must anyone approve my draft before it is typed and sent?"

If you take the time to anticipate how much work a piece of writing involves and how much time to allow for the various steps, you can make the process of

I have enclosed a quotation on AMP's AMP-O Lectric Automachine. We lease the machine and dies to you at a minimal monthly charge, leaving AMP Incorporated responsible for correcting any malfunctions or repairs. A principal service to you is an AMP engineer, available to assist you when your equipment arrives. Our engineer will assist in setting up the tooling and will review proper maintenance and operating procedures with your personnel. Our engineer will also periodically inspect the AMP machine and check on the product quality. This after-the-sale service will ensure that you are obtaining the maximum potential from AMP products and machines.

The machine I recommend for you is bench-mounted, stands 24 inches high, 21 inches wide, 20 inches deep, and requires an air supply of 80-120 pounds per square inch (psi). The operator simply places a wire in the anvil of the applicator and operates the crimper by pressing the foot pedal. The self-supporting machine performs a perfect mechanical and electrical crimp every crimp.

The machine will crimp 1800 wires in one hour compared with manual crimping at a maximum 300 an hour. An operator can crimp 4000 wires, the number you crimp in less than three hours—without human error.

Figure 2-4   A sales letter. (Yvonne Walko, AMP Incorporated.)
This excerpt from a sales letter shows how the writer presented information to a customer who was unfamiliar with automated wire crimpers. Notice how the writer leads into the matter-of-fact description of the machine with a persuasive paragraph about how the machines are serviced. Discuss the other strategies the writer uses to present information persuasively to her reader.

writing less overwhelming. Conscientious writers often sketch a work plan to forecast the steps and time needed to plan, draft, revise, and format the final copy of a complex piece of writing. Of course, the best plans can go astray. Even so, planning and remaining flexible are better strategies than not planning at all.

Represent the Problem

A linear representation of composing

The way you think about the composing process can affect the way you write. Some people assume that good writers never struggle to get words on paper. These people imagine that good writers move almost effortlessly from the top of a page to the bottom, without crossing out, rereading, or starting over. Envisioning a linear model of composing simplifies a complicated process, but can be mislead-

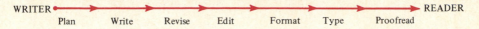

WRITER   READER

Plan   Write   Revise   Edit   Format   Type   Proofread

Figure 2-5 A representation of composing as a linear process.

ing. Such a model encourages the belief that writing is always a neat and predictable activity. A visual representation of this view of composing might look like the one in Figure 2-5.

    If you picture composing as a neat, linear process, the accounts that expert writers give us may surprise you. These writers claim to make false starts and to loop back and forth as they write and reread their drafts. These writers are aware of the interconnections among the choices they make about content, presentation, and meeting deadlines.

A recursive representation of composing

Even though thoughtful writers frequently plan the content and presentation before they compose a full draft, the process of planning does not necessarily stop once and for all. Making choices about words, ideas, and ways of organizing them for particular readers is a writer's sustained concern. The act of writing itself often sparks new ideas about what to say and how to say it. That is, writing generates further thinking. You will often find that when you reread and review what you have written, you will discover new ideas about how to proceed. Or you might make an entirely new plan. Figure 2-6 represents writing as a recursive process.

    After writing a draft, writers usually need time to step away from it. When they return to the draft, they are better judges of what they have written and what they need to do next. Often writers call on a reader to help them make that judgment and, possibly, to offer other strategies. As writers move toward a finished piece of writing, the process of revising is sometimes so recursive that drafts overlap, becoming indistinguishable from one another.

Understand and Vary Your Processes of Composing

Different kinds of writing require different kinds of composing strategies. For example, simple or familiar kinds of writing, such as a routine memo, can take only one draft. However, complex or unfamiliar kinds of writing can require several drafts and several reviews by readers before the work can be considered finished. Projects sufficiently complex to require several drafts give writers a chance to focus on different problems in each draft.

    You might find that a useful strategy is to avoid stopping in the middle of writing a sentence to puzzle over a word you are unsure of. Stopping to find just the right word can sometimes help you clarify what you mean and move you along. But too often such stops bog down the process. Instead, try writing the best word

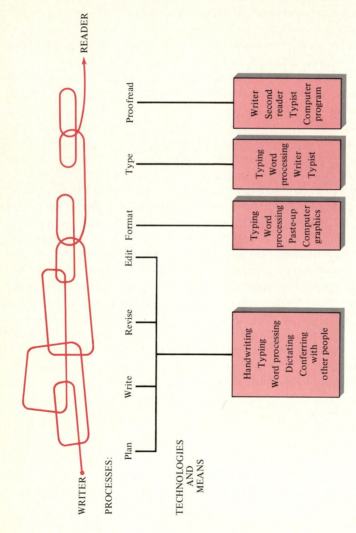

WRITER

READER

PROCESSES:

| Plan | Write | Revise | Edit | Format | Type | Proofread |

TECHNOLOGIES
AND
MEANS

Handwriting
Typing
Word processing
Dictating
Conferring
with
other people

Typing
Word
processing
Paste-up
Computer
graphics

Typing
Word
processing
Writer
Typist

Writer
Second
reader
Typist
Computer
program

Figure 2-6 A representation of composing as a recursive process.
This representation illustrates the way a writer can loop back and forth in the process of composing a written communication. Variables shaping this process include: individual habits, deadlines, situational contexts, degrees of familiarity with particular issues and types of documents, the length and importance of a document, the number of writers, and the technologies and human assistants available. Writers need constantly to ask themselves what composing process is best under each new set of circumstances.

you can think of, underline it, and change it later. Likewise, circle or type a symbol next to any words you suspect are misspelled. Look them up after you have finished writing. References such as a dictionary and a thesaurus will be available whenever you need them, but good ideas can be ephemeral.

The more you write, the more you will be able to anticipate the time and complexities involved in writing various kinds of documents. As you compose the documents introduced in the sections that follow, you will take longer to complete them now than after you have written them at work several times. The process of making certain choices will become automatic for the documents you write frequently.

Nonetheless, the time spent composing needs to be weighed against the time you can take. Deadlines can prime your imagination and motivation. They can also reduce the number of drafts you can compose and revise. You might wonder whether you will have the time at work to draft and redraft to the extent that we show you in some of the examples in later chapters. Obviously, some documents will be worth the effort it takes to make them the best you can. However, writers need to ask, ''What is the best possible job I can do in the time I have and with the resources available to me?''

Eventually, you will see that there is no single composing process or schedule suitable for all writers or all circumstances. One goal of the procedures followed in this book is to help you become more aware of your processes of composing. Another goal is to help you develop the most useful composing habits you can to prepare for writing in workplaces.

Word processing programs have added other variables to strategies for composing. We are only beginning to see research on ways computer technology can assist us as we write. Composing on a monitor allows us a certain playfulness, an ability to make easily erasable changes as we go. This ability can assist us while we initially plan our writing and while we revise, edit, format, and proofread it. Using computers certainly eliminates the drudgery of retyping entire documents for major or minor changes. For that reason, computers might encourage us to make bolder and more frequent changes, giving us the incentive to make each piece of writing the best we can.

1. Think of a problem you would like someone to solve in an organization you are a part of. The organization could be your college or university, your place of work, your church or synagogue, or a community or volunteer organization. The problem may involve the actual running of the organization; a need the organization could address; or a plan for increasing profits, membership, or contributions. Write as complete an analysis of the problem as you can, using the four questions in Figure 2-1 as a guide. What discoveries do you make about solving that organizational problem as a result of answering those four questions?

2. If one of the operators for solving the problem you wrote about in Exercise 1 was to write a document, plan that document by asking and answering appropriate questions about the information you will need to include (the content problem); the strategy you will use to make the document effective for your readers (the presentation problem); and the steps you need to plan, research, and write the document (the composing process problem). Then write a work plan to guide your composing process. Review pages 29–32 in this chapter before you write your analysis of these three problems.

CHAPTER

3

STRATEGIES FOR GETTING STARTED AND DRAFTING

GETTING STARTED

Until recently, the part of the composing process that has been virtually ignored in books like this one is the process of getting started. Conventional wisdom encouraged the view that good ideas either come to us or they don't. That view led us to believe we could do nothing but wait for inspiration to come along. Yet few of us have the luxury of time to wait around for good ideas. Besides, someone who needs to read a particular document can become irritated just waiting for the writer's inspiration to strike.

Fortunately, we can encourage good ideas. Experienced writers, cognitive psychologists, classical and modern rhetoricians, language specialists, and writing teachers have all developed heuristics to initiate the process of writing and to start ideas flowing. These strategies are operators for meeting the goal of finishing a written document. The more such strategies you know how to use, the better your chances for meeting your goals. The next few pages illustrate some useful heuristics you can refer to and experiment with as you prepare to write various documents for this course.

Strategy One: Identify Your Purpose, Your Readers, and the Problem You Are Solving

Look back at "A Checklist of Questions Writers Need to Ask" to help you identify your purpose and your readers. Use your answers to those questions to guide you as you decide what to write and how to write it. Similarly, find the words to describe the problem you are attempting to solve, including its goal, initial state, operators, and restrictions. Use this problem analysis to double check your reasons for writing in the first place and to anticipate difficulties in reaching your goal.

Strategy Two: Brainstorm

Some people use the word "brainstorm" only when referring to group processes for generating ideas. We are following the convention of using this term to describe individual creative efforts as well.

Once you have your goal in mind, brainstorming can be a useful way to recover ideas and information. You can try two different forms of brainstorming, focused and unfocused, to see which is more useful. To brainstorm in an unfocused way, quickly jot down whatever comes into your mind without stopping to judge what you have written. You can write questions, words, phrases, whole sentences, or paragraphs, as long as you avoid stopping to perfect them. This kind of brainstorming allows you to unload your mind, to jettison unrelated material that can get in the way, before you direct your efforts toward your project. In the process of brainstorming for ten minutes or more, you can discover some useful ideas among your jettisoned words.

Use focused brainstorming when you know what you want to accomplish and feel ready to begin. As with unfocused brainstorming, you proceed by writing quickly without stopping to correct spelling or grammar. Even though you restrain your correction editor, you keep your idea editor active and focused on solving the problem at hand. Focused brainstorming usually produces more usable material than unfocused brainstorming.

To focus your thinking, you can begin with a question (e.g., "How can we improve our training program?") or a statement of purpose (e.g., "I want this memo to convince management that we need a new training program."). Most likely, as you put your words on paper, other ideas will occur to you, or you will notice inconsistencies or gaps in your thinking. When you stop writing, you can edit your brainstorming by adding, deleting, and rearranging your ideas, and by substituting some words and ideas for others.

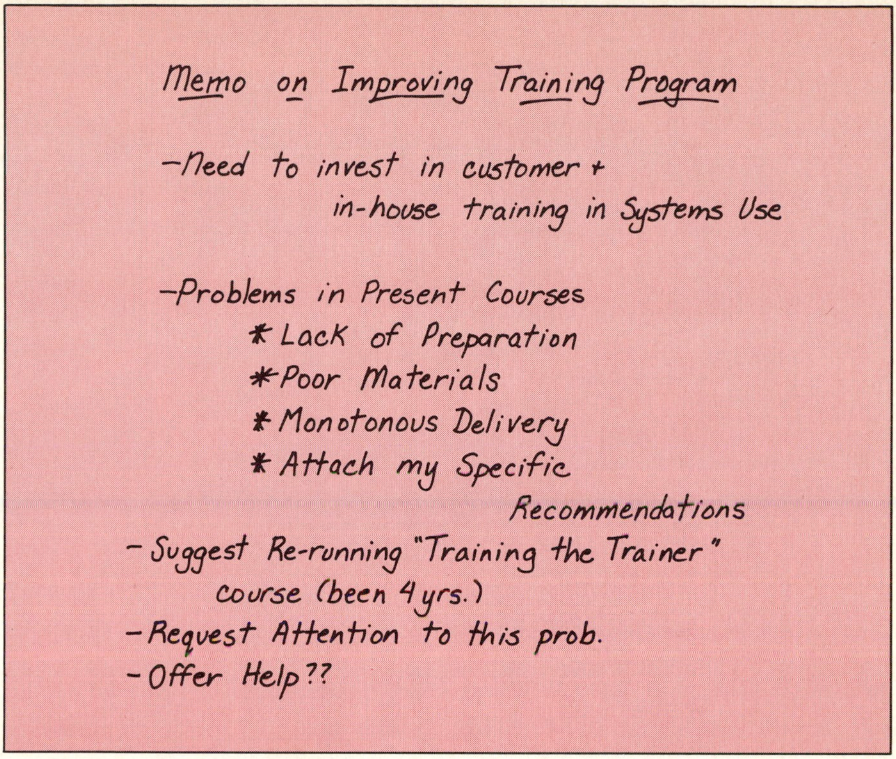

Memo on Improving Training Program

—Need to invest in customer +
                in-house training in Systems Use

—Problems in Present Courses
        * Lack of Preparation
        * Poor Materials
        * Monotonous Delivery
        * Attach my Specific
                                Recommendations
 — Suggest Re-running "Training the Trainer"
        course (been 4yrs.)
 —Request Attention to this prob.
 — Offer Help??

Figure 3-1   Focused brainstorming.
An engineer quickly wrote these notes to himself before he composed his memo recommending changes in his company's training program. Although he might add new points, delete others, or rearrange them, at least he has saved his initial ideas before they escaped him.

Figure 3-1 shows an example of focused brainstorming. The writer used a modified outline form that moves from stating the problem to suggesting solutions.

Besides brainstorming on paper, you can also brainstorm into a tape recorder. Whether you simply play back your words or have them transcribed for revising, at least you will have captured your ideas before they escape you.

Strategy Three: Respond to Questions

Asking and answering a series of questions can help you identify the information you need to include in a document. One useful set of questions is the one journalists depend on: "Who?" "What?" "When?" "Where?" "Why?" "How?" This strategy works especially well when you are writing announcements and certain kinds of informative letters and memos.

WHO is eligible?
- Elementary and secondary schools, if they
  - Purchase equipment that we will match in kind
  - Submit periodic evaluation reports
- Schools proposing innovative uses for teacher training or curricular development will be given preference

WHO will judge applications?
- Committee of elementary, secondary, and university educators and members of my staff

WHAT kind of grants are being offered?
- Matching grants in kind on hardware only

WHERE must applications be sent?
- To me at above address

WHEN must applications be received?
- By March 15, 1988
- We will notify winners in early June

WHY have we started this grant program?
- To promote excellence in the use of computer learning
- To establish an Educational Resource Network so that ideas can be shared among schools using computers

HOW should proposals be submitted?
- Submit written proposal on enclosed form
- No preliminary proposals required

Figure 3-2   Using journalists' questions.

Figure 3-2 shows how one writer began with this strategy to help her make sure that she included all the information her readers needed to have. In this case the writer works for a computer manufacturer who is sponsoring a matching grant program to help schools purchase computer hardware. As the company's education projects coordinator, she had to compose a cover letter to accompany the grant application forms sent to interested schools. Before she composed her letter, the coordinator asked herself what information the application recipients would need to understand the grant program and to fill out and return the application form correctly.

Strategy Four: Look at a Model

Find an example of a document that is like the one you must write. Notice how another writer has solved a problem similar to the one you are working on. From this example, develop a checklist of the kinds of information you will need to include in your document. Or you can develop a checklist by recalling a similar piece of writing you previously composed. Each of the following sections in this book introduces you to models you can refer to as you write.

Strategy Five: Imagine Your Reader Is with You

Ask yourself what you would say to your readers in a face-to-face discussion. Imagine that your various readers are present, and talk to them. How would they respond to what you are saying? What objections might they have? What questions might they ask? Consider moving around the room as you talk. You can use a tape recorder to keep track of your words. Or, if you can, keep a pencil in hand to jot down words and phrases as they come to you. If these devices inhibit you, don't use them. Just talk. In the process you will discover what you most need to say, and you might also find a plan for deciding how to arrange your ideas.

Strategy Six: Talk to a Friend or Co-worker

Instead of imagining that you are talking to your reader, speak face-to-face to someone you know. Begin by saying, "What I want to tell [Alex] is . . ." and explain what you want to say. Ask your friend to take notes as you speak and to ask you questions as you go along. Once you have explained your purpose, discuss what you need to say, what you can leave out, and what specific words and pattern of arrangement would work best. You can also discuss whether you should write this message in the first place. Maybe a phone call or a conversation would be better. Maybe you should wait longer before you decide to commit the message to writing.

Strategy Seven: Make a Visual Representation

Make a quick drawing, diagram, or sketch to help you envision what you want to say and to help you connect pieces of information. Some visual representations, such as a branching outline, can help you see which points are major and which

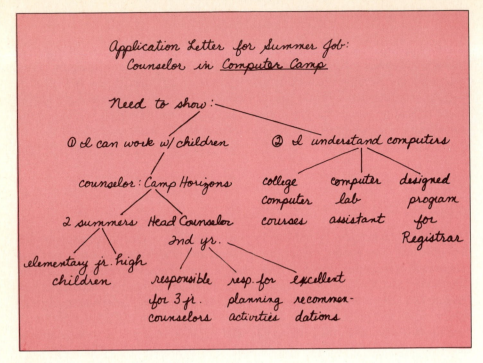

Figure 3-3   A branching outline.

are subordinate. Branching outlines also allow writers to add information to different sections of their outlines as new ideas occur. With the information in view, writers can decide how to arrange paragraphs and what information to highlight for readers. Writers can also rearrange the information in different hierarchical structures and find different ways of classifying it.

Figure 3-3 illustrates how one writer used a branching outline to generate information about his background for a letter of application.

Strategy Eight: Ask Yourself What You Have to *Do* In Your Writing

Refer to your goal and purpose statement and ask yourself how you can achieve what you want to. For example, will you need to make comparisons, describe a process, or support a claim? What other *means* will you use in your writing?

Define

Do you need to *define* any concrete or abstract terms? Write out definitions that your readers can understand by answering some or all of the following questions:

- What category does the thing or concept you are defining belong to?
- What specific characteristics separate it from things that are like it?
- How many varieties of it are there?
- Where do you find it, or when does it occur?
- What systems make it up?
- What systems is it a part of?

When you write your definition, avoid using ambiguous, obscure, or figurative language. Also avoid using the term itself as a part of your definition.

Classify

Do you need to *classify* anything? You can classify items under ready-made categories, or you can begin with a list of items and look for ways to divide them into categories. There are several ways to group items under headings and subheadings. For example, you can group by

- Common categories (animal, vegetable, mineral)
- Priority (first, second, third)
- Frequency (from most to least common)
- Magnitude (from best to worst)
- Intensity (from most to least severe)

There is never just one way to classify; all classification systems depend on circumstances and judgments. The two points to keep in mind are to classify in a way that suits your purpose and that is familiar to your reader. If you think your system is unfamiliar to your reader, explain the basis for your classification.

Divide

Do you need to *divide* an object, system, or issue into its constituent parts? The process of dividing is called *analysis*. To analyze, list all the parts you observe or all the parts that are generally thought to exist. Then decide whether your method of dividing suits your purpose and readers. For example, listing the parts of an automobile as the exterior, interior, engine block, and wheels would be too elementary for a class of auto mechanics. However, the division might be appropriate in the section of a user's manual that explains how to care for a car.

Sequence steps or narrate events

Do you need to *sequence* steps in a *process* or *narrate* a *sequence* of *events?* First determine the focus and scope of your sequence. What aspect of the process or event do you want to emphasize? How much of the process do you need to present? At what points do you need to begin and end? If you are sequencing the steps in a process, begin by stating the task and your reason for describing it. List all the equipment or ingredients needed to begin the process. Write any warnings or cautions you need to issue. Then list all the steps as you perform them. Test your preliminary instructions on a reader.

    If you are narrating a sequence of events, review what your purpose for narrating them is and what you want your reader to understand about them. Will a chronological sequence serve your purpose? Or would another arrangement work better? Perhaps you could begin at the most crucial point in the narrative; then summarize the events leading up to that point. If you are not sure, write more than one sequence and decide, perhaps with the help of a reader, which one seems best.

Show cause and effect

Should you show *cause and effect?* Write down what the consequences of a particular action or decision will most likely be. Or write down all the possible actions or decisions that could have led to present conditions. Figure 3-4 illustrates this heuristic.

Evaluate

Do you need to *evaluate* anything? List the criteria, the norms or goals, you will use as the basis for your evaluation. Rank them in order of importance. List the tests or conditions you are using to apply the criteria to the object or issue you are judging. Summarize the ways the criteria have or have not been met. Decide how close the object being evaluated comes to meeting the stated criteria.

Compare

Do you need to *compare* two items to show their similarities or differences?

    The process of comparing is similar to the process of evaluating. You can begin your comparison by making a column for each thing you want to compare. Write down as many features that are similar or different that you can think of or that you have observed. Then decide which points of comparison you want to call to your reader's attention and what the points of comparison are. To decide, you will need to think about the aim of your comparison. For example, do you want to show that one of the things you are comparing is better than the other, or will you let your readers make that judgment?

    Figure 3-5 shows the beginning of a writer's side-by-side comparison. Notice that the criteria for his evaluation are implicit in the points the writer chose to

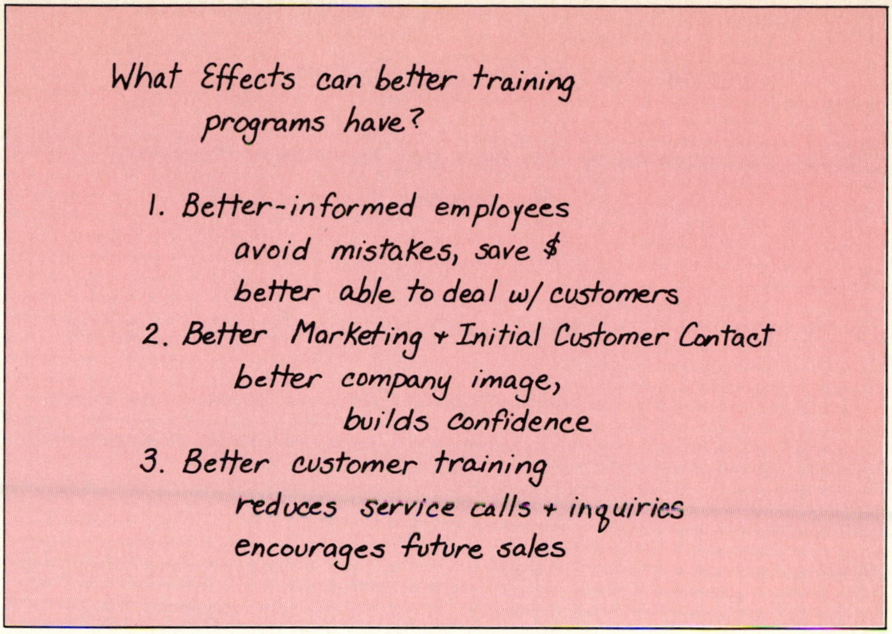

> What Effects can better training
>   programs have?
>
>   1. Better-informed employees
>   avoid mistakes, save $
>   better able to deal w/ customers
>   2. Better Marketing + Initial Customer Contact
>   better company image,
>   builds confidence
>   3. Better customer training
>   reduces service calls + inquiries
>   encourages future sales

Figure 3-4   Using cause-and-effect thinking to generate ideas.
The engineer who used this heuristic to generate preliminary writing for a memo wanted to persuade his readers to improve certain training programs. He can use all the ideas he wrote here and arrange them in a paragraph; he can summarize them selectively in a single sentence; or he can use each point as the kernel of a separate paragraph. Write this information in a paragraph, or summarize it selectively in a sentence.

compare: (1) lecturers should be well prepared, (2) teaching methods should involve students, and (3) manuals should be pedagogically organized.

Create an analogy

Do you need to create an *analogy* to help readers understand something complex or unfamiliar? An analogy is an imaginative comparison, a way of showing the similarities between two dissimiliar things. Using an analogy helps readers understand a new concept in terms of one they are already familiar with. Frequently, unfocused brainstorming can help you discover analogies. Some will be usable; others will not. For example, if you want to explain a new fringe benefits package, you would write

The new fringe benefits package is like a _____ .

Comparison of Training Systems

Reason for comparing: to persuade my readers to change
                          the present training system

Points of comparison	Present System	Proposed System
lectures :	lacked preparation	Provide prep. time (maybe rehire Marj?)
teaching methods :	lectures overheads some rote exercises	Interactive teaching Use problems/cases to solve + discuss Small group discussions
manuals :	not arranged from learner's point of view	Write new teaching materials based on key concepts — move from simple to complex

Figure 3-5   A side-by-side comparison.
The writer can use the information he generated in this comparison in one or more paragraphs of his persuasive memo. Arrange the information in one or more paragraphs in one of the following ways: (1) Write all points under ''Present System'' in sequence, and then all points under ''Proposed System'' in parallel sequence; or (2) work across the grid, considering each point of comparison, first in the ''Present System,'' then in the ''Proposed System,'' in alternating sequence.

Then let your brain freewheel, listing as many possibilities as you can, no matter how ridiculous they seem:

Buffet
Smorgasbord
Repertory theater
Grocery store
Menu
Multiple-choice exam

Then decide which analogy corresponds best. You can extend the analogy by listing the similarities between the two things you are comparing.

Describe

Do you need to *describe* something—a mechanism, a place, or an idea? List as many details as you observe or think of. Decide which ones you need to include to serve your purpose and suit your readers. Also decide how you want to arrange your description: from top to bottom, from front to back, from outside to inside, from most familiar part to least familiar part, by attributes (color, shape, dimensions, texture), or by functions. Do you need to make any generalizations about the description or provide background information before you begin?

Explore a problem and offer solutions

Do you need to explore a *problem* and offer *solutions*? Write down everything you can think of about the problem, its background, and its significance in as much detail as you can. Let this preliminary writing help you determine how much research you will need to do to define the problem and generate solutions. Try to anticipate what some solutions may be, and write them down also. List tentative operators for carrying out the solutions.

Support a claim

Will you need to *support a claim with evidence*? A claim states what you are asserting or proposing. It is like the thesis statement of an essay. First write your claim in a complete sentence. Then as quickly as you can, write down all the reasons you can think of to show why your claim is plausible. Or write down all the reasons your research supports.

Use this list to help you decide whether you need to carry on further research. Also ask yourself whether your readers will find the reasons you have listed as compelling as you do. Why or why not? Then select and organize your reasons in a convincing way for your readers. One effective presentation strategy is to list

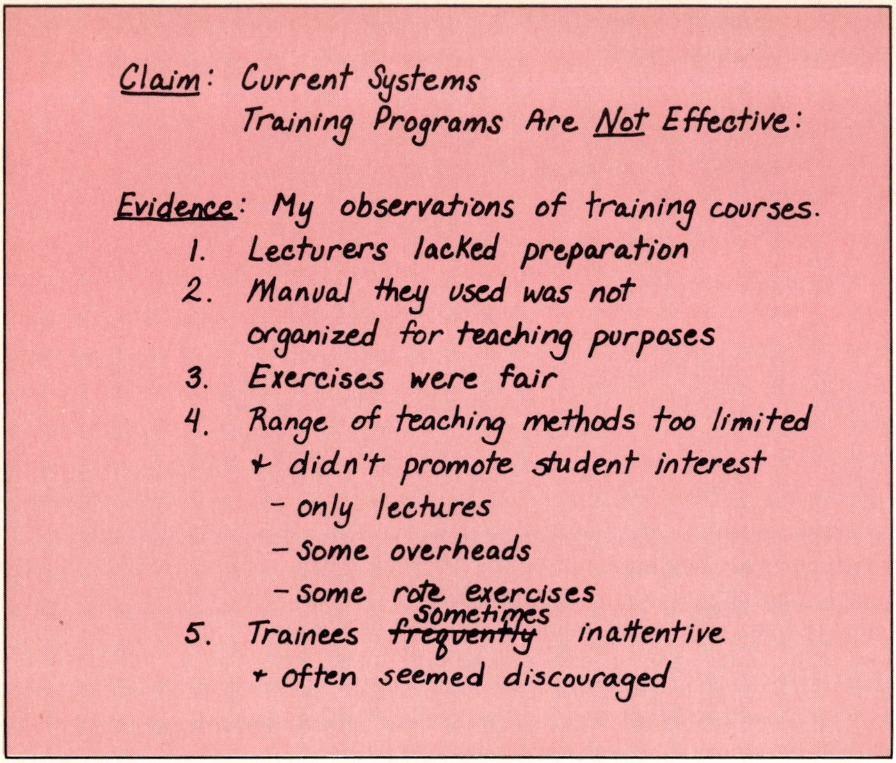

Claim: Current Systems
        Training Programs Are Not Effective:

Evidence: My observations of training courses.
    1. Lecturers lacked preparation
    2. Manual they used was not
       organized for teaching purposes
    3. Exercises were fair
    4. Range of teaching methods too limited
       + didn't promote student interest
        – only lectures
        – some overheads
        – some rote exercises
                    Sometimes
    5. Trainees frequently inattentive
       + often seemed discouraged

Figure 3-6 Supporting a claim with evidence.
Using the list above, write a paragraph, or more, that supports the writer's claim about the training programs.

your strongest points at the beginning and end, and your weakest points in the middle. Figure 3-6 shows one writer's preliminary list.

WRITING A TEST DRAFT

Writing an initial draft, or test draft, gives you a chance to pull together the fragments of your preliminary writing and to test a way of arranging them. Drafts also allow you a chance to find the best words to explain your ideas. The process of drafting is the process of discovering both what you mean to say and how to say it best to your reader.

   To watch an example of this process at work, look back at the preliminary writing in Figures 3-1, 3-4, 3-5, and 3-6. These notes, written by a manager in an engineering firm, provide the substance for his memo to superiors. The manager's primary purpose for writing the memo is to persuade his readers to *do* something—to remedy an organizational problem by improving certain customer and employee training sessions. To persuade his readers, he must inform them that the problem exists and persuade them that he is a reliable informant. The problem he must solve as a writer is finding a way to persuade his readers to restructure the training program.

As you review the manager's preliminary writing in Figure 3-1, notice that he includes two kinds of notes to himself: notes on what to *say* and notes on what to *do*. The last two points, ''Request attention to this'' and ''Offer help?'' are notes on what to do. In both his notes and memo, the writer uses a problem-solving framework to organize his request by (1) defining the problem and offering a solution, (2) supporting with examples his claim that a problem exists, (3) describing the beneficial effects of his solution, and (4) suggesting a procedure, by naming the operators, to put his solution into effect. Look at the memo in Figure 3-7 to see how the writer used his preliminary writing as the starting point for his test draft.

Like this writer, you can use the heuristics in Strategy Eight as ways of thinking about the subject of your writing. Then you can use them as patterns for arranging your message.

Finally, look at the way the engineer changed his test draft after he reread it. Figure 3-8 shows how messy and tentative these drafts can be.

ASKING SOMEONE TO REVIEW YOUR DRAFT

Test drafts are made to be changed. Yet sometimes we have trouble knowing what changes to make. Sometimes we are so close to our writing that we are unable to see it the way our readers will. One way to help ourselves see our writing as others do is to ask someone to review it.

You might think that asking someone else to read your writing is asking for trouble. Certainly no one likes criticism. Yet we think you will agree that it's better to have a draft reader tell you about any problems in a piece of writing while you still have a chance to make changes. Once your letter, memo, or report is sent, you surrender any hope of recalling your words.

As you write various documents for this course, we recommend that you review each other's drafts. We have found that this process helps in two important ways. First, it gives you useful responses to your writing. The process helps you see the difference between what you think you wrote and what others think they read. In addition, carefully reading others' drafts helps you become a better writer. You have most likely heard the conventional wisdom that teachers learn as they teach. You will experience this learning process as you work with other people's

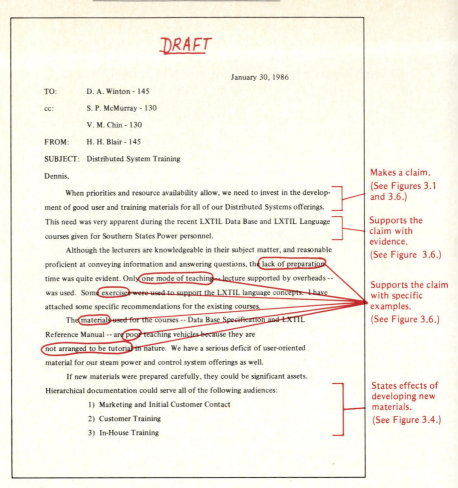

Figure 3-7   A test draft. (Used by permission from Leeds and Northrup Systems, North Wales, Pennsylvania.)
Notice how the writer used material from his preliminary writing—which helped him explore and understand the problem he was solving—in his initial draft. Test drafts, such as this one, contain errors of word choice, grammar, spelling, and typing. Perfection, however, is not the goal of writing a test draft. Instead, this draft helps you find ways to put information together.

writing and become their teacher. In other words, by helping others, you will help yourself.

     Besides being a good strategy for revising, reviewing each other's drafts prepares you for a procedure you are likely to encounter in workplaces. Writing

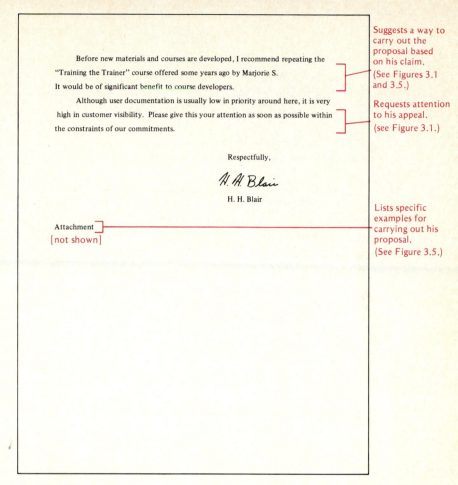

Before new materials and courses are developed, I recommend repeating the "Training the Trainer" course offered some years ago by Marjorie S. It would be of significant benefit to course developers.

Although user documentation is usually low in priority around here, it is very high in customer visibility. Please give this your attention as soon as possible within the constraints of our commitments.

Respectfully,

H. H. Blair

H. H. Blair

Attachment
[not shown]

Suggests a way to carry out the proposal based on his claim.
(See Figures 3.1 and 3.5.)

Requests attention to his appeal.
(see Figure 3.1.)

Lists specific examples for carrying out his proposal.
(See Figure 3.5.)

Figure 3-7   (*Cont.*)

that is sent on organizational stationery is frequently reviewed by someone in authority. As a member of an organization, you will find yourself both giving your writing to someone else to review and reviewing and authorizing other people's writing. If you begin that process now, you'll be better prepared to identify elements of writing that need changes and to find tactful ways to make suggestions. Throughout this book, you will see review forms that you can use as a guide. We also encourage you to review your own writing in as objective a way as you can before you show your work to others.

Chapter 4 introduces you to useful strategies for revising and editing your own and other people's drafts.

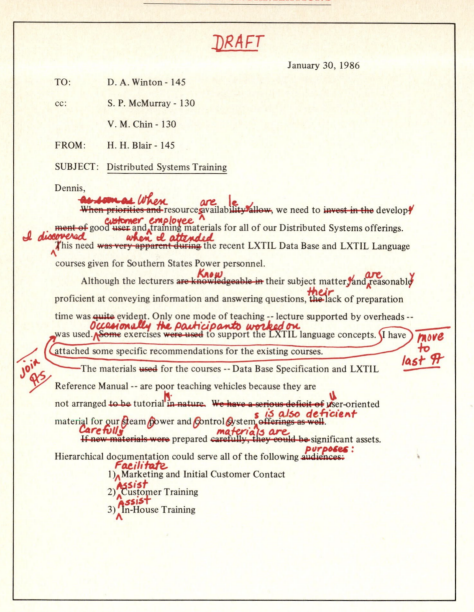

The draft memo reads, with handwritten red editing marks:

DRAFT

January 30, 1986

TO: D. A. Winton - 145

cc: S. P. McMurray - 130

           V. M. Chin - 130

FROM: H. H. Blair - 145

SUBJECT: Distributed Systems Training

Dennis,

~~as soon as~~ *When* ~~When priorities and~~ resource availability ~~allow~~, we need to ~~invest in the~~ develop-ment of good ~~user~~ *customer* *employee* and training materials for all of our Distributed Systems offerings. *I discovered* This need ~~was very apparent during~~ *when I attended* the recent LXTIL Data Base and LXTIL Language courses given for Southern States Power personnel.

Although the lecturers ~~are knowledgeable in~~ *Know* their subject matter, and ~~reasonable~~ *are* proficient at conveying information and answering questions, ~~the~~ *their* lack of preparation time was ~~quite~~ evident. Only one mode of teaching -- lecture supported by overheads -- was used. *Occasionally the participants worked on* ~~Some exercises were used~~ to support the LXTIL language concepts. ~~I have attached some specific recommendations for the existing courses.~~ *move to last ¶*

join ¶'s

The materials ~~used~~ for the courses -- Data Base Specification and LXTIL Reference Manual -- are poor teaching vehicles because they are not arranged ~~to be~~ tutorial ~~in nature~~. ~~We have a serious deficit of~~ user-oriented *s is also deficient* material for our steam power and control system offerings ~~as well~~. *Carefully* *materials are* ~~If new materials were~~ prepared ~~carefully, they could be~~ significant assets. Hierarchical documentation could serve all of the following ~~audiences~~ *purposes:*

Facilitate
1) Marketing and Initial Customer Contact
Assist
2) Customer Training
Assist
3) In-House Training

Figure 3-8   Initial changes made on the engineer's test draft. (Used by permission from Leeds and Northrup Systems, North Wales, Pennsylvania.)

Compare this revised test draft with the final draft the engineer eventually sent to his superiors (Figure 4-2).

Before new materials and courses are developed, I recommend repeating the "Training the Trainer" course offered some years ago by Marjorie S. ~*check name!* ~ *This course is valuable.* ~~It would be of significant benefit~~ to course developers.

Although user documentation is usually low in priority around here, it is very high in customer visibility. Please give this your attention as soon as possible within the constraints of our commitments.

Respectfully,

H. H. Blair

H. H. Blair

Attachment
[not shown]

For that reason, I would enjoy participating in the course developement. (add: "I have attached..." here.)

Figure 3-8 *(Cont.)*

1. Use at least four of the strategies for getting started described in this chapter (pages 38 through 48) to begin writing a letter or a memo. (You can use the document you worked on in Exercise 2 in Chapter 2.) Use this preliminary writing as the basis for composing a test draft. When you have finished the test draft, experiment with another way to present your message to your reader in a second test draft.

2. Consider the following case. You have a part-time job working in the office of a group of psychologists who conduct various self-help clinics, such as weight loss, assertiveness training, and parenting clinics. These clinics are conducted in a large metropolitan area. Your employers have decided to add a time-management clinic for procrastinators as a pilot project. The aim of the project is to help people break patterns of procrastination that keep them from meeting their educational, career, or other life goals. To start this project, your employers have decided to solicit undergraduate and graduate students from colleges and universities located in the metropolitan area.

    Your employers ask you to write the initial draft of the cover letter they will distribute to students in area universities and colleges. The letter will accompany a brochure explaining procedures used in the time-management clinic in more detail. You are given a rundown of the facts about the program that you can use in your draft of the letter. Then you are left with the directive to "write a letter that will motivate procrastinators to call us." To begin this letter, analyze the problem you must solve. Write explanations of how you intend to solve the composing process, content, and presentation problems that writing this letter raises. Pay particular attention to the challenges of solving the presentation problem in this case. To review ways to analyze your readers, look back at Chapter 1. Then write down what you think your readers' knowledge and motivation are and what use you think your readers will make of this cover letter. What strategies can you think of to make procrastinators *act* on the information they receive about the time management workshop? Before you write the letter, study the information provided below and decide which is useful and motivating to your readers and which you can omit. Do you need any information that is not provided below? The facts of the case are:

    - The clinic has been operating for seven years.
    - It offers a wide variety of services to adults and children.
    - The time management workshop is new.
    - Applicants to the program who have more serious problems than ones this workshop can address will be directed to other sources of help.
    - The program is staffed with experienced, licensed psychologists.
    - Procrastination can take a range of forms from mild to extreme.
    - Participants must agree to attend sessions on five consecutive days lasting six hours each day.
    - Applicants are screened.

- The workshop includes lectures, working in small groups, and some individual conferences.
- Participants must bring with them a project they have been putting off.
- The total cost is $300 (considered low).
- Some health insurance plans will defray the cost or pay it in full.

In addition to this information, make up the name of a clinic or psychologist, an address, and a phone number to include in your letter. Explain why you decide to include or exclude particular pieces of information in your persuasive letter. Use several of the strategies for getting started presented in this chapter to explore the problems involved in writing this letter. Choose three strategies from Strategies Three through Seven, and ask yourself all the questions in Strategy Eight. Go back to the ones in Strategy Eight that you answered ''yes'' to and write out your answers to those. Compare your heuristics for getting started with the ones used by other students in the class. Use your preliminary writing to compose a test draft. Compare your test draft with ones written by other students in the class. Discuss your processes of planning and writing the test drafts. Then discuss the various strategies you used to motivate your readers to act. After your discussion, write a work plan to help you anticipate the steps you will need to take to finish the draft. Write a test draft of the letter.

CHAPTER

4

STRATEGIES FOR REVISING AND EDITING

Revising and editing are processes of clarifying your meaning and intentions for both yourself and your readers. These processes put your meaning into focus just as adjusting a camera lens focuses an image.

Revising begins with reading your draft—not just once, but several times. Revising can also include giving your draft to someone else to review. This chapter leads you through four review processes to help you revise and edit your drafts. Later chapters alert you to the special concerns that editing particular documents raises. Nonetheless, you can practice the four review processes explained here on any piece of writing:

First Review
Read for Purpose and Appropriateness
Second Review
Read for Arrangement and Cohesion
Third Review
Read for Sentences and Language
Fourth Review
Read for Accuracy

Of course, we don't recommend that you adhere rigidly to the order of these four reviews. As you become a more practiced writer, the distinctions among the reviews, especially between the second and third, are likely to blur. We do recommend, however, that you concern yourself with the larger issues of purpose and arrangement before you look for spelling and punctuation errors. Why bother to fine-tune the grammar on a draft that you might decide to scrap altogether?

FIRST REVIEW: READ FOR PURPOSE AND APPROPRIATENESS

Sometimes when we write, we get so caught up in what we're doing or in a particular part of the writing, that we lose sight of our initial purpose. Even if you took stock of your purpose and your reader's background before you started a draft, you could still benefit from reviewing your initial reasons for writing. You could also review your reasons for writing to your readers and ask whether the document and its format serve your purpose.

Strategy One: Write a Purpose Sentence

One way to carry out this review is to compose a sentence that summarizes the organizational problem you wrote your document to solve. Your sentence might look like this:

```
To ensure that our staff and our customers
                 (state problem-solving goal)

know how to use our products correctly, / I must

persuade my readers, / Winton, McMurray, and Chin, /
(state primary                     (name readers)
 purpose of memo)

to allocate time and funds to improve our in-house and
                      (list operators)

customer training programs.
```

Now ask someone else to read your draft and write a sentence summarizing what that reader understands to be the goal and purpose of your writing. If your reader's statement looks like yours, you have probably accomplished what you intended to. If your reader's statement is different, try to figure out why. Do you need to revise anything to make your point clearer to your reader?

Strategy Two: Answer Questions about Your Document's Purpose and Appropriateness

Questions for reviewing your purpose are:

- Is writing this document the best way to solve this problem?
- Have I told my readers why I'm writing?
- Have I let my readers know why they should read this?
- Have I supported each claim? With what information?
- Do I stick to the issue at hand or go off on tangents I could delete?
- Do I need to add information?
- Do I need to rearrange any information?
- Have I accomplished my primary and secondary purposes?

Questions for reviewing appropriateness are:

- Have I written to the appropriate readers?
- Am I the right person to be dealing with this issue and writing about it to these readers?
- Have I written the appropriate kind of document?
- Is it too long or too short?

We suggest that you scan your draft as quickly as you can for this first review.

SECOND REVIEW: READ FOR ARRANGEMENT AND COHESION

Once you've decided that you've written a purposeful document, you can take a long, hard look at how you've put your draft together. That is, you can analyze what each part of your writing says and how you've arranged and connected the parts. This process moves far more slowly than the first review. At first, you may wonder whether this review is worth the time and effort, yet after a while you may agree with us that this reading can help you improve your writing.

Read for Arrangement

To get an idea of how well you have organized what you've written, you need to find a way to see it all at once. This process isn't easy. One reason is that a draft you've just written is so much a part of you that you can't really see it. It's like trying to look at your own face. To do that, you need the help of a mirror. You can, however, see a mirror image of your draft in an outline you can create.

Strategy One: Write a Descriptive Outline

We suggest that you sketch a descriptive outline of your draft in the following way:

1. Read each paragraph slowly enough to absorb its meaning.
2. After you read each paragraph, write a single sentence that summarizes what the paragraph says.
3. Then write a verb that describes what each paragraph does. Does it describe a problem, offer a solution, support a claim with evidence, illustrate what you mean with an example, thank someone, scold someone, congratulate someone, emphasize a point, or make a comparison?
4. Read your summary sentences from beginning to end and see whether each sentence seems to say what you wanted to say in each paragraph. Did you fulfill your intentions?
5. Reread your summary sentences to determine whether the sequence of your paragraphs is likely to make sense to your reader.
6. Reread your verbs describing what each paragraph does to see whether each separate paragraph and all the paragraphs working together seem to do what you intended your writing to do. Does the order seem to make sense?

You will find a sample descriptive outline of a letter in Figure 4-1. To get an even clearer picture of what your draft looks like, let another reader review your draft and write a descriptive outline of it. Then see if you find any differences between your account of what your draft says and your reader's account.

Discuss any differences you and your reader have found. Try to figure out why you've disagreed. That is, try to understand why a reader came away from your draft thinking it said or did something different from what you identified. What else could you do to clarify what you mean? Also discuss the arrangement of your message. Does your reader suggest another plan? Do you think it's a good one or not? Why? You might want to call in a third opinion, or even a fourth or more, if you think that would be helpful.

These descriptive outlines help your reader focus on important issues while reviewing your draft. Such outlines discourage readers from making trivial or useless comments that waste time without moving you forward.

	SAYS	DOES
Paragraph 1	We spoke about giving me credit for Speech Communications 20.	Reminds
Paragraph 2	I am also able to document my claim that I'm an experienced public speaker.	Supports a Claim
Paragraph 3	I've never challenged a course before this request.	Requests
Paragraph 4	(I realize that) this issue is taking your time.	Thanks

Figure 4-1   A descriptive outline of a student's letter.

If you are generally satisfied with the way the message in your draft is arranged on paper, you can take a closer look at how you've helped your reader connect the parts. We call this element making your writing *cohere*, or stick together. Sometimes readers don't get what you're saying simply because you haven't made explicit connections. In other words, your arrangement can be fine, yet your readers won't follow you because you haven't marked the path of your thinking clearly enough with sign posts. Strategies for making your writing cohesive begin on page 61.

However, don't move on to them if you need to reorganize your draft. Go back, reorganize, and then proceed.

Strategy Two: Sketch a Branching Outline

A branching outline gives you a visual representation of your draft. This representation allows you to see at a glance just what you have written and how the parts of your writing fit together. You've already seen an example of a branching outline that a writer used to plan a piece of writing. That illustration appears in Figure 3-3. Here is another example:

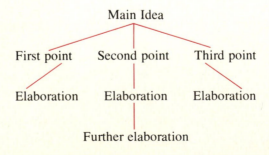

Sometimes you can write a branching outline more quickly than a descriptive outline. Both allow you to see what your entire draft looks like. Once you do, you can identify whether and how you need to revise. Ask yourself: "Where are the gaps?" "What is incomplete?" "What is unnecessary?" "What could I classify or arrange differently?"

Strategy Three: Write a Conventional Outline

Of course, you can also develop a conventional outline of your draft, an outline that looks like this:

    I.

      A.

          1.

          2.

              (a)

              (b)

      B.

          1.

          2.

   II.

and so on.

Such an outline can also be a useful and efficient way to see how your draft fits together.

Whatever method you use for surveying the arrangement of your draft, ask yourself if you need to *add*, *delete*, or *rearrange* anything. Or do you need to *substitute* any part of the contents with other information, to clarify your meaning for your readers?

Read for Cohesion

Once you feel reasonably sure about what you have included in your draft and how you have arranged the contents, you can review your draft to judge whether it is cohesive. Cohesive writing seems to flow. It gives readers the impression that the words poured out of the writer's pen or appeared on the computer monitor with little effort. However, you probably realize by now how false that impression must be.

Even though cohesive writing takes an effort to compose, the effort is worth your trouble for two reasons: (1) readers appreciate prose that moves them smoothly through the parts of a message—from paragraph to paragraph, sentence to sentence, word to word; and (2) as you check for cohesive devices when reviewing and revising your draft, you will actively and critically question what you wrote. For example, when you notice that you haven't made explicit connections between two sentences, you need to search for a transitional word or phrase that signifies that connection. As you search, you will be forced to clarify the logical relationship between the two sentences. Do the sentences show cause and effect? Does one sentence give an example of the other? Does one sentence contradict the other or offer a qualifying statement?

Your search can even reveal that the two sentences simply don't belong next to one another. This discovery sometimes signals a gap in your thinking, which can cause you to reexamine the problem you are working on.

You can achieve cohesion in your writing through paragraph sequences, sentence sequences, word choices, and punctuation. Use your descriptive outline to see if your paragraphs follow in a sensible order. Then refer to the following sections to learn how to use other cohesive devices.

Strategy One: Check Sentence Sequences

When you state a generalization in a sentence and follow it with sentences that show examples of your generalization, you are using a cohesive device. That is, you are sequencing your sentences in a way that allows your reader to move with understanding from one sentence to the other. Your sequence follows a logical pattern of thinking—moving from general to specific, for example. If your paragraph consists of a string of generalizations, however, you leave your readers wondering what the connection is among those generalizations.

Study the paragraph below to see how one writer sequenced general and specific information.

```
Our training department is now offering employees oppor-
tunities to improve their job skills.  We have established
a tuition assistance program, through which we will reim-
burse employees two-thirds of the cost of a course taken at
a local college or university.  We also provide a variety
of in-service training programs during the workday.  These
include management development and supervisory development.
```

Logical sentence sequences include moving

from cause to effect
from effect to cause
from conditions to consequences
from if... to then...
from problem to solution
from impossible to possible
from possible to impossible
from most to least
from least to most
from similarity to difference
from difference to similarity
from first step to next step
from first event to next event
from one location to another
from statement to restatement
from whole to parts
from parts to whole
from general to specific
from specific to general

Strategy Two: Check for Cohesive Language

You can choose words that make your writing cohesive—words that denote specific relationships. For instance, "however" and "but" signify a contrast. In addition, certain repetitions and substitutions of words can be powerful ways of connecting ideas and clarifying your meaning. The following list illustrates ways you can use words to make your writing more cohesive.

1 USE ADVANCE ORGANIZERS.
   Purpose statements, proposition statements, and other orienting sentences (such as "We have identified four workable solutions.") help readers to anticipate and connect parts of your writing.
2 REPEAT KEY WORDS AND PHRASES.
   If you write in the beginning of a letter that you will compare the "old system" to the "proposed system," include the phrases "old system" and "proposed system" frequently in the rest of your letter.
3 SUBSTITUTE WORDS WITH SIMILAR MEANINGS.
   Synonyms: for "system," you could substitute "method" or "operation."

Pronouns: for "system," substitute "it"; for "systems," substitute "they," "their," "theirs," and "them."

Other forms of the word: system, systematic, systematically, systematized.

4 REFER TO THE PARTS OF THE WHOLE.

Refer to the introduction, body, and conclusion or to the front, back, and sides, and so on.

5 USE "THIS," "THAT," "THESE," AND "THOSE" FOLLOWED BY A NOUN.

Avoid using these demonstrative adjectives by themselves. "This system offers several advantages." Not: "This offers several advantages."

6 USE CONJUNCTIONS.

"And," "but," "or," "nor," "for," "so," and "yet" can connect all elements of your sentences: words, phrases, and clauses. They can also connect sentences.

7 USE NUMBERS.

"First," "second," "third," and so forth help your readers connect steps and events that occur in sequence. Numbers also indicate priorities.

8 USE TRANSITIONAL WORDS.

You can use the following list as a ready reference:

CONDITION	TRANSITIONAL WORDS
ADDITION	again, also, besides, furthermore
CAUSE AND EFFECT	as a result, because, therefore, thus
SIMILARITY	likewise, similarly
DIFFERENCE	however, differently, unlike, on the other hand, but, yet
CONCESSION	after all, although, at the same time, even though, nonetheless
EXEMPLIFICATION	for example, that is, for instance
SUMMATION	to conclude, in conclusion, in summary
TIME	at the same time, now, before, after, when, then, first, second, third, initially, finally
PLACE	here, there, where
SPATIAL RELATIONSHIPS	next to, behind, in front of, attached to
ADDITION	further, furthermore, in addition, also, too, besides, and
RESULTS	as a result, finally, therefore, then, thus
QUANTITY AND DEGREE	more, most, fewer, less, moreover

Look back at the paragraph on training programs on page 62. Circle words the writer used to help readers move from point to point. What other devices suggested in the preceding list could the writer have included? How can they help readers?

Strategy Three: Use Punctuation to Connect Ideas

You can also make your writing cohesive by using punctuation marks accurately and effectively. Some uses of punctuation are closely rule-governed. For example, periods mark the end of sentences. That convention leaves us little to discuss. However, you can also use punctuation to emphasize a point or to clarify a relationship between parts of a sentence.

Colons

Colons (:) signal your reader that whatever follows will further elaborate on what you just wrote. Colons usually announce that you are moving from general to specific information.

1 Colons precede a list. Example: Our Open House will provide your employees with the following opportunities:
    * To evaluate their present skills
    * To assess the role of continuing education in career advancement
    * To understand recent technological changes
2 Colons alert readers to anticipate a point you want to emphasize. Example: There's one question I hear too often around here: ''What's the bottom line?''

Dashes

Dashes (—) also connect general and specific information. However, dashes are more appropriate in informal writing, while colons suggest more serious and formal writing.

1 Dashes can emphasize information at the end of a sentence. Example: Why do we use ''prioritize,'' when a simpler word would do—''rank''?
2 Dashes can signal a parenthetical thought, one that is less important than the thought it interrupts. Example: The new office computer—a welcome relief after years of manual filing—will be installed next week.

Semicolons

Semicolons (;) connect independent clauses. Use semicolons when you want to stress the equality or close relationship of the information or ideas in each clause.

1 Semicolons can signal a contrast. Example: We did not reach our long-term goals; we did reach our short-term goals.

2 Semicolons can signal a cause-and-effect relationship. Example: No one showed up for the meeting; it was apparently scheduled for a time when committee members had other meetings.

3 Using a semicolon with conjunctive adverbs (such as *however, consequently, nevertheless*) makes the relationship between the clauses more explicit than the semicolon alone does. Example: We originally scheduled the shipment for January 21; however, we will be unable to ship until March because the Z components are now out of stock.

THIRD REVIEW: READ FOR SENTENCES AND LANGUAGE

Once you see that you have organized your message in a clear, effective, and cohesive way for your reader, you can focus on reviewing your sentences and language. An excellent strategy is to read your draft aloud to yourself or to someone else. You'll discover that your sentences are smooth or awkward. You'll hear whether your voice sounds authentic. You'll stumble over phrases that you read over silently without questioning.

Another useful strategy is to look back over any paragraphs that your draft reader had trouble understanding. Any paragraph your reader had trouble understanding is probably a paragraph with incoherent sentence sequences, overloaded sentences, vague or inappropriate language, or any combination of those problems. As you get to know what kind of writer you are, you can focus on only those problems that seem to recur in your drafts. For example, some of us know that we have a tendency to write long sentences. Once we identify that problem, we can read our drafts with a conscious effort to locate and unpack the excess baggage in each sentence.

Reread Your Sentences

Strategy One: Unpack Overweight Sentences

Like some suitcases that passengers try to take on airplanes, some sentences carry excess weight. Understanding sentence patterns and becoming a skillful manipulator of those patterns will help you avoid overloading your sentences. The process of arranging those patterns takes some time to describe. We do just that in the next section.

First, however, we can show you two quick fixes for some overloaded sentences. You can easily think about these strategies as you write each sentence or as you read over your draft to revise it.

Find Hidden Verbs

Sometimes we refuse to use verbs to name the actions we are describing. Instead, we hide the action in a noun. The English language allows us this flexibility. For example, we can write:

It was our decision to...

Now watch what happens when you uncover the verb hidden in the noun "decision." You can write a shorter and more direct clause:

We decided to....

We usually hide primary verbs when we depend on forms of the verb "to be" to carry the weight of our sentences. That was the case in "It was our decision to...." If the writer had named the action—"decided"—and named the agent of that action—"we"—first, the verb "to be" would be unnecessary.

"To be" isn't the only verb that causes writers to hide the action in a noun. Other commonly used verbs include "to make," "to take," "to give," "to have," and "to hold." Here are some examples of how they work:

MAKE INQUIRY REGARDING	hides	INQUIRE
TAKE INTO CONSIDERATION	hides	CONSIDER
GIVE CONSIDERATION TO	hides	CONSIDER
HAVE NEED FOR	hides	NEED
HOLDS THE BELIEF	hides	BELIEVES

How would you rewrite the following sentences to release the hidden verbs?

1 We will make a recommendation for his promotion at the next board meeting.
2 It was our decision to postpone development of the drug until next year.
3 To make a determination of the sales potential of the new product, we made a survey of the target market.

Question Your Use of Passive Constructions

The passive voice of verbs robs your sentences of an agent–action sequence. As a result, you wind up loading your sentences with additional nouns and prepositional phrases. For example, notice the difference between these two sentences:

PASSIVE VOICE
It *was recommended* by the budget *committee* that the program *be discontinued* by this *department*.
ACTIVE VOICE
The budget *committee recommended* that *we discontinue* the program.

Certainly the active voice is more readable. It also forces you to name the agent of each action. Many passive constructions are leaner than the example above, but they refuse to tell the reader *who* did what. Notice, for example, what happens to the agent in the following sentence:

It *was recommended* that the program be discontinued.

This construction leaves your reader wondering, "*Who* recommended this action? *Who* will discontinue the program?"

In some contexts, however, both reader and writer understand exactly *who* recommended and *who* will discontinue the program. Naming the agents would be unnecessary in such a context.

Strategy Two: Check Sentence Patterns

Recognize basic sentence patterns

Sentences begin with an unadorned independent clause:

He called me.

If you need to elaborate on that statement, you can place the additional information before, after, or in the middle of the independent clause. When you place the additional, modifying information first, you construct a *left-branching sentence:*

When he finished reading the report, he called me.

This construction tends to emphasize the importance of the *time* when "he called." Similarly, if you want to name a condition that affects the action named in the main clause, you would construct a left-branching sentence. It would look like this:

If the committee decides to vote tomorrow, call me.

In *midbranching* sentences, modifying information appears between the subject and the verb, interrupting the main clause. This interruption tends to emphasize the information suspended between the subject and the verb. Notice, for example, how this principle works in the following sentence:

The program *developed by our training department* will begin next week.

In *right-branching* sentences, you follow the main subject and verb with the modifying information. This pattern tends to emphasize the information in the main clause. Read the following right-branching sentence as it is written:

We will discuss your proposal *after we review the budget for the next fiscal year.*

Now see what happens when you move the modifying information in front of the main clause. Go back to the other examples in this section to see how many ways you can rearrange them. How does each new pattern affect the way you interpret the meaning of the sentence?

Look for heavy branches

Too much modifying information in any part of a sentence strains the whole structure along with your reader's attention. Parcel the modifying information sparingly. Notice what happens, for example, when too many prepositional phrases are strung together:

During her examination of the records of the sales department in November, the accountant found incomplete sales records for several customers.

The following revision reduces the number of those phrases:

When she examined the sales department's records in November, the accountant found incomplete sales records for several customers.

Another way you can lighten the load on a heavy branch is by writing two, or even three, sentences instead of one. Go back to the above sentence with the string of prepositional phrases and see what happens when you rewrite the information in more than one sentence.

Place modifying information next to the word it modifies

Sometimes what seems clear to you is ambiguous to your readers. Readers, especially ones who don't understand the context of a statement, will have trouble understanding the following sentence:

He only asked for a leave of absence.

Was he the only one who asked for a leave of absence? Or did he ask for a leave of absence and nothing else, such as a raise or a promotion? How would you rewrite the sentence to answer those questions?

Readers could also be stumped by this sentence:

The committee decided to extend library hours on Friday.

Is Friday the only day that library hours will be extended? Why only Friday? Or did the committee decide on Friday, rather than on some other day, to extend the hours? If the committee decided on Friday, how would you rewrite the sentence?

Introductory verbal phrases, the ones in the left branch of a sentence, almost always refer to the subject of the sentence. That is the case in the following example:

After deciding to extend library hours, the committee set the agenda for the next meeting.

In other words, the action named in the introductory phrase was performed by the committee, the subject of the sentence. Notice what happens, however, in the following sentence:

By extending library hours, the campus will offer more opportunities for students to study productively.

This sentence claims that the campus extended library hours. Didn't the committee do that? The following revision avoids the dangling modifier:

Now that the library is open longer, students have more opportunities to study productively.

Some dangling modifiers produce humorous results:

> When inflated with hot air, four people can lift off in the balloon.

How would you revise that sentence to deflate those four uncomfortable people?

Vary your sentence patterns and sentence lengths

Readers enjoy a change of pace. Yet there are other reasons for varying sentence patterns. Notice what happens when a writer depends on a single sentence pattern and length:

> Thank you for your order of 5000 batteries. We will send them in one week. We will call you the day we ship. We hope you are satisfied.

By composing a series of short, simple sentences, the writer has given the reader the job of connecting the information in those sentences. What is the relationship, for example, between sending the batteries in one week and calling on the day they are shipped? If no relationship exists, why is the information in these two sentences placed side by side? Vary the length and patterns of the sentences in the example given above by using some of the editing strategies and cohesive devices you just learned about.

Choose the Best Words

The moment we run a pencil across a piece of paper or begin typing, we think about the words we are using. Finding the best words is a sustained concern as we write. Yet sometimes we let inappropriate word choices slip into a draft. Sometimes, just to keep rolling, we allow ourselves to write the first words that come to mind. That is, we postpone choosing the best word until we can take the time to consider our choices.

Suggestions for making those choices follow. Even though these suggestions appear at the end of this chapter on editing, you can keep them in mind any time you write.

Strategy One: Check for an Authentic Voice

Although writing replaces human voices, writing is not simply transcribed speech. If it were, we would not have to work so hard to learn how to write.

However, our writing does not need to sound labored, stiff, or artificial. The writing we compose in organizations is no exception. Writing that sounds authentic—as if the writer is sitting down and talking to the reader—is more engaging. Such writing is also more readable.

In fact, some states have recently passed ''Plain English'' laws that require certain public documents and legal contracts to be written in accessible, jargon-free language. The following suggestions offer you ways to avoid stilted, clichéd, and inaccessible language.

Delete ''grab-bag'' expressions

These expressions do not help a writer sound authentic. They are the tired clichés that a writer can thoughtlessly grab from a bag and place in almost any document. What are some of them?

> This is in regard to. . . .
> Thanking you in advance. . . .
> Enclosed please find. . . .
> Pursuant to your inquiry. . . .
> Thank you for your attention to this matter.

Such phrases give readers the impression that you are not paying particular attention to them or to the issue at hand. These phrases make you sound more like a preprogrammed robot than an alert human being. You will find a fuller list of these expressions in Appendix A.

Question jargon

Jargon consists of specialized, technical language that members of a particular professional community understand. However, jargon is likely to baffle other people. Sometimes these other people are your readers.

Stockbrokers, for example, talk about *price-earnings ratios*. Could these brokers expect first-time clients to know that the term refers to the ratio of a stock's price to its earnings per share? Would all clients understand how this ratio is used to make investment decisions?

Messages containing jargon that a reader does not understand sound garbled to that reader. They also make the writer sound distant and uncommunicative. On the other hand, using jargon when you speak or write to other members of your professional community can be appropriate.

Rewrite word strings

Stringing together too many words of the same part of speech also makes your writing less readable and less inviting. The effect of the number of adjectives strung in front of ''hardware'' in the following sentence, for example, is deadly:

> We expect to develop our *multicomponent, systematized third-generation* hardware by the end of the 1980s.

How would you recast that sentence to avoid the string of adjectives?

Notice how verbs and verbal forms can pile up as well:

We *are beginning to make* progress toward *achieving* our first quarter goals.

Besides being clumsy to read, such verb strings make writers sound as if they are fudging. The verb string in the preceding sentence leaves the reader wondering whether the goals have been met. If they were, say so:

We have reached our first quarter goals.

If your progress is stalled, explain what you have accomplished and what your setbacks have been.

Revise inflated language

Like balloons, words can be filled with gaseous substances. Inflated language strains a reader's patience. Such language also makes writers seem pompous, dishonest, or unsure. The novelist Charles Dickens, for example, often endowed pretentious characters with inflated language, using their words as a source of humor. Dickens's inept businessman Wilkins Micawber is one such character. For example, when writing to his friend David Copperfield, Micawber cannot bring himself to say simply, ''I haven't told my wife that I plan to go to London.'' Instead, he writes in a postscript:

P.S. It may be advisable to superadd to the above, the statement that Mrs. Micawber is *not* in confidential possession of my intentions.

More contemporary examples of inflated language include the use of:

finalize	for	end
subsequent to	for	after
at this point in time	for	now
fashion distribution center	for	clothing warehouse

Strategy Two: Use a Precise Vocabulary

Of course, what is precise in one context can be ambiguous in another. The best any of us can do is be aware of subtle differences between the denotations of words and be attentive to their connotations. Notice, for example, how the writer's verb choice would alter the reader's perception of what the committee in the following sentence did:

The committee $\begin{Bmatrix} \text{discussed} \\ \text{considered} \\ \text{evaluated} \end{Bmatrix}$ the proposal.

If you develop the habit of asking questions about what you have just written, you can more easily choose precise words for your readers. Notice the questions that the following imprecise statement can generate:

The *report* analyzes *central issues* about *opportunities* for our *organization*.

1 Report. Which report?
2 Central issues. Which issues are they? Central to whom? For what reasons?
3 Opportunities. What kind of opportunities? Who will benefit? How?
4 Organization. All departments in our organization? Some? Which ones?

Strategy Three: Use Unbiased Language

Be aware of the biases—social, racial, and gender biases in particular—that certain expressions and titles contain. Practices such as addressing all unspecified letter readers as ''Dear Sir'' or ''Gentlemen'' are examples of such biases. While such addresses are more specific than ''To Whom It May Concern,'' they exclude all female readers. A guide to using unbiased language appears in Appendix B.

FOURTH REVIEW: READ FOR ACCURACY

Regardless of whether you type your own documents, you are responsible for the accuracy of any work bearing your name. You would be embarrassed, for example, if your reader found misspellings, grammatical or typographical errors, or inaccurate information. While correct spelling is the good grooming rather than the heart of a piece of writing, some readers take spelling seriously. They let a misspelling or a typographical error distract them from reading the meaning of your message. Some readers even tend to judge a writer's character and intellect by the way the writer has followed the grammatical and spelling conventions of written English.

Today, writers who have access to word processing systems can use preprogrammed spelling and grammar verifiers to assist them with the proofreading process. But these electronic assistants might not be 100 percent reliable. There are some kinds of information that only the writer or another person can verify. Besides, if the system is down, writers must depend on themselves or draft readers. Using the following strategies will help ensure the accuracy of each document you send.

Strategy One: Check the Accuracy of Information

1 NAMES. Be sure you have included the names of all the people you need to. Check the spelling of each.
2 DATES. Be sure the dates of meetings, deliveries, deadlines, agreements, and other events are correct.
3 LOCATIONS. Be sure to include locations, especially of meetings, and any directions readers need to find them. Double-check for accuracy.
4 TIMES. Verify times of events and recheck them in the final copy.
5 NUMBERS. It is easy to type wrong numbers. Avoid assuming they must be correct.
6 CALCULATIONS. Recalculate mathematical operations and check your calculations against the ones in the typescript.
7 ABBREVIATIONS. Write out complete names in the first citation. Follow the name with its abbreviation in parentheses. For example, write ''the College of Arts and Sciences (CAS)'' the first time you mention it. After that, you can refer to it as CAS. If you are using many abbreviations in a long document, you need to rewrite the full name at least in the beginning of each new section. Check for consistency.

Strategy Two: Check the Mechanics and Conventions of the Language

Knowing yourself as a writer means knowing what kind of grammar, spelling, punctuation, and language usage mistakes you most frequently make. If you do not know, monitor your mistakes for a week or so and list the ones you find. Your instructor can help you identify patterns of mistakes you are making. That way you may discover, for example, that although you have made eleven mistakes in several pieces of writing, you have actually been repeating the same three errors. Once you know your pattern of errors, you can look for them as you proofread.

Even the most experienced writers need to turn to a handbook to check points of grammar, punctuation, and standard usage. In fact, good writers keep a handbook and dictionary close at hand.

Strategy Three: Proofread in a Novel Way

Moving your eyes across your lines of type will not help you find all your mistakes. You are too likely to see what you thought you wrote rather than what is actually on a page. Instead, you need to find some novel strategies. Try the ones listed below and find out which work best for you.

1 Read each line of type backward.
2 Cut a word-length rectangle out of the corner of an index card. Move the card along each line of type so that only one word appears at a time. You

February 2, 1986

TO: D. A. Winton - 145
cc: S. P. McMurray - 130
            V. M. Chin - 130
FROM: H. H. Blair - 145
SUBJECT: Distributed Systems Training

Dennis,
        When resources are available, we need to develop good customer and employee
training materials for all of our Distributed Systems offerings. I discovered this need
when I attended the recent LXTIL Data Base and LXTIL Language courses given
for Southern States Power personnel.

        Although the lecturers know their subjects well and are reasonably proficient
at conveying information and answering questions, they could have benefitted from
more preparation. Only one mode of teaching -- lecture supported by overheads --
was used. Occasionally the participants worked on exercises to practice the LXTIL
language concepts. The materials for the courses, the LXTIL reference manuals,
are poor teaching vehicles because they are not arranged tutorially. Our Steam Power
and Control Systems also lack user-oriented materials.

        Carefully prepared materials could be significant assets, serving the following
purposes:

        (1)   To improve marketing and customer relations

        (2)   To assist customer training

        (3)   To assist in-house training for employees

        Before new materials and courses are developed, however, I recommend repeating
the "Training the Trainer" course offered some years ago by Marjorie Swartley. This
course is valuable to course developers.

        Customers need good user manuals and first-hand instruction. I would enjoy con-
tributing to the process of developing such materials and courses. To begin, I have attached
some specific recommendations for the existing courses. Please give these suggestions
your attention as soon as you can.

                                Respectfully,

                                H. H. Blair
                                H. H. Blair

HHB/jap

Attachment: Recommendations

[not shown]

Figure 4-2   Final copy of a memo. (Used by permission from Leeds and Northrup Systems, North Wales, Pennsylvania.)

will see the sequence of letters that you actually typed rather than the
sequence you assume is there.

3   Reading from left to right, move a ruler or a piece of firm paper down
    the lines of types as you read. This strategy also controls your line of
    vision.

4 Read a copy of your finished writing to another person. This strategy works even better if you give your listener a duplicate copy to look at as you read.

5 Ask another person to read your final copy aloud as you simultaneously run your eyes across the draft your final copy was typed from.

6 Ask someone who has never seen a copy of your document to read it over.

Figure 4-2 shows the final copy of the engineer's memo you watched being drafted in Chapter 3. The writer used a dictionary and grammar handbook to check some words and constructions before giving the draft to the typist. He then proof-read the final copy before signing it at the bottom.

1. Combine the following sentences into a single left-branching sentence, then a midbranching sentence, and finally a right-branching sentence. Explain how each of these sentence patterns affects the way readers will understand the information.

   1 We received the returned units.
   2 Our programming staff tested them.
   3 Our tests showed that these units were inaccurate.
   4 We will replace these units with our newer ones.

2. Use some of the strategies presented in this chapter to revise the following sentences. Compare your revisions with ones made by other students in your class.

   1 At the request of Mr. Lovejoy, we wish to advise you that the electric nozzle tilt control drives can be replaced by pneumatic cylinders for a price reduction of $24,000 per control system.
   2 This price includes the deletion of the power switch cabinet, which is no longer necessary.
   3 Regarding the fuel management program, we have concluded that this could not be done satisfactorily.
   4 It is our understanding that the 32-bit machine would not have been backed up by a second machine.
   5 Given below is our conformance status with respect to the recommendation made by your audit team in the audit report attached to your letter dated July 28, 1986.
   6 To terminate these unnecessary delays, a rather tough study was made, in accordance with standard engineering procedures, during which a number of reliable sources agreed that all laboratory design information reports should be accompanied with the following information: a listing of computer output, a sketch of the board to enable us to review the output, and a statement of the need for a solder mask.

3. Many of the cohesive devices used to connect ideas and clarify meanings in the following paragraph have been circled. Follow the lines connecting the circles to see how the writer leads his readers through the paragraph. Identify the cohesive devices, such as word repetition and substitution, transitional words, and sentence sequences.

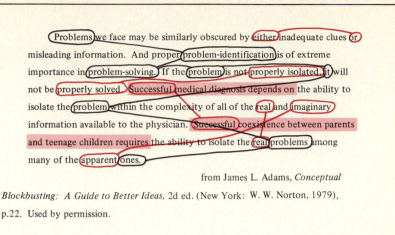

Problems we face may be similarly obscured by either inadequate clues or misleading information. And proper problem-identification is of extreme importance in problem-solving. If the problem is not properly isolated, it will not be properly solved. Successful medical diagnosis depends on the ability to isolate the problem within the complexity of all of the real and imaginary information available to the physician. Successful coexistence between parents and teenage children requires the ability to isolate the real problems among many of the apparent ones.

from James L. Adams, *Conceptual Blockbusting: A Guide to Better Ideas,* 2d ed. (New York: W. W. Norton, 1979), p.22. Used by permission.

4. Select a paragraph from something you have written to test for cohesion. Circle, connect, and identify the cohesive devices you have used. How could you revise your paragraph as a result of this test?

5. If you wrote a draft of the letter in Exercise 2 in Chapter 3, review and revise that letter by following the strategies suggested in this chapter. Be sure to write a descriptive outline of your letter. Then ask another student to write a descriptive outline. Compare your outlines and discuss suggestions for revising your draft. Write a descriptive outline for another student's letter and exchange suggestions for revising it. When you are satisfied with your revisions, type a final copy.

SECTION TWO

STRATEGIES FOR DESIGNING A DOCUMENT

CHAPTER

5

DESIGNING A DOCUMENT

The first thing a reader notices about a document is its overall appearance. Whether the document is a letter, a memo, a set of instructions, a report, or a proposal, readers notice how it looks. Some documents invite readers' attention and encourage them to take the message seriously. Others make readers turn away. A clumsy format can even mislead readers, causing them to misread a message.

Planning how a document looks is *document design*. When you design a document, you consider how to arrange copy and graphic elements to achieve the purpose of your document for your readers. *Copy elements* are visual devices writers use to focus readers' attention on the text. *Graphic elements* are visual devices writers use to complement or supplement the text. In some documents you write, you may use only copy elements; in others, you may use both copy and graphic elements. The arrangement of all the copy and graphic elements on a page, including the spaces left around them, is called page *layout*.

In this chapter we discuss when to use copy and graphic elements, what kinds there are, and where to place them in your document. In your own writing on the job you may be responsible for setting up copy and graphic elements in your document. Other times you may work with a professional graphic artist. The principles

83

of design we discuss in this chapter are those you can carry out with a typewriter, a word processor and printer, a computer graphics program, or by hand.

COPY ELEMENTS

Understanding how your reader will read and use your document helps you to design that document. Some readers scan a document because they want to familiarize themselves with the general contents. Others, such as those who read reports and proposals, often jump to the introduction and recommendations to understand how a document has solved a problem and how that solution affects the reader's organization. Understanding your readers' purposes in reading should help you decide how to design your text. Copy elements are one of your design tools.

When to Use Copy Elements

Writers use copy elements in a document to achieve the following purposes:

1 TO HELP READERS PREVIEW AN ENTIRE DOCUMENT.
2 TO HELP READERS LOCATE CERTAIN KINDS OF INFORMATION IN A DOCUMENT.
3 TO EMPHASIZE RELATIONSHIPS AMONG ITEMS IN A SERIES, such as relationships of time (first, next, then) or order of importance (most to least).
4 TO CALL ATTENTION TO IMPORTANT PIECES OF INFORMATION, such as definitions, warnings, or results.

What Kinds of Copy Elements to Use

To make their messages more readable, writers depend on the following kinds of copy elements. As you read about each one, locate it in the pamphlet in Figure 5-1.

Master Headlines: These are the most visible cues which give readers an overview of the information provided in a document. By providing a way for readers to scan a document, headlines help readers select sections of documents they need to read.

Subheadings: These indicate subordinate information, reveal the plan of organization, and, thereby, help readers locate information within a document.

Body Copy: These consist of the largest blocks of text in a document. Readers generally have more difficulty compre-
hending information contained in a thick block of copy.
They often need to reread it. Readers also have difficulty locating specific pieces of information in a large
copy block.

Short copy blocks: These are single words, phrases, sentences, or brief
paragraphs. These small units of information interrupt
or introduce the body copy and are separated by spaces.
Writers place information they want to call to their
readers' immediate attention in short copy blocks. The
use of white space between short copy blocks prevents
crowding of information and separates one section of
text from another.

Once you have located these four copy elements in Figure 5-1, look at the
figure again to discover the *highlighting techniques* writers used to call readers'
attention to certain parts of the text. These devices include the following:

BOLDFACE TYPE

Large Type

CAPITAL LETTERS

Italics

Underlining

Numbers (1, 2, 3 . . .)

Bullets (•)

Dashes (—)

Asterisks (*)

Check marks (✔)

Boxing

Color

Shading

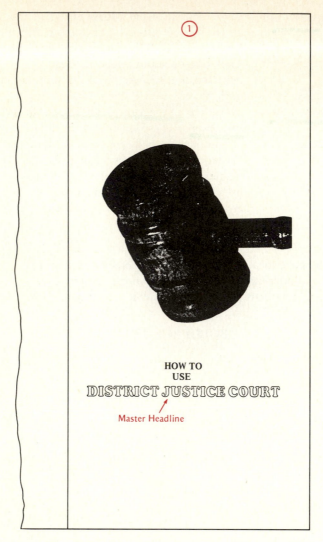

Figure 5-1   Good use of copy elements in consumer affairs pamphlet. (By permission from Montgomery County Department of Consumer Affairs, Pennsylvania.)

After you have located as many highlighting techniques as possible in Figure 5-1, explain how each of these makes the message more readable.

All copy elements call attention to important information within a document, but overuse of any one of them can confuse readers and clutter a page.

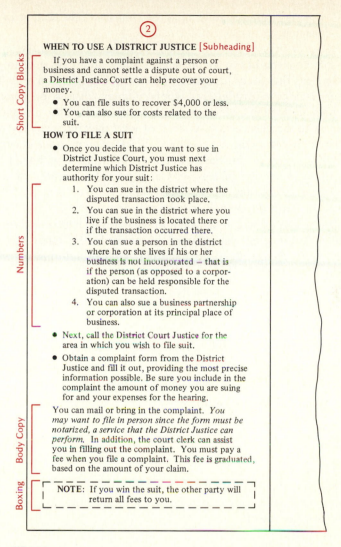

Short Copy Blocks

②

WHEN TO USE A DISTRICT JUSTICE [Subheading]

If you have a complaint against a person or business and cannot settle a dispute out of court, a District Justice Court can help recover your money.

- You can file suits to recover $4,000 or less.
- You can also sue for costs related to the suit.

HOW TO FILE A SUIT

- Once you decide that you want to sue in District Justice Court, you must next determine which District Justice has authority for your suit:

Numbers

1. You can sue in the district where the disputed transaction took place.
2. You can sue in the district where you live if the business is located there or if the transaction occurred there.
3. You can sue a person in the district where he or she lives if his or her business is not incorporated – that is if the person (as opposed to a corporation) can be held responsible for the disputed transaction.
4. You can also sue a business partnership or corporation at its principal place of business.

- Next, call the District Court Justice for the area in which you wish to file suit.
- Obtain a complaint form from the District Justice and fill it out, providing the most precise information possible. Be sure you include in the complaint the amount of money you are suing for and your expenses for the hearing.

Body Copy

You can mail or bring in the complaint. *You may want to file in person since the form must be notarized, a service that the District Justice can perform.* In addition, the court clerk can assist you in filling out the complaint. You must pay a fee when you file a complaint. This fee is graduated, based on the amount of your claim.

Boxing

NOTE: If you win the suit, the other party will return all fees to you.

Figure 5-1.   *(Cont.)*

Where to Use Copy Elements

Where you decide to use copy elements will depend on the type of document you are designing, the purpose of the document, and your reader's use of the document. For example, an organization's booklet explaining its various medical plans should use short copy blocks and headings to help employees locate information about the kinds of questions they would have about each plan.

As you design your document for a reader, consider where you want to use copy elements. Look at Figure 5-1 again and notice where copy elements occur to signify different kinds of text:

1 *Before the entire text* to identify the contents of the text, as in the title of a document.

2 *Before or in between major divisions or subdivisions of the text*, marking different levels of text for the reader. Subheadings are an example of copy elements that occur before or in between divisions of a text. They function as *advance organizers*—words, phrases, clauses, or sentences which announce the topic of a following section of text. They also provide readers with the chance to take stock of what they have already read before they move on to the next segment of information in the document.

3 *Within the text* to emphasize important information within a paragraph or section of writing, such as a warning printed in capital letters or italics.

4 *Next to subdivisions of the text* to signal the relationship of these subdivisions, such as numbers indicating orders of priority.

5 *Around the text* to distinguish or to separate one kind of text from another, as in information that is boxed off or shaded in. Often the text that is enclosed speaks about an important kind of information that readers should remember.

Compare Figure 5-2, a rough draft of a memo, to Figure 5-3. What kinds of copy elements did the writer use in the final copy? Where did the writer place them so that readers would understand the message?

As you read about the different kinds of organizational writing in this textbook, notice how writers used copy elements to help readers better understand information in a document.

GRAPHIC ELEMENTS

Perhaps you assume that you will never need to know anything about illustrating the documents you write. You may believe that graphic artists or other specialists will be responsible for those concerns. Or you may foresee yourself writing letters and memos and, therefore, believe you have no need to learn about the graphic elements used in a document. However, part of your responsibility in designing a document may be to know when graphic elements need to be included, what kinds to recommend, and where to place them in the document. Or you may be responsible for approving documents that contain graphics. In that case, you will need to be able to assess whether the graphic elements someone else has designed are appropriate for the readers and the use they will make of the graphics.

The Purchasing Department has reported that a large percentage of EN's* cannot be processed because the P. O.* value exceeds the amount authorized on the EN. To avoid delays in processing these notices, please prepare the EN's as follows: Determine the material cost. When in doubt, especially on low cost items, add 10% for inflation. Purchasing should be contacted for material costs, if possible. Add 10% of the above cost to cover taxes, shipping and insurance. On orders of $250 or less that require expedited delivery, this percentage should be increased to 20% to cover the higher than normal shipping costs. Round off total cost to the nearest dollar. Indicate this total on the EN in the following way: Cost Not to Exceed $_____.

*Note: The readers to whom this memo was sent understand that the abbreviation EN
         (Engineering Notice) refers to a specific kind of order form and that P. O. refers
         to Purchase Order.

Figure 5-2   Draft of memo without copy elements.

The Purchasing Department has reported that a large percentage of EN's cannot be processed because the P. O. value exceeds the amount authorized on the EN.

To avoid delays in processing these notices, please prepare the EN's as follows:

1. Determine the material cost. When in doubt, especially on low cost items, add 10% for inflation. Purchasing should be contacted for material costs, if possible.

2. Add 10% of the above cost to cover taxes, shipping and insurance. On orders of $250 or less that require expedited delivery, this percentage should be increased to 20% to cover the higher than normal shipping costs. Round off total cost to the nearest dollar.

3. Indicate this total on the EN in the following way:
    Cost Not to Exceed $_____.

Figure 5-3   Final copy of memo with copy elements. (By permission from RCA, New Jersey.)

When to Use Graphic Elements

Writers include graphic elements in a document to achieve the following purposes:

1   TO ILLUSTRATE THE TEXT.   Graphic elements complement the various purposes of a text: they provide readers with information, document

actions or results of actions, represent the results of exploring an issue, instruct, and persuade. For example, to instruct readers how to assemble a mechanical object, including a diagram of the steps required to assemble the object would complement, perhaps even replace, text.

2   TO SUBSTITUTE FOR TEXT. Readers' styles of reading vary according to what they are reading, how motivated they are, how complicated the information is, and how much time they have to read. Many readers prefer to read graphic elements instead of text either as a ready reference or as a summary that writers can understand "at a glance." Some readers immediately look at the graphic elements in a document to understand the message.

3   TO CLARIFY THE TEXT. If some readers should have questions about your text, a graphic element can help to answer these questions. For example, if you expect that a reader may question how you arrived at a total cost for a program you are proposing, you would document individual expenses totaling that final cost. Graphic elements also help readers monitor their understanding of information. For example, to perform a task, many readers shift their attention from the text to a graphic element to verify their understanding.

4   TO MOTIVATE. Most readers are not motivated to read thick copy blocks or page after page of text. They need to know that there is some relief from the text and that they can learn from a visual representation what they might not have time to read or learn from the text—especially in long documents, such as reports, proposals, or a set of instructions.

5   TO SIMPLIFY COMPLICATED INFORMATION. Sometimes explaining relationships among categories of information, tracing a sequence of actions, or discussing numerical data in the text is difficult for readers to understand. Providing a visual summary simplifies what is often difficult to explain in words.

6   TO PROVIDE ADDITIONAL INFORMATION. Graphic elements can help readers understand information better by filling in gaps or pieces of information that text cannot supply. For example, sketching a map and including it along with written directions helps readers gain a better understanding of where they are going and how they will get there. By showing other information, such as the placement of landmarks, the map provides information that supplements the text.

Although you have just read that graphic elements have numerous purposes, visuals do need to be accompanied by words. Specifically, graphic elements require *labels*, *call-outs*, and *captions*. You can find illustrations of these copy elements in Figure 5-4.

As you look at Figure 5-4, notice the layout of the page—the arrangement of all the copy and graphic elements, including the spaces left around them. Notice the ways the illustrator avoided crowding too much into one space. Also, notice how the illustrator outlined graphic elements or the combination of graphic ele-

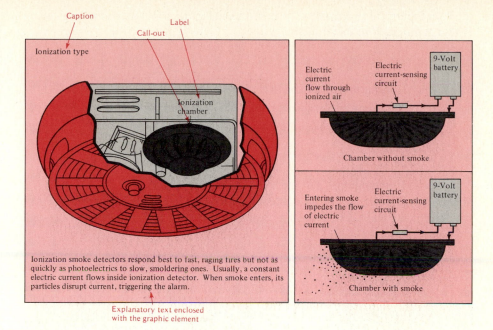

Figure 5-4   **Cutaway of smoke detector and closeups of ionization chamber.** (Copyright by Consumers Union of United States, Inc., Mount Vernon, N.Y. 10553. Reprinted by permission from *Consumer Reports:* October 1984 report on "Smoke Detectors.")

ments and copy elements with a solid line. This technique, called *framing*, creates a boundary between the graphic element and text or encloses explanatory text and graphic elements as a unit.

What Kinds of Graphic Elements to Use

Now that you know when to use graphic elements, you should know some of the kinds writers use to represent information; these include photographs, drawings, charts, tables, and graphs.

Photographs

Photographs function to verify an action, event, or activity or the results or effects of an action, event, or activity. For example, in a medical report, photographs might show a patient's condition before and after a treatment. These photographs help readers better understand the effects of a treatment, because the reader "sees" the effects. However, the primary purpose of these photographs in a medical report could be to persuade the medical community that this particular treatment does work or may be more effective than another one.

In Figure 2-3 in Chapter 2, you saw a catalog description of a crimper, along with a photograph of the crimper.

> Refer to that photograph of the crimper. What is the
> purpose of the photograph? Why are both the text
> and photograph necessary for a potential customer?

Because photographs do not always reproduce clearly, readers often have difficulty distinguishing details in a reproduction. If you decide to use photographs in a document, make sure you get a clear glossy photograph that reproduces well.

Drawings

Within organizations, writers use drawings to represent objects, spatial relationships among objects, or steps in a process. Drawings may be two- or three-dimensional and include varying amounts of detail. Deciding how detailed to make a drawing depends on how much your readers need to see.

> Why do you think the illustrator of Figure 5-4 drew
> both two- and three-dimensional illustrations of the
> smoke detector?

The two-dimensional drawing in Figure 5-5, a floor plan, appeared in a student's proposal for a college gymnasium. The drawing illustrates the structure of the gymnasium, as well as the interior design.

The three-dimensional drawing of the smoke alarm in Figure 5-4 is also an example of a *cutaway* drawing. In this kind of drawing, the artist cuts away an exterior section of an object to reveal an interior view. Notice how the illustrator of the smoke detector cut out a section of the detector to show readers the ionization chamber and also shaded the ionization chamber to focus readers' attention on it.

To show readers an inside view of all parts of the smoke detector, as well as their placement in relation to each other, the illustrator could have drawn a *cross section*. A cross section shows what an object would look like if it were sliced in half and viewed from the side.

In a *close-up*, illustrators focus on a particular part of an object to eliminate unnecessary or confusing details for a reader. In Figure 5-4, the close-ups of the chamber focus readers' attention on one part of the smoke detector to illustrate how the chamber operates with and without smoke.

To emphasize how parts of the chamber fit together the illustrator could have

REQUIRED GYMNASIUM DIMENSIONS

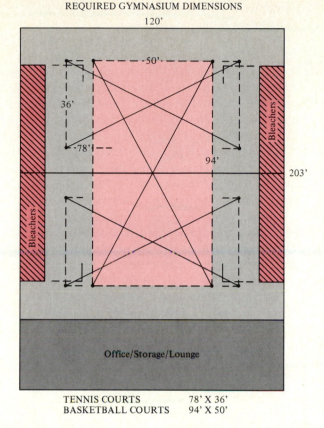

| TENNIS COURTS | 78' X 36' |
| BASKETBALL COURTS | 94' X 50' |

Figure 5-5   Floor plan for a gymnasium. (By permission from Gayle Assetto.)

used an *exploded drawing*. As the name suggests, an illustrator shows how separated parts of a disassembled object fit together to make the object. This kind of drawing is especially helpful when you want to explain how to assemble parts to make a whole mechanism.

In Figure 5-4, would photographs have been as effective as drawings in helping readers locate the ionization chamber or understand how the chamber looks before and after smoke? Explain your answer.

Charts

Charts, another type of graphic element, use geometric shapes connected by lines to represent components of a whole, such as steps in a process, or components or units comprising a whole. Charts become a visual shorthand for representing how smaller units work together to form a larger unit.

One of the most common diagrams you may have to draw on the job is an *organization chart*, which provides an overview of an organization or system. At a glance, a reader can understand the relationships among and between departments, divisions, or actions. Perhaps you have seen an organization chart for your school's student government organization. It represents a hierarchical structure of how the organization works—a skeleton of the organization—or how responsibilities are delegated. Areas of responsibility may be designated in geometric shapes, such as diamonds, squares, or rectangles; lines connecting these shapes represent lines of responsibility or communication among these areas. The organization chart in Figure 5-6 shows the relationship of various subdivisions of a department.

Another common chart is a *flowchart*. This type of diagram helps readers construct a mental picture of how a system or process works. Figure 5-7 shows you one kind of flowchart, representing how departments work together to manufacture an aircraft carrier. Often, as in this one, flowcharts arrange information so that a reader reads from top to bottom (hierarchically) or from left to right. At a glance, a reader gains an understanding of the hierarchical relationships among actions, as well as the temporal sequence of movements.

As you have seen in Figure 5-7, one way to represent steps in a procedure is with rectangles. Each rectangle represents a separate step, and arrows connect the sequence of actions.

To represent decision-making as part of a process, some illustrators use diamond shapes. Diamonds represent decisions that must be made under certain conditions. Think of these conditions as "if ... then" statements. For example, "If the light is on, then press switch 3. If the light is off, then press switch 2." Labels indicating the reader's response, as "Yes" or "No," along with directional lines

Organizational Development and Training

Figure 5-6   Organization chart. (By permission from Rodney Stevens, RCA, New Jersey.)

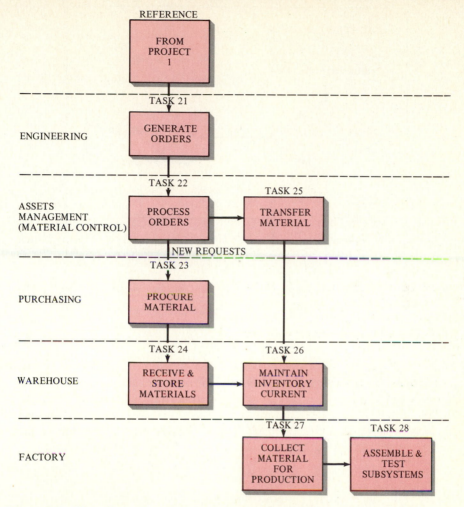

Figure 5-7 Flow chart. (By permission from Rodney Stevens, RCA, New Jersey.)

or arrows, signal the action readers should take under each condition. Actions are represented in squares or rectangles. Writers may also use ovals to signal beginning and ending points. Look at the flowchart in Figure 5-8 to see how an illustrator represented a process for monitoring a control panel. This segment of a complicated flowchart in an operator's manual represents the end of a process. After completing this section, an operator can go off duty.

What is the primary purpose of the flowchart in Figure 5-8?

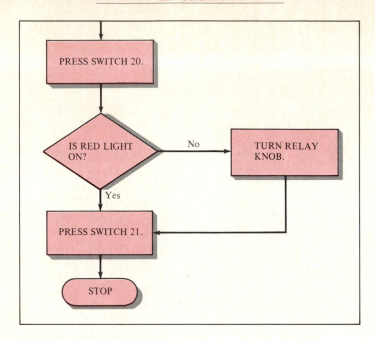

Figure 5-8   Concluding segment of a flow chart.

Sometimes directional lines trace cyclical processes, such as in a flowchart representing the recurring processes of evaporation and condensation. Directional lines may also loop back to steps to signal that the reader should repeat or return to a step.

To represent the procedure you read in the memo in Figure 5-3, draw a flowchart that includes decisions and actions.

The principle of directional movement in flowcharts may also be combined with drawings. The drawing in Figure 5-9 is an example of this combination, called a *pictorial flowchart*. This pictorial flowchart illustrates the greenhouse effect, a process which takes place as carbon dioxide and water vapor are released into the atmosphere. Arrows trace the process within the picture.

When illustrators want to represent subdivisions of an entire amount, they frequently use a *pie chart*. Slices in a circle represent percentages of a whole. The pie chart in Figure 5-10 illustrates the distribution of retirement account funds held

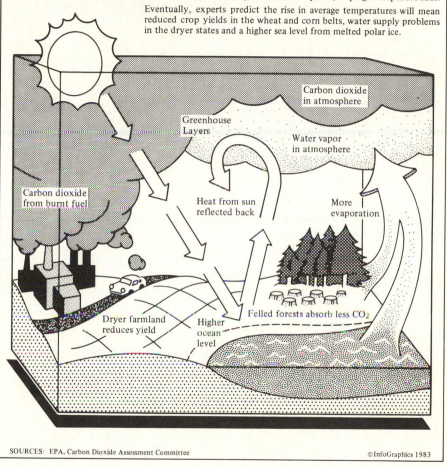

THE GREENHOUSE EFFECT

Recent studies have renewed interest in the "greenhouse" effect, caused by increased levels of carbon dioxide and water vapor in the atmosphere. Carbon dioxide is released when fuels are burnt and it is absorbed by growing plants. Two factors are increasing the amount of CO_2 — the burning of fossil fuels, producing CO_2, and the felling of the tropical forests, resulting in less absorbtion.

The extra carbon dioxide is forming a layer in the atmosphere like glass in a greenhouse-allowing heat from the sun in, but not letting it escape again. The heating process is accelerated by the rising temperature causing more evaporation. This in turn adds more water vapor to the atmosphere, helping to trap more heat.

Eventually, experts predict the rise in average temperatures will mean reduced crop yields in the wheat and corn belts, water supply problems in the dryer states and a higher sea level from melted polar ice.

Carbon dioxide in atmosphere

Greenhouse Layers

Water vapor in atmosphere

Carbon dioxide from burnt fuel

Heat from sun reflected back

More evaporation

Dryer farmland reduces yield

Higher ocean level

Felled forests absorb less CO_2

SOURCES: EPA, Carbon Dioxide Assessment Committee   © InfoGraphics 1983

Figure 5-9   Pictorial flow chart. (Source: InfoGraphics.)

in one year by savings institutions, commercial banks, and money market mutual funds.

Subdivide slices of a pie clockwise, labeling either inside (if there is enough room) or outside of each piece. The more subdivisions in a pie, the harder it usually is to demonstrate the relative proportions of all the pieces.

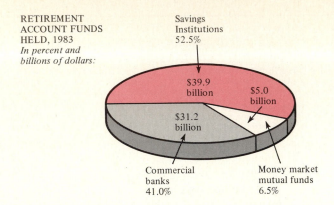

RETIREMENT
ACCOUNT FUNDS
HELD, 1983
*In percent and
billions of dollars:*

Savings
Institutions
52.5%

$39.9
billion

$5.0
billion

$31.2
billion

Commercial
banks
41.0%

Money market
mutual funds
6.5%

Total $76.1 billion

**Figure 5-10   Pie chart showing percentage of retirement account funds held in 1983
by savings institutions, commercial banks, and money market mutual funds.** (Source:
InfoGraphics.)

Tables

To simplify readers' understanding of quantities of numerical data or other units
of information, writers may use *tables*. Tables are parallel columns of data that
help readers compare changes in units of information.

To see how to set up a table, refer to Figure 5-11. Notice how the illustrator
centered, labeled and spaced that table so that units of information do not crowd
each other. Notice, also, that the illustrator captioned the table. Captions occur
either above or below tables.

TABLE 1: CRITERIA FOR EVALUATING BASE AND ENHANCED SSD MODELS

	BASE MODEL	ENHANCED SSD MODELS
Microprocessor	16/24-bit; Intel 80286	16/24-bit; Intel 80286
Permanent Memory (ROM)	64KB (killobyte)	64KB
User memory (RAM)	256KB standard; expandable to 3 MB (megabyte)	512KB standard; expandle to 3MB
On-line storage	1.2MB standard (one diskette drive)	21.2MB standard (one diskette drive and one 20 MB fixed disk drive)
System expansion	8 expansion slots	8 expansion slots
Operating System	Disk Operating System (DOS)	DOS
Cost	$ 2595.00	$ 4395.00

Figure 5-11   Format for a table. (By permission from Michele DiCarlo, Delphi Systems
Associates, Pennsylvania.)

What do you think might be the purpose or purposes of the table in Figure 5-11?

Writers may also use tables to enumerate options, decisions, operations, commands or steps. For example, Figure 5-12, part of a page from a manual accompanying a computer printer, lists possible problems a user might encounter, causes of these problems, and solutions.

In Figure 5-12 how does the illustrator use highlighting devices to call attention to significant pieces of information? Why do you think a table is effective in enumerating decisions, actions, or options?

Troubleshooting

Problem	Possible Cause	Solution
Power lamp does not light.	*AC plug is not connected to an AC receptacle.	*Connect AC input plug to AC receptacle.
	*Circuit breaker is open.	*Turn OFF AC Power switch. *Remove access cover. Press down breaker pushbutton. (Refer to Fig. 3-1.)
Paper lamp lights.	*Paper has run out, or is close to running out.	*Install new paper.

Figure 5-12   Section of a page from a printer manual.

Graphs

Graphs consist of lines or bars that trace trends in statistical information. By following a line or comparing bars, a reader can quickly generalize about trends. Line graphs use one or more lines to depict changes in values of a variable quantity or quantities. They trace trends, amounts, and results over a period of time. You may have read the Dow Jones market analysis graphs in the *Wall Street Journal*, which trace gradual or sudden shifts in the stock market.

Line graphs are especially effective for comparing two or more items over a period of time or two or more items at the same time. Figure 5-13 compares total disbursements in hospital insurance trust funds to total income in hospital insurance trust funds from 1966 until a projected date of 1990.

Bar graphs are rectangular blocks of color or shading that allow comparisons among items. The bars may be drawn horizontally or vertically and may measure one or more quantities over time. The vertical bar graph in Figure 5-14 compares the percentage of elderly eligible for Medicare from 1966 to 1982. Because the illustrator also wanted to show relative percentages of parts of a whole, different subgroups of the elderly, the illustrator used shading to indicate these percentages over time.

> Convert either Figure 5-13 or 5-14 into prose.
> Compare your prose explanation to another
> student's explanation.

Here are some guidelines for constructing bar or line graphs. As you read these guidelines, refer to Figures 5-13 to 5-16 to see how various illustrators incorporated these guidelines into their graphs.

1 Use the horizontal line of a graph to mark off your independent variable, such as time periods.
2 Use the vertical line to mark off your dependent variable, the quantity that you are measuring, such as amounts or costs.
3 Label both the horizontal and vertical lines so that readers know what variables you are using. When you are measuring quantities, begin at zero to give a truthful representation of increase or decrease. It is possible to distort readers' impression of change in a graph by purposely starting a measurement scale much higher than zero. For example, in Figure 15-15, if the illustrator had begun measuring sales along the $110,000–$130,000 scale, instead of from the zero point, the increase in sales in

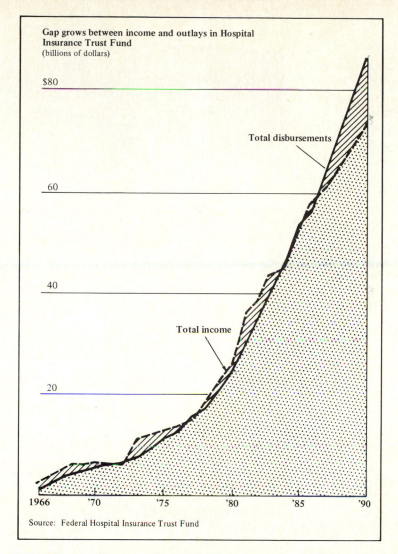

Gap grows between income and outlays in Hospital
Insurance Trust Fund
(billions of dollars)

Total disbursements

Total income

$80

60

40

20

1966   '70   '75   '80   '85   '90

Source: Federal Hospital Insurance Trust Fund

**Figure 5-13   Line graph comparing total disbursements to total income in hospital
insurance trust funds.** (Copyright © 1983 by The New York Times Company. Reprinted
by permission.)

the winter months would have seemed far greater than it does in the $0–
$130,000 scale.

4   Use a legend if you are comparing two or more quantities. A legend is a
    key that identifies the quantities your lines or bars are measuring. Gen-
    erally, place that legend inside the frame surrounding your graph. Figure
    5-14 uses a legend to identify two kinds of populations.

5   Title your graph above it, below it, or within the frame surrounding it.

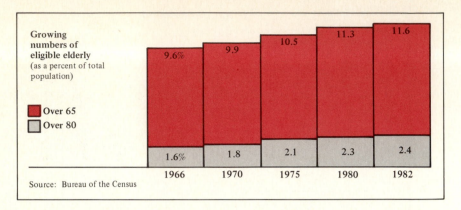

Figure 5-14 Bar graph comparing percentages of elderly eligible for medicare. (Copyright © 1983 by The New York Times Company. Reprinted by permission.)

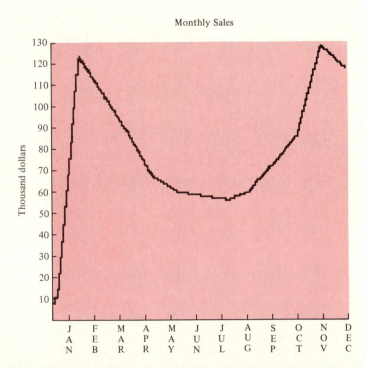

Figure 5-15   Line graph illustrating monthly sales. (By permission from Andrew Leschak.)

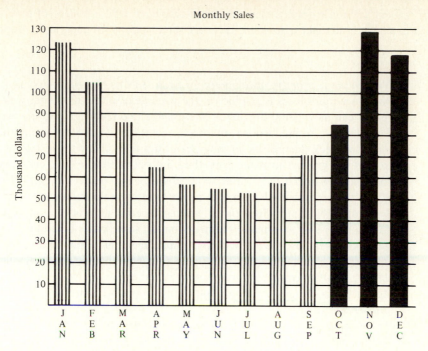

Figure 5-16   Bar graph illustrating monthly sales. (By permission from Andrew Leschak.)

Figures 5-15 and Figures 5-16 were plotted on a computer. Both illustrate the same kind of information—monthly product sales in thousands of dollars for one year.

Even though they both illustrate the same information, how does each representation affect your interpretation of the information?

Where to Integrate Graphic Elements

Where do writers integrate graphic elements in a document? There are three options for incorporating graphics. Deciding where to place a graphic depends on your purpose in using it—to inform, document, show the results of exploring information, instruct, or persuade. Placement also depends on understanding how your readers will use a graphic element, for example, to read it instead of text, to perform a task, or to make a decision. Here are three options for integrating graphics:

1   *Next to the text on an accompanying page*. In this design, called *storybook*, a writer places a graphic on the page next to the text. That way a reader can move from the text to the graphic and back again to the text. For example, in instructional manuals, many readers rely on visual material to check themselves as they perform a step. They move from the text to the graphic to make sure they are performing a task correctly. Imagine how much more difficult it would be for readers to perform a task if they constantly had to turn pages to refer to the relevant graphic.

2   *Integrated in the text*. Sometimes writers integrate graphics in their texts so that the visual information appears on the same page as the text. Or, writers may enclose the text within a graphic element to reinforce readers' understanding of the graphic. You have already seen an example of a text enclosed with a graphic (Figure 5-4).

3   *Appended to the document*. In some cases, graphic material cannot be placed next to or integrated in the text because the graphic element takes up more than a page. In such instances, writers append a pull-out page, conveniently located for readers to refer to numerous times. At other times graphic elements may be important for only some, and not all, readers. Or, elements may support information in a document but may not be essential in the text for all readers. Under these conditions, writers include graphics in an appendix. (You will read more about appendices in Chapter 13.)

How to Integrate Graphic Elements and Text

After determining where to place graphic elements, writers have to determine how to tie them in with the text. We have already discussed the importance of using captions and labels to identify graphics and parts of graphics. Now we need to discuss how writers connect graphic elements with their text.

Within the text of a document writers lead into a graphic or refer readers to an accompanying graphic. Effective writers alert readers to what a graphic element is designed to illustrate—trends, proportions, changes or cycles, projected costs. For example, in Figure 5-17, notice how a writer prepares readers for a table by referring to the table and explaining what it measures. Writers often fail to prepare readers for graphic elements: they fail to tell readers what to focus on in a figure or table.

With the exception of tables, refer to all graphic elements as "Figures." Number all graphic elements in a document sequentially, such as Figure 1, Figure

A summary of proposed facilities for the county is presented in Table 6. This summary includes the length of gravity sewers and force mains. It also lists the gallons per minute (gpm) that will flow through the three proposed pumping stations.

Figure 5-17   Introductory text preparing reader for a table.

2, Figure 3, and so on. It is important that you identify the source of a graphic, if you have not designed it yourself. If that is the case, document your source above or below the graphic. Notice, for example, in this chapter how we indicated our sources of graphic elements. If you draw a graphic element based on data from another source, you also should document that source beneath the graphic. Acknowledging sources of information not only is a courtesy, but also adds to the credibility of your document.

Once you have reviewed your graphic elements to make sure that you have labeled them sequentially, review your text to make sure that references in your text correspond to the figure and table numbers accompanying your visual material.

Whether you write a one-page memo or a 200-page report, consider how you will design your document for your readers. In essence what you will be doing is making your document "look good."

CHECKLIST FOR LAYOUT

To design your documents for readers, answer the following questions:

Copy Elements

1   What use will the reader make of this document?
2   Will copy elements help the reader achieve that purpose?
3   What kinds of information do I want to draw my reader's attention to?
4   What kinds of copy elements should I use?

Graphic Elements

5   For what purpose or purposes would I use a graphic element for my reader?
6   What kind of graphic element should I use to achieve this purpose or purposes?

7   Where should I include graphic elements for my reader?

8   How will I refer the reader to graphic elements?

9   How will I introduce graphic elements in my text?

10 Where will I place captions, labels, call-outs, and legends?

11 If I use graphic elements, do my textual references to graphic elements correspond to figure and table numbers, captions, labels, and call-outs in my graphic elements?

1. How could you use a graphic element in the following letter explaining two insurance policies?

Dear Mrs. Smith:

You have two hospital policies with our insurance firm. Policy 171--the basic hospital plan--allows $90 a day for hospital room and board charges with a ninety-day maximum and a $10/day hospital miscellaneous charge with a thirty-day maximum. Policy 172--the supplementary hospital plan-- allows an additional $10/day for room and board charges to a maximum of thirty days and $5/day from the thirty-first day of the hospital miscellaneous charges to a maximum of sixty days and $100 maximum allowance for surgical benefits.

Very truly yours,

Claim Approver
Health Claim Division

---

2. The manager of a savings and loan bank believes that customers need more information about how to establish credit. Read the following information about how to establish a good credit history and prepare a flowchart to send to customers.

How to establish a good credit history

Your record at a credit bureau is a crucial item in obtaining credit. It's a good idea to check your credit history periodically at various credit bureaus. It's especially important to check before applying for a large loan. Nothing can be more frustrating than to apply for a mortgage loan and find that an error made on a department-store account three years ago is still on your record.

Finding the credit bureaus may be tricky, however. A particular bureau covering an area may not necessarily be listed in the yellow pages under credit bureaus. At the end of this box, we've given the five major credit bureaus and their addresses. If you write to them, they may be able to furnish your report themselves or at least put you in contact with their office in your area.

You have a right to know what's in your bureau report although, except in New York and California, a bureau doesn't have to give you a copy of the report itself. The Fair Credit Reporting Act gives you the right to insist that a credit bureau recheck any wrong or incomplete information in your report. If, after investigation, the bureau claims the information is correct, you can put a 100-word statement in the record to explain your side of the dispute.

Credit bureaus are allowed to charge a fee—usually $5 to $8—for giving you the information in a report. But if you've been turned down for credit in the last 30 days, the bureau cannot charge.

Besides maintaining a good credit-bureau record, there are some specific things you can do to help establish a good credit history:

1. Open both a checking and a savings account

2. Establish credit with a local department store. Department-store credit is often easier to obtain than bank credit, and many creditors look favorably on that type of credit when judging your application.

3. Take out a small installment loan from a bank and pay it back promptly. Some creditors look for evidence that you can successfully handle different types of credit.

4. Do not borrow from a small-loan company if you can help it. Its rates are

likely to be high, but more importantly, listing a small-loan company as a credit reference could hurt you in obtaining other credit (see text).

5. If a bank or major department store offers you a credit card, take it. Use it to help establish a credit history. As we've pointed out, credit may be harder to obtain if you apply for it.

6. Obtain credit from creditors who report to credit bureaus—banks, large department stores, and the like. Many small stores, credit card companies, and the oil companies don't routinely report their accounts to credit bureaus.

7. If you move and continue to have accounts with creditors in your old city, make sure that the accounts are reported to the credit bureaus with your new address.

8. Don't apply for credit too often in a six-month period. If you're turned down, that fact stays on your credit record. Creditors judge that unfavorably.

9. Pay all bills promptly, including those from utility companies. While utilities don't report their customers' accounts to credit bureaus, your promptly paid receipts may persuade prospective creditors to take a chance with you.

10. If you have a joint credit account with your spouse, make sure that it's reported to the credit bureau in both your names. If you're a woman, the account should be reported in your given name—Mary Smith, for example; not Mrs. John Smith.

11. If you're going through a divorce or separation, make sure payments are made on all joint accounts. Even after a divorce, you're responsible for payments on a joint account. Joint accounts often become delinquent in this situation. That can blemish both parties' credit records. Under the law, however, you have the right to present evidence to the creditor that the delinquency is not your fault.

12. If an unexpected large expense or a loss of income causes you to miss payments, try to work out alternative arrangements with your creditors. Since a creditor will report your account as "late" to a credit bureau, contact the credit bureau and enter a 100-word explanation on your record.

3. You are a staff member in an organization called Citizens for Peace. Your project supervisor asks you to investigate attendance percentages for members in this organization for the period from November through February. Draw a line graph comparing the following percentages of members' attendance in the organization. (The section numbers represent areas that members come from within the community.)

	SECTION 1	SECTION 2	SECTION 3	SECTION 4
November	40%	66%	40%	64%
December	40%	70%	40%	66%
January	35%	72%	36%	65%
February	42%	72%	28%	66%

After you draw the graph, summarize the trends presented in the graph.

4. Investigate how long it would take and how much it would cost for you to take a train, a bus, or an airplane to a major city at least several hundred miles away. Present this information in a decision table so that your classmates can compare the differences to decide which way they might choose to go.

5. Sometimes writers must convert information in a graphic element into prose. Read the following bar graph about increases and decreases in areas of employment from 1981 to 1995. In a paragraph addressed to your classmates, who are all interested in the potential job market, summarize the trends this graph traces.

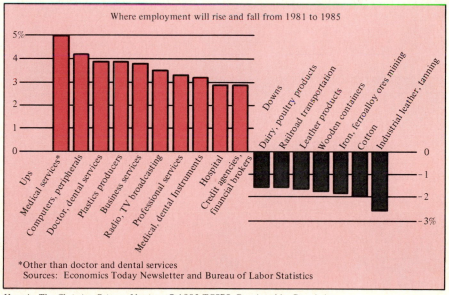

Where employment will rise and fall from 1981 to 1985

*Other than doctor and dental services
Sources: Economics Today Newsletter and Bureau of Labor Statistics

Horn in *The Christian Science Monitor*, © 1983 TCSPS. Reprinted by Permission.

6. In the *Occupational Outlook Handbook*, find the research hiring trends for the next five years in the profession that you are interested in entering. Draw a line graph or a bar graph showing this trend; then write an introduction for your graph that explains what the graph is measuring.

7. Draw an organization chart for an organization or department you are familiar with. Convert that chart into explanatory text.

8. Find a product manual or a description of how to perform a process. Draw a flowchart that would accompany the text in the manual or in the description.

9. Find a piece of text that contains numerical data. Convert these data into three different kinds of graphics. Write an explanation of how each kind affects readers' understanding or interpretation of the data.

10. Write a summary of the results reported in Table 5-2. The results came from a 1984 national survey of Americans' concerns about economic issues.

Table 5-2 Could You Tell Me to What Extent You Are Concerned About the Following Issues

	VERY CON- CERNED, %	SOME- WHAT CON- CERNED, %	NOT CON- CERNED, %	DON'T KNOW OR NO ANSWER, %
Future reductions in Social Security benefits you will be eligible for when you retire	68	18	12	2
The need to retrain should you ever have to change jobs	38	20	39	3
Computers or robotics threatening your job in the future	29	17	50	4
Your employer moving away from your area	27	13	55	5
A corporate takeover or merger of your company	24	19	51	6
(Number of respondents)	(1006)			

The American Public's Knowledge of Business & The Economy: A National Survey of Public Awareness and Personal Opinion, A Hearst Report, 1984. Used by permission of The Hearst Corporation, New York.

APPLICATIONS
SECTION THREE

STRATEGIES FOR WRITING CORRESPONDENCE

CHAPTER 6

PURPOSES FOR WRITING CORRESPONDENCE

Jan Holcombe, a program director for a county-sponsored recreation program for girls, has numerous responsibilities. She seeks financial support from local, state, and federal funding agencies to operate recreation programs. Once she receives financial support, she reports to funding agencies, informing them of the success of the county programs. She participates in regional and national conferences, during which directors exchange information about activities and programs. To understand the needs of her county, Holcombe meets with representatives from communities. These conferences and meetings help her decide what kinds of programs to offer. In addition, she supervises a staff of twenty who help her administer these programs by planning and evaluating them, hiring instructors, and writing publicity.

All of these responsibilities require Holcombe to spend a considerable part of a day writing correspondence. Woven throughout her day are periods of planning, drafting, revising, editing, and proofreading letters and memos. For example, in a typical day she

- Proofreads a letter to the state requesting additional funds to offer a community workshop on understanding adolescents

- Drafts a memo to her staff, instructing them how to fill out and submit travel vouchers after they have visited a club
- Writes a memo informing her staff of a time change for the next monthly meeting
- Plans a letter to another program director who is interested in finding out which of Holcombe's programs have been the most successful over the past year
- Redrafts a letter to the director of a local program, recommending that the director drop a program that has been poorly attended during the past year
- Writes the final copy of a letter inviting a job applicant to an interview for a staff position

Composing correspondence—memos and letters—is a routine kind of writing at work. *Memos* are brief messages, sometimes containing only one paragraph and frequently taking no more than a page. Most of the time, you will write memos to internal readers—those who are familiar with your organization and who may have established a working relationship with you. For example, Holcombe writes memos to such internal readers as co-workers, staff members, and her county supervisor. They understand how the community organization works and achieves its goals. Because most readers in organizations receive numerous memos a day, the more concisely you can write memos, the more satisfied your readers will be. Busy decision makers, in particular, appreciate brief memos.

Letters are also brief messages, ranging from one paragraph to several pages. Generally, you will write letters to external readers—those outside your organization who are not necessarily familiar with how your organization works, what services it performs, or what products it sells. Your external readers will differ from your internal readers. Because outside readers will be less familiar with your organization, they will have different motivations for reading your messages. As a result, you will have to take the time to represent yourself and your organization and orient these readers to your message.

Having written and received letters yourself, you are probably more familiar with this form of communication than with others presented in this book. As a consumer, you may have written to an organization requesting information about its product. As a concerned citizen, you may have written a letter to your congressional representative to influence that individual's votes. As a participant in a social, religious, political, or business organization, you may have written to members, informing them of an upcoming event.

In this chapter you will see examples of representative letters and memos and of the problems they solve. Of course, we can't offer you examples of every type of letter or memo that you might have to write. Your position within your organization will determine what, when, why, and to whom you write. However, we can explore the kinds of problems writers solve in correspondence, explain the purposes for writing correspondence and describe its general features.

EXPLORING THE PROBLEMS
MEMOS SOLVE

Probably, the most frequent form of communication that you will write on the job is the memo because it is a daily vehicle for circulating information about an organization's activities. The diverse kinds of problems memos solve are represented in the following list. Memos are useful when you need

1. To convey social responses, such as thanks, congratulations, praise, or sympathy
2. To admonish or warn, such as voicing concern about a danger or oversight
3. To inform readers about an event, issue, decision, or person
4. To verify or document information for future reference, such as recording the results of a meeting
5. To confirm information, such as meeting times or travel arrangements
6. To call attention to an organizational problem, such as ineffective work procedures
7. To instruct readers what to do or how to perform a task, such as filling out a form
8. To clarify an issue, such as a misunderstanding about a decision or an action
9. To evaluate a situation, condition, decision, object, or choices for solving a problem
10. To summarize information, such as the results of an on-site investigation, a meeting or conference, or research
11. To identify the contents of attached documents, such as reports and proposals, circulated within an organization or sent to another organization
12. To request information, such as organizational data
13. To provide information in response to an inquiry
14. To require action, such as following a new procedure

EXPLORING THE PROBLEMS
LETTERS SOLVE

The same occasions for writing memos that we just listed are also the occasions when you may write letters. Usually, however, your readers will be external ones. In addition to the occasions you just read about, you may also have to write letters when you need

1. To sell an organization's products or services
2. To convince others about your qualifications

3   To price a job
4   To confirm a sale
5   To respond to a customer's complaint
6   To motivate a customer to pay an overdue bill

PURPOSES OF CORRESPONDENCE

To solve organizational problems, writers compose correspondence that achieves one of the following primary purposes or aims:

- To express
- To inform
- To document
- To explore
- To instruct
- To persuade

Sometimes, however, writers need to accomplish two or more of these purposes at the same time. For example, Holcombe's memo to her staff about a new procedure for filling out travel forms both instructed workers how to fill out the forms and persuaded them that it was important to follow these new procedures. Or, the purpose of a letter or memo may extend beyond the event that prompted it. Holcombe had to write a letter responding to another program director's request for information about successful programs. Holcombe saw this initial situation—calling for a letter of response—also as an opportunity to persuade this director to work with Holcombe to develop some new county-sponsored programs.

Because letters and memos may have one or more purposes or may go beyond their original purpose, we will classify the correspondence in this chapter according to both its primary and secondary purposes. Table 6-1 previews and classifies correspondence according to primary and secondary purposes. Classifying correspondence according to its primary aim will help you understand the features of each aim. Classifying correspondence according to secondary aims will help you understand how coequal or subordinate aims work together in letters and memos.

After you read about the general features of each purpose—its focus, content, strategies for arrangement, and style—you will read several cases. These cases explain the occasions that prompted writers to compose correspondence. As you read each case, *analyze the organizational problem each writer faced.* Then *focus your attention on how each writer composed correspondence to achieve one primary aim, and one or more secondary aims.*

Table 6-1   Primary and Secondary Purposes of Correspondence

PURPOSES OF CORRESPONDENCE

PRIMARY PURPOSE	SECONDARY PURPOSE(S)	EXAMPLES OF CORRESPONDENCE
To Express	To Persuade and to Inform	Goodwill Memo (Figure 6-1)
	To Inform	Rejection Letter (Figure 6-2)
To Inform	To Instruct	Response Letter (Figure 6-4) to Letter of Inquiry in Figure 6-3
To Document	To Inform and to Explore	Documentary Memo (Figure 6-5)
To Explore	To Inform, to Document, and to Persuade	Progress Memo (Figure 6-6)
To Instruct	To Inform	Instructional Memo (Figure 6-7)
To Persuade	To Express, to Inform, and to Instruct	Donation Letter (Figure 6-8)
	To Inform, to Document, and to Express	Job Application Letter and Résumé (Figures 6-9 and 6-10)
	To Document to Inform, and to Express	Collection Letter (Figure 6-11)

WRITING TO EXPRESS

General Features

Focus

When you write correspondence that aims to express, you focus on your reactions or responses to the subject or issue under discussion. You may express your responses, using "I," or those of your organization, using "we."

Content

The content of correspondence that aims to express consists of your feelings, personal experiences, opinions, beliefs, values, goals, social responses (such as "congratulations''), or ideologies. Often, the content of expressive correspondence is designed to keep channels of communication open.

Strategies for Arrangement

The strategies you use to arrange information in expressive correspondence will depend on whether you are writing favorable or unfavorable messages to your readers. Favorable messages acknowledge the accomplishments of an individual or group by expressing praise, congratulations, or appreciation.

You usually open your good news correspondence by expressing your feelings of appreciation or goodwill. Then, you state the event or issue you are responding to. Your strategies for developing your message can range from a chronological pattern or autobiographical pattern to associative patterns of thinking in which you draw on personal experiences, emotions, or reactions to support your favorable response. Some writers close their expressive correspondence by restating their positive response or by suggesting positive consequences or future hopes.

Messages that report unfavorable information are likely to disappoint your reader. When you have to write this kind of information, such as disappointment about the quality of an employee's work, you have to decide if your strategy should be to open with a negative statement or to withhold the negative statement until you first explain why you are expressing an unfavorable reaction. You need to justify the basis of your response. Your closing can state your unfavorable response or open up channels to resolve an unpleasant or difficult situation.

Vocabulary and Style

Connotative words, exclamatory words, and superlatives (such as ''most remarkable'' or ''most extraordinary'') characterize writing that aims to express.

Case: Occasion for Writing a Goodwill Memo

What Problem Must the Writer Solve?

John Hill has been working for four years as a sales representative at Landowe's, Inc., a manufacturer of industrial shelving units. In this position, he frequently takes phone orders from customers and has orders shipped directly from his organization's warehouse. However, complications can occur when customers make last-minute changes in their orders. Over the years, Betty Simmons in the Ship Direct Department has helped Hill resolve numerous complications in customer orders. Recently, she helped save the organization $20,000 because she was able to make several last-minute changes in a customer's order and still ship it on time. This occasion prompts Hill to think about Simmons's contribution to Landowe's over the years.

Since the goal of Hill's organization is to sell shelving units, the shipping department is an essential means, or operator, for meeting that goal. Someone as reliable and knowledgeable as Simmons makes the company operate more effectively. Identifying who the valuable employees are helps the company meet its goal.

How Does the Memo Solve the Problem?

Hill decides to send a memo to Simmons's supervisor expressing appreciation of Simmons. Hill knows that supervisors periodically evaluate their staff. As you read Hill's memo in Figure 6-1, look at how he achieved his primary purpose, to express his thanks for a job well done. Hill also writes to inform and to persuade. He writes to inform about Simmons's most recent help—a piece of "news" for the reader—to persuade Simmons's supervisor that Simmons is a valuable employee.

His strategy is to open by expressing thanks and stating the reason for that response. To develop the memo, he draws on his personal experiences and his observations which persuade readers to accept Hill's judgment of Simmons.

> Notice that Hill sends a copy not only to Simmons's supervisor, but also to the Director of Human Resources. What does including those readers suggest about Hill's purposes for writing?

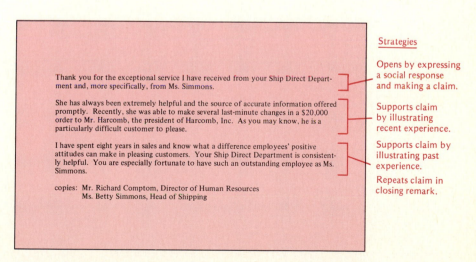

Strategies

Opens by expressing a social response and making a claim.

Thank you for the exceptional service I have received from your Ship Direct Department and, more specifically, from Ms. Simmons.

She has always been extremely helpful and the source of accurate information offered promptly. Recently, she was able to make several last-minute changes in a $20,000 order to Mr. Harcomb, the president of Harcomb, Inc. As you may know, he is a particularly difficult customer to please.

Supports claim by illustrating recent experience.

I have spent eight years in sales and know what a difference employees' positive attitudes can make in pleasing customers. Your Ship Direct Department is consistently helpful. You are especially fortunate to have such an outstanding employee as Ms. Simmons.

Supports claim by illustrating past experience.

Repeats claim in closing remark.

copies: Mr. Richard Comptom, Director of Human Resources
       Ms. Betty Simmons, Head of Shipping

Figure 6-1   Goodwill memo. (By permission from Yvonne Walko.)

Case: Occasion for Writing a Rejection Letter

What Problem Must the Writer Solve?

Margaret Harding, Director of Human Resources at Data, Inc., a distributor of data bases, has the unfortunate task of writing rejection letters to applicants who were not hired for an advertised position as telemarketing representative. One of the rejected candidates, Amanda Jones, was well qualified but did not have as much sales experience as the hired candidate. Harding knows that rejection is difficult for anyone to accept—even highly qualified job applicants. She thinks about her operators—what she can say that will not offend Jones.

How Does the Letter Solve the Problem?

Thinking about her reader's feelings prompts Harding to write a letter that expresses gratitude and regret (see Figure 6-2).

Specifically, she opens her letter by expressing gratitude and regret to her reader. She continues her rejection letter by describing how difficult it was to select one candidate. Her closing paragraph expresses another personal response—a wish for the applicant's eventual success.

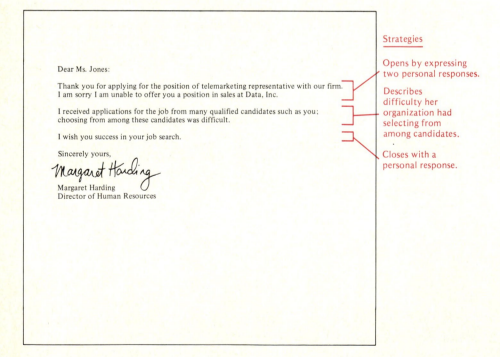

Strategies

Opens by expressing two personal responses.

Describes difficulty her organization had selecting from among candidates.

Closes with a personal response.

Dear Ms. Jones:

Thank you for applying for the position of telemarketing representative with our firm. I am sorry I am unable to offer you a position in sales at Data, Inc.

I received applications for the job from many qualified candidates such as you; choosing from among these candidates was difficult.

I wish you success in your job search.

Sincerely yours,

Margaret Harding

Margaret Harding
Director of Human Resources

Figure 6-2   Rejection letter.

Why is Harding's strategy an appropriate way to reject a candidate? Circle the words that indicate that
Harding is writing primarily to express.

WRITING TO INFORM
General Features

Focus

When you aim to inform readers, you focus on the subject or issue under discussion
to help your reader become knowledgeable.

Content

Informative correspondence is factual and comprehensive, and it contains ''news''
for a reader. That is, it contains verifiable information, includes *all* the information
that is necessary for a reader, and contains information that your reader does not
already know. One useful way to determine whether you have included *all* the
necessary information for your reader is to ask the journalists' questions: ''Who?''
''What?'' ''When?'' ''Where?'' ''Why?'' ''How?''

Strategies for Arrangement

Expressing a social response to a reader, stating a topic, or summarizing a situation
are some of the ways in which you might choose to open correspondence that
informs. Memos, especially one-paragraph ones, often dispense with a formal
opening when both reader and writer share a common context for understanding a
topic or an issue. Letters to external readers, however, need opening paragraphs
to orient readers to a topic or an issue.

To develop the body of your correspondence, use any of the patterns or
combination of patterns that you read about in Chapter 3, Strategy Eight: ''Ask
What You Have to *Do* in Your Writing.'' Deciding what patterns to use will depend on the kinds of information your reader needs to become more knowledgeable
about.

Some correspondence ends with a closing paragraph that summarizes the
contents or encourages future communication. Other correspondence, usually
memos more than letters, may not have a separate conclusion, especially when
readers share an informal work relationship.

Vocabulary and Style

In contrast to correspondence that aims to express, correspondence that aims to inform primarily uses denotative language. Use objective, accurate language to provide your readers with information about the "who," "what," "when," "where," "why," and "how."

Case: Occasion for Writing a Response Letter

What Problem Must the Writer Solve?

Pat McClosky, a staff assistant in the headquarters of an agency that administers certifying examinations for real estate agents, receives a letter of inquiry from a real estate broker. This broker, unfamiliar with how the agency administers tests, wants to know if the testing center provides accommodations for a disabled candidate. The inquiry letter appears in Figure 6-3, along with some of the staff assistant's notes to herself about how to respond.

    The problem is to discover what the candidate can or must do to take the test. Because the assistant is familiar with the testing center, she jots down some initial notes based on what she already knows. During a phone call to the center, she finds out that the broker has to document the candidate's disability on the examination registration form. Drawing on what she already knows and what she finds out, the staff assistant writes the response letter shown in Figure 6-4.

How Does the Letter Solve the Problem?

McClosky's primary purpose is to inform by responding to her reader's request. Since she has good news to deliver, she opens the letter by immediately responding to the broker's question. Because her answer is "yes," she writes to instruct Williams about the "how," the arrangements.

    To help solve the problem, McClosky uses the following strategies to arrange information: she opens by immediately responding to the reader's question, describes the process the center will use, and closes with information that keeps channels of communication open.

Dear Ms. McClosky:

Jeffrey Waters, one of my candidates for a real estate license, is scheduled to take his certifying examination in Dover on April 30, 1987. However, he cannot write answers to the questions because he is a disabled veteran who has lost the use of his hands. *Phone Dover!*

Do you have a way to accommodate this candidate? If you do, what special arrangements, if any, must he make in advance? If you do not, what should this candidate do next to find an appropriate testing arrangement? You can imagine how eager Mr. Waters is to take his exam and become certified.

Thank you for any information you can offer us.

Sincerely yours,

John Williams

John Williams
Director

– yes, we notify person in charge that day.
– oral test?
– notify us about disability so we can make arrangements.

Figure 6-3   Letter of inquiry.

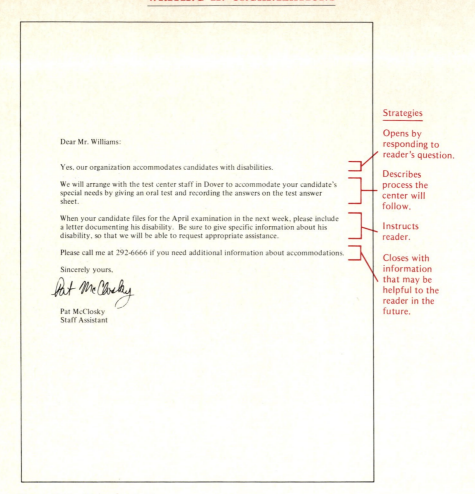

Dear Mr. Williams:

Yes, our organization accommodates candidates with disabilities.

We will arrange with the test center staff in Dover to accommodate your candidate's special needs by giving an oral test and recording the answers on the test answer sheet.

When your candidate files for the April examination in the next week, please include a letter documenting his disability. Be sure to give specific information about his disability, so that we will be able to request appropriate assistance.

Please call me at 292-6666 if you need additional information about accommodations.

Sincerely yours,

Pat McClosky

Pat McClosky
Staff Assistant

Strategies

Opens by responding to reader's question.

Describes process the center will follow.

Instructs reader.

Closes with information that may be helpful to the reader in the future.

Figure 6-4   Response letter.

Discuss how this response letter fulfills the criteria of informative writing: is it factual and comprehensive? Does it provide the reader with new information? What are some examples of her objective language? Suppose that the staff assistant could not help the broker because the test center did not provide accommodations. Do you think it would have been just as appropriate for her to begin her response letter with a negative response such as, "No, we cannot accommodate you"? Explain your answer.

WRITING TO DOCUMENT
General Features

Focus

When your aim is to document, you focus on establishing or verifying facts about the subject or issue under discussion.

Content

Documentary correspondence records yours or others' verifiable observations, facts, or data, such as proceedings of a meeting or conference, or quotations or paraphrases from an eyewitness. Documentary correspondence is an organization's historical record of events and as such may have immediate or future use. Decision makers may refer to documentary correspondence to confirm information or make decisions. When you write documentary correspondence to external readers, you write to verify your or your organization's activities. The contents of documentary correspondence include responses to such questions as: Who said or did what? When? Where? What did *X* look like? What happened?

Documentary information includes names, places, events, times, dates, facts, statistics, verifiable observations, direct or indirect quotations, or paraphrases. Precise descriptions of people, places, things, actions, and conditions are also characteristic of documentary writing.

Strategies for Arrangement

Because so many readers and writers work in the same organizational context, in documentary correspondence you often can eliminate a formal introduction and simply list categories of information that establish or verify a topic or an issue. When your readers are unfamiliar with a topic or an issue, begin your correspondence with a sentence or a paragraph that orients your readers to the subject or issue you are documenting. Your introduction might state the purpose of your documentary correspondence, the ways you collected data, and the sources you consulted.

You can rely on any one or more of the patterns you read about in Chapter 3, Strategy Eight: ''Ask What You Have to *Do* in Your Writing,'' to develop a strategy for your body paragraphs. Usually, you will classify your information in alphabetical, sequential, numerical, categorical, or spatial order (such as when you record observations at an accident site).

If it is necessary or important for your reader to know what you conclude about your information, develop a closing paragraph. Otherwise, let your readers draw their own conclusions based on your data.

Vocabulary and Style

Denotative and precise language marks the style of documentary writing. You may also use technical language and abbreviations that your readers understand. Passive voice verbs have traditionally been one of the characteristics of documentary writing, especially when writers record what they have observed or what they or others have done (the effect of actions). Although many organizations are encouraging employees to use the active voice instead of the passive voice to record observations, you may find that the organization you work for will not tolerate this change.

Case: Occasion for Writing a Documentary Memo

What Problem Must the Writer Solve?

A county recreation program offers after-school sports for girls. However, to the surprise of the program director, no one has enrolled, even though she had expected the sports program to be a success. To understand why girls are not enrolling, the coordinator asks her staff assistant, Julie Lopez, to find out if other community organizations may be offering similar programs that are competing with the county program.

> Analyze the organizational problem the coordinator
> is facing in terms of the four components of a
> problem.

How Does the Memo Solve the Problem?

After interviewing directors of community organizations, Lopez writes a memo that aims to document her interviews (see Figure 6-5). She also writes to inform— to convey ''news'' to the coordinator. The new pieces of information she includes are the reasons why girls are not attending.

Lopez opens her documentary memo by identifying the purpose of her interviews and the kind of problem she hoped to solve. She arranges her documentary information chronologically to verify when she spoke with directors. Under

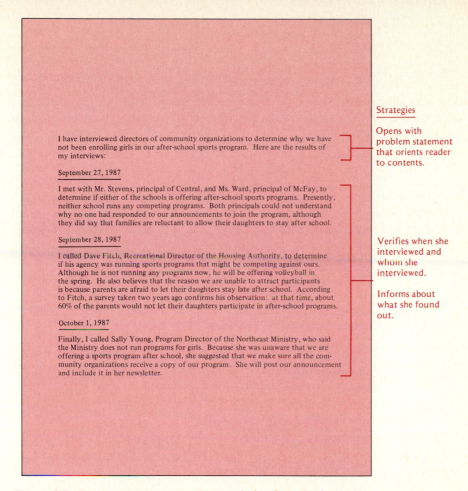

I have interviewed directors of community organizations to determine why we have not been enrolling girls in our after-school sports program. Here are the results of my interviews:

September 27, 1987

I met with Mr. Stevens, principal of Central, and Ms. Ward, principal of McFay, to determine if either of the schools is offering after-school sports programs. Presently, neither school runs any competing programs. Both principals could not understand why no one had responded to our announcements to join the program, although they did say that families are reluctant to allow their daughters to stay after school.

September 28, 1987

I called Dave Fitch, Recreational Director of the Housing Authority, to determine if his agency was running sports programs that might be competing against ours. Although he is not running any programs now, he will be offering volleyball in the spring. He also believes that the reason we are unable to attract participants is because parents are afraid to let their daughters stay late after school. According to Fitch, a survey taken two years ago confirms his observation: at that time, about 60% of the parents would not let their daughters participate in after-school programs.

October 1, 1987

Finally, I called Sally Young, Program Director of the Northeast Ministry, who said the Ministry does not run programs for girls. Because she was unaware that we are offering a sports program after school, she suggested that we make sure all the community organizations receive a copy of our program. She will post our announcement and include it in her newsletter.

Strategies

Opens with problem statement that orients reader to contents.

Verifies when she interviewed and whom she interviewed.

Informs about what she found out.

Figure 6-5   Documentary memo. (By permission from Gayle Assetto.)

each heading, she continues to document by stating the names and positions of those she interviewed and by summarizing their comments.

Why would it not have been appropriate for Lopez to express her reactions to these interviews? What word choices indicate that Lopez is writing primarily to document?

WRITING TO EXPLORE
General Features

Focus

In correspondence that aims to explore, you focus on identifying or defining a problem about the subject or issue under discussion, or you ask a question about the subject or issue.

Content

To achieve this aim, your content will consist of verifiable observations, facts, data, and speculations about solutions to problems. Often you may explore a problem without stating a solution to that problem, or you propose possible solutions to a problem.

Strategies for Arrangement

Exploratory correspondence generally opens by identifying a problem, posing a question, establishing reasons for investigating a problem, or describing the methods.

Writers use any of the paragraph patterns you read about in Chapter 3, Strategy Eight: "Ask What You Have to *Do* in Your Writing," as strategies to develop the body of exploratory correspondence. Of these patterns, claim-support, cause and effect, comparison, problem and solution, and chronological patterns tracing how you investigated a problem are predominant.

To investigate a problem, you need to establish a method and a set of criteria that will show your reader how you weighed the solutions. Some criteria that are important to organizations are the following:

Efficiency	Profit	Effectiveness
Accuracy	Speed	Reliability
Time savings	Quality	Improved communication

You can weigh criteria in the body of your correspondence to show how you arrived at your conclusions. Or, you can summarize your findings or recommended solutions to a problem in a concluding paragraph.

Vocabulary and Style

To achieve an exploratory aim, follow the principles of style under "Writing to Inform." In addition, conditional words, such as "perhaps," "could," "probably," "is likely," and "it appears," may also characterize exploratory language. These words reflect the tentativeness of your exploration.

Case: Occasion for Writing a Progress Memo

What Problem Must the Writer Solve?

As part of his semester project in a career-writing course, Roger Dunham is required to submit a progress report in memo form. For his project, he has chosen to investigate career opportunities in solar energy for math majors. In his memo, he needs to identify the problem he has chosen, describe how he has explored this problem, and make some tentative conclusions based on his exploration so far. He also knows that his instructor will use this memo to determine whether Dunham has made progress.

How Does the Progress Memo Solve the Problem?

Dunham writes a progress memo that aims primarily to explore. To achieve that aim, he focuses on describing how he has explored career opportunities and what he tentatively believes his conclusion will be. (See Figure 6-6.) He writes to inform about what he has discovered and to document what he has accomplished. His information about what he has done, what he has found, and what he has yet to do also functions to persuade his instructor that he is "making progress."

He uses the following strategies to open, develop, and close his progress memo:

1 Identifies the problem
2 Justifies the importance of the problem
3 Documents the method he has used to explore the problem
4 Speculates about what he will find
5 Isolates a problem that he at present believes will restrict him from achieving his goal—writing his report
6 Describes future work

Specifically, how does Dunham explore his problem? Do you think he should have considered any other methods? If so, which ones? What word choices suggest his findings are tentative?

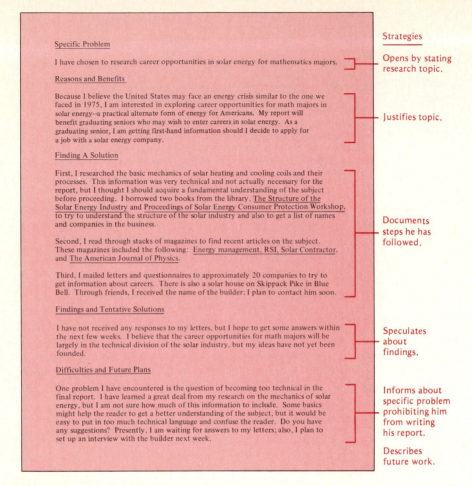

Figure 6-6   Progress memo.

WRITING TO INSTRUCT

General Features

Focus

When you aim to instruct in your correspondence, you focus on directing readers how to perform the task under discussion or on explaining to readers how something operates. You place equal emphasis on the reader and the subject of your instructional writing. (You will read more about this aim in Chapters 9 through 11.)

Content

The content consists of explaining concrete or abstract operations so that a reader or readers can perform or understand those operations.

Strategies for Arrangement

Summarizing the principle of operation, generalizing about the procedure, stating the purpose of the procedure, listing material (if readers need equipment to perform a task), describing conditions necessary to perform a task and explaining why it is important to perform a task are some of the ways writers begin correspondence that instructs.

When you write to instruct, you use a chronological strategy to list steps and substeps in a procedure. This strategy guides readers through a task. A conclusion is necessary if you want to summarize the effects or results of a procedure.

Vocabulary and Style

So that readers can perform a task, your language must be denotative and accurate. Often, it will be technical. Numbers or expressions of time guide readers through steps or stages of a procedure. Abbreviations are appropriate when your readers understand them. When you list steps in a procedure, use short, imperative sentences. (See Chapter 9 for further discussion of the stylistic features of "Writing to Instruct.")

Case: Occasion for Writing an Instructional Memo

What Problem Must the Writer Solve?

On Tuesday, Walter Leakey, vice president of finance for a large toy manufacturer with subsidiaries in numerous West Coast states, calls in one of his senior accountants, Kathleen Shorner. Leakey asks Shorner to travel to one of the subsidiaries in Oregon to investigate accounting procedures in this subsidiary's accounting department and recommend corrective actions for the department. The controller of this accounting department has not demonstrated strong management skills. As a result, work is late, inaccurate, and incomplete.

Leakey expects to make an unofficial visit to this department Thursday to give the controller directions for improving the department. To prepare for this visit, Leakey needs to know what the problems are and how, according to Shorner's expertise, to correct them. Leakey plans to be out of town until Wednesday night, but en route to Oregon on Thursday he will stop by the office to pick up Shorner's memo. With the information in Shorner's memo, Leakey will be able to speak knowledgeably to the controller about departmental problems and solutions.

> What is the organizational problem that Shorner
> knows she has to solve? What do you think her
> operators are once she gets to Oregon?

How Does The Memo Solve the Problem?

Because Leakey wants to know how to correct problems, Shorner writes a memo that aims primarily to instruct (see Figure 6-7). But, because it is also important for Leakey to understand the problem he will face, Shorner writes to inform him about what she discovered.

Shorner opens her memo by stating the purpose for the memo. Knowing how Leakey will use her memo, Shorner continues by using a two-part strategy. She informs him about ''news''—what he does not already know about the situation—by using a claim-support strategy in her ''Findings.'' Then she enumerates corrective actions in her ''Recommendations.'' Notice how each step she enumerates corrects a specific problem.

> Why are Shorner's two strategies, claim-support
> and a list of corrective actions, useful for how
> Leakey intends to use the memo. Point to examples
> of her objective and accurate use of language in her
> memo. Why is it appropriate for her to use
> abbreviations?

WRITING TO PERSUADE

General Features

Focus

A frequent aim of your correspondence will be to persuade: to motivate a reader to accept your point of view about the subject or issue under discussion. To accomplish this aim, you focus primarily on the ''you''—your reader's values, perspectives, beliefs, needs—to motivate your reader to act or think a particular way.

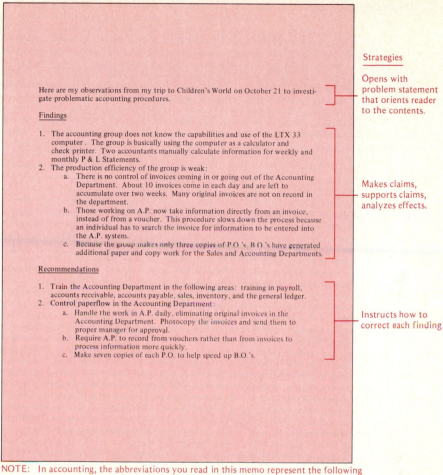

Here are my observations from my trip to Children's World on October 21 to investigate problematic accounting procedures.

Findings

1. The accounting group does not know the capabilities and use of the LTX 33 computer . The group is basically using the computer as a calculator and check printer. Two accountants manually calculate information for weekly and monthly P & L Statements.
2. The production efficiency of the group is weak:
    a. There is no control of invoices coming in or going out of the Accounting Department. About 10 invoices come in each day and are left to accumulate over two weeks. Many original invoices are not on record in the department.
    b. Those working on A.P. now take information directly from an invoice, instead of from a voucher. This procedure slows down the process because an individual has to search the invoice for information to be entered into the A.P. system.
    c. Because the group makes only three copies of P.O.'s, B.O.'s have generated additional paper and copy work for the Sales and Accounting Departments.

Recommendations

1. Train the Accounting Department in the following areas: training in payroll, accounts receivable, accounts payable, sales, inventory, and the general ledger.
2. Control paperflow in the Accounting Department:
    a. Handle the work in A.P. daily, eliminating original invoices in the Accounting Department. Photocopy the invoices and send them to proper manager for approval.
    b. Require A.P. to record from vouchers rather than from invoices to process information more quickly.
    c. Make seven copies of each P.O. to help speed up B.O.'s.

Strategies

Opens with problem statement that orients reader to the contents.

Makes claims, supports claims, analyzes effects.

Instructs how to correct each finding.

NOTE: In accounting, the abbreviations you read in this memo represent the following terms:

P & L — Profit & Loss
A.P. — Accounts Payable
P.O. — Purchase Order
B.O. — Back Order

Figure 6-7   Instructional memo. (By permission from Wanda Burke.)

Content

The content of persuasive correspondence can range from facts, statistics, or other verifiable information, to expressions of values, beliefs, or opinions. To motivate readers to act or respond, you can rely on one or more of the traditional persuasive appeals: logic, emotions, and ethos. That is, you can persuade by emphasizing the logic of your proposition, by engaging your reader's emotions, and by presenting yourself as trustworthy and capable.

Logical appeal

When you make logical appeals, you speak to your reader's powers of reasoning by making claims based on common assumptions you and your reader share. According to the philosopher Stephen Toulmin, a *claim* makes an assertion that is based on facts, statistics, observations, or other verifiable information. The *ground* provides the support you use to substantiate your claim: the specific facts, statistics, or observations that can be verified. A *warrant* is the more general law, rule, or common assumption that allows you to make a connection between your claim and the ground. The warrant consists of the general beliefs that you and your reader share.[1] The following sentence shows you how the logic of *claim-ground-warrant* works:

"We believe the county will have to develop more ways to dispose of waste products because population in the county will double by the year 2000."

Claim: The county will have to develop more ways to dispose of waste.
Ground: The population will double by the year 2000 (based on population growth studies in the community)
Warrant: Rapid growth in a community necessitates increasing waste disposal facilities.

When you appeal to your readers' powers of logic through *claim-ground-warrant*, you usually inform them of the *ground*, persuade them of the *claim*, and assume you and your readers share the *warrant*.

Emotional appeal

Appealing to your readers' emotions, values, or attitudes is another kind of appeal that you may incorporate into correspondence that aims to persuade. These emotions, values, or attitudes may be held by individuals or by groups. For example, since most of us believe that animals should be treated humanely, letters from animal protection societies describing inhumane treatment of animals arouse our anger. This arousal of anger causes us to want to support the efforts of animal protection leagues.

You can make emotional appeals to you reader through documenting responses from people your reader respects, wishes to emulate, or wants to identify with. For example, a long-time customer's testimonial about the effectiveness of a training seminar could serve to persuade a new customer to purchase this seminar.

[1] *The Uses of Argument* (New York: Cambridge University Press, 1958, and Stephen Toulmin, Richard Rieke, and Allan Janik, *An Introduction to Reasoning* (New York: Macmillan, 1979). Toulmin analyzes three other components of an argument besides these three.

Ethical appeal

You may also persuade readers based on your ethos—the sense of self you project. When you make ethical appeals (not to be equated completely with "moral" appeals), you create an image of yourself that persuades readers that you are a certain kind of person or represent a certain set of values. The three components of ethical appeal that Aristotle identified to instruct speakers are also the ones writers may use to persuade readers: the writer must demonstrate he or she knows the issue and is confident of that knowledge; the writer must demonstrate he or she has good intentions toward readers; and the writer must display good moral character, specifically honesty and trustworthiness. A candidate who is running for a position in a local community election might decide to persuade community members to vote for her by sending them a letter. Presenting herself as knowledgeable about the community issues, identifying with voters' values, such as their concern for air and water pollution, and demonstrating her trustworthiness (by documenting that she accomplishes what she sets out to do) contribute to her persuasiveness.

Strategies for Arrangement

When you write to persuade, you can use any of the patterns or combinations of patterns for developing paragraphs that you read about in Chapter 3, Strategy Eight: "Ask What You Have to *Do* in Your Writing." The strategies you use to open, develop, and close persuasive correspondence depend upon your reader's situational context and point of view. If you know your reader will accept your claims or be receptive to them, then you can begin your correspondence by stating your claim or claims and substantiating your claim in the body of your correspondence. For example, in the opening paragraph of a sales letter to a potential customer, you might make a claim about your organization's product. In the body of your letter, you can support that claim by using the following patterns of arrangement: a narration of the improvements in this product over the years, a description of the salient features of the product, and an analysis of how this product could meet your reader's needs. You might conclude by restating your claim or spurring your reader to take a course of action—such as calling you for a product demonstration.

If you know your reader will resist what you are claiming or proposing, then you may choose to refute your reader's beliefs or position to clear the ground for your assertion. For example, if you know that the readers of your sales letter will not be interested in your product because they are satisfied with the product they use at present and think your product is too expensive, then your strategy might consist of refuting each of the views your reader holds *before* you assert your claim. You might open your letter by restating your reader's views. In the body of the letter you could refute these views by describing the advancements in your product and by analyzing how cost effective this product would be for the potential client. Then you could close your letter by stating your claim(s) about your product. In addition, you might want to close by spurring your reader to call you to demonstrate the product.

Another strategy that you might use to persuade resistant readers is the strategy developed by the psychologist Carl Rogers. This strategy helps to establish understanding between you, the writer, and your reader. It asks you to discover what you and your reader have in common and to understand your reader's point of view as thoroughly and as objectively as you can. This strategy is particularly effective when you face resistance or even hostility. A Rogerian approach helps people listen to one another.

If you use the Rogerian strategy in correspondence, for example, you could begin by acknowledging your reader's situation, opinion, or point of view. This kind of opening begins with the reader's perspective and helps you establish a trusting relationship. Once you have established this relationship, your reader is more likely to go along with you as you present the value of your position or ideas.

Maxine Hairston[2] lists the elements of this non-threatening strategy as follows:

1   A brief and objectively phrased statement that defines the issue.
2   A complete and neutrally worded analysis of the other side's position. This should demonstrate that you understand the other's position and reasons for holding it.
3   A complete and neutrally worded analysis of the position you hold. You should carefully avoid any suggestion that you are more moral or sensitive than your audience.
4   An analysis of what your positions have in common and what goals and values you share.
5   A proposal for resolving the issue in a way that recognizes the interests of both parties.

Determining what strategy or combination of strategies to use will depend upon how well you understand your readers: the more you know about their values, beliefs, and organizational context, the greater your chances of developing a successful persuasive strategy.

Vocabulary and Style

Because persuasive writing can contain logical, emotional, and ethical appeals, your word choice will vary from denotative to connotative. Also characteristic of persuasive writing are word plays (''tourrific'' a combination of tour and terrific), rhythmic sentences or phrases, exclamations, superlatives, grammatical flexibility

[2]*Contemporary Rhetoric*, 3d edition, 1982, page 345. By permission from Houghton Mifflin Company, Boston.

(such as incomplete sentences or unusual positionings of words in a sentence), and informal language. Often, writers of persuasive correspondence will integrate proverbs or maxims as a means of establishing shared values with readers.

Case: Occasion for Writing a Donation Letter

What Problem Must the Writer Solve?

The Abington Choral Club relies on community financial support. The club must rent auditoriums, buy uniforms, and pay for the club's transportation costs. Each year the president, Marie Lawrence, must write to long-time and potential community supporters to request their support. Each year she thinks about how she can best motivate former and potential sponsors to contribute to her choral group. Because she does not want to write a boilerplate letter, a letter like last year's, she spends considerable time thinking about what she can say that will sound refreshing and motivating to both kinds of readers.

How Does the Letter Solve the Problem?

Lawrence's letter aims primarily to persuade readers to donate to her club (see Figure 6-8). To achieve that aim, she also expresses her enthusiasm about her club's recent activity, expresses thanks to previous and new sponsors, informs about the club's successes, and instructs readers how to send their donations.

   On behalf of her organization, she opens the letter with two sentences: one expresses her enthusiasm; the other informs readers about her organization's "news." She continues to provide readers with news in paragraph 2 to prove that her organization is successful. In her third paragraph she makes a claim about the effect of sponsorship. On the basis of this claim, she makes her request for donations. Having made the request, she instructs readers how to send contributions. She concludes by expressing thanks and hope.

> How does Lawrence use logical, emotional, and ethical appeals to persuade her readers to act? What are some examples of her persuasive use of language? Why is it important that Lawrence also include the aim of writing to instruct in this persuasive letter?

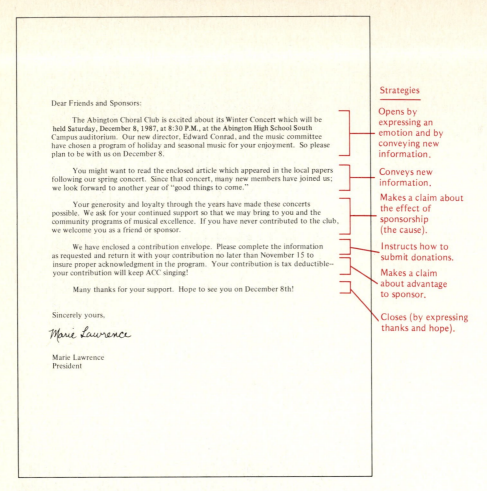

Figure 6-8   Donation letter. (By permission from Marie Lawrence.)

Case: Occasion for Writing a Job Application Letter and Résumé

What Problem Must the Writer Solve?

A graduating senior, Gayle Assetto, wants a position in public relations, even though her major has been art. During her last year and a half at college, she realized she was becoming increasingly interested in public relations and decided to minor in writing. During her four years she was also actively involved in public relations work on campus, writing proposals for college athletic equipment and raising funds for her college. Further, she held a part-time public relations job during her senior year.

Although she did not major in communications, she wants to persuade potential employers that her background suits her for public relations jobs. Assetto realistically understands what could prevent her from achieving her purpose—more experienced competition. Accepting the reality of her chances, she spends time thinking about how she can overcome that restriction. In particular she is interested in applying to a local nonprofit organization that has recently advertised a position in program promotion. She writes a letter, accompanied by her résumé, to L. Kirkpatrick, Director of Personnel, to document her work experience in public relations and to demonstrate how part of her education has prepared her for public relations work.

> On the basis of what you know about Assetto,
> analyze the problem she faces in terms of the four
> components of a problem.

How Do the Letter and Résumé Solve the Problem?

In her letter, Assetto aims to persuade Kirkpatrick that she possesses the skills, experience, and education required for a public relations position. To achieve this aim, she writes to inform about herself and to document her qualifications and achievements. (See Figures 6-9 and 6-10.)

Her strategy is to begin by referring to the job announcement to which she is responding and then to make a claim about her qualifications. To demonstrate that she is qualified, she makes claims about her achievements, which she supports with verifiable documentation—job titles, places of employment, and dates. Although she has other kinds of work and study experience, she chooses to highlight only those accomplishments that she knows her reader is most interested in. Her résumé in Figure 6-10 further documents her work experience by job title rather than place of work. She concludes by calling for action and expressing a social response, "Thanks."

> How does classifying her experience in her résumé
> according to job title help her show that her
> qualifications match the job? What kind of "self"
> does she express, and why do you think she
> projects that image of herself? How does that image
> help her achieve her primary purpose? Does she use
> appeals to logic and emotion?

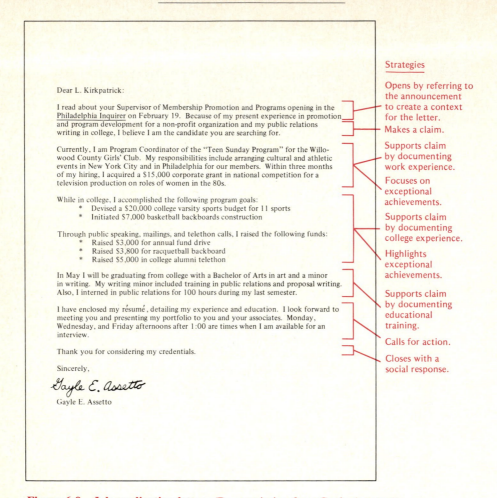

Figure 6-9   Job application letter. (By permission from Gayle Assetto.)

Case: Occasion for Writing a Collection Letter

What Problem Must the Writer Solve?

Although Lee Warren has already written two collection letters to William Laird requesting that Laird pay an overdue bill for electrical work, Warren still has not received payment. It is now three months since Warren has completed the work and one month since he sent his second reminder letter. In thinking about what his operators are to achieve his goal—to convince Laird to pay—Warren considers writing one more letter or turning over the account to a collection agency. The latter choice is both bothersome and costly. So, he decides to write one more time.

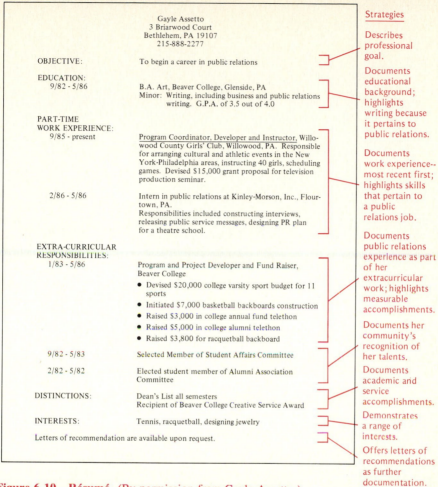

Gayle Assetto
3 Briarwood Court
Bethlehem, PA 19107
215-888-2277

Strategies

OBJECTIVE: To begin a career in public relations

Describes professional goal.

EDUCATION:
9/82 - 5/86   B.A. Art, Beaver College, Glenside, PA
                              Minor: Writing, including business and public relations
                              writing. G.P.A. of 3.5 out of 4.0

Documents educational background; highlights writing because it pertains to public relations.

PART-TIME
WORK EXPERIENCE:
9/85 - present   Program Coordinator, Developer and Instructor, Willo-
                              wood County Girls' Club, Willowood, PA. Responsible
                              for arranging cultural and athletic events in the New
                              York-Philadelphia areas, instructing 40 girls, scheduling
                              games. Devised $15,000 grant proposal for television
                              production seminar.

2/86 - 5/86   Intern in public relations at Kinley-Morson, Inc., Flour-
                              town, PA.
                              Responsibilities included constructing interviews,
                              releasing public service messages, designing PR plan
                              for a theatre school.

Documents work experience-- most recent first; highlights skills that pertain to a public relations job.

EXTRA-CURRICULAR
RESPONSIBILITIES:
1/83 - 5/86   Program and Project Developer and Fund Raiser,
                              Beaver College
                              • Devised $20,000 college varsity sport budget for 11
                                sports
                              • Initiated $7,000 basketball backboards construction
                              • Raised $3,000 in college annual fund telethon
                              • Raised $5,000 in college alumni telethon
                              • Raised $3,800 for racquetball backboard

Documents public relations experience as part of her extracurricular work; highlights measurable accomplishments.

9/82 - 5/83   Selected Member of Student Affairs Committee

2/82 - 5/82   Elected student member of Alumni Association
                              Committee

Documents her community's recognition of her talents.

DISTINCTIONS: Dean's List all semesters
                              Recipient of Beaver College Creative Service Award

Documents academic and service accomplishments.

INTERESTS: Tennis, racquetball, designing jewelry

Demonstrates a range of interests.

Letters of recommendation are available upon request.

Offers letters of recommendations as further documentation.

Figure 6-10   Résumé. (By permission from Gayle Assetto.)

Given his initial state (his reader's unresponsiveness to previous letters) what kinds of things do you think Warren could say to convince his reader?

How Does the Letter Solve the Problem?

Warren writes a letter to persuade Laird to pay. To achieve this primary purpose, Warren also writes to document, express, and inform. (See Figure 6-11.)

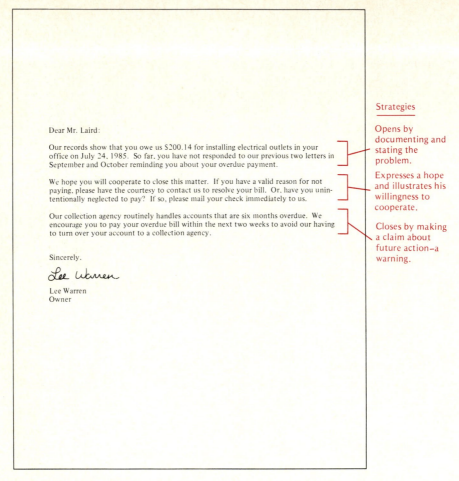

Strategies

Opens by documenting and stating the problem.

Expresses a hope and illustrates his willingness to cooperate.

Closes by making a claim about future action–a warning.

Dear Mr. Laird:

Our records show that you owe us $200.14 for installing electrical outlets in your office on July 24, 1985. So far, you have not responded to our previous two letters in September and October reminding you about your overdue payment.

We hope you will cooperate to close this matter. If you have a valid reason for not paying, please have the courtesy to contact us to resolve your bill. Or, have you unintentionally neglected to pay? If so, please mail your check immediately to us.

Our collection agency routinely handles accounts that are six months overdue. We encourage you to pay your overdue bill within the next two weeks to avoid our having to turn over your account to a collection agency.

Sincerely,

Lee Warren

Lee Warren
Owner

Figure 6-11   Collection letter.

His persuasive strategy consists of three parts: (1) he begins by documenting previous efforts to collect; (2) he expresses hope that he and Laird will be able to settle the account and, in a gesture of understanding, shows his willingness to cooperate; and (3) he concludes by making a claim about a future action.

> Why do you think Warren used this three-paragraph strategy to persuade his reader? Why do you think it is important that Warren opened by writing to document?

In this chapter you have seen some representative occasions when writers in organizations compose letters and memos. Like these writers, you will have to understand the organizational problem your correspondence will solve—either a problem that exists within your organization or in another organization. Thinking about that problem and your readers will help you decide what the purpose or purposes of your correspondence should be and what strategies you should use to achieve your aims.

In Chapter 7 you will see how three of the writers you just read about composed their correspondence.

1. Read the following letter from a business machines company addressed to a customer who has recently bought a computer. What are the primary and secondary purposes of this letter? What strategies does the writer use to present information? How effectively do you think the letter achieves its purposes for the reader?

Dear Ms. Goldman:

I certainly enjoyed your recent visit, and want to thank you sincerely for your first order. I am sure you will be pleased once you have had a chance to install your new computer and let it go to work for you.

We have been welcoming new customers for many years now, but you may be sure that our interest in you will not stop with your first order. In fact, if you ever feel that there is a let-down in our service or interest, just let me know so that I can straighten things out immediately. We are ready and willing to serve you in any way possible for many years to come.

---

2. Read the following memo from a store manager to his boss, the advertising manager. In this memo the store manager wants to persuade his boss that regional advertising procedures should be changed. Analyze the problem that the writer is attempting to solve in the memo according to the four components of a problem. What are the writer's primary and secondary purposes in writing this memo? What strategies does the writer use to achieve his purposes? Then evaluate how effectively he solves his problem. Can you think of other kinds of information that might more effectively persuade the advertising manager?

Ron Tyler, store manager of the other Philadelphia branch
of Gatsby and Fitzgerald, and I met last week to discuss
improving advertising strategies in our Philadelphia area
stores. Agreeing that the present strategies we receive
from New York are not attracting our Philadelphia clientele,
we propose that New York hire a regional advertising manager
for Philadelphia.

Under our present advertising campaign strategy, New York
develops all promotional material for Gatsby and Fitzgerald
and sends that material to all stores in New York and
Philadelphia. In turn, store managers send out this material
to their clientele. Because New York has made few attempts
to survey the advertising needs of the Philadelphia area and
the material we receive is developed for New York customers,
Ron and I believe most of the promotional material we receive
is inappropriate for our Philadelphia area customers.

We, therefore, propose that you hire a regional advertising
manager who is familiar with the Philadelphia area. This
manager would develop advertising strategies and campaigns for
our Philadelphia-based stores and report to you about our
campaigns. Rather than using promotional material developed
for a New York audience, Philadelphia stores would be using
material developed by those familiar with Philadelphia and
aimed at Philadelphia clientele, not New York clientele.

Both Ron and I would like to set up a conference call with you
next week to discuss the possibility of creating this new
position in Philadelphia. I will call your secretary at the
end of this week to set up a convenient time for all of us
to talk.

3. Read the following memo addressed to staff members in a community organization. What problem is this memo written to solve? What are the primary and secondary purposes of the memo? What strategy did the writer use? Why do you think this strategy is effective or ineffective? Would you have added or deleted any information to achieve the purpose?

We recently purchased a Cycle 9200 copier for the office. Most of you have been impressed with the copy quality and speed but unimpressed by the frequent periods of down time because of a variety of malfunctions. We have been assured that the operation of the machine will improve with the acquisition of appropriate supplies and service.

Please note the following changes:

1. The new machine now requires a ''key'' to operate. The key-counter used on the old copier will operate the new copier. I am interested in monitoring the number of copies, but I am also concerned that unauthorized use of the machine be eliminated (especially during evening hours). The number of copies on the old copier averaged 17,000 to 20,000 each month. We have averaged 40,000 each month since the new copier arrived and have made 30,000 copies in the last two weeks. The machine was not built for that volume, and our department is not budgeted for that amount. The overuse has also contributed to down time. We must find ways to reduce the volume.

4. Suppose that you faced the following problem as president of the political science club on your campus. Your political science club has sponsored two on-campus debates this semester to get students involved in the political issues at stake in a forthcoming state and local election. Unfortunately, only a handful of students showed up for these debates. Low attendance was embarrassing for you, the president of your club, as well as for the candidates. In fact, one candidate stated it was hardly worth his while to debate. However, you have

already scheduled one more debate for the week before the election. Consider how you would write two memos to your peers or two letters to your school newspaper—one *to express* your reactions to peers' lack of interest on your own campus and the other *to persuade* peers on your campus to attend the next debate. Discuss what kinds of information you would use in each memo and what strategies you would use to express or to persuade. Which memo would you send? Why?

5. Describe how you would handle the following problem. You are an office manager in an office which has flex time (flexible working hours.) According to flex time, workers must log eight hours of work each day, but they may choose when to begin those eight hours. However, many of your staff have been taking advantage of this informal work arrangement: they come in late and leave earlier than they should. You have no objections to people coming in late and leaving early if they have legitimate health or personal reasons. You do object to those who have been taking advantage of the new system. Their behavior may cause you to go back to the "fixed" eight-hour workday because office productivity may suffer. If you wanted to write a memo to your employees informing them about what is happening and motivating them to stay within the eight-hour flex time schedule, how would you analyze your problem? Use the problem-solving model to analyze the problem. What strategy would you follow to accomplish your aims?

6. Make a list of five organizational problems that exist within an organization that you are a part of. Think about whom you could write a letter or memo to within your organization to solve these problems. Isolate one of those problems and analyze the problem according to its components:

   1 What is a goal of your organization?
   2 What is your organization's initial state—the situation it is in right now?
   3 What are its restrictions—obstacles that are preventing your organization from attaining its goal?
   4 What are your operators—actions you can take to achieve this organizational goal?

WRITING CORRESPONDENCE

Perhaps you assume that you don't have time to plan and draft the letters and memos you compose at work. After all, you read in Chapter 6 that you write correspondence to solve problems as they occur. Certainly, many problems demand immediate attention and quick responses.

Yet planning a letter or memo and finding a solution to your problem work hand in hand. As you think about *how* to express your ideas, you also reconsider the substance of what you are saying. Furthermore, you might find yourself taking more time to undo the damage caused by a hasty piece of writing than to plan and draft it carefully in the first place.

In Chapter 6 you read about some organizational problems writers face and the strategies they use to write correspondence to solve those problems. In this chapter we will survey some strategies writers use *to compose* correspondence—strategies for getting started, drafting, revising, editing, designing a finished document, and proofreading. Once you have read this chapter, you can use it as a ready reference as you write your own correspondence in this course.

GETTING STARTED

The strategies writers choose to begin writing their letters and memos vary. Their heuristics depend on their work habits, the circumstances that prompt them to write, the amount of time they have to write, and their experience with having written similar correspondence.

Before writing a draft, writers need to explore the organizational problem they are solving. (Refer to Chapter 2 to review how to explore a problem.) Then they determine the purpose of their writing and ask questions about their readers. (Refer to ''A Checklist of Questions Writers Need to Ask'' in Chapter 1.) Having answered those questions, writers use one or more of the heuristics for getting started that you read about in Chapter 3.

To give you an idea of the diverse ways in which writers get started, observe how three writers planned their correspondence before they wrote drafts.

> Read the following descriptions of the ways each of these three writers got started and decide how useful each strategy is under the circumstances. Could you suggest other strategies to them? Why do you think your alternate or additional strategies would be useful under the circumstances?

Comparing Three Writers' Strategies

Strategy One: Using Models

As president of her choral club, Marie Lawrence was responsible for soliciting financial support for her club from the local business community. Lawrence had seen many solicitation letters go out over the years; she had even helped the past president draft some of the letters. Lawrence had a minimum amount of information to convey about the process of sending in a contribution, but she had to think about what she could say about the club to persuade people to support it. Lawrence knew that the community was accustomed to receiving the yearly requests. As a result, she was writing to readers who were essentially familiar with her organization. Their familiarity meant that she didn't have to provide a lot of background information, but that she ran the risk of sounding repetitious.

To get started, Lawrence looked at the file of past letters sent from her choral group to see what kinds of information other writers used to write a persuasive letter. One of the models Lawrence looked at appears in Figure 7-1. Lawrence analyzed each paragraph to discover what the writer did. Her descriptive outline looked like this:

PARAGRAPH	WHAT DOES IT DO?
1	INVITES sponsors to participate
2	ANNOUNCES the winter concert and RESTATES the invitation
3	SOLICITS support
4	INSTRUCTS readers on the way to return their contributions and INFORMS them about the reserved seats
5	THANKS readers

Under the circumstances, how useful do you think Lawrence's strategy was for getting started? Could you suggest other strategies for planning the letter? Why do you think your strategies or additional strategies would be useful under the circumstances?

Strategy Two: Anticipating Readers' Questions

Gayle Assetto, a student applying for a job, also had to write to persuade her reader to act—specifically, to call in Assetto for an interview. To motivate her reader to act, Assetto had to show that she was qualified. She assumed that her reader would ask questions about a recent college graduate's qualifications in public relations. To anticipate these questions, Assetto relied on the newspaper ad she was answering:

Nonprofit organization seeking individual with college degree for position of Supervisor of Membership Promotion and Programs. Candidate must be a ''self-starter'' and demonstrate strong communication skills. Some experience is desirable, but not essential. Send résumé to L. Kirkpatrick, Box 222, Philadelphia, PA 19038.

October, 1977

PATRONS, FRIENDS, ASSOCIATE MEMBERS AND BUSINESS SPONSORS:

Join us for our 30th Year!

Plans are in full swing for a super season. Rehearsals have begun for our 30th Annual
Winter Concert to be held Saturday, December 17, 1977, at 8:30 P.M., Abington High
School South Campus Auditorium. We hope you will join us in celebrating our 30th
year.

Each year we ask for your support, and we welcome the many friends who have so
generously assisted us. Abington Choral Club continues in its desire to bring quality
entertainment, enjoyment and fellowship to the community through music. You have
helped us to achieve that goal, so once again we ask for your generous support.

A new contribution envelope has been enclosed. Please complete the information
requested and return with your contribution no later than November 17th, to insure
proper acknowledgment in our program. Reserve seat tickets will be sent to you for
both the Winter and the Spring Concerts.

Dear Friends, our sincere THANKS for your continued generosity.

ABINGTON CHORAL CLUB

Figure 7-1   Model of donation letter. (By permission from Marie Lawrence.)

Keeping this job description in mind, she posed questions she believed her
reader would ask. You see these questions in Figure 7-2.

Strategy Three: Dictating

Typically, Kathleen Shorner, a senior accountant, had much less time than Lawrence and Assetto to compose her correspondence. Usually, she had to write letters

DO YOU HAVE A COLLEGE DEGREE? IN WHAT?

DO YOU HAVE EXPERIENCE IN PROMOTION AND PROGRAM DEVELOPMENT?

WHAT, SPECIFICALLY, DID YOU DO IN YOUR INTERNSHIP OR IN OTHER WORK EXPERIENCES THAT DEMONSTRATES YOUR ABILITIES TO DEVELOP AND PROMOTE PROGRAMS?

DO YOU HAVE WRITING SAMPLES?

WHAT KINDS OF EXTRA-CURRICULAR ACTIVITIES WERE YOU INVOLVED IN AT COLLEGE?

HOW CAN YOU DEMONSTRATE THAT YOU ARE A SELF-STARTER?

Figure 7-2 Questions Assetto assumed her reader would ask.

and memos at the end of a day after she had investigated an accounting department. To write within such a time constraint, she learned how to dictate letters and memos. Because her organization had a central dictating system, she could call any time of the day or night to dictate.

To compose summary memos of her trips, Shorner learned how to ask the ''right questions'' during her on-site visits and to record what she observed so that she could submit a summary memo to her boss the next day. What she recorded about what she asked or observed became the skeleton of the memo she wrote or dictated at the end of a day.

Shorner learned how to comb through her notes to select and order information for her reader. Further, she was able to plan a draft or final copy because she knew what her boss wanted in situations such as this one—a summary of findings and recommendations.

In Figure 7-3 you see her annotated notes. Her system of lines, circles, numbers, letters, and boxes indicates how she planned to sequence information in her dictated memo. She did not plan to include everything she wrote down. For example, at the top of the first page she recorded the names of people in the department. She needed this information to help her learn names and positions during her on-site visit, but they weren't important to her boss. Once she identified the relevant information, she classified and sequenced it before she dictated.

How does she classify her notes to prepare to dictate a memo?

To dictate the memo, Shorner followed the checklist you see in Figure 7-4.

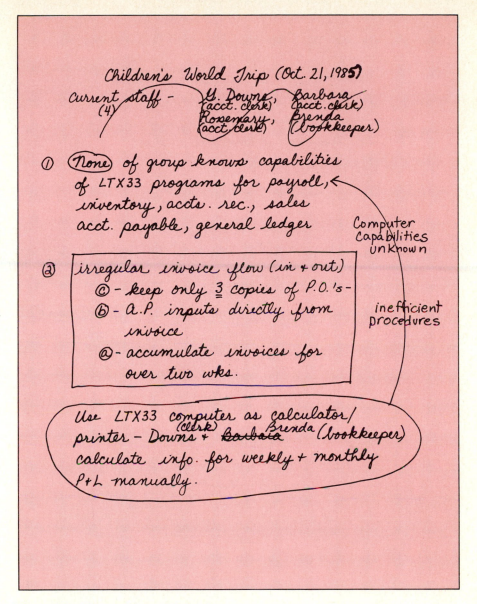

Figure 7-3   Shorner's annotated notes.

DRAFTING

When it comes to beginning a draft for a letter or memo, writers also vary their strategies. Some feel compelled to get the first line, sometimes the first paragraph, right before they go on. They use what we call the *top-down strategy*. Others are more comfortable when they begin writing the body and concentrate on openings and closings at a later time. They use the *outline strategy* or the *focused freewriting strategy*. (For a list of other strategies you might want to use, refer to Chapter 3.)

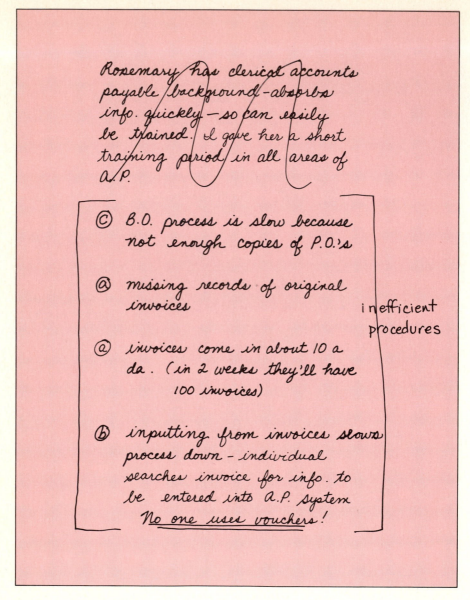

Figure 1-3 *(Cont.)*

Top-Down Strategy

Lawrence, the writer of the donation letter, was particularly fond of getting the first sentence right when she wrote. She believed that if she got the tone she wanted in the first sentence, she would have an easier time writing the rest of the draft. As a result, she composed several opening sentences and used them as starting points for different drafts. These openers are as follows:

This past year has been challenging in many ways for the club. First, our director of twenty-six years has had to resign his position with us.

We have a wonderful program of music planned for your entertainment.

We invite you to join us on Saturday, December 8, at the Abington High School for an evening of holiday music.

We are very excited about our winter concert and know that you will be, too.

We have a wonderful year of music planned for your entertainment beginning with an evening of holiday and seasonal music on Saturday, December 8.

What are some of the main differences you notice about the opening sentences you just read? What is the purpose of these openings? What various assumptions do they make about the readers' interests? How do they establish a context for reading the letter? How do they orient readers to the information that will follow?

Some Purposes of Openings in Correspondence

Opening sentences and paragraphs provide readers with an advance organizer. Perhaps, more importantly, opening sentences and paragraphs establish a relationship between the writer and reader. Knowing the range of purposes that first sentences in correspondence can serve helps you decide how to begin. Consider, as Lawrence did, some of the frequent purposes of openings:

The following are reminders of important points which the dictator must remember.

AT THE START

1.   Identify yourself—name, department.
2.   State type of dictation: This is a . . . . letter, memo, report, proposal, etc.
3.   Indicate type of stationery or form.
4.   State number of extra copies.
5.   State special instructions (format, spacing, "confidential letter").
6.   Spell out names and addresses.
7.   State whether you want a draft or finished copy.
8.   If draft is requested, state whether it should be double-spaced and approximately when you will return it for final typing.
9.   State when dictation begins.

DURING DICTATION

1.   Spell names, unusual words, technical terms, etc.
2.   Dictate the following punctuation marks and other special typing requirements:
      Colon
      Semicolon
      Exclamation Point
      Quote . . . .   End quote
      Paren. . . . .   End paren
      Underline . . . .   End underline
      Bracket . . . .   End bracket
      All CAPS. . . . .   End all caps
      Initial Caps . . . .   End initial caps
3.   Indicate paragraphs.

AT THE END

1.   Indicate signature (your own or other) and title to be used.
2.   Identify names of persons receiving copies (spell names).
3.   Identify enclosures.
4.   State special instruction(s)—forgotten or out-of-sequence instructions.
5.   State when dictation ends.

Figure 7-4   Dictation checklist. (By permission from Sumner Peirce, Leeds & Northrup.)

- To confirm telephone conversations or previous correspondence
- To explain circumstances leading up to the present correspondence
- To clarify a point of misunderstanding
- To acknowledge your reader's position or point of view
- To argue against a particular point of view
- To reaffirm a commitment
- To flag the reader's attention or interest
- To describe an existing condition
- To summarize information
- To explain a problem
- To alert readers to an impending problem
- To announce a change

- To express personal responses, such as congratulations, compliments, thanks, disappointment, or sympathy
- To boost morale
- To create an image of yourself and/or your organization

Opening sentences are usually more effective when they focus on the reader's concerns. Some examples of "you-message" openings follow:

1 Since you have expressed interest in our retirement plan, I would like to. . . .
2 We understand that you are disappointed about having to change planes so many times.
3 Thank you for your patience. We are sorry that. . . .

Unfortunately, we have seen numerous writers who fail to think of the social importance of their correspondence. Instead, they draw from a grab bag of stale expressions that fail to ingratiate or motivate readers. In drawing on these expressions, these writers focus immediately on the issue, not the reader. Here are some examples of these stale expressions used to open correspondence:

1 Reference is made to. . . .
2 In accordance with Regulation 210, it is hereby requested that. . . .
3 This is to acknowledge receipt of Form 322.
4 With regard to our agreement to. . . .
5 Per our agreement. . . .

> What kind of message do these expressions send about the writer?

Refer to Appendix A for a list of some other grab-bag expressions that you want to avoid using.

Outline Strategy

Other writers develop drafts by fleshing out an outline or plan based on what they initially recorded. Assetto followed this strategy to make sure she grouped her answers to anticipated questions into the following categories: education, college experience in program development and promotion, and part-time work in program development and promotion. You can see how she expanded an outline in Figure 7-5.

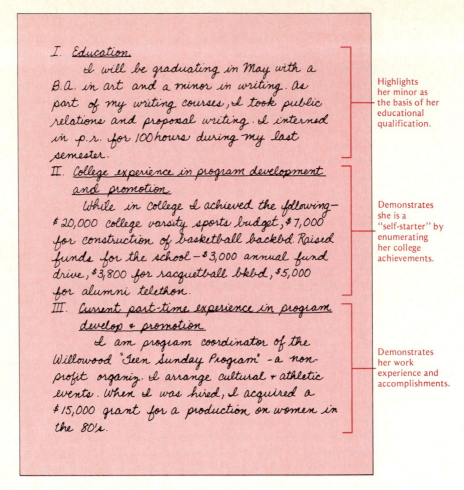

I. Education.

I will be graduating in May with a B.A. in art and a minor in writing. As part of my writing courses, I took public relations and proposal writing. I interned in p.r. for 100 hours during my last semester.

Highlights her minor as the basis of her educational qualification.

II. College experience in program development and promotion

While in college I achieved the following— $20,000 college varsity sports budget, $7,000 for construction of basketball backbd. Raised funds for the school — $3,000 annual fund drive, $3,800 for racquetball bkbd, $5,000 for alumni telethon.

Demonstrates she is a "self-starter" by enumerating her college achievements.

III. Current part-time experience in program develop + promotion

I am program coordinator of the Willowood "Teen Sunday Program" - a non-profit organiz. I arrange cultural + athletic events. When I was hired, I acquired a $15,000 grant for a production on women in the 80's.

Demonstrates her work experience and accomplishments.

Figure 7-5 **Assetto's expanded outline.** (By permission from Gayle Assetto.)

COMPOSING A TEST DRAFT

Asking Journalists' Questions to Test for Completeness and Accuracy

Once Lawrence composed an opening that satisfied her, she jotted down a few notes about what she wanted to include in each paragraph of her letter. From those notes, she composed a "test draft" (Figure 7-6) to check for completeness and accuracy.

Lawrence read her draft to make sure that she included all the necessary information about the holiday concert and about forwarding the contributions. To check her draft for completeness, she applied the series of journalists' questions she had learned: Who is giving the concert? What is it about? Where will it be held? When will it take place? Why is it being given? How are contributions made?

See if you can find the answers to those questions
in the draft in Figure 7-6. Then ask the same
questions of the information in the paragraph on
making a contribution. Do the readers know
everything they need to know to send in a contribution? Take the role of an interested draft reader
and comment on Lawrence's draft. What do you
think she has done well? What changes would you
suggest?

Asking What Each Paragraph Does and Says to Test Strategies for Arrangement

As Assetto wrote her test draft, she reordered her information. To test her strategies for arrangement, she wrote a descriptive outline in the margin of her test draft,
asking herself what each paragraph *does* and *says*.

As you read Assetto's descriptive outline in Figure
7-7, explain why you think she used these strategies
for arrangement. How do her arrangement strategies
help her achieve her primary purpose better than the
strategies she used in her expanded outline in
Figure 7-5?

Patterns of Arrangement in Paragraphs

As Assetto read over her descriptive outline, she also reviewed the paragraph patterns she used in the body of the letter. (Refer to Chapter 3 to review patterns of
arrangement for paragraphs.) Entire letters or memos can consist of one or more
of these patterns of arrangement. Each pattern can also be used to compose individual paragraphs, or patterns can work together in a paragraph. In the process of
drafting, you can boldly cut, paste, scratch out, and add on, or you can silently
push the DELETE key or move blocks of your text to create these patterns.

The Abington Choral Club is very excited about its winter concert which will be held
Saturday, December 8, 1987, 8:30 PM at the Abington High School South Campus
auditorium. Our new director Edward Conrad and the music committee have selected
a program of holiday and seasonal music for your enjoyment. So please plan to be
with us on December 8th.

You might want to read the article which is enclosed which appeared in the local
papers following the spring concert.
Since that concert, many new members have joined us and we look forward to another
year of "good things to come".

These
have   concerts
Your generosity and loyalty through the years has made our programs possible.
continued
We ask for your support so that we may bring to you and to the community
programs of musical excellence.

We have enclosed a contribution envelope. Please complete the information as
requested and return with your contribution no later than November 15 to insured
proper acknowledgment in the program. Your contribution can be deducted from
your taxes--your contribution will keep ACC singing!

For those of you who have never contributed to the club, or who have not been a
contributing member for sometime we welcome your support too.
as a friend or sponsor.

Thinks of new
information
to add.

Figure 7-6   Lawrence's test draft. (By permission from Marie Lawrence.)

> Look again at paragraph patterns in Assetto's test
> draft in Figure 7-7. What patterns does she use in
> each paragraph?

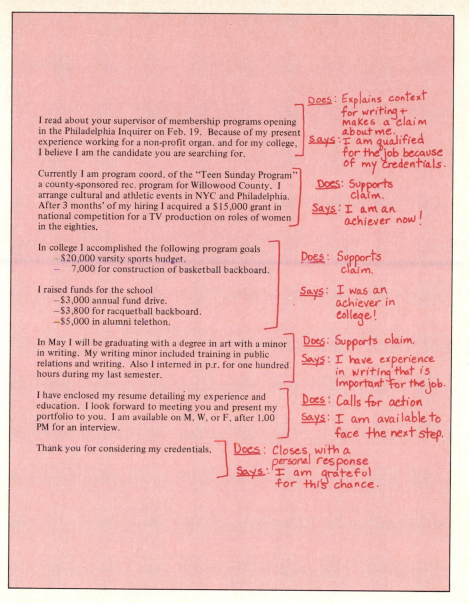

I read about your supervisor of membership programs opening in the Philadelphia Inquirer on Feb. 19. Because of my present experience working for a non-profit organ. and for my college, I believe I am the candidate you are searching for.

Does: Explains context for writing + makes a claim about me.
Says: I am qualified for the job because of my credentials.

Currently I am program coord. of the "Teen Sunday Program" a county-sponsored rec. program for Willowood County. I arrange cultural and athletic events in NYC and Philadelphia. After 3 months' of my hiring I acquired a $15,000 grant in national competition for a TV production on roles of women in the eighties.

Does: Supports claim.
Says: I am an achiever now!

In college I accomplished the following program goals
- $20,000 varsity sports budget.
- 7,000 for construction of basketball backboard.

I raised funds for the school
- $3,000 annual fund drive.
- $3,800 for racquetball backboard.
- $5,000 in alumni telethon.

Does: Supports claim.
Says: I was an achiever in college!

In May I will be graduating with a degree in art with a minor in writing. My writing minor included training in public relations and writing. Also I interned in p.r. for one hundred hours during my last semester.

Does: Supports claim.
Says: I have experience in writing that is important for the job.

I have enclosed my resume detailing my experience and education. I look forward to meeting you and present my portfolio to you. I am available on M, W, or F, after 1.00 PM for an interview.

Does: Calls for action
Says: I am available to face the next step.

Thank you for considering my credentials.

Does: Closes with a personal response
Says: I am grateful for this chance.

Figure 7-7 Assetto's test draft and descriptive outline. (By permission from Gayle Assetto.)

Some Purposes of Closings in Correspondence

Depending on the purpose and length of a letter or memo, writers may end these documents with a closing paragraph—often only one or two sentences. One-paragraph memos and letters, such as a one-paragraph memo announcing a change in a meeting time, rarely require a concluding sentence. In your correspondence, consider what ideas, attitudes, feelings, values, or, perhaps, instructions you want to leave your reader with. More than a signal that concludes the correspondence, a closing paragraph or sentence may function in one or more of the following ways:

- To encourage future communication or action
- To emphasize a point
- To reinforce reader's perception of the writer and or the organization
- To motivate a reader to act or think a certain way
- To summarize the contents of a letter or memo
- To warn of a consequence
- To express feelings, attitudes, reactions, or values
- To restate a problem
- To give instructions
- To express personal responses, such as congratulations, compliments, gratitude, disappointment, and sympathy

> Explain the different relationships that Lawrence and Assetto established in the concluding paragraphs of their test drafts (Figures 7-6 and 7-7). What other kinds of closings might they have used?

Like openings, closings serve a social function. They are particularly important because they leave a reader with a final impression of you. They are also your last chance to motivate readers to act. That is why we suggest you consider using "you-message" closings.

Here are two examples of "you-message" closings:

1   Thank you for your continued support. We look forward to a successful year.
2   We apologize for the inconvenience you experienced while traveling to the West Coast on our airline. We hope this inconvenience will not deter you from making reservations with us on your next trip.

REVISING AND EDITING CORRESPONDENCE

Once writers have a test draft, they continue to refine their writing to achieve their primary and secondary purposes. They review their correspondence for content, strategies of arrangement, patterns of arrangement in individual paragraphs, sentence structures, and language. Reviewing at any one of these levels may cause writers to start over again or rewrite the draft. To edit and revise your own correspondence, follow the four review steps you read about in Chapter 4:

First Review
Read for Purpose and Appropriateness
Second Review
Read for Arrangement and Cohesion
Third Review
Read for Sentences and Language
Fourth Review
Read for Accuracy

Compare Lawrence's and Assetto's final letters in Chapter 6 (Figures 6-8 and 6-9) with their test drafts in this chapter (Figures 7-6 and 7-7). Discuss how each writer revised and edited her test draft. Why were these changes effective?

DESIGNING A FINISHED DOCUMENT
Letter Format

First impressions count. That is why you will want to be particularly careful when you plan and type your correspondence. Your reader's first impression of you will be based on how that document looks. When you type your final copy, choose one of the formats we show you in Figures 7-8 to 7-11: block, *full block, modified block*, or the *simplified* letter format. The simplified letter format, recommended by the National Office Management Association, differs from the other formats primarily by omitting two lines of social convention—the salutation and complimentary close—and by capitalizing the writer's name and title in the signature block. Although the simplified letter format is more efficient to type than the other formats, consider what image you may be projecting about your organization by using this format. In all formats, use ample margins, usually 1 inch on either side and $1\frac{1}{2}$ inches on the top and bottom. Wide margins invite readers to read and also give them space to jot down notes.

Here are the various parts of a letter. Locate them on each of the formats to familiarize yourself with them. As you write a letter, refer to the spacing indicated in each format.

HEADING. If you are writing on non-letterhead stationery, type your address and a date line. Follow these general guidelines for typing the heading: (1) write out the words "Street" and "Avenue;" (2) use the Postal Service's two-letter abbreviations for your state; (3) include your zip code after your state; and (4) write the date either as October 1, 1987 or as 1 October 1987. If you are writing on an organization's letterhead, all you have to include is the date line.

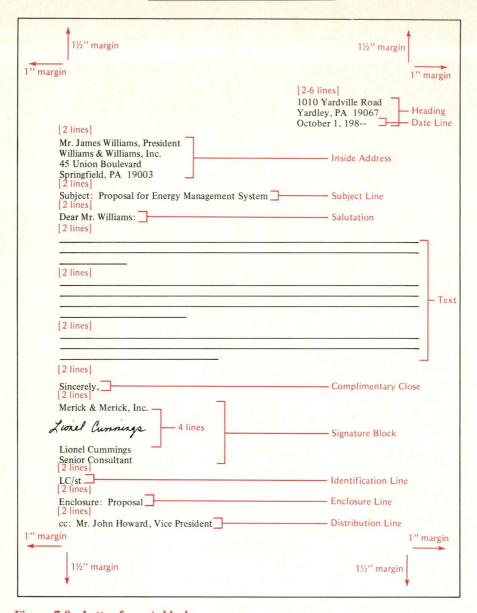

Figure 7-8   Letter format: block.

INSIDE ADDRESS.   Next, type the name, title, and address of your reader. Place a comma after the name, when the reader's title appears on the same line.

> Short title: Mr. James Smith, President
>
> Long title: Ms. Elizabeth Gaston
>   Vice President and General Manager

If you do not know someone's name, use the next best option: (1) a person's professional or occupational title (Personnel Director) or

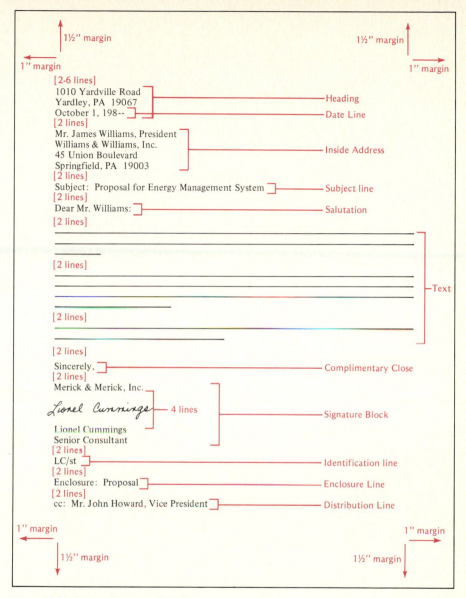

Figure 7-9   Letter format: full block.

(2) a division or department within an organization (Personnel Department). Along with the designations "Mr.," "Mrs.," and "Miss," the title "Ms." is now widely used. Unless a woman specifies otherwise, use Ms. If you are not sure how to address a reader, use the person's first initial, such as J. Williams, or use the person's full name, such as Jan Williams. (Refer to Appendix B, "Guidelines for Avoiding Biased Language.") If you are writing to several people, place each person's name on a separate line:

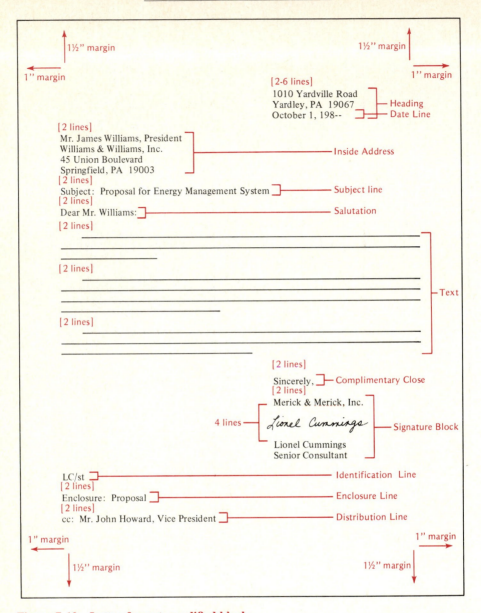

Figure 7-10   Letter format: modified block.

J. Thompson, President

Rebecca Smith, Vice President

Type the reader's address after his or her name.

SUBJECT LINE.   Some letters contain subject lines. This line, indicated as "Re:" or "Subject:," should state the issue or topic of the letter in terms your reader will understand. Subject lines ease the burden of locating letters in a file. Identify your subject as briefly and concisely as possible, avoiding strings of nouns, verbs, and prepositional phrases.

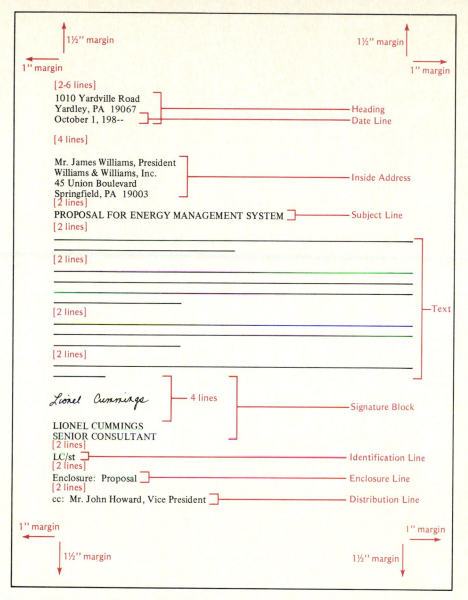

Figure 7-11 Letter format: simplified.

      Poor: ''Measurement of the Effects of the Incentive Plan
                     on Productivity''
   Better: ''Effects of the Incentive Plan on Productivity''
SALUTATION.   The salutation begins with ''Dear.'' Follow the reader's
name with a colon. When you want to signify a less formal relationship
with your reader, such as in a social or informal letter, use a comma.
When you are addressing a large number of readers or unknown readers, find a designation other than ''To Whom It May Concern.'' Use

an appropriate designation, such as "Dear Neighbor," "Dear Sponsor," or "Dear Member." (Refer to Appendix B.)

If you are writing to more than one male, write:

Messrs. Williams, Stone, and Smith

If you are writing to more than one female, write:

Mses. Lind, Quaker, and Stern

If you are writing to individuals with separate titles, write:

Dr. Sarah Williams and Mr. John Hardy

TEXT.   Single-space your text and double-space between paragraphs. Let your sense of balance and proportion guide you as you set up paragraphs on a page. Also, avoid long paragraphs; they discourage readers who need time to comprehend one sequence of information before they move on to the next. Use short copy blocks, headings, bullets, numbers, or letters, to emphasize important information or divisions in your text. (Refer to Chapter 5 for a discussion of principles of copy elements.)

COMPLIMENTARY CLOSE.   Conventional closings express degrees of formality between the writer and the reader. They range from the more formal closings, such as "Sincerely," "Sincerely yours," or "Yours truly" to the informal "Cordially" or "With best wishes." In closings, capitalize only the first letter of the first word; follow the closing with a comma.

SIGNATURE BLOCK.   The signature block includes the writer's signature with the writer's name and title typed underneath.

IDENTIFICATION LINE.   The identification line acknowledges who typed your letter, if you did not type it yourself. The line consists of your capitalized initials separated from your typist's initials by a colon or slash mark: SK: lct

ENCLOSURE LINE.   The enclosure line verifies that you have enclosed important information with your correspondence.

Enclosure: Proposal

You may use the abbreviation "Enc.:." If you are sending more than one enclosure, indicate how many you are sending by placing the number in parentheses after "Enclosure: (2)" and/or titling the enclosures:

Enclosures: (2) Signature Card
                          Contract

DISTRIBUTION LINE.   The distribution line lists other people to whom you are sending a copy of your correspondence. Use the word "Copy" or "Copies," or the abbreviation "c:" or "cc:" followed by the names and titles of those who are receiving copies:

cc: Mr. Hill, Manager
        Mr. L. Higgins, Director of Plant

ENVELOPE.   Figure 7-12 shows you the format for an envelope. If the information you are sending is confidential, then write "Personal" or "Confidential" on the envelope.

```
┌─────────────────────────────────────────────────────────────┐
│  Lionel Cummings                                              │
│  Merick & Merick, Inc.                                        │
│  1010 Yardville Road                                          │
│  Yardley, PA  19067                                           │
│                                                               │
│                       Mr. James Williams, President           │
│                       Williams & Williams, Inc.               │
│                       45 Union Boulevard                       │
│                       Springfield, PA  19003                  │
│                                                               │
│                                                               │
│                                                               │
└─────────────────────────────────────────────────────────────┘
```

Figure 7-12   Envelope Format.

MEMO FORMAT

Figures 7-13 and 7-14 illustrate two conventional memo formats. You may find that some organizations consistently follow one format. Or you may find that there are other formats which differ from the conventional ones we show you. (For example, look at the in-house memo format in Figure 4-2, "Chapter 4.")

Single-space each paragraph; double-space between paragraphs.

```
┌─────────────────────────────────────────────────────────────┐
│                                                               │
│                         M E M O R A N D U M                   │
│                  [2 lines]                                    │
│          TO:     R. Lewis, Manager of Inventory Control       │
│                  [2 lines]                                    │
│          FROM:   J. Syms, General Manager   JS                │
│                  [2 lines]                                    │
│          RE:     New Procedures for Recording Stock Inventory │
│                  [2 lines]                                    │
│          DATE:   October 1, 1985                              │
│                  [2 lines]                                    │
│          ─────────────────────────────────────────────       │
│          ─────────────────────────────────────────────       │
│          ──────────────────────                               │
│                  [2 lines]                                    │
│          ─────────────────────────────────────────────       │
│          ─────────────────────────────────────────────       │
│          ──────────────────────                               │
│                                                               │
└─────────────────────────────────────────────────────────────┘
```

Figure 7-13   Memo format.

INTERNAL CORRESPONDENCE

[2 lines]

TO: R. Lewis, Manager of Inventory   DATE: Oct. 1, 1985

[2 lines]

FROM: J. Syms, General Manager

[2 lines]

RE: New Procedures for Recording Stock Inventory

[2 lines]

[2 lines]

Figure 7-14   Memo format.

The **TO** line identifies the name and title of those who are supposed to read the memo.

The **FROM** line includes the writer's name and title. Most memo writers write their initials next to their names to confirm that they have written the information.

The **RE** line or the **SUBJECT** line announces the subject of a letter.

The **DATE** line identifies the month, day, and year a memo is written. If a date is important for a reader to see immediately, you may separate it from the other lines, as in Figure 7-14.

PROOFREADING

Although you may have tried to correct grammar, punctuation, capitalization, spelling, and usage errors by the time you type your final copy, there still may be some slips—even typing errors. Therefore, we suggest you follow the strategies we listed under the *Fourth Review* in Chapter 4 when you proofread your final copy.

Compare Lawrence's and Assetto's final letters in Chapter 6 (Figures 6-8 and 6-9) with their test drafts in this chapter (Figures 7-6 and 7-7). List the kinds of changes each made and why.

A CHECKLIST FOR CORRESPONDENCE

Content

1   Have I included accurate and comprehensive information to achieve my purpose for my reader?
2   Have I checked the accuracy of my information?

Strategies for Arrangement

1   Have I oriented my reader to the contents of the correspondence?
2   Have I reviewed the strategies for arranging the body of my correspondence to make sure they achieve the purpose I intend?
3   Have I used cohesive devices—including headings, if necessary—to guide my reader through the information from sentence to sentence and paragraph to paragraph?
4   Have I concluded appropriately?

Vocabulary and Style

1   Have I unpacked weighty sentences?
2   Have I varied my sentence structures to achieve the emphasis I want and to avoid repetitious sentence structures?
3   Do my word choices consistently convey the relationship I want to establish with my reader?
4   Do my word choices project the image of myself and my organization that I want to project?
5   Have I avoided biased language?
6   Have I used fresh language?

Conventions of the Language

1   Have I followed the conventions of spelling, punctuation, and grammar?

Layout

Have I applied the principles of effective document design? (See the checklist at the end of Chapter 5.)

Format

1   Have I followed an appropriate format for correspondence?

As you write the letters and memos in assignments 1 through 4, use the strategies you read about in this chapter and in Chapters 3 and 4. To begin thinking about what you will say in your correspondence, analyze the organizational problem you will be attempting to solve using the four components of the problem-solving model.

When you have written a test draft, your instructor may ask you to copy and fill out the "Writer Review" at the end of the projects and exercises and may ask a peer to copy and fill out the "Reader Review" for your test draft.

Your instructor may also ask you to dictate one of these pieces of correspondence into a taperecorder or to another person. Use the "Dictation Checklist" in Figure 7-4 to help you dictate a draft or final copy. Before you hand in your final copy, use the checklist for correspondence and follow the four review steps.

1. Since you have already decided how to solve the organizational problems in Exercises 4 and 5 in Chapter 6, write the memos you would send.
2. In Chapter 6, Exercise 6, you listed organizational problems that exist within an organization you are a part of. You analyzed one of the problems according to the four components of a problem. Now write the letter or memo that solves that problem.
3. In the newspapers or in your school's job placement center, find a job description for a part-time summer job and a job description for a full-time job that you would apply for when you graduate. Write a job application letter and résumé for each of these job descriptions. Discuss how you determined what kinds of information to include in each letter and résumé. You might want to look at Assetto's job application letter in Chapter 6 as a model for getting started. Or, you might want to collect other kinds of models to see which one would be most appropriate for you.
4. Write a letter to an organization complaining about a product you just purchased. Ask one of your peers to role play a representative of that organization and write first a favorable reply and then an unfavorable reply.
5. How would you rewrite the paragraphs in the following memo to develop a "you-message"?

> This is to advise you that this office cannot process your
> application form for funding in fiscal year 1986 under the
> Regional Act unless its attachment is signed by your
> supervisor.
>
> It is hereby requested that a signed copy of this applica-
> tion be mailed to this regional office as soon as possible.

6. Edit the following memo and discuss the kinds of changes you made:

> Reference is made to your letter of November 15, 198_, in
> which you state that you have an interest in the work mea-
> surement program which this office has instituted which was
> brought to your attention at a conference which was held
> recently the Agency Management Conference. In accordance
> with your stated desire to obtain more information, the
> undersigned is pleased to attach hereto several reports of
> progress which have been attained as a result of the insti-
> tution of said program.

7. Read the following opening lines of introductory paragraphs to letters. How would you describe the sense of "self" or of the organization that the writer projects in each of these opening sentences? How would you rewrite these sentences to change the "self" the writer projects?
   (a) Your attention is called to the printed terms of this quotation, listed on the back of the quotation sheet, which apply to this project.
   (b) Enclosed is a list of algorithms that are being supplied for New York by R&T.
   (c) You letter of November 3, 198___, regarding the payment bond to the City of New York, has been reviewed.
   (d) Per our discussion, the glycol temperature override setpoint will be located in the control cabinet.
8. Look back at the letters in Chapter 6 and decide the purpose or purposes each opening paragraph serves. Do you recommend a different approach for any of them? What changes do you recommend, and why?
9. Look back at the letters in Chapter 6 and locate examples of the patterns of arrangement you read about in Chapter 3. How many combinations of these patterns do you find within paragraphs and within entire letters? Analyze one of the letters and explain how the patterns of organization contributed to your understanding of the message and your likelihood of acting on it. Do you recommend any changes in the pattern of organization?

WRITER AND READER REVIEW SHEETS

Writer Review of A Test Draft

Readers and Purpose

1 Who are my readers? What do I know about their interest in and motivation for reading this correspondence? (Recall "A Checklist of Questions Writers Need to Ask" in Chapter 1.)
2 What is my purpose or purposes in writing this correspondence? (To express, to inform, to document, to explore, to instruct, or to persuade?)

Strategies for Arrangement

1 Trace the strategies for arrangement that you have used in this correspondence by filling out the following descriptive outline:
   PARAGRAPH 1
       What does it do (e.g., states the problem, expresses a personal response)?
       What does it say (e.g., says I can respond to a reader's request; says I have received the reader's request)?
   PARAGRAPH 2
       What does it do?
       What does it say?
   PARAGRAPH 3
       What does it do?
       What does it say?
   PARAGRAPH 4
       What does it do?
       What does it say?
   (Continue using the outline if you have more paragraphs.)

Reader Review of a Test Draft

Readers and Purpose

1 Who will read this correspondence? What do you know about the reader's interest in and motivation for reading this correspondence? (Recall "A Checklist of Questions Writers Need to Ask" in Chapter 1.)
2 What is (are) the purpose (purposes) of the document? (To express, to inform, to document, to explore, to instruct, or to persuade?)

Strategies for Arrangement

1 Trace the writer's strategies for arrangement by filling out the following descriptive outline:

PARAGRAPH 1

What does it do (e.g., states the problem; expresses a personal response)?

What does it say (e.g., says the writer can fulfill the reader's request; says the writer has received the reader's request)?

PARAGRAPH 2

What does it do?

What does it say?

PARAGRAPH 3

What does it do?

What does it say?

PARAGRAPH 4

What does it do?

What does it say?

(Continue using the outline if there are more paragraphs.)

2 Do you agree that the strategies for arrangement achieve the purpose(s) of the document for the intended reader(s)? Explain your response.

Content

1 Do you agree that the writer has included comprehensive and appropriate information to achieve the original purpose? If not, what kinds of information do you think are missing?

Vocabulary and Style

1 Do you agree the style is appropriate for the intended reader and for the purpose of the document? Explain you response.

CHAPTER 8

A WRITER AT WORK: CASE STUDY OF COMPOSING A LETTER

We have given you a close look at some of the problems writers solve in their correspondence and at the strategies writers use to plan, draft, revise, edit, design, and prepare a finished document. Now, we want to give you an overview of the process of writing correspondence by showing you the path one writer took to write a response letter to a long-standing customer.

You will follow Mark Williams' strategies and processes of writing from the time he learned about the organizational problem he had to solve to the time he prepared a finished letter. He progressed through the writing process by following these activities:

Part 1: Identifying the problem within the reader's and writer's organizational context
Part 2: Getting started
Part 3: Writing and revising drafts
Part 4: Preparing the finished letter

176

PART I: IDENTIFYING THE PROBLEM WITHIN THE READER'S AND WRITER'S ORGANIZATIONAL CONTEXT

Leeds & Northrup (L&N), a leading manufacturer of electrical power systems, received a letter of inquiry from a customer who purchased one of L&N's boiler systems approximately forty years ago. Read that incoming letter in Figure 8-1, along with Williams' annotations. To develop a response to that letter, Mark Williams, Manager of System Sales at L&N, explored the problem—the inquiry—from the perspectives of both the customer and L&N.

As he read the incoming letter, he used a question-answer strategy to think through Southern's organizational problem. So that you understand how he did this, we have written out his questions and responses:

---

1 What is Southern Station's present situation?
   (They are operating a boiler system which is over
   forty years old.)

2 What does Southern Station want given this situation?
   (To maintain this system.)

3 What action does Southern Station want L&N to take to
   maintain this system? (To provide long-term maintenance contracts for present parts. . .to rebuild old
   components for the system or supply manufacturing
   drawings for components so that Southern Station or an
   engineering firm could rebuild parts.)

4 What problems must Southern Station be experiencing
   with this system? (Difficulty in replacing or having
   components rebuilt since the system is so old.)

By exploring Southern Station's request through a series of questions, Williams effectively began the problem-solving process in writing. He defined Southern Station's problem according to the four components of any problem:

1 The *goal*—the point where an individual wants to be
2 The *initial state*—the point where an individual is

September 18, 1985

Mr. Mark Williams, Manager
System Sales
Leeds and Northrup
Dickerson Road
North Wales, PA 19454

Re: Cost Estimates--Long-Term Maintenance Support for Southern Station

Dear Mr. Williams:

In the late 1940s, L & N manufactured Southern Station's System II boiler control
equipment. We would like to ask you some questions about cost estimates for long-
term (30 years) maintenance support for this existing control equipment at our
Southern Station.

Would you provide cost estimates for the following alternatives:

1. A long-term maintenance contract to provide spare
   parts to Southern Station as required for the control   *support for 10 yrs for*
   equipment L & N originally supplied   *this equipment - but*
2. A long-term maintenance contract to rebuild used   *we phased-out equipment.*
   controllers L & N provided
3. Acquisition of required drawings and patent rights for   *ask Systems*
   the existing controls so that we can manufacture or   *Design about this.*
   have a machine shop manufacture spare parts when
   they are required

I have attached the equipment lists for the existing L & N controls at our Southern
Station.

Because we will begin discussing our options to maintain the System II within the next
two weeks, we would appreciate hearing from you within the next week.

Sincerely yours,

Thomas Syms

Thomas Syms
Procurement Assistant

TS/re
                              Northern's situation
                              was similar -
Enclosures: Equipment lists   *gradually modernized*
                              in Unit 3 plant!

Figure 8-1   Letter of inquiry and Williams' annotations.

3 The *operators*—the actions individuals take to move from where they are
   to where they want to be
4 The *restrictions*—the limitations which prevent an individual from taking
   those actions which help to achieve a goal

> How do Williams' questions and answers
> correspond to the four components of a problem?

Williams understood what Southern Station wanted—he understood the problem—but he also had to explore L&N's perspective. What could L&N do to help Southern Station? Because he knew about developments in systems since 1940 and about growing demands for making electrical control systems more efficient, he immediately jotted down some responses in the margins of the incoming letter (Figure 8-1).

Based on what he already knew, he generated ideas for his response. For example, he knew that since 1940 L&N had developed new technology in steam plant control systems. As a result, L&N began to phase-out older equipment, although it maintained older equipment for ten years after purchase. Read his notes beside paragraph two of the incoming letter. As he thought about Southern Station, he remembered a similar problem with another customer, Northern Electric. Also facing the prospects of having to replace old parts, that customer decided to begin modernizing its boiler system. Read Williams' notes about this thought at the end of the incoming letter.

There were two questions Williams could not answer: Did L&N still have manufacturing drawings? Would L&N necessarily have to rebuild components? To find out what he did not know, he wrote a memo to System Design. You see his memo in Figure 8-2. To gather all the information he needed to respond to Southern Station, he recalled what he did know and found out what he did not know.

PART 2: GETTING STARTED

After receiving the memo in Figure 8-3, researching information about energy systems, and drawing on his understanding of his work environment, Williams thought about how he would respond to Southern Station's inquiry. This time, though, he thought about the problem from L&N's point of view. He anticipated what effect meeting the customer's request would have on his company.

He knew that replacing and rebuilding parts would be difficult for L&N, let alone any other manufacturer. He also knew that replacing parts, even if it could be done, was not a long-term solution to Southern Station's problem, because technological advances had made it possible to develop more efficient systems. Certainly, Southern Station would experience a drain on its present system as demands for greater efficiency and more energy increased. Such was the case with Northern Electric. This customer, instead of rebuilding old parts, decided to mod-

INTER-OFFICE MEMO

TO: *Harriet Quills, Research Assistant, System Design*
FROM: *Mark Williams, Manager, System Sales*
RE: *Manufacturing Drawings for 40's Southern Station System II*
DATE: *Sept. 20, 1985*

Do we still have manufacturing drawings for Southern Station's System II built in the 1940s?

Have our patent rights expired so that another firm could rebuild parts?

Figure 8-2   Memo to System Design.

INTER-OFFICE MEMO

TO: Mark Williams, Manager, System Sales

FROM: Harriet Quills, Research Assistant, System Design

RE: Manufacturing Drawings and Patents for Southern Station

DATE: September 20, 1985

We would have to search for documentation on the Southern Station. Such a search would cost $94 an hour to see what we still have in our records.

Patent rights have passed into the public domain so this aspect is no longer a consideration. Parts would have to be made on a customer service basis.

Figure 8-3   Response to memo of inquiry.

ernize its system gradually. Modernizing, then, could be the solution to Southern Station's problem. Williams decided that the best strategy to follow was to compare Southern's short-term solution—rebuilding parts—with L&N's long-term solution—phased modernization.

How did Williams analyze Southern Station's
problem from his company's point of view? What
did he see as his goal, initial state, operators, and
restrictions?

Listing Issues

With his marginal notes on the incoming letter, information from System Design,
information he already knew, and a plan for how he would address his reader,
Williams began to list his responses to his reader and his thoughts about the prob-

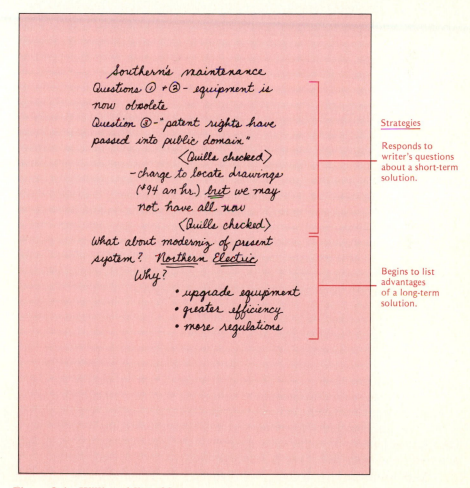

Southern's maintenance
Questions ① + ② - equipment is
now obsolete
Question ③ - "patent rights have
passed into public domain"
⟨Quills checked⟩
- charge to locate drawings
($94 an hr.) but we may
not have all now
⟨Quills checked⟩
What about moderniz. of present
system? Northern Electric
Why?
• upgrade equipment
• greater efficiency
• more regulations

Strategies

Responds to
writer's questions
about a short-term
solution.

Begins to list
advantages
of a long-term
solution.

Figure 8-4   Williams' list of issues

lem. In Figure 8-4 you see how Williams recorded ideas by responding to Southern's questions, writing down what he had found out, and elaborating on his idea about Northern Electric's experience. He recorded some ideas in complete sentences. He asked himself a question about modernization to cause him to think further about "why" Southern Station should modernize. He underlined *Northern Electric* as a reminder that he intended to discuss this company in his letter. By moving from his marginal notes to a list of issues he intended to cover in his letter, he developed his rhetorical plan.

> At this point, what kinds of information did he
> think were important?

PART 3: WRITING AND REVISING DRAFTS

Looking at his list, Williams began to draft a response (Figure 8-5). He began to flesh out his rhetorical plan and thoughts; yet he still questioned some of what he wanted to say and the order in which he wanted to say it. He placed a question mark next to his first sentence and questioned whether he should begin a new paragraph after the first two sentences.

He drew an arrow from his marginal note on "efficiency" to the end of paragraph two to signal to himself that he intended to include more information about this advantage.

> At this point in the drafting process, how did
> Williams intend to organize his letter? Why do you
> think he questioned the first sentence?

As you can see, in the process of writing his first draft, Williams came to terms with what he wanted to say. He left the draft to continue other work, although he never completely forgot the problem he was attempting to solve. After some time away from the draft, he returned to it with some new insight about how he would develop the letter. His second draft appears in Figure 8-6.

As he wrote his second draft, he developed information he wrote in his first draft and sequenced that information for his reader. While writing, he remembered

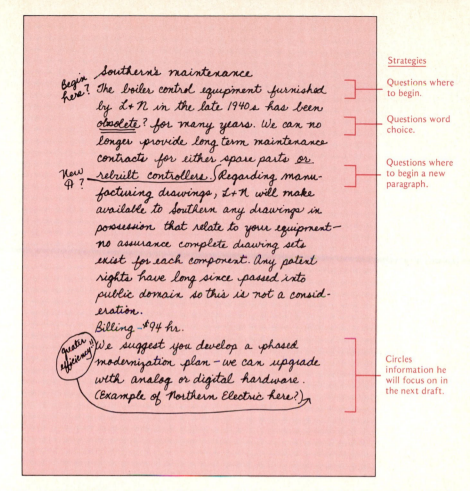

The handwritten draft reads:

Begin here? Southern's maintenance

The boiler control equipment furnished by L+N in the late 1940s has been obsolete? for many years. We can no longer provide long term maintenance contracts for either spare parts or rebuilt controllers. Regarding manufacturing drawings, L+N will make available to Southern any drawings in possession that relate to your equipment—no assurance complete drawing sets exist for each component. Any patent rights have long since passed into public domain so this is not a consideration.

Billing—$94 hr.

We suggest you develop a phased modernization plan—we can upgrade with analog or digital hardware. (Example of Northern Electric here?)

Marginal notes: "Begin here?" / "New ¶?" / "greater efficiency!!"

Strategies

Questions where to begin.

Questions word choice.

Questions where to begin a new paragraph.

Circles information he will focus on in the next draft.

Figure 8-5   William's first draft. (By permission from Leeds & Northrup, Pennsylvania.)

something else to add, an article he read about energy efficiency; he decided to summarize information from this article and include it in his draft.

What was originally a two-paragraph letter became a seven-paragraph letter. As Williams put the letter into a conventional letter format, he developed an introduction to orient his reader and to express L&N's desire to help Southern. He also developed a concluding paragraph. This paragraph stated Williams' future action—a telephone call to discuss what L&N was recommending. This conclusion established grounds for future communication between L&N and Southern Station.

In his first draft Williams was more concerned with recording *what* he thought he needed to include in the letter. In his second draft he began to consider *how* he is was going to convey that information to his reader. He even circled a punctuation mark that he was not sure he was using correctly, and he circled the word "this" because he knew it did not have a clear reference for his reader. However,

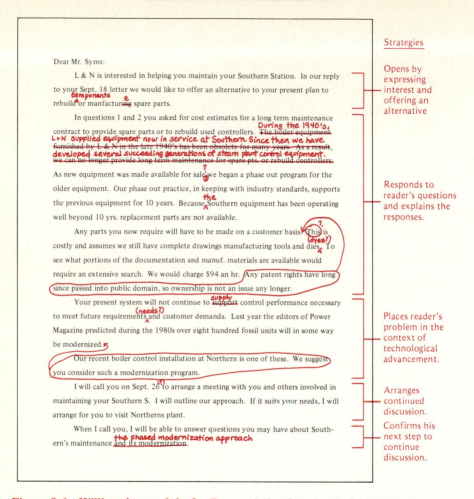

Figure 8-6   Williams' second draft. (By permission from Leeds & Northrup.)

issues of grammar, punctuation, and spelling were not a major concern at this point.

Compare draft 1 to draft 2. In his second draft, what kind of information did he add and how did this information affect the organization of the letter? Classify the kinds of changes he made to prepare a ''you message'' letter.

Revising and Editing a Final Draft

Williams continued to revise his second draft. Instead of using a descriptive outline, he preferred to summarize each paragraph in the margin and then review the
sequence he had followed. He was confident that each paragraph contributed to
the central issue—finding a solution for Southern Station. As he reviewed cohesive
devices from sentence to sentence, he saw places where he could add words to
clarify meaning for his reader. For example, in his last sentence he changed " . . .
about Southern's maintenance and its modernization" to "about Southern's maintenance and the phased modernization approach." The addition of these words
extended meaning from his earlier discussion and repeated a key phrase—*phased
modernization*—in his letter.

He also asked a co-worker to read over his final draft to get another perspective on how clearly he had structured his letter and conveyed his information.
His co-worker suggested Williams delete the first sentence of the second paragraph
because that sentence did not relate to the topic of the second paragraph. Paragraph
two did not focus on cost estimates, but rather on L&N's history of technological
developments since the 1940s. Agreeing with this advice, Williams deleted that
sentence in his final copy.

PART 4: PREPARING THE
FINISHED LETTER

When Williams was satisfied with the organization of his letter and the continuity
of his paragraphs, he read it to make sure that it conformed to the conventions of
the language—grammar, spelling, capitalization, punctuation, and usage. After he
had carefully proofread the final draft, he sent it to a secretary who typed it in
conventional full-block format.

Compare the final copy of this letter in Figure 8-7
with the second draft. Circle all the changes he
made in the final copy as he proofread. Explain the
conventions of the language that he followed.

After Williams received the typed copy from his secretary, he proofread it
once more. What you see in Figure 8-7 is what he sent to Southern.

September 23, 1987

Mr. Thomas Syms
Procurement Assistant
Southern Station
2 Ninth Avenue
Edgeway, PA 19067

Re: Long-Term Maintenance Support for Southern Station

Dear Mr. Syms:

L & N is interested in helping you maintain your Southern Station. In our reply to
your September 18 letter, we would like to offer an alternative to your present plan to
rebuild components or manufacture spare parts.

During the late 1940s, Leeds & Northrup supplied equipment now in service at Southern Station. Since then, we have developed several succeeding generations of steam
plant control equipment. Each generation took advantage of the latest technological
advances. Our goal was to bring to the market equipment that would improve plant
safety and produce more fuel-efficient operations.

As new equipment was made available for sale, we began a logical phase-out program
for the older equipment. Our phase-out practice, in keeping with industry standards,
supports the previous equipment for 10 years. Because the Southern Station equipment has been operating well beyond 10 years, replacement parts are unavailable.

Any parts you now require will have to be made on a customer basis. Any patent
rights have long passed into public domain, so ownership is not an issue any longer.
Manufacturing parts is costly and assumes we still have complete drawings, manufacturing tools and dies. To see what portions of the documentation and manufacturing
material are available would require an extensive search. To locate this information,
we would charge $94 an hour.

Even in the best state of repair, your present system will not continue to supply
control performance necessary to meet future needs. Last year the editors of Power
Magazine predicted that during the 1980s over 800 fossil units will be modernized in
some way. Our recent control installation at Northern is one of these. We suggest you
consider a phased modernization program, such as the one we installed at Northern's
Long Island Unit 3 plant.

Figure 8-7 Williams' response letter. (By permission from Leeds & Northrup.)

Either draw a branching outline or write a
descriptive outline of Williams' final letter in
Figure 8-7. Then explain why he followed this
strategy to respond to Southern Station.

To help you evaluate a phased approach, I will call you on September 26 to arrange a meeting with you and others involved in maintaining your Southern Station system. In this meeting I will outline our approach. If it appears to suit your needs, I will arrange for you to visit Northern's Long Island Unit 3 plant. There, you will be able to see our equipment, ask questions, and talk with the operators.

I will call you around 9:00 A.M. on September 26 to arrange a meeting time. During our phone call, I will be able to answer any other questions you may have about Southern Station's maintenance and the phased modernization approach.

Sincerely yours,

Leeds & Northrup

Mark Williams

Mark Williams
Manager
System Sales

MW/cd

Figure 8-7   (Cont.)

In this chapter you have seen how a writer solved a problem by taking his assignment through various stages of writing. Initially, he generated ideas or plans for what he wanted to say. As he wrote, he continued to rethink what he wanted to say and how he wanted to say it, conscious of what his reader needed to know to solve Southern Station's problem.

For this particular writing assignment, Williams took two drafts to discover and polish what he had to say and how he had to say it. In composing other letters or memos, Williams may write more drafts or only one draft or may dictate or write a final copy without using drafts. Writers differ in the amount of time it takes them to write a final copy. The more experienced they become, the less time it takes them to compose correspondence. What they develop is the ability to generate information and organize ideas in their heads before they begin to translate these ideas onto paper.

In your own writing on the job, you will learn how to write routine letters that may take you a few minutes to compose. However, much of what you write will take you more than a few minutes because you will have to explore a new or difficult organizational problem and then develop a rhetorical plan to solve that problem. In such instances you will find that you will probably write several drafts to discover what to say and how to say it. Like Williams, you will discover which strategies and processes will be most useful as you write different kinds of correspondence. The strategies you decide to use in your own writing will depend on what type of problem you are solving, how much time you have to write, and how the stimulus to write begins—with a telephone call, an incoming letter, a memo, someone's spoken request, or your own initiative.

SECTION FOUR

STRATEGIES FOR WRITING INSTRUCTIONS, DIRECTIVES, AND OTHER PROCEDURAL DOCUMENTS

CHAPTER 9

PURPOSES FOR WRITING INSTRUCTIONS, DIRECTIVES, AND OTHER PROCEDURAL DOCUMENTS

Tom McCormick is manager of a battery plant that manufactures wet cell automotive batteries. As manager, he is responsible for making sure his plant operates twenty hours a day, seven days a week with a force of 300 workers. That means workers must consistently rotate shifts and the physical plant must operate so as to maintain production quotas. To assure that employees follow similar procedures in manufacturing batteries and rotating work schedules, he frequently writes to instruct. Instructing employees how to perform a task, establishing procedures, or explaining procedures is a routine part of his job. Some of the routine documents he writes are:

- Training manuals instructing new employees how to perform technical tasks, such as how to secure batteries into casings

- Job descriptions specifying the tasks a worker must perform
- Directives establishing policies about an organizational objective and instructing workers how to carry out that objective
- Appraisal reports that document workers' performance on the job

In all these cases, McCormick has to solve a problem by getting readers to understand how to do something and, possibly, why to do it; how something operates; how something happened; or how something will happen. To make an organization work, someone writes the responsibilities of each department and position. Someone describes how to carry out procedures or how to do them differently. Someone investigates several ways of carrying out a procedure and evaluates them according to criteria. In addition, to make the goods or services that an organization produces useful to those outside the organization, someone writes instructions for using those products or services or describes how a product or service operates.

In this chapter we will survey representative kinds of documents that instruct readers to perform a procedure or help them understand how something operates. The importance of cooperation in an organization explains why documents that aim at instructing employees to perform a task or inform them how a task is, was, or will be performed are among the most frequent kinds of writing you can expect to do at work.

Instructions are documents that instruct readers how to perform either a physical task, such as an on-line computer search, or a mental activity, such as computing an income tax return or a grade-point average. Instructions list the steps a reader needs to follow to accomplish a task. If you have taken a laboratory science course, you have already read, and may even have written, a rather complex set of instructions for an experiment. The conventions of the scientific method require that someone else can replicate an experiment. However, one difference between writing a set of instructions for a scientist and writing an instructional document for an organization is that your reader may not bring an expert's understanding to your instructions. Instructions to workers may be separate documents posted on a bulletin board or included in an office manual directing employees to perform routine or nonroutine tasks. Or they may be included in other documents, such as letters, memos, reports, and proposals (which you will read about in Chapters 12 and 13).

Directives are orders or commands issued by authorities in an organization. Like instructions, directives instruct readers to perform a task by breaking it down into subtasks. Whereas instructions direct readers to follow a task by following certain steps, directives command readers to follow a task because they are mandated by someone who has authority. Directives can be conveyed in a memo. Or they can be separate documents that are included in office manuals. They can also be posted on a bulletin board to alert employees to newly established procedures.

We use the term *procedural documents* to include any documents that inform readers how something does, did, or will work. These documents consist primarily of *process descriptions*. Process descriptions explain how a product, process, or service operates. They inform readers, rather than direct readers to perform. There are numerous kinds of procedural documents, such as service contracts or maintenance agreements. Process descriptions may be integrated into other documents, such as letters, memos, instructional manuals, reports, and proposals.

After you read more about the kinds of problems instructions, directives, and procedural documents solve and the purposes for which writers compose them, we will describe five occasions that prompted writers to compose these documents and show you the documents they wrote.

EXPLORING THE PROBLEMS INSTRUCTIONS SOLVE

Within an organization, instructions solve the problem of how to get people to work together to achieve organizational goals. By explaining how to perform a task, instructions establish consistency and continuity in the way workers carry out a task. They describe what actions an agent must take, along with conditions affecting those actions, to achieve a goal, such as manufacturing a product. Instructions to workers may be conveyed in letters or memos or in manuals that contain all the procedures workers should memorize or refer to while performing a task.

Between an organization and someone outside it, instructions solve the problem of describing how to operate a product or use a service. Instructional sheets or manuals usually accompany a product or service that you buy so that you understand how to use it.

EXPLORING THE PROBLEMS DIRECTIVES SOLVE

Authorities in an organization find it necessary to issue directives, or orders, to enforce already existing procedures or to establish new ones. A common kind of directive is called *policy and procedures*. A policy announces a principle that authorities believe will achieve an organizational objective; procedures specify how employees must carry out this policy. Within an organization, management develops policies to correct problems that occur in an organization, such as workers' careless handling of dangerous chemicals. Often management establishes a policy to comply with local, state, or federal regulations. For example, state agencies issue regulations guiding the operation of day-care centers. To fulfill these regulations, directors of day-care centers circulate policy and procedures to personnel to enforce compliance with these regulations. Failure to comply may mean that a day-care center will lose its license.

Some Occasions for Writing Instructions and Directives

Here is a list of some of the occasions when you may have to write instructions or directives to solve organizational problems. Write them when you need to:

1   Direct employees to perform routine and nonroutine tasks, including how to handle emergencies
2   Teach readers how to use a product or service
3   Command readers to comply with a policy

EXPLORING THE PROBLEMS OTHER PROCEDURAL DOCUMENTS SOLVE

Within an organization, procedural documents explain how something does, did, or will work. Strategic plans, goal statements, or statements of objectives describe the steps a writer or a department will follow to accomplish tasks. Job descriptions outline responsibilities of employees in an organization to establish continuity and stability within an organization. These procedural documents aim to inform readers about a procedure.

Procedural documents also solve the problem of explaining to readers outside your organization how your product or service operates. Sales brochures explain how a product or service operates; service contracts explain what kinds of repairs a firm guarantees.

A description of how something operates (process description) can also be a part of a document that has another purpose. For example, an organization's annual report to shareholders aims at persuading readers that an organization is achieving its goals. As part of that report, writers may describe what their organization has achieved during a year and what it plans to do in the next year. Many manuals accompanying products open with a description of how a product works before they instruct readers to operate that product.

Some Occasions for Writing Other Procedural Documents

Here is a list of some of the occasions when you may have to write other procedural documents to solve organizational problems. Write them when you need

1   To describe a system that establishes lines of authority and areas of responsibility and, thus, provides stability and continuity in the way an organization accomplishes its goals
2   To specify strategies for achieving an organizational objective
3   To inform customers or clients about an organization's products or services
4   To document how a task was performed

PURPOSES OF INSTRUCTIONS, DIRECTIVES, AND OTHER PROCEDURAL DOCUMENTS

To solve the kinds of organizational problems you have just read about, writers compose instructions, directives, and other procedural documents either to instruct or inform.

Because instructions, directives, and other procedural documents can have one or more purposes, we will classify some representative documents that aim to instruct or to inform according to their primary and secondary purposes. Table 9-1 previews and classifies instructions, directives, and other procedural documents according to primary and secondary purposes.

Table 9-1 Primary and Secondary Purposes of Instructions, Directives, and Other Procedural Documents

Primary Purpose	Secondary Purpose	Examples of Instructions, Directives, and Other Procedural Documents
To Instruct	To Inform	Memo Directive (Figure 9-1)
	To Inform	Policy and Procedures in a Hospital Manual (Figure 9-2)
	To Inform	Instructional Panel for a Product (Figure 9-3) (See Also Figure 6-7 in Chapter 6)
To Inform	To Persuade	Consultant's Letter Outlining Firm's Services (Figure 9-4)
	To Document and Persuade	Page of Report Explaining Training Procedures (Figure 9-5) (See also Figure 6-6 in Chapter 6)

After you read about the general features of each aim, you will read several cases. These cases explain the occasions that prompted writers to compose instructions, directives, or other procedural documents that instruct or inform. *As you read each case, analyze the organizational problem each writer faced. Then focus your attention on how each writer composed a document to achieve one primary aim, and one or more secondary aims.*

WRITING TO INSTRUCT

General Features

Focus

When you write to instruct, you focus on directing your reader to *perform* a task. That is, you focus both on information you are conveying and on your reader.

Content

The content of writing to instruct consists of steps or stages that help your reader perform a task.

Strategies for Arrangement

Writing to instruct may consist of three parts:

1 An *introduction* that orients a reader to the instructions (see also Chapter 10, section entitled ''Some Purposes of Introductions in Instructional and Procedural Documents'')
2 *Major steps* that divide a task into substeps usually following a chronological sequence (see also Chapter 3, ''Ask What You Have to *Do* In Your Writing,'' Strategy 8.)
3 A *conclusion* that describes the effects or results of the procedure (see also Chapter 10, section entitled ''Some Purposes of Conclusions in Instructional and Procedural Documents'')

Your directions to perform a task may also integrate sentences, clauses, or phrases that provide answers to questions about when, where, how, or why to perform a step or who should perform a step. These pieces of information help readers monitor their progress. For example, conditional statements such as ''If...'' or ''When...'' guide readers through difficulties they may experience while performing steps in a task. Describing results of actions, such as ''When the red light turns on, push button 5,'' helps readers confirm that they are ''on track.'' Further, sections of text labeled ''Notes,'' ''Cautions,'' and ''Warnings'' alert readers to additional important information: conditions that might occur (''Notes); safety measures (''Cautions''); and possible dangers (''Warnings'').

Numbers, letters, other highlighting devices, as well as words indicating time, help readers connect steps.

Vocabulary and Style

Writing to instruct uses imperative sentences to command readers to act (''Take...'' ''Adjust...''). You write as an authority directing readers. Imperative sentences are usually short: each sentence commands a reader to perform one action or simultaneous actions. Maintain parallelism in each imperative sentence so that readers can consistently locate the verb that instructs them. Variation in this sentence structure occurs when you have to introduce conditions that affect when or how your reader performs a step. If you have one conditional statement to make, write that clause or phrase; then connect your command to it. In the following sentence, notice how the conditional clause precedes the command:

If the temperature rises quickly, pour in the coolant.

If you need to include more than one conditional statement, list the command first, and then number the conditions after it.

Your language must be denotative and accurate so that readers can operate a product or perform a procedure. Achieving accuracy may mean defining terms for your readers and making sure that your descriptions of things and actions are specific. Directing someone to ''turn'' something is not the same as directing someone to ''twist'' it.

Writing to instruct uses parallelism in headings and subheadings to classify steps or to classify kinds of information in a set of instructions. For example, questions that anticipate what readers will ask as they read instructions are one way of establishing parallelism in headings. Notice how instructions to applicants who want to take a certifying examination use the following questions to establish parallel headings: ''When Should You Apply?'' ''How Should You Apply?'' ''Where Can You Apply?'' and ''When Will You Be Notified?'' Parallelism in headings, like the consistency of tenses, helps readers comprehend or memorize steps by patterning information.

Illustrations and flowcharts are common graphic elements you can use to complement your text and assist your reader in performing a task. Copy elements help readers follow instructions and directives. Highlighting devices, such as underlining and boxing, cause readers to focus on important pieces of information, such as warnings. (See Chapter 5 for a review of copy and graphic elements in document design.)

Case: Occasion for Writing a Memo Directive

What Problem Must the Writer Solve?

Lynn Rogers is office manager of a new mail-order firm that promises customers ''fast delivery'' on all items. Having spent two evenings after hours randomly inspecting outgoing packages, she has found many inconsistencies in the ways in which clerks prepare packages for shipping. Many clerks do not completely fill out shipping orders. Some do not secure customer address labels securely on boxes. Furthermore, several customers have complained that they never received their merchandise.

To solve the problem of inconsistency, Rogers writes a memo directive establishing a new procedure and outlining steps in the procedure.

> Analyze the organizational problem Rogers faces in terms of the four components of a problem.

How Does the Memo Directive Solve the Problem?

To enforce procedures for correctly preparing packages, Rogers issues a memo directive that commands workers to follow a new set of procedures (Figure 9-1).

Her strategy for arranging information is to explain the reason for the new procedure and then state her new procedure. She instructs workers to carry out steps by using a chronological pattern.

> Why do you think Rogers includes an introductory paragraph explaining her reasons for establishing this procedure? What effect do you think that introduction has on her readers? How does her language indicate that she is writing as an authority? How does Rogers specify conditions affecting actions?

Case: Occasion for Writing Policy and Procedures

What Problem Must the Writer Solve?

According to periodic reports on work-related illnesses or injuries among hospital personnel, there has been an increase in infections and injuries among personnel who give patients injections. After investigating the causes of this increase, Jerome Fox, a hospital administrator, finds that nurses have been depositing used syringes and needles into plastic bags. Often the syringes and needles poke through the bags, thereby contaminating those who dispose of the bags. Because this method of disposal is not a healthful one, Fox establishes a new policy for disposing of syringes and needles.

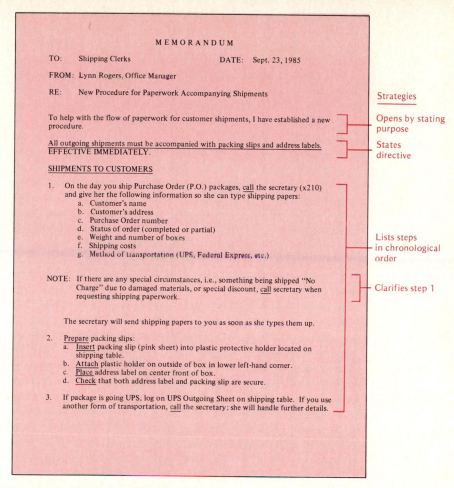

Figure 9-1   Memo directive. (By permission from Lynn Rogers.)

Analyze Fox's problem according to the four components of a problem.

How Does the Policy and Procedure Document Solve the Problem?

In the procedural manual directing nurses to perform various tasks for patients, Fox inserts a page which states a new policy and describes how nurses and staff must follow that policy (Figure 9-2).

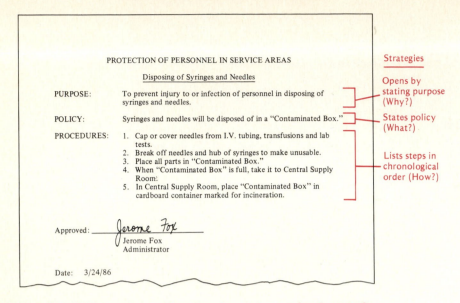

Figure 9-2   **Policy and procedures in a hospital procedural manual.**

Like all the other directives in this hospital manual, this page follows a specified order of information: a statement of the purpose, followed by the policy the hospital has established, followed by step-by-step procedures. The strategy for arranging information moves from "why," to "what," to "how."

> Even though the administrator had to follow a prescribed order for sequencing information, why do you think the document follows this pattern of arrangement?

Case: Occasion for Writing an Instructional Panel for a Product

What Problem Must the Writer Solve?

Nashua Corporation, a manufacturer of thermal transparencies, packages its transparencies in an $8\frac{1}{2} \times 11$ inch box—the size of standard paper. Because the writer wants customers—usually office workers—to use the transparencies correctly and to be able to locate the instructions easily, he considers where and how to include directions for these readers.

What are the restrictions in this problem? What do
you see as operators?

How Does the Instructional Panel Solve the Problem?

The writer decides to write the directions on the back of the cardboard packaging
so that readers can quickly locate and refer to them (Figure 9-3). Although the
writer also considers writing a separate sheet of instructions, he believes that in a
busy office someone might easily lose or misplace it.

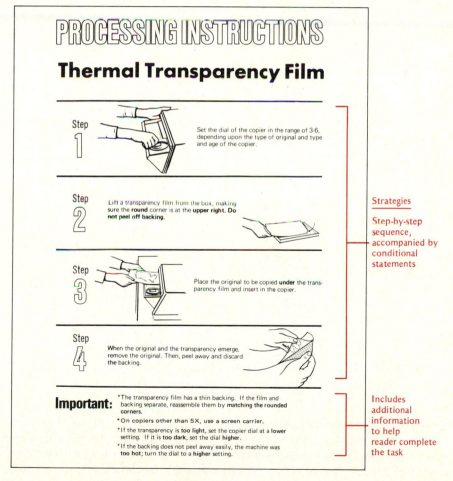

Figure 9-3   Instructional panel. (By permission from Nashua, Corp., New Hampshire.)

The writer's strategy for arranging information is to integrate graphic elements with the text to instruct readers. Each step (and its illustration) becomes a scene in a story; illustrations assure that readers will be able to perform the process. The steps are presented in chronological order and are accompanied by conditional statements. These conditional statements alert readers to considerations or adjustments they need to make during the process.

> Discuss the importance of the section entitled
> "Important" at the bottom of Figure 9-3. On the
> basis of this instructional panel, what generalization
> can you make about where to place a single conditional statement in a command?

WRITING TO INFORM

General Features

Focus

When you want to describe how something works, how it did work, or how it will work, you write to inform.

Content

Primarily, you describe actions that animate or inanimate agents perform: "*Who* (human agent) does, did, or will do *what*" or "*What* (inanimate agent) does, did, or will perform an action?"

Strategies for Arrangement

To inform about how something works, so that readers can understand a procedure or memorize it, follow the same strategies for arrangement that you read about in this chapter under "Writing to Instruct."

Vocabulary and Style

When you write to instruct, you command readers to perform a task as they read. When you write to inform about a procedure, you describe how something operates. Ask:

Am I describing how something does operate? (Present tense)
Am I describing how something did operate? (Past tense)
Am I describing how something will operate? (Future tense)

Follow the principles of parallelism and sentence structure that you read about in this chapter under "Writing to Instruct."

Case: Occasion for Describing Procedures in a Sales Letter

What Problem Must the Writer Solve?

John R. Mills works as a consultant in a management consulting firm, Morton & Morton Associates. As a management consultant, he and his co-workers specialize in diagnosing and solving managerial problems, such as financial problems, inventory problems, or production problems. Preston Smith, President of Ridley and Delta Manufacturers (R&D), a manufacturer of valves, calls in Mills to diagnose why R&D is experiencing a reduction in valve production. Mills is not the only consultant Smith calls in; he also calls in other consultants from competing firms. Smith will then choose one of these consulting firms to solve his problem.

> Analyze the problem that Mills faces as he writes his letter to Smith.

How Does the Letter Solve the Problem?

Mills writes a letter (Figure 9-4) that informs Smith about how Morton & Morton Associates *will* diagnose R&D's problems. In addition to this primary aim, Mills also writes to persuade Smith that Morton and Morton Associates is capable of doing an effective job.

> Since you have already read about persuasive strategies in correspondence in Chapter 6, classify the kinds of appeals Smith makes and discuss his persuasive use of language.

Mills' strategy is to open his letter by expressing a belief and describing a future effect. He uses a chronological sequence in the future tense to describe what

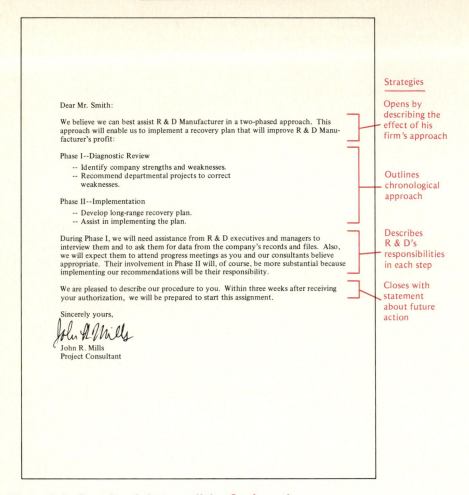

Dear Mr. Smith:

We believe we can best assist R & D Manufacturer in a two-phased approach. This approach will enable us to implement a recovery plan that will improve R & D Manufacturer's profit:

Phase I--Diagnostic Review

    -- Identify company strengths and weaknesses.
    -- Recommend departmental projects to correct weaknesses.

Phase II--Implementation

    -- Develop long-range recovery plan.
    -- Assist in implementing the plan.

During Phase I, we will need assistance from R & D executives and managers to interview them and to ask them for data from the company's records and files. Also, we will expect them to attend progress meetings as you and our consultants believe appropriate. Their involvement in Phase II will, of course, be more substantial because implementing our recommendations will be their responsibility.

We are pleased to describe our procedure to you. Within three weeks after receiving your authorization, we will be prepared to start this assignment.

Sincerely yours,

John R. Mills

John R. Mills
Project Consultant

Strategies

Opens by describing the effect of his firm's approach

Outlines chronological approach

Describes R & D's responsibilities in each step

Closes with statement about future action

Figure 9-4   Consultant's letter outlining firm's services.

his firm will do: Phases I and II. This pattern helps him explain how he and his co-workers will diagnose problems and implement a plan "that will improve R&D Manufacturers' profits."

> What tense does Mills use to describe the procedure? Why does he use this tense?

After describing what his firm will do, Mills focuses on what his client must do to assure effective results. Again, Mills writes in the future tense to talk about actions that will take place once Mills agrees to buy Smith's service. He closes his letter encouraging his reader to act.

Case: Occasion for Describing Procedures in a Report

What Problem Must the Writer Solve?

Gary Walkins, project supervisor in a research firm, has just completed an extensive research project for a county health commissioner in South Carolina. The commissioner wants to know "How effective are our county's alternative long-term care facilities for the elderly?" Over the last five years, the county has established several alternative long-term care facilities. These include in-home, community, and other institutional facilities. To justify federal support of these facilities, the county health commissioner asked Walkins' firm to interview elderly citizens receiving care from these facilities. Walkins and his staff trained fifty people to interview county residents receiving long-term care.

Although his goal is to report the results of these interviews, Walkins also describes how he and his staff trained interviewers. He does this to verify and, thereby, demonstrate his organization's professional approach.

How Does the Page of Procedures Solve the Problem?

Although the majority of Walkins' report to the county health commissioner summarizes the results of the interviews, Walkins decides to begin his report by writing to inform the commissioner about how Walkins' staff trained interviewers (Figure 9-5). By describing what his staff did, Walkins achieves the additional purpose of writing to document.

> How does writing to document achieve Walkins'
> goal of illustrating his firm's professional approach
> to handling this project?

Walkins' strategy for arranging information is, first, to introduce the commissioner to the objectives of interviewer training. Then he documents the procedures his staff followed step-by-step. He arranges these tasks according to degree of difficulty—from simple tasks, reading about interviewing, to more complex tasks, performing the interviews and filling out routine administrative forms.

This sequencing of tasks, not only according to chronological order, but also according to an order of increasing complexity, documents how the research firm achieved its goal—interviewing senior citizens. Notice how each step achieves one of the goals specified in the introductory paragraph.

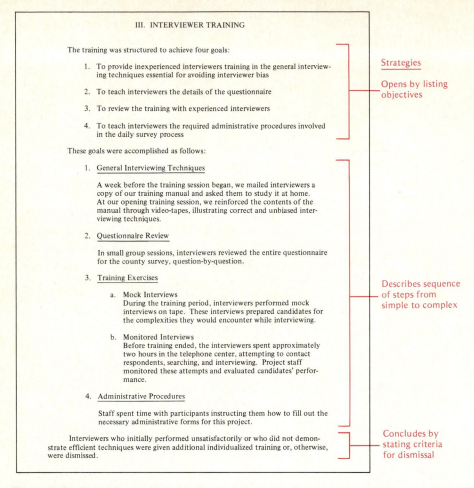

III. INTERVIEWER TRAINING

The training was structured to achieve four goals:

1. To provide inexperienced interviewers training in the general interviewing techniques essential for avoiding interviewer bias

2. To teach interviewers the details of the questionnaire

3. To review the training with experienced interviewers

4. To teach interviewers the required administrative procedures involved in the daily survey process

Strategies

Opens by listing objectives

These goals were accomplished as follows:

1. General Interviewing Techniques

A week before the training session began, we mailed interviewers a copy of our training manual and asked them to study it at home. At our opening training session, we reinforced the contents of the manual through video-tapes, illustrating correct and unbiased interviewing techniques.

2. Questionnaire Review

In small group sessions, interviewers reviewed the entire questionnaire for the county survey, question-by-question.

3. Training Exercises

a. Mock Interviews
During the training period, interviewers performed mock interviews on tape. These interviews prepared candidates for the complexities they would encounter while interviewing.

b. Monitored Interviews
Before training ended, the interviewers spent approximately two hours in the telephone center, attempting to contact respondents, searching, and interviewing. Project staff monitored these attempts and evaluated candidates' performance.

4. Administrative Procedures

Staff spent time with participants instructing them how to fill out the necessary administrative forms for this project.

Describes sequence of steps from simple to complex

Interviewers who initially performed unsatisfactorily or who did not demonstrate efficient techniques were given additional individualized training or, otherwise, were dismissed.

Concludes by stating criteria for dismissal

Figure 9-5   Page of report explaining training procedures.

What kind of sentence pattern does he repeat to establish parallelism in his document? In the concluding paragraph, Walkins provides additional information about the training. Why do you think he felt it was important to include that information?

In this chapter you have seen some of the occasions when writers solve problems by writing instructions, directives, or other procedural documents. How writers compose these documents is the subject of Chapter 10.

1. Ask three people familiar with your campus to give you the directions they would use to tell someone unfamiliar with your campus how to get from place A on campus to place B on campus (preferably on the other side of campus). Record each person's directions. Then evaluate how successful each person's directions are. How effective are each person's directions for an unfamiliar reader? How well organized is each set of directions? What assumptions does each writer make in giving directions? What kinds of information would you add or delete to improve the directions? After evaluating each set of directions, write what you think are the best directions. Be prepared to justify your directions to your classmates.

2. Within your organization, or from examples you have read or received on campus, bring to class as many as you can of the following documents:

   (a) Instructional memos
   (b) Instructional letters
   (c) Directives
   (d) Manuals accompanying a product
   (e) Instructions within another document, such as a brochure or a catalog
   (f) Documents containing descriptions of procedures
   (g) Other procedural documents, such as service contracts or job descriptions

   Define the kind of problem the writer of each document had to solve. Define the purpose of each document. What features of "Writing to Instruct" or "Writing to Inform" does each document use?

3. Make a list of five organizational problems that require individuals to follow instructions or directives or to understand how a procedure works. Select one problem; think about who the readers would be. Finally, consider how you would solve your problem for those intended readers by thinking about these questions:

   (a) What kinds of information would you need to include?
   (b) What strategies for arrangement would you use?
   (c) What features of writing to instruct or to inform would you use in your document?

4. Read the following instructional memo sent to plant employees. The purpose of this memo is to outline procedures plant employees should follow when bad weather conditions occur. Discuss how effectively the writer explains these procedures and list changes you would make:

By means of this memorandum, I want to clarify management's policy on early closings of plants because of hazardous working conditions or other emergencies.

The decision to close the plants will be made by Operations or, in the absence of Operations, the designee. This decision will be made only after a careful review of the specific conditions. It should be noted that no administrator or individual supervisor is authorized to approve the departure of employees or to close plants except as noted below:

    A. Employees who feel that weather conditions are hazardous may be permitted to depart work early, but annual, personal, or compensatory leave time must be used to cover their departure. When the closing of plants is authorized, employees in non-essential operations will be permitted to be absent from work. Employees who are considered essential and are required to work may not depart. Any employee on annual, personal, sick, or compensatory leave when the closing of plants is authorized will be charged with the period of such leave. This applies to all employees except Unit 1 members who accumulate only sick leave, which cannot be used for this purpose.

    B. Supervisors are requested to report through the appropriate channels to the Operations office to secure approval prior to closing an entire office because of weather conditions.

    C. Employees who feel that working conditions make it necessary for them to leave work cannot be released by their supervisors unless the following procedures have been observed:

       1. Individual essential employees may be released only after clearance from the Personnel office.

2. Closing of an office should occur only after clearance through appropriate channels from the Operations office.

3. In either case, such departures will not normally be approved if it is possible for the employee's plant's work to continue either to a lesser degree in the present location or another location or if it should be possible to utilize the employee(s) to assist another plant.

4. Employees must use leave time unless approval has been received from the Operations office to close the plant in question.

D. Supervisors should assume responsibility in emergency situations which consitute a clear and immediate danger to the safety of employees to the extent of evacuation or reassignment on a temporary basis.

5. Refer to Figures 5-8 and 5-10 in Chapter 5. Convert each flowchart into explanatory text, describing how each procedure works. As you write to inform, consider what features of ''Writing to Inform'' you will use to describe these procedures.

6. In the profession or field that you intend to enter, select a professional article that contains a flowchart or a diagram that illustrates a process. Convert that graphic element into a process description for your classmates who do not share your area of expertise.

7. In the profession or field you intend to enter, select an article that describes a process or contains a description of a process. Convert that process into a set of instructions for others in your field or profession.

CHAPTER

10

WRITING INSTRUCTIONS, DIRECTIVES, AND OTHER PROCEDURAL DOCUMENTS

Knowing or learning how to perform a task or understanding how a process works does not guarantee that you can write instructional or procedural documents that are clear for your readers. Writing these kinds of documents to achieve a purpose for your readers—to instruct or to inform—requires that you be willing to explore or question what information will be useful to your readers.

In Chapter 9 you read about some of the organizational problems writers face that require them to write instructions, directives, or other procedural documents. In this chapter we will show you the strategies two writers used to compose these documents—strategies for getting started, drafting, revising and editing, designing a finished document, and proofreading. As you write instructional or procedural documents in this course, use this chapter as a ready reference.

GETTING STARTED

As you have already read in Chapter 9, the occasions that prompt writers to instruct or to inform about a procedure or process vary. Similarly, the ways in which writers plan instructional or procedural documents also vary. In all cases, however, writers get started by exploring the organizational problem they are solving. (Refer to Chapter 2 to review how to explore a problem.) Then they determine the purpose of their writing and ask questions about their readers. (Refer to section entitled "A Checklist of Questions Writers Need to Ask" in Chapter 1.) Of specific importance to writers of instructions and procedures are questions about how readers will use these documents. For example, will they

- memorize information?
- explain information to someone else?
- refer to the information while performing a task?
- read selectively for only one step?
- make a decision?
- understand a procedure better?
- buy or use a product or service?

Further, writers must determine their readers' background by asking:

- What are my readers' levels of understanding?
- How often will they read the document?
- What is their motivation for reading the document?

Having answered those questions, writers use one or more heuristics for getting started that you read about in Chapter 3.

To give you an idea of how writers of instructions, directives, or other procedural documents may get started, observe how two writers, Gary Walkins, who wrote a page describing training procedures for the commissioner, and Lynn Rogers, who wrote the directive memo, planned their documents before they wrote drafts.

Read the following descriptions of the ways each of these writers got started and decide how useful each strategy is under the circumstances. Could you suggest other strategies to them? Why do you think your alternatives or additional strategies would be useful under the circumstances?

Comparing Two Writers' Strategies

Strategy One: Classifying Steps

In his report to the commissioner about long-term care facilities, Walkins wanted to include a section on how he and his staff trained people to interview the elderly. Although this section was a small part of the report, it was significant to include because it informed the commissioner and documented Walkins' method of training. Walkins considered simply inserting his training director's schedule into the report. This schedule specified the steps trainers followed to prepare interviewers.

As he thought about the commissioner, Walkins asked himself, "How much does the commissioner need to know about how we trained people, especially since this kind of information is not a central part of the report? Surely the commissioner is not interested in knowing all the steps we took. Yet, he must want to know how we prepared for this project. And I want to document how we trained our staff to demonstrate my staff's professionalism. After all, that's why he hired our firm. He believed that we could do the job."

To achieve his primary purpose of informing, as well as his secondary purposes of documenting and persuading, Walkins decided to classify the training director's schedule according to topics. Although the schedule was already in step-

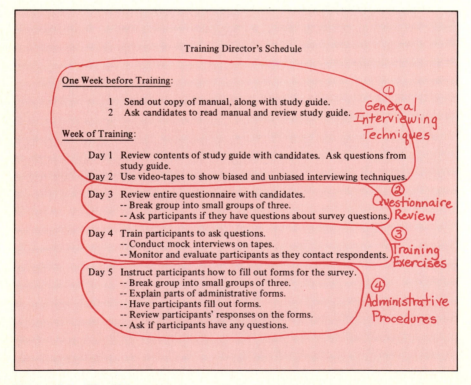

Figure 10-1   Classifying steps.

by-step sequence, Walkins saw another way to classify those steps. Figure 10-1 shows you how he classified the training director's schedule.

> How does Walkins decide to classify the schedule? Why do you think this classification system accomplished his purposes in writing: to inform, to document, and to persuade?

Strategy Two: Listing Steps

To plan her directive to shipping employees, Rogers faced a different kind of problem. Unlike Walkins, who had more than enough information to start with, Rogers had to ask herself, "What are all the steps my readers have to follow to ship packages correctly?" She knew what she wanted employees to do, but she wasn't sure just how many steps to include, especially since she didn't want employees to think that this new procedure was a complicated one. In Figure 10-2 you see how Rogers began to develop a plan for her directive. Her strategy was to list all the steps she could think of.

DRAFTING

Writers also vary their strategies for writing a draft. Classifying and listing steps help writers develop the plot of their instructions, directives, or procedural documents—the movement or sequence of actions readers should be able to perform or understand. In the process of writing a draft, writers may find that their original list of steps does not suit the way their readers intend to use the information. Steps may be out of order for readers, or each step may not have enough information to help a reader understand or perform a task.

To make sure that readers have all the information they need, some writers compose a draft by using the *journalists' strategy*—asking questions to develop a scene for each step. Another strategy is the *visual representation strategy*. Instead of beginning to write the text, some writers represent a procedure visually.

Journalists' Strategy

Because getting a reader to understand a procedure is like getting a reader to understand scenes in a play, writers of instructions, directives, and other procedural documents often ask the following journalists' questions to cause them to think about the kinds of information they need to provide readers:

Who performed the action or actions in the process?
What action or actions did the agent perform?
When and where did the agent perform this action or actions?
Why did the agent perform an action?
How did the agent perform an action or actions?

Asking these questions caused Walkins to include information that he thought would be important for the commissioner to know about, such as what trainers

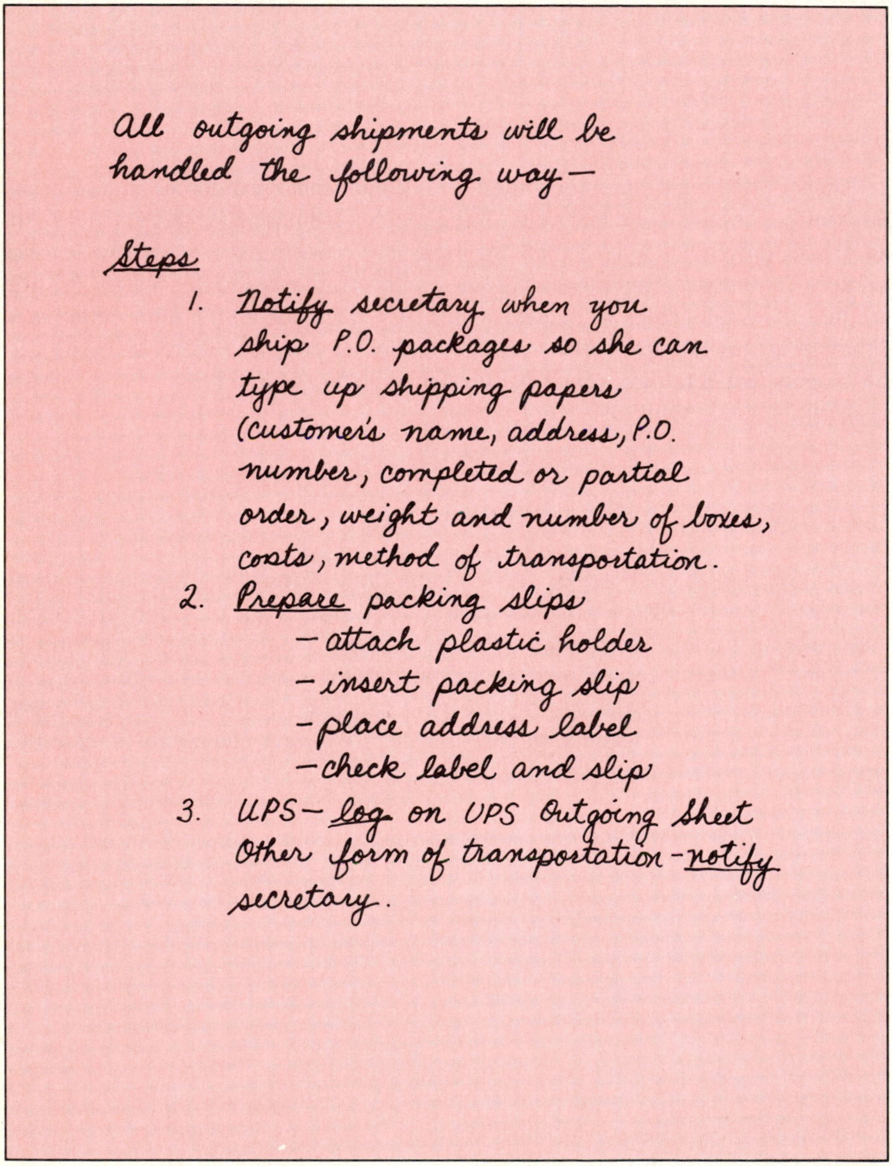

All outgoing shipments will be handled the following way—

Steps
1. Notify secretary when you ship P.O. packages so she can type up shipping papers (customer's name, address, P.O. number, completed or partial order, weight and number of boxes, costs, method of transportation.
2. Prepare packing slips
   — attach plastic holder
   — insert packing slip
   — place address label
   — check label and slip
3. UPS — log on UPS Outgoing Sheet Other form of transportation — notify secretary.

Figure 10-2 Listing steps.

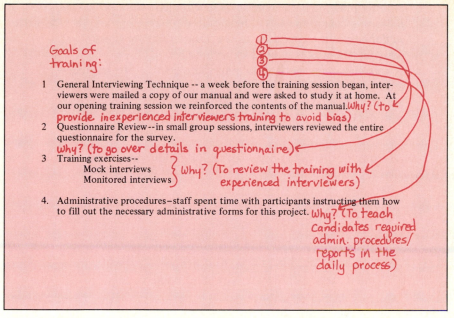

Goals of training:

1 General Interviewing Technique -- a week before the training session began, interviewers were mailed a copy of our manual and were asked to study it at home. At our opening training session we reinforced the contents of the manual. *Why? (to provide inexperienced interviewers training to avoid bias)*

2 Questionnaire Review--in small group sessions, interviewers reviewed the entire questionnaire for the survey. *why? (to go over details in questionnaire)*

3 Training exercises--
   Mock interviews
   Monitored interviews   *Why? (To review the training with experienced interviewers)*

4. Administrative procedures--staff spent time with participants instructing them how to fill out the necessary administrative forms for this project. *Why? (To teach candidates required admin. procedures/ reports in the daily process)*

Walkins asks the journalists' questions to include relevant information under each topic. His answer to the question "Why?" prompts him to develop an introduction justifying why he and his staff trained interviewers a certain way.

Figure 10-3   Journalists' strategy.

did, what trainees did, and how trainees completed steps. You see his first draft in Figure 10-3.

As Walkins asked the question "Why?" after each step, he began to realize how important it was to explain the purpose of these steps to the commissioner. Responding to this question for each step prompted Walkins to write down the purpose of each step. Writing down these purpose statements prompted him to develop an introduction justifying the purpose of the steps.

The journalists' strategy helps you add essential information to your steps, and, as with Walkins, also helps you determine whether your readers need introductory information about what you are describing or narrating. For example, Walkins believed he needed an introduction that answered the question "Why?" The following is a list of some other purposes of introductions and the questions they answer for readers.

Some Purposes of Introductions in Instructional and Procedural Documents

1 A summary of the number of steps necessary to perform a task—often to motivate a reader to believe the task is not difficult to perform. Or, a description of how a document is organized, or how someone should use a document   **How?**

2 A description of the conditions when someone can or should ⎤ When?
   perform a task (time, place, temperature)   ⎦ Where?
3 A definition of terms used in the instructions or a listing of ⎤
   materials the user may need to perform a task   ⎦ What?
4 A rationale statement, explaining the objective of the proce- ⎤
   dure   ⎦ Why?
5 An identification of the person or persons who should use or ⎤
   read the instructions or directives   ⎦ Who?

Introductory sections of instructions and procedures may include one or more of these purposes.

> Review the examples of instructions and procedures
> in Chapter 9. What kinds of introductions, if any,
> did writers use? Why do you think some writers
> included introductions?

Visual Representation Strategy

Rogers preferred to represent the procedure for preparing packages by relying on a visual: a flowchart. She believed that if she could represent the sequence of actions and decisions clerks would have to follow, she would write more accurate instructions than if she merely wrote a draft based on her list of steps. In Figure 10-4 you see her flowchart.

> Compare her flowchart with her original list of
> steps in Figure 10-2. How did the flowchart help
> her develop more accurate information about the
> last step?

COMPOSING A TEST DRAFT

Satisfied with the skeleton of their steps, writers then compose a test draft to check for completeness, accuracy, and strategies for arrangement.

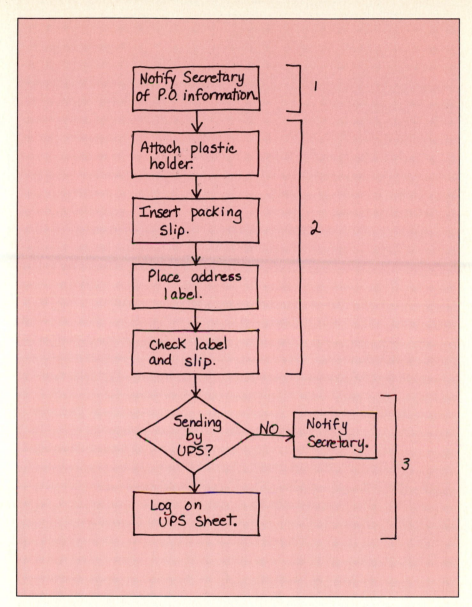

Figure 10-4   Visual representation strategy.

Asking Journalists' Questions to Test for Completeness and Accuracy

Based on his first draft, Walkins wrote the test draft you see in Figure 10-5. To check his test draft, he continued to ask journalists' questions about each step: "Do I have to provide more information about Who? What? When? Where? Why? and How?" His handwritten notes in Figure 10-5 show what kinds of information he still thought he should include.

Interviewer Training

The training was structured to achieve four goals

1. to provide inexperienced interviewers training in the general interviewing techniques essential for avoiding interviewer bias

2. to teach interviewers the details of the questionnaire

3. reviewing the training with experienced interviewers

4. to teach interviewers the required admin. procedures and reports involved in the daily *survey* process

Goals accomplished

1. General interviewing technique--a week before the training session began, interviewers were mailed a copy of our training manual and were asked to study it at home. At our opening training session, we reinforced the contents of the manual. *through video-tapes, illustrating correct and unbiased interviewing techniques.*

2. Reviewing Questionnaire--in small group sessions, interviewers reviewed the entire questionnaire for the county survey. *question-by-question*

3. Training exercises

   Mock Interviews

   during the training period interviewers performed mock interviews on tape. These prepared candidates for the complexities they would encounter. *while interviewing*

   Monitored Interviews

   Before training ended the interviewers spent approximately two hours in the telephone center, attempting to contact respondents, searching, and to interview. Project staff monitored these and evaluated candidates performance.

4. Administrative procedures--staff spent time with participants instructing them how to fill out the necessary administrative forms for this project.

Interviewers who initially performed unsatisfactorily or who did not demonstrate efficient techniques were given additional individualized training or otherwise were dismissed.

Figure 10-5   Walkins' test draft.

> Compare his first draft in Figure 10-3 with his test draft in Figure 10-5. What kind of information did he add? Why do you think he added this kind of information?

Viewing Each Step as a Problem to Test for Completeness and Accuracy

Rogers wrote a test draft based on her flowchart, but she was still concerned that she may have left out important information. She decided to use another strategy to test her draft: viewing each step as a problem.

Because you are already familiar with the components of a problem and have been using the problem-solving model in this textbook, you know how this strategy works. Rogers asked herself the following questions about each step:

What is the reader's goal in this step or stage?
What is the reader's initial state in this step or stage?
What restrictions would prevent a reader from completing the goal in this step or stage?
What actions should I specify, or what pieces of information should I include to help a reader overcome those restrictions?

Asking herself these problem-solving questions about each step caused her to add the note you see in her test draft in Figure 10-6.

How does this piece of information overcome a restriction that could prevent shipping clerks from carrying out the procedure?

Observing Readers to Test Strategies for Arrangement

Walkins had already established a chronological arrangement taken from his training director's schedule. Rogers, however, wanted to test the sequence of her steps because all shipping clerks would have to follow the directive. Therefore, she asked several clerks to try out her test draft. By observing them using her directive and asking them what kinds of problems they experienced, she was able to find out whether she had mistakenly ordered the steps.

Two workers told her that the sequence of actions in her second step was awkward to perform. They said, ''Why would someone want to attach the plastic holder to the package and then try to insert the packaging slip? It would be easier if clerks first put the packing slip into the holder and then secured the holder on

To: Shipping Clerks   Date: Sept. 23

From: Lynn Rogers, Office Manager

Re: New Procedure for Paperwork Accompanying Shipment

To help with the flow of paperwork for our shipments I have established a new procedure.

All outgoing shipments will be accompanied with the following paperwork. Effective immediately.

1. When materials are being shipped to our customers as a result of a Purchase Order (P.O.) placed with us on the day the order is to be shipped notify secretary of the following information; customers name, customers address, purchase order number, completed or partial order, weight and number of boxes, shipping costs, method of transportation.

The secretary will then send shipping papers as soon as she types them.

2. Prepare packing slips

   a. attach plastic holder on outside of box

   b. insert packing slip (pink slip) into plastic protective holder located on shipping table

   c. place address label on center front of box

   d. check that both address label and packing slip are secure.

3. If package is going UPS log on UPS Outgoing Sheet. If you use another form of transportation, notify the secretary; she will handle further details.

Note: If there are any special circumstances, i.e., something being shipped "no charge" due to damaged materials, or special discount, call secretary when requesting shipping paperwork. *(Insert after Step 1.)*

Figure 10-6   Rogers' test draft. (By permission from Lynn Rogers.)

the package." As a result of this observation, Rogers reordered the first two steps under step two as you see in Figure 10-6.

      Also notice in Figure 10-6 that Rogers chose a memo format to send to all clerks. This format provided her with the opportunity to state her purpose before she instructed workers. She believed that providing readers with a purpose statement would help them understand why she was establishing this directive.

Some Purposes of Conclusions in Instructional and Procedural Documents

Although Rogers did not see the necessity of including a conclusion in her directive, some documents may have concluding sentences or paragraphs. Walkins, as you recall, did conclude with a paragraph explaining how unsuccessful trainees were dismissed. Here is a list of some functions of conclusions:

- To describe the result or end product
- To describe the effects of a procedure
- To compliment the reader on being able to perform an entire task

REVISING AND EDITING INSTRUCTIONS AND DIRECTIVES

To make sure they order events or actions correctly and include accurate and complete information to help readers perform a task or understand how an action is or was or will be performed, writers review their documents at four levels. Follow the four review steps you read about in Chapter 4 to check your documents:

First Review
Read for Purpose and Audience
Second Review
Read for Arrangement and Purpose
Third Review
Read for Sentences and Language
Fourth Review
Read for Accuracy

Compare Walkins' and Rogers' final documents in Chapter 9 (Figures 9-1 and 9-5) with their test drafts in this chapter (Figures 10-5 and 10-6). Discuss how each writer revised and edited the test draft.

DESIGNING A FINISHED DOCUMENT
Formats for Instructional and Procedural Documents

As you may have already read in Chapter 5, knowing who your readers are and how they will use a document will affect how you design your document. Whether your readers will be using your document as a ready reference or reading it to understand how a process was or will be performed, you will want to design your document to enable readers to focus on individual steps and scan the document for information that they need.

As you have already seen in Chapter 9, there are numerous formats for instructional and procedural documents. You may be writing a memo, a letter, an instructional sheet, an operator's manual, an office manual, or representing a procedure in a flowchart. Because there are so many formats, we will list the principles of format that you should consider. Listing these does not mean that you have to include all of them. Your purpose, your readers, and their use of a document will help you determine which ones to include.

> *Introduction* answering the questions Who? What? When? Where? Why? How?
> *Body* classifying and listing steps
> *Conclusion* specifying the result or the effect

Copy Elements

Here are the copy elements that you will want to consider using as you design your final document:

> *Title* (in a master headline) to define the document or specify the purpose of the document
> *Subheadings* to signal major divisions of the text, such as a section on materials or major steps in a procedure
> *Short copy blocks* to call attention to steps or substeps
> *Highlighting devices* to call attention to notes, cautions, warnings, or important words in a sentence

As you prepare a final document, review the section entitled "Copy Elements" in Chapter 5. You might also want to review some of the examples in Chapter 9, although they do not represent all the possible formats that are appropriate for instructions or other procedural documents.

> Look at Rogers' final copy of the directive she sent
> to shipping clerks in Chapter 9 (Figure 9-1). List
> all the copy elements she used to prepare that final
> document. Discuss the effectiveness of all those
> devices in achieving the purpose of her document.

Graphic Elements

As you prepare a finished document, you may consider integrating one or more graphic elements into your document. If graphic elements will assist your reader in performing a task or understanding how a task was or will be performed, you will want to include them.

> Look at Figure 9-3 in Chapter 9. Explain why
> illustrations help readers perform the task of mak-
> ing a transparency.

Deciding to include graphic elements means that you will have to answer the following questions:

1 Where should I place my graphic element so that it assists my readers' understanding of the text?
2 How will I refer readers to the graphic element in my text?
3 Where will I caption my graphic element, and how will I label it?

If you want to review principles of graphic elements, refer to Chapter 5.

PROOFREADING

Even though you probably will have checked for spelling, punctuation, grammar, and capitalization in the process of writing your document, you still need to check your final copy one more time. Follow the strategies for proofreading that you read about in Chapter 4.

CHECKLIST FOR INSTRUCTIONAL OR PROCEDURAL DOCUMENTS

Content

1   Have I included accurate and comprehensive information to inform or help my reader carry out a procedure?
2   Have I provided sufficient context for my reader? Or does my reader already understand the context?

Strategies for Arrangement

1   If necessary for my reader, have I opened with an introduction?
2   Have I grouped steps chronologically so that my reader can understand a procedure or perform a task?
3   If necessary, have I ended with a conclusion?
4   Have I used cohesive devices—including headings—to guide my reader through the steps to understand or perform a procedure?

Vocabulary and Style

1   Have I unpacked weighty sentences?
2   Have I followed the principle of parallelism in listing steps, in listing commands, or in listing several conditions affecting how someone performs an action or how an action occurs?
3   Have I used accurate word choice to describe who does "what?" "when?" "where?" "why?" and "how?"
4   Do my word choices convey the tone I wish to establish? Am I explaining a procedure or am I commanding readers to carry out a procedure?

Conventions of the Language

1   Have I followed the conventions of spelling, punctuation, and grammar?
2   Have I avoided biased language in naming or referring to the reader?

Layout

1   Have I applied the principles of effective document design to list steps and/or conditions; to call attention to notes, cautions, warnings, or pieces of important information; and to integrate graphic elements with the text?

Format

1 Have I followed an appropriate format, such as for one of the following:
- ☐ Instructional sheet?
- ☐ Procedural manual?
- ☐ Instructional manual?
- ☐ Pamphlet or brochure?
- ☐ Memo?
- ☐ Letter?
- ☐ Other format?

REVISING INSTRUCTIONS OR OTHER PROCEDURAL DOCUMENTS FOR A SPOKEN PRESENTATION: A CHECKLIST

Frequently you will have to revise instructions, directives, or other procedural documents for a spoken presentation. You might, for example, have to train employees to use a new piece of office equipment. You might have to explain to a potential customer how your product or service operates or instruct a customer to use your product. The following checklist will help you think through how you should prepare for these kinds of presentations.

Purpose

What is (are) the purpose(s) of this spoken presentation?

- ☐ To inform about what is happening, what happened, or what will happen?
- ☐ To instruct listeners to perform a task?
- ☐ To persuade listeners to perform a task?
- ☐ To persuade listeners to purchase a service or a product?
- ☐ Other?

Listeners

Who are my listeners? Are they members of my organization or outsiders? What is their level of expertise? What is their motivation for listening?

- ☐ Asked to attend?
- ☐ Required to attend?
- ☐ Volunteered to attend?

What use will they make of my instructions or procedures?

- ☐ Memorize them?
- ☐ Explain them to someone else?
- ☐ Follow them as I speak?
- ☐ Recall them in the future?
- ☐ Make a decision based on them?
- ☐ Understand a process better?
- ☐ Buy a product or service?
- ☐ Other?

What kind of relationship do I want to establish with my listeners?

- ☐ Formal?
- ☐ Informal?
- ☐ Other?

What preconceptions do they have about me?

- ☐ See me as an authority within my organization?
- ☐ See me as an expert within my field?
- ☐ Other?

Strategies for Arrangement

- ☐ How many steps are in this procedure?
- ☐ How will I group them?
- ☐ What transitional words or phrases should I use to move from one major step to the next?
- ☐ How will I open my presentation?
- ☐ Should I give an overview of the major steps to orient listeners?
- ☐ Should I state how simple the procedure is to motivate listeners?
- ☐ Should I list the advantages or benefits of the procedure to motivate listeners?
- ☐ Other?

How will I conclude the presentation?

- ☐ Restate the major steps?
- ☐ Emphasize the advantages of the procedure?

☐ Emphasize the simplicity of the procedure?
☐ Emphasize the effects or results of the procedure—especially in solving a problem?
☐ Other?

Format

Where will I be speaking? What format should I use for this location?

☐ Read the presentation?
☐ Memorize the presentation?
☐ Speak from notes or an outline?
☐ Speak without notes?
☐ Incorporate question and answer period?
☐ Other?

How long should I speak?

☐ How much time is available?
☐ How long can I expect listeners to want to pay attention?
☐ How long should I allow for questions?
☐ Should I invite questions during or after my presentation?

What steps should I take so that I speak neither too fast nor too slowly?

Audiovisual Media

What kinds of audiovisual media should I use to help my listeners understand or perform a procedure? What is the advantage of using one or more of these media for this presentation?

☐ Flowchart?
☐ Diagram?
☐ Organization chart?
☐ Model?
☐ The product itself?

What media should I use to achieve my purpose and make it possible for all listeners to hear or see audiovisual media?

1 Visual media:
   - ☐ Slide projector?
   - ☐ Overhead projector?
   - ☐ Chalkboard, clothboard?
   - ☐ Flipchart?
   - ☐ Handout?
2 Audiovisual media:
   - ☐ Videotape?
   - ☐ Videodisk?
   - ☐ Film or motion picture?
   - ☐ Tape recorder?
   - ☐ Record?
   - ☐ Other?

1st - Job description for adults
2nd - Job description for children

Child

purpose: explain How you do your job, etc.

→ simplify
show - demonstrate
personify - relate to
something familiar
- Shorter sentences
- more breaks / new ¶
- illustration

Successor

- instruct so successor will be able to carry out procedure

- illustration?

In the following projects or exercises you will either write or revise instructions or other kinds of procedural documents. When you write a document, begin by thinking about the kind of problem you are solving; then make sure you follow the strategies that you read about in this chapter or in Chapters 3 and 4. Once you have a test draft, your instructor may ask you to fill out a Writer Review for that draft. Then, your instructor may ask one of your peers to fill out a Reader Review. Examples of these review sheets are presented following the projects and exercises in this chapter.

Before you hand in your final copy, make sure you follow the four-step review process and the "Checklist for Instructional or Procedural Documents" that you read toward the end of this chapter.

1. In Chapter 9, Exercise 3, we asked you to list five organizational problems that require individuals to follow instructions or directives. Select one organizational problem and write a document that solves this problem.

2. List the procedures you follow in performing a specific task for a campus job or an off campus job. Write an instructional memo to a newly hired person who has to perform this task for the first time. Make sure that you consider how to classify steps. Write another memo to a superior in your work place, describing how you perform the task.

3. Think of a mental or physical task that you could instruct readers to perform. Decide what kind of document you would write to each of the readers listed below. Select two out of the following three groups of readers and write instructions for the same operation to each group.

   (a) Readers who must perform the procedure but do not have any previous knowledge about the procedure
   (b) Readers who are reluctant to try a procedure because they believe it is too difficult
   (c) Readers who must perform the procedure and do have previous knowledge about the procedure or, at least, understand the context in which they will have to perform the procedure

4. Write an instructional manual to accompany a mechanism. As you plan that document, think about who your readers will be, how they will use the document, when or how often they will use it, and why they will use it.

5. Find a technical manual written to instruct experts to carry out a procedure, such as operating a computer, repairing household equipment, or assembling a product. Decide how you would change the instructions to make them more readable and useful for nonexperts. Rewrite the manual for readers without technical expertise.

6. Rewrite the following instructional sheet accompanying a drafting table. Add, delete, substitute, or rearrange pieces of information. To test the accuracy of each step, view each step as a problem.

DRAFTING TABLE

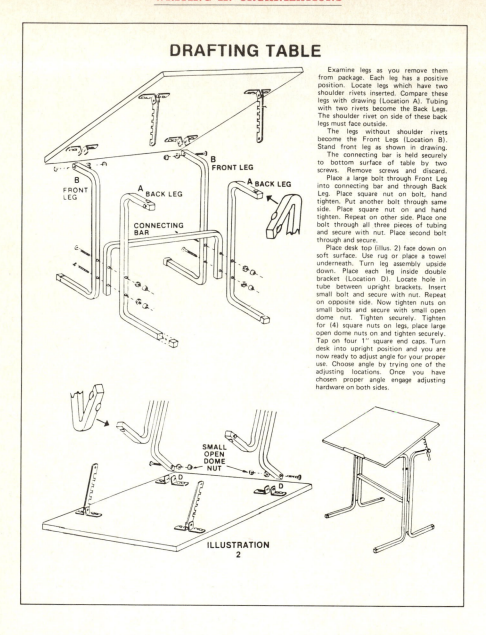

Examine legs as you remove them from package. Each leg has a positive position. Locate legs which have two shoulder rivets inserted. Compare these legs with drawing (Location A). Tubing with two rivets become the Back Legs. The shoulder rivet on side of these back legs must face outside.

The legs without shoulder rivets become the Front Legs (Location B). Stand front leg as shown in drawing.

The connecting bar is held securely to bottom surface of table by two screws. Remove screws and discard. Place a large bolt through Front Leg into connecting bar and through Back Leg. Place square nut on bolt, hand tighten. Put another bolt through same side. Place square nut on and hand tighten. Repeat on other side. Place one bolt through all three pieces of tubing and secure with nut. Place second bolt through and secure.

Place desk top (illus. 2) face down on soft surface. Use rug or place a towel underneath. Turn leg assembly upside down. Place each leg inside double bracket (Location D). Locate hole in tube between upright brackets. Insert small bolt and secure with nut. Repeat on opposite side. Now tighten nuts on small bolts and secure with small open dome nut. Tighten securely. Tighten for (4) square nuts on legs, place large open dome nuts on and tighten securely. Tap on four 1″ square end caps. Turn desk into upright position and you are now ready to adjust angle for your proper use. Choose angle by trying one of the adjusting locations. Once you have chosen proper angle engage adjusting hardware on both sides.

ILLUSTRATION 2

7. Imagine that you are the public relations director of a company that wants to build a "trash to steam" recycling plant in your particular city or county. Write a news release or design a brochure that explains the process to the citizens of your city or county.

8. Think of ways to improve an invention that already exists, or make up your own invention. To a financial backer, describe how useful it would be and what its advantages are over anything that already exists, *or* write a set of instructions for potential users.

9. Rewrite the following instructional sheet so that it instructs homeroom teachers how to hand out and collect ticket forms for a school event. Add, delete, substitute, or rearrange information to write a document that will achieve this purpose. When you have a test draft that you are satisfied with, go through the four-step review process. Then write your final copy.

1983–84 FUND RAISING DRIVE

1. The fund raising drive will begin on Friday, September 23rd, with a special school schedule. The students will report to their homerooms and be given instructions at that time.

2. In the homeroom each student will be issued an envelope on which his name will have been printed. Inside the envelope will be three (3) 10 Week Club Tickets, some information about the Activity Drive and a copy of Form B. The students' names, sections, and ticket numbers will have been written on Form B. When the student makes his first returns, he will submit Form B, along with the ticket stubs and the money. He should have written on Form B the name of the person who has purchased the ticket (next to the corresponding ticket number) and the amount of money he is returning with that ticket.

3. Each ticket will cost $20.00. Every student will be expected to sell a minimum of three (3) tickets. As has been the practice for the past three years, and, indeed, as is the policy in other archdiocesan high schools, if a student does not sell his quota, he will not be allowed to continue in or join any activities for the school year. For every ticket a student sells beyond the quota, he is eligible for one (1) chance in an incentive cash prize drawing. Thus, if a student sells five (5) tickets, he is entitled to two (2) free chances on a cash prize. If he sells six (6) tickets, he is entitled to three (3) free chances on a cash prize. Special cash prizes will also be awarded to the ten (10) highest student sellers.

4. Ticket returns will be collected by members of the Mothers' Association on Monday, Tuesday and Wednesday at all the lunch periods in the cafeteria.

5. When a student returns tickets/money, a record of the returns will be kept in two files. A "master file" print-out of the student's name and ticket numbers will be kept in the office records. Student returns will be indicated in the master file on a weekly payment basis. Space will be provided in the master file for any additional "homeroom files." In the homeroom files there will be one sheet of paper for each payment that each student returns.

6. The tickets will be in three (3) detachable sections; the first section will be kept by the buyer and will include the ticket number, club rules, prizes and a weekly record of payments made on the ticket.

    A second section of the ticket will include the ticket number, the name, address, and phone number of the buyer and the name of the seller. This second section will be deposited in the drawing barrel.

    The third section of the ticket will include the name, address, and phone number of the buyer and the name and homeroom section of the seller. This third section of the ticket will be filed in the office records and will indicate how much money has been paid for that ticket. The third section will verify if a person whose name has been drawn from the barrel is eligible to win in any one of the weekly drawings. (To be eligible to win in the weekly drawing the ticket must be paid for that particular week). If the person is not eligible, his/her name will be returned to the barrel and another ticket will be drawn.

WRITER AND READER REVIEWS
Writer Review of a Test Draft

Readers and Purpose

1 Who are my readers and how will they use this document? (Refer to section entitled "A Checklist of Questions Writers Need to Ask" in Chapter 1.)

2 What is my purpose in writing this document? (To inform or to help perform?)

Strategies for Arrangement

1 How did I begin the document? (With an introductory paragraph? The first step?)
2 How did I sequence information? (Step by step, along with description of conditions or results of actions?)
3 How did I establish cohesion from step to step and sentence to sentence? (Numbers? Words indicating time?)
4 Did I include notes, warnings, or emergency procedures? Which ones? Why? Where did I include them?
5 How did I conclude or close the document? Why?

Copy Elements

1 Did I title the document or name the product or process?
2 What have I done to set off headings and subheadings? Have I followed the principle of parallelism in developing headings and subheadings?
3 How have I indicated lists and made them easy to follow?
4 Are the copy blocks small and visually clear?

Vocabulary and Style

1 Have I used the correct tense and voice to inform about actions or command actions?
2 Are commands short?
3 How have I indicated conditions if there are any?
4 Are my word choices accurate?
5 Have I rewritten negative statements into positive ones?
6 Have I followed the principle of parallelism in the steps?

Graphic Elements

1 If I have used graphic elements, are they placed next to or near the instructions they illustrate?
2 Are the diagrams labeled? How?
3 Are the call-outs clear?
4 Are the call-outs parallel?
5 Are textual references to the graphic elements clear?

Format

1   How is the format of the document suited to the readers and to the way they will use it?

Reader Review of a Test Draft

Readers and Purpose

1   Who are the readers of this document, and how will they use this document? (Refer to section entitled ''A Checklist of Questions Writers Need to Ask'' in Chapter 1.)
2   What is the writer's purpose in writing this document? (To inform or to help perform?)

Strategies for Arrangement

1   How does the writer begin the document? (With an introductory paragraph? The first step?)
2   How does the writer sequence information? (Step by step, along with description of conditions or results of actions?)
3   How does the writer establish cohesion from step to step and sentence to sentence? (Numbers? Words indicating time?)
4   Does the writer include notes, warnings, or emergency procedures? If not, should they be included? Which ones? Why? Where?
5   How does the writer conclude or close the document? Why?

Copy Elements

1   Does the writer title the document or name the product or process?
2   What has the writer done to set off headings and subheadings? Has the writer followed the principle of parallelism in developing headings and subheadings?
3   Has the writer listed information and made it easy to read?
4   Are the copy blocks small and visually clear?

Style

1   Has the writer used the correct tense and voice to inform about actions or command actions?

2 Are commands short?
3 How has the writer indicated conditions if there are any?
4 Are all word choices accurate?
5 Are there any negative statements that are difficult to follow?
6 Has the writer followed the principle of parallelism in each step?

Graphic Elements

1 If the writer used graphic elements, are they placed next to or near the instructions they illustrate?
2 Are the diagrams labeled? How?
3 Are the call-outs clear?
4 Are call-outs parallel?
5 Are textual references to the graphic elements clear?

Format

1 How is the format of the document suited to the readers and to the way readers will use it?

CHAPTER

11

A WRITER AT WORK: A CASE STUDY OF COMPOSING A SET OF INSTRUCTIONS

PART 1: IDENTIFYING THE PROBLEM

Gina Recigno was majoring in computer science and taking an advanced writing course. Her writing instructor asked members of the class to design and write a set of instructions or directives. To get started, students had to decide what process they aimed to teach, who their primary and secondary readers would be, and where and how those readers would use the instructions. Recigno's part-time work in her college's computer center gave her the idea for her project.

She planned to design a simplified manual of instructions for college students just learning how to use the computer. Recigno noticed that the computer manuals her college received from the manufacturers were usually written by experts, and only other experts could make sense of them. These manuals were troublesome because they did not provide useful guides for all the inexperienced students learning to use the machines. As a result, these students routinely asked the computer center assistants, like Recigno, for help when something went wrong. It frequently did.

The assistants were hired to help the computer users and to carry out other responsibilities in the center as well. Most assistants agreed that they were spending too much time answering the routine questions of novices and not enough time on the more challenging responsibilities they had. Clearly, providing an instructional manual for new computer operators would give them the help they needed and would relieve the assistants.

Recigno decided she first wanted to teach how to log on and off the computers. She also considered offering some programming instructions. Her primary readers would be new computer users. However, she thought a basic instructional manual would be a useful ready reference for previous users who needed to refresh their memories. Readers would use the manual while they were at the keyboard. Recigno needed to figure out a format that was convenient yet didn't require much space on the computer tables. Gina's notes for her preliminary thinking appear in Figure 11-1.

PART 2:   GETTING STARTED
Planning the Composing Process

Recigno's instructor sketched a sample work plan on the chalkboard and told the students to adapt the plan to their projects. The plan contained the due date for the final project and the dates to submit drafts for the instructor and peers to review.

Work plans help writers map the composing process for a particular piece of writing. Sketching such a plan helps you break your project down into smaller steps. It also helps you anticipate and sequence those steps, as well as estimate the amount of time to allow for each one.

Recigno realized that writing the copy is only a small part of preparing most instruction manuals. She also needed time to make illustrations or figures and to work on the layout. She anticipated making several ''pasteups'' to test ways to put the text and illustrations together. Only after trying several strategies would she format the document in its final form.

Recigno's work plan appears in Figure 11-2. Notice that she sketched in target dates to correspond with the due dates of her rough drafts, commentary sheets, and the finished manual.

Planning Ways to Sequence the Instructions

Once Recigno figured out the time frame for her project, she still had to devise another plan: one for organizing the manual itself. She predicted that she could

Purpose
- to get new computer users started
- to make them able to log on + off w/out help from computer center assistants
- (maybe) to teach elementary programming

Readers
  Primary - 1st time computer operators
  Secondary - experienced operators who get into trouble

Uses
  Primary Readers will read it step-by-step as they work at the machines
  Secondary Readers will use it to look up specific pieces of information

Format
- Inst. should lie flat on computer tables -- on right side of machines -- 2 page fold out?
- Should be small
- How many copies will I need??

Figure 11-1   Preliminary Planning.
Recigno wrote a preliminary plan to help her think about the purpose of her document, its readers, and the use they would make of it.

divide it into two main sections: one for logging on the computer and one for logging off. She quickly jotted down the steps she thought of for each category. Her list of steps appears in Figure 11-3.

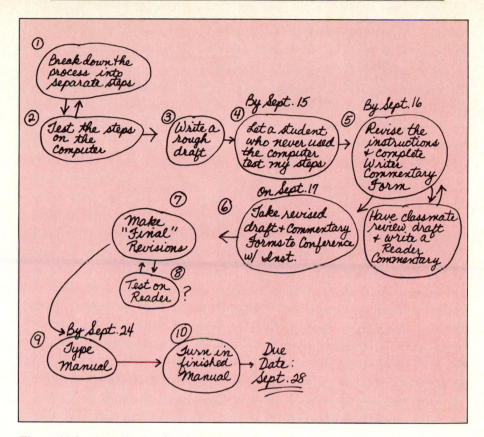

Figure 11-2   A work plan for the computer manual.

At this point, Recigno thought illustrations would be unnecessary, except perhaps for a diagram of the keyboard. Her readers would need this illustration to locate the RETURN key. However, Recigno wasn't sure where to place the diagram in the document. Would readers want to locate the key first or wait until they saw a command to push RETURN?

Testing the Steps

Recigno decided that since she knew the process she was describing so well, she did not need to test the steps on the computer. Sometimes, of course, writers are not as familiar with the procedures they must write about as Recigno was. However, even Recigno might have benefited from working at the computer rather than at her desk. If she had carried out the procedure herself, she would have more easily identified the steps in greater detail than her memory recalled.

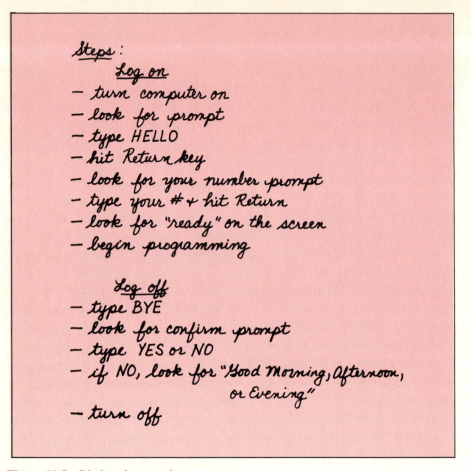

Figure 11-3   Listing the steps in a process.

PART 3: WRITING AND REVISING DRAFTS

Writing a Test Draft

As Recigno started to write her draft, she realized that some of the steps on her original outline were more complex than she thought. A simple command, such as "turn computer on," required an explanation of where to locate the ON-OFF switch. Furthermore, she realized that no operator could get the terminal going without a user number and a password. As she was writing the draft, Recigno also remembered that new operators often strike the wrong keys and don't know how to correct their errors. To solve that problem, she decided to include instructions for using the DELETE key, along with directions for logging on.

Recigno's goal for writing this test draft was to sequence and explain the directions as quickly as she could. She particularly needed to know how long each explanation would be so that she could estimate the length of her manual. At first, she thought she could fit everything on a two-page foldout that would lie flat on each computer table. Once she saw the explanations written out, however, Recigno realized they were too long for such a format.

Recigno also realized that some of her sentences were awkward. Cleaning them up might shorten the instructions. However, she decided to watch a reader actually use her instructions before she took the time to rewrite her prose. The draft Recigno gave to her reader appears in Figure 11-4.

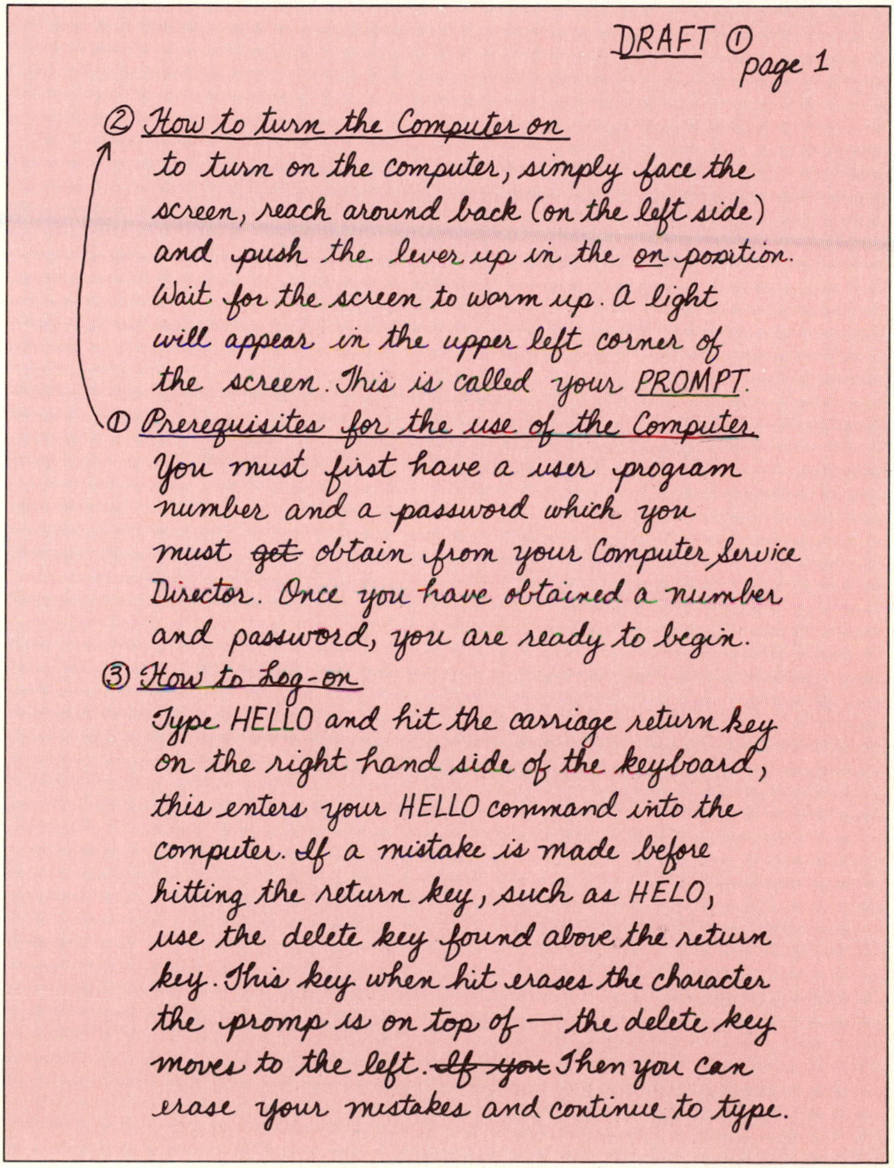

DRAFT ① page 1

② How to turn the Computer on
to turn on the computer, simply face the screen, reach around back (on the left side) and push the lever up in the _on_ position. Wait for the screen to warm up. A light will appear in the upper left corner of the screen. This is called your PROMPT.

① Prerequisites for the use of the Computer.
You must first have a user program number and a password which you must ~~get~~ obtain from your Computer Service Director. Once you have obtained a number and password, you are ready to begin.

③ How to Log-on
Type HELLO and hit the carriage return key on the right hand side of the keyboard, this enters your HELLO command into the computer. If a mistake is made before hitting the return key, such as HELO, use the delete key found above the return key. This key when hit erases the character the promp is on top of — the delete key moves to the left. ~~If you~~ Then you can erase your mistakes and continue to type.

Figure 11-4 Recigno's test draft.

Testing the Draft

Recigno observed her reader as he tried to follow the instructions in the first draft. The operator was able to log on, get ready to program, and log off. However, he couldn't find the ON-OFF switch simply by reaching around the terminal. In addition, he made no mistakes, so the directions for correcting errors simply got in his way.

After observing the reader, Recigno decided to make the following revisions on her next draft:

1 To use shorter copy blocks
2 To separate and bullet each step
3 To revise most of her sentences, especially to write imperative verbs
4 To add a simple program from which the operator could log off
5 To divide the manual into three separate major sections: "How to Log on," "How to Program," and "How to Log off"
6 To place all the information on correcting errors in a separate section at the end called "Send Help"
7 To place the information about the user's number and password in a prefatory note
8 To rephase each subheading so that it gave a command

PART 4:   REVISING AND EDITING THE DRAFT

Observing a reader follow the instructions helped Recigno think about revising as a process of rethinking her writing, not simply of correcting it. She typed another draft (Figure 11-5) and filled out a Writer Review to show her instructor during their conference. She also had another student in the class review her draft and write a Reader Review. (Review forms appear in Chap. 10, pp. 232–235.)

Conferring with a Reader

After Recigno and her instructor reviewed the drafts and review forms, they discussed making still more changes. For example, they agreed that illustrating the text with graphics would be helpful to a new operator. Recigno initially resisted this idea because she didn't feel capable of making the illustrations. The two also agreed that some of the graphics should show the reader what would appear on the computer screen. That way the operators could check the responses they saw on the screen against the ones they were supposed to see.

HOW TO LOG ON

Turn the Computer ON

- Place the ON-Off switch, located on the back of the terminal, up to the "on" position.

- Face the terminal and look for a flashing rectangular light, known as the cursor, in the upper left hand corner of your screen. Your terminal is now on.

Log In to Your Account

- Type HELLO and hit the carriage return key, located on the right side of your key board. The symbol "CR" will appear when the user is to hit the return key.

- Type your account number when the symbol "#" appears on the screen. The password you type will not appear on the screen, so type carefully.

- If "INVALID ENTRY TRY AGAIN" appears on the screen, you made an error. Look for another "#" prompt and carefully retype your account number and password.

- Once you have successfully entered your account, a message will appear on your screen followed by a READY prompt. The computer is ready for you to program.

HOW TO PROGRAM

Create a New File

- Type "NEW" [CR] to enable you to name a new program.

- Wait for "OLD FILE NAME --" to appear.

- Type a 1-6 letter and/or number name for your new program.

Figure 11-5   Draft 2 of the computer manual.

By conferring with other students about her draft and looking at her classmates' rough drafts, Recigno figured out how to make simple yet useful illustrations. These appear in her final draft (Figure 11-7). Before tackling those illustrations, however, she made some changes in the wording and layout of her draft. You can find those changes in Figure 11-6.

HOW TO LOG ON   *Draft 2*

Turn the Computer ON

- *Turn* ~~Place~~ the ON-Off switch, located on the back of the terminal, up to the "on" position.

- Face the terminal and look for a flashing rectangular light, known as the cursor, in the upper left hand corner of your screen. Your terminal is now on.

Log In to Your Account

press caps.   *[CR]*

- Type HELLO and ~~hit~~ the carriage return key, located on the right side of your key board. The symbol "CR" will (appear) when ~~the user is to hit the~~ return key. *where?* *you are to use* *caps*

Add Diagrams →

- Type your account number *[CR]* when the symbol "#" appears on the screen. The password you type will not appear on the screen, so type carefully. ** Add: new step — Wait for PASSWORD to appear on screen.*

- If "INVALID ENTRY TRY AGAIN" appears on the screen, you made an error. Look for another "#" prompt and carefully retype your account number and *Then type your password [CR]."* password.

- Once you have successfully entered your account, *look for* a message ~~will appear~~ on your screen (followed by a READY prompt.) The computer is *now* ~~ready~~ for you to program.

HOW TO PROGRAM

Create a New File

- Type "NEW" [CR] to enable you to name a new program.

- Wait for "OLD FILE NAME --" to appear.

- Type a 1-6 letter and/or number name for your new program.

Figure 11-6   Editing draft 2 of the computer manual.

PART 5: DESIGNING THE FINAL DOCUMENT

Recigno saw that her original idea of putting her instructions on a foldout was unworkable. There were too many instructions, and she had to work with 8½ × 11 inch paper. She decided to fasten the top of the pages with rings, allowing the

HOW TO OPERATE THE CT-100

HOW TO LOG ON

NOTE: Before you can log on, you must obtain an account number and a password from the Director of the Computer Center.

Turn the Computer ON

- Turn the ON-OFF switch, located on the back of the terminal, up to the "on" position.

- Face the screen and look for the cursor, a flashing rectangular light, in the upper left hand corner of your screen. The terminal is now on.

Log On to Your Account

- Type HELLO and press the CARRIAGE RETURN KEY <CR> located on the right side of your key board. The symbol "<CR>" will appear in this manual when you are to press the CARRIAGE RETURN KEY.

- Type your account number <CR> when the symbol "#" appears on the screen.

- Wait for "PASSWORD" to appear on screen. Then type your password <CR>. The password you type will not appear on the screen, so type carefully.

- If "INVALID ENTRY TRY AGAIN" appears on the screen, you made an error. Look for another "#" prompt and carefully retype your account number and password.

- Once you have successfully entered your account, look on the screen for a message followed by a READY prompt. The computer is now ready for you to program.

Figure 11-7   The final draft of the computer manual. (Used by permission from Gina Recigno.)

reader to flip one page behind the other. That way the instructions would fit on the table space to the right of each computer.

Before typing and formatting the final draft, Recigno reviewed the information in Chapter 5 about designing a document and in Chapters 9 and 10 about writing instructions. She carefully went over the checklist at the end of Chapter 10. The text and illustrations of Recigno's final draft appear in Figure 11-7.

HOW TO PROGRAM

Create a New File

- Type "NEW" <CR> to enable you to name a new program.

- Wait for "NEW FILE NAME -------" to appear.

- Type a 1-6 letter and/or number name for your new program.

Write a Program

- Type the following program written in the BASIC language. (NOTE: If you already have a program to type, ignore this one and proceed to type your own.)

```
10 REM this is my first program on a CT100.
20 LET A = 235
30 LET B = 99.3
45 LET D = A * B
50 PRINT "C = "; C
55 END
```

- Type SAVE <CR> to save your program.

Figure 11-7   (Cont.)

- Type DIR <CR> for a directory of your account.

```
READY
DIR
RSTS * Job Pc *  123.45  * ...
NAME          SECURITY  DATE
PROG I. BAS      <60>    10/7/81
```

Access Old File

- Type OLD <CR>, then type your file name in order to see, change, or use your program.

- Wait for your READY prompt.

```
OLD
OLD FILE NAME: PROG I

READY
■
```

- Type LIST <CR> to see a listing of your program.

- Type an entire line over or add new lines for changes.
  Type the line number <CR> to erase an entire line.
  After a change is made, type REPLACE.

- Type RUN <CR> to execute your program.

```
30 LET B = 27.3
REPLACE
READY
RUN
PROG I.
C = 6415.5
```

LOG OFF

Exit from Your Account

- Type BYE <CR> to exit from your account.

```
BYE
■
```

- Type YES <CR> after the CONFIRM: prompt.
  A message will be printed on your terminal with information about your account. This is your last message from the terminal. You have just logged off your account.

```
BYE
CONFIRM: YES

GOOD AFTERNOON
■
```

Figure 11-7 (Cont.)

Turn the Terminal Off

- Reach around the left side of your terminal and find the same ON/OFF switch you used to turn the computer on.

- Turn the switch down to the OFF position. The screen will flash, then darken.

SEND HELP

A GUIDE FOR CORRECTING ERRORS

Typing Error

- If you notice that you have made an error typing the line you are on, press the DELETE key to back space the cursor and type your correction. DO NOT USE THE BACK SPACE KEY!

Computer Responses

If you made an error, the following responses may appear on the screen:

- ?CAN'T FIND FILE OR ACCOUNT
  You have tried to access a file you do not have on your account. If you mistyped the name, correct your typing. If you cannot remember the correct name, type DIR <CR> for your account name.

- ?ILLEGAL FILE NAME
  You used characters other than letters and numbers to name your file. Type the NEW command again and choose a file name consisting of 1 to 6 alphanumeric (letters and numbers) characters.

- ?SYNTAX ERROR
  You have incorrectly typed a BASIC command. Retype the line.

- ?WHAT?
  You have typed a command the computer cannot process. First check the screen to see if you can find your own error. If not, check one of the manuals listed below:

  - the RSTS/E USER MANUAL
  - the BASIC-PLUS PROGRAMMING MANUAL, Vol. 3.

  These manuals are located on the bookshelves in the back of this room.

NOTE: IF YOU NEED FURTHER HELP, ASK YOUR FRIENDLY COMPUTER ASSISTANT. ONE IS ON DUTY AT ALL TIMES.

Figure 11-7   (Cont.)

What do you think are the strong points of the computer manual? What would you suggest doing differently?

SECTION FIVE

STRATEGIES FOR WRITING REPORTS AND PROPOSALS

CHAPTER
12

PURPOSES FOR WRITING REPORTS AND PROPOSALS

Along with the numerous letters and memos he writes each day, Sam McMillan routinely sets aside a part of each workday to write reports. He is the assistant director of marketing at a subsidiary of a consumer products firm that manufactures household cleaning products. As assistant director of marketing, he has to explore markets, develop marketing strategies, manage a staff, and transmit information about his activities to others in his organization. In the past month he has written the following reports:

- A report evaluating options for improving a liquid cleanser
- A report outlining marketing strategies for selling a new kitchen cleanser that will be placed on the market in six months
- A report projecting sales for the next quarter
- A report reviewing recent research in marketing journals about sales strategies
- A report appraising his new sales manager's performance over the last three months

In your routine writing on the job, you also may have to write reports. *Reports* are documents that focus on the status of a topic or issue, such as a progress report, or on the information you research about a topic or an issue, such as a marketing survey report. Reports can be as short as one page or as long as several hundred pages.

In this chapter you will see representative examples of reports and the kinds of problems they solve. You will also see *proposals*, documents that focus on persuading readers to support an idea, plan, or project or to buy a product or service. They, too, can be as short as one page or as long as several hundred pages—even volumes! We discuss both of these documents in this chapter because often proposals follow closely on the heels of reports. Reports can document the need for a change, such as a plan or program; proposals persuade readers to support a specific plan or program. Like reports, proposals often identify a problem, but they focus on a particular solution.

So that you understand when writers in organizations are prompted to write these documents, we will explore the kinds of problems writers solve when they write reports and proposals, explain the purposes of these documents, and show you how several writers solved organizational problems by writing reports and proposals.

EXPLORING THE PROBLEMS REPORTS SOLVE

Internal Reports

Reports can convey information about the internal activities of your organization, such as the proceedings of a meeting or the accomplishments of a committee toward achieving its goal. Or, they can convey information about your organization's external activities, such as its product sales. Reports are also vehicles for transmitting information about the activities outside of an organization, such as technological advances or demographic changes, to readers within your organization. These reports alert decision-makers to activities that may affect how an organization operates, what kinds of products it will manufacture, what kinds of services it will offer, or where it will sell its products or services. For example, a marketing survey measuring consumers' reactions to a test product will determine whether a manufacturer believes it would be profitable to market that product. Decision-makers use reports as ready references to make on-the-spot decisions or to plan for the future.

External Reports

You will also write reports for external readers to communicate information to those who have an interest in your organization's operations or achievements, such as stockholders, special-interest groups, potential customers, or financial investors. Outside readers use these reports to remain informed of your organization's activities.

Reports can follow letter or memo formats or conventional report formats. (You will read more about these formats later in this chapter and in Chapter 13.) Generally, the more complex the issue or problem is, the longer the report and the greater the need to use a formal report format. The format you choose will also depend on your reader's familiarity with the information in your report and your reader's context. For example, the memo length report may be appropriate for a quarterly sales report to a department head, whereas a regional manager would expect a longer formal report.

SOME OCCASIONS FOR WRITING REPORTS

The following occasions are some of the times when you will write reports to solve organizational problems. You may have to write a report when you need to:

- Document "for the records" what happened during an event or activity, such as a committee meeting or an on-site investigation
- Summarize results of research, such as research of in-house records
- Describe a department's or organization's activities, such as accomplishments toward fulfilling an organizational objective
- Describe a strategy or plan of action, such as a marketing strategy for the next quarter
- Investigate the causes or effects of problems that are occurring in an organization, such as a decline in a division's productivity
- Evaluate a worker's job performance

EXPLORING THE PROBLEMS PROPOSALS SOLVE

Because his job also requires that he explore market opportunities and develop plans to market his products, McMillan writes proposals. Here is a list of the proposals he has worked on over the last month:

- A proposal persuading his director of marketing to increase the advertising budget for the next year
- A proposal suggesting ways to launch a new advertising campaign for an improved product
- A proposal persuading a chain of discount stores to carry his division's product line

Frequently, after a report demonstrates the need for a product, service, or plan, or recommends a solution to a problem, someone or a group of people writes a proposal. A proposal is a persuasive document, designed to convince readers to sponsor, accept, or support an idea, method, plan, project, or activity, or to buy a product or service. These readers may be either internal or external ones.

In a proposal, you will begin either by establishing a need for your proposed plan or by responding to an already acknowledged need for a plan, system, product, or service. There are two types of proposals: solicited and unsolicited.

Solicited Proposals

You will have the occasion to write a *solicited proposal* when someone asks you to propose a solution to an individual or organizational problem. In many cases, an organization will state its need for a solution to a problem in a "Request for Proposal," a published announcement requesting that qualified candidates or organizations submit proposals to solve an organization's problem.

When you write this kind of proposal, you must demonstrate how your organization's solution will solve your reader's problem. Also, you need to keep in mind that your proposals will be competing against others.

Unsolicited Proposals

When you write to readers who do not request your proposal, you will have the occasion to write an *unsolicited proposal*. In this kind of proposal, you first have to convince your readers that they have a problem worth solving. Then you demonstrate how your plan or service will solve that problem or need.

Just as the formats of reports may vary depending on the formality of the occasion and the complexity of the problem, so do the formats of proposals: the formats can follow the conventions of a memo, letter, or a long proposal.

SOME OCCASIONS FOR WRITING PROPOSALS

Here is a list of some of the occasions when you may have to solve organizational problems by writing a proposal. You may have to write a proposal when you need to:

- Sell an organization's product or service
- Motivate readers to financially support a plan or program, such as a research project
- Motivate readers to support a plan or program, such as a request for an independent study

PURPOSES OF REPORTS AND PROPOSALS

Once writers understand the problem that their report or proposal will solve, they consider the purpose or purposes of their documents. Writers compose reports and proposals that primarily achieve one of the following purposes or aims:

- To inform
- To document
- To explore
- To persuade

Because reports and proposals may have more than one purpose, we will classify these documents according to both their primary and secondary purposes. Table 12-1 previews and classifies reports and proposals according to primary and secondary purposes so that you understand how purposes may work together. As you look at this table, notice that whereas reports may vary in their primary aim, proposals always aim primarily to persuade. Even so, proposals also rely on other purposes to persuade readers.

Table 12-1 Primary and Secondary Purposes of Reports and Proposals

PRIMARY PURPOSE(S) OF REPORTS AND PROPOSALS	SECONDARY PURPOSE(S)	EXAMPLES OF REPORTS AND PROPOSALS
To Inform	To Document	Periodic Memo Report (Figure 12-1)
To Document	To Inform	Minutes of a Meeting (Figure 12-2) (See also Figure 6-5 in Chapter 6)
To Explore	To Inform, Document, and Instruct	Evaluation Report (Figures 12-3 to 12-8) (See Also Figure 6-6 in Chapter 6)
To Persuade	To Inform, Explore, and Instruct	Unsolicited Proposal (Figure 12-9)
	To Inform, Explore, and Instruct	Solicited Proposal (Figure 12-10)

After you read about the general features of each purpose—its focus, content, strategies for arrangement, and style—you will read one or two cases. These cases explain the occasions that prompted writers to compose reports or proposals. As you read each case, *analyze the organizational problem each writer faced. Then focus your attention on how each writer composed a report or a proposal to achieve one primary aim, and one or more secondary aims.*

WRITING TO INFORM

General Features

Focus

When you write reports that aim primarily to inform or when a secondary aim of a report or proposal is to inform, you will focus on the information you are conveying about an issue.

Content

When you inform, you write to convey factual, comprehensive, and surprising information. That is, the information is verifiable; it includes all that a reader needs to know about the issue; and it contains some information that your reader does not already know. New information can include answers to the questions: "Who?" "What?" "When?" "Where?" "Why?" and "How?" A report that aims to inform may contain answers to one, some, or all of these questions.

Strategies for Arrangement

The strategies you decide to use will depend on the kind of format you will be following. You may write in a letter or memo format and, thus, want to follow the strategies for arrangement we described in Chapter 6 under "Writing to Inform." Or you may write a formal report similar to ones you will see in Figures 12-3 through 12-8.

In a formal informational report, you may open your report with an abstract or an executive summary that briefly summarizes the topic or problem you researched and the results of your research, such as results of a survey. Even if you do not need to write an abstract or summary, you will want to write an introduction that orients your readers to the content and design of the report by describing the issue or problem, the context of the issue or problem, and your method of gathering information. Sections in the body of the report may be organized according to one or more of the patterns you read about in Chapter 3, Strategy Eight: "Ask What You Have to *Do* in Your Writing." Some reports do not include a conclusion that shows readers the significance of your research. Instead, they let readers draw their own conclusions to make decisions or to monitor a situation or condition.

Integrating graphic elements into or along with your text may help readers better understand your information. A bar graph measuring product sales over a year would help to inform a busy reader about the trends that you are reporting on. (Refer to Chapter 5 to review graphic elements.)

Vocabulary and Style

You will use denotative and precise language to record your data, statistics, or observations. Your word choices may range from technical to non-technical, depending on your reader's understanding of an issue. You may use abbreviated terms when you and your reader share the same understanding of what abbreviations mean. If there is a chance your readers may not be familiar with an abbreviation, write it out the first time you use it, perhaps define it, and then indicate the abbreviated form in parentheses, e.g., Computerized Payroll System (CPS).

Case: Occasion for Writing a Periodic Memo Report

What Problem Must the Writer Solve?

As a routine part of his job, Robert Holt, accountant for a small, privately owned trucking company, is responsible for investigating company records to determine the cost of diesel breakdowns. He does this twice a year to help the owner of the company monitor expenses. If the costs are out of line or if one truck costs more than usual, the owner investigates the reason for increased maintenance costs—perhaps his own crew's negligence in maintaining the trucks. To gather this kind of information, Holt looks through repair bills for the trucks and summarizes the results of his investigation.

> What is the organizational problem that Holt has to solve? Analyze the problem according to the four components of a problem.

How Does the Periodic Memo Report Solve the Problem?

Holt writes his periodic report in the form of a memo because he does not need to provide background information for the owner (Figure 12-1). In his report, he aims simply to inform the owner about costs over the last six months.

Holt's strategy is first to orient his reader to the topic of the memo by documenting what he did and, generally, what he found—his claim. He supports his

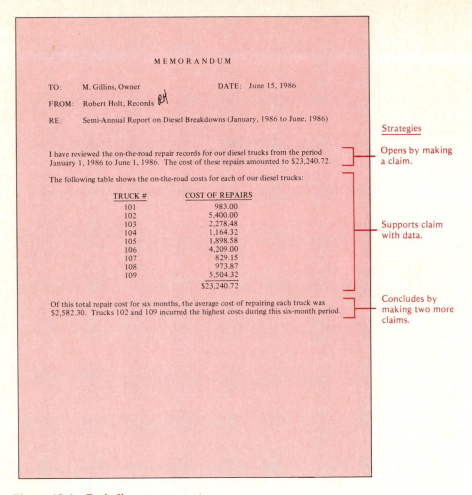

Figure 12-1   **Periodic memo report.**

claim with data he collected and concludes with two other claims that are important for his reader and that are based on the data.

To present comprehensive information, as well as to point out "new" information, Holt integrates a table in the second paragraph. This graphic provides the owner with all the information he needs to compare costs among the trucks and to single out trucks that have incurred the highest costs.

> What action do you think the owner of the company might take after reading this report?

WRITING TO DOCUMENT
General Features

Focus

When you aim to document information in a report or proposal, you focus on establishing or verifying facts about a topic or issue under discussion. You record what you or others witnessed, such as a decision made during a meeting. Or you record how you investigated a problem or issue and what you discovered.

Content

A report that aims to document or a proposal that includes documentary information may consist of the following kinds of information that verify the subject or issue under discussion: facts, data, statistics, verifiable observations, quotations or paraphrases from eyewitnesses. Often, writers keep logs in which they record observations, such as descriptions of an accident site, that they will later use in a documentary report.

Strategies for Arrangement

You may write documentary reports in letter or memo formats. If you use these formats, follow the strategies we described in Chapter 6 under "Writing to Document."

Formal documentary reports may begin with an abstract or an executive summary that briefly summarizes the problem or issue you are reporting on, your method of research, and the results of your research. Even if you do not write an abstract or executive summary, you will want to introduce your readers to the subject of your report in an introduction. The introduction orients readers to the content and design of the report by describing the problem or issue, the context of the problem or issue, and ways you gathered your documentary information. To develop the body of a documentary report, you can use any one of the patterns for organizing information that you read about in Chapter 3, Strategy Eight: "Ask What You Have to *Do* in Your Writing." Ordinarily, you categorize documentary information by alphabetical, numerical, chronological, or spatial order. In some documentary reports you will summarize what you or others witnessed or discovered and draw conclusions about your information in a summary. In other documentary reports, your reader may only be interested in the kinds of information that you offer as proof or verification.

Consider using graphic elements to record the information that you are documenting, such as a photograph of an accident site. (Refer to Chapter 5 to review graphic elements.)

Vocabulary and Style

Use denotative language to record your information, being careful to select words that your readers understand. Depending upon your reader's expertise, your word choice can range from a technical to nontechnical vocabulary. Follow the guidelines for using abbreviations under "Writing to Inform." (See also the discussion of style under "Writing to Document" in Chapter 6.)

Case: Occasion for Writing Minutes of a Meeting

What Problem Must the Writer Solve?

As secretary of his college's Student Affairs Club, a club that sponsors various social events for college students, Bob Quincy is responsible for recording the proceedings of each of his club's monthly meetings. Among the proceedings are discussions of how to raise money to sponsor events and what kinds of events to offer. From all that he hears at each monthly meeting, he selects information about what the members discussed, voted on, and agreed to do. Because his club follows an agenda—a chronological listing of subjects that members discuss—he records his notes according to each agenda.

> Why is it important for organizations to document the proceedings of every meeting?

How Do the Minutes Solve the Problem?

Bob works from his meeting notes to write a report that aims primarily to document who did or said what. His report, minutes of the meeting (Figure 12-2), achieves the goal of continuing, initiating, or concluding discussions about organizational issues. His secondary aim is to inform members about the news—new developments that they should be aware of.

His strategy is to record the names of those officers who were present and then to categorize the events of the meeting chronologically. Roman numerals document the order of events.

> Do you think Quincy could have classified the sequence of events any other way? If so, how? What kinds of documentary information does he use in the minutes?

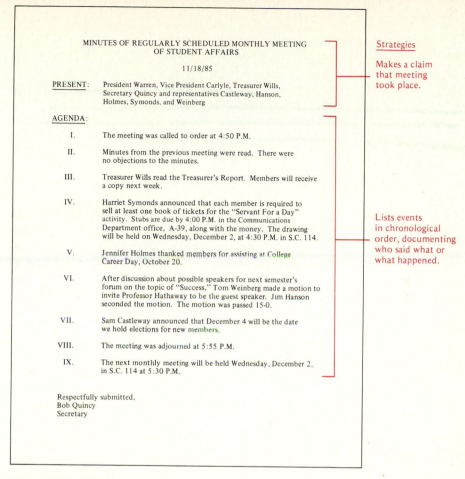

MINUTES OF REGULARLY SCHEDULED MONTHLY MEETING
OF STUDENT AFFAIRS

11/18/85

PRESENT: President Warren, Vice President Carlyle, Treasurer Wills,
            Secretary Quincy and representatives Castleway, Hanson,
            Holmes, Symonds, and Weinberg

AGENDA:

I.   The meeting was called to order at 4:50 P.M.

II.   Minutes from the previous meeting were read. There were
        no objections to the minutes.

III.   Treasurer Wills read the Treasurer's Report. Members will receive
        a copy next week.

IV.   Harriet Symonds announced that each member is required to
        sell at least one book of tickets for the "Servant For a Day"
        activity. Stubs are due by 4:00 P.M. in the Communications
        Department office, A-39, along with the money. The drawing
        will be held on Wednesday, December 2, at 4:30 P.M. in S.C. 114.

V.   Jennifer Holmes thanked members for assisting at College
        Career Day, October 20.

VI.   After discussion about possible speakers for next semester's
        forum on the topic of "Success," Tom Weinberg made a motion to
        invite Professor Hathaway to be the guest speaker. Jim Hanson
        seconded the motion. The motion was passed 15-0.

VII.   Sam Castleway announced that December 4 will be the date
        we hold elections for new members.

VIII.   The meeting was adjourned at 5:55 P.M.

IX.   The next monthly meeting will be held Wednesday, December 2,
        in S.C. 114 at 5:30 P.M.

Respectfully submitted,
Bob Quincy
Secretary

Strategies

Makes a claim
that meeting
took place.

Lists events
in chronological
order, documenting
who said what or
what happened.

Figure 12-2   Minutes of a monthly meeting.

WRITING TO EXPLORE

General Features

Focus

When you aim primarily to explore, you focus on identifying or defining a problem
and possibly on weighing solutions to solve it. Or you ask questions about the
subject or issue under discussion.

Content

Exploratory writing consists of observations, facts, data, and speculations about
solutions to a problem. In some exploratory reports, you investigate a problem
without stating a solution to that problem. In other exploratory reports, you investigate a problem and speculate about or propose solutions or alternative solutions.

Strategies for Arrangement

You may write exploratory reports in letter or memo formats. If you use these formats, follow the strategies we described in Chapter 6 under "Writing to Explore."

Formal exploratory reports may begin with an abstract or executive summary that briefly summarizes the problem or issue you explored, your method of exploration, criteria you used to evaluate solutions to a problem or alternative choices in a situation, and your proposed solution or choice. Following the abstract or summary is an introduction that orients your readers to the content and design of the report.

In the body of an exploratory report, you may use any of the patterns for organizing paragraphs that you read about in Chapter 3 under Strategy Eight: "Ask What You Have to *Do* in Your Writing." To analyze a problem and evaluate alternative choices or solutions to a problem, you will rely primarily on patterns of cause and effect, comparison and contrast, problem and solution, and claim and support. Because you often evaluate solutions to a problem or evaluate alternative choices, you need to establish criteria to compare these choices or alternatives (refer to a representative list of organizational criteria in Chapter 6 under "Writing to Explore"). When you describe your method of exploring a problem or issue, you will rely on a chronological pattern.

After you have explored an issue or problem or have evaluated alternative choices or solutions to a problem, you state your findings in a conclusion and, perhaps, propose that your readers take a course of action or select a proposed alternative.

To present the results of your exploration, consider integrating graphic elements into or along with your text. (Refer to Chapter 5 to review graphic elements.)

Vocabulary and Style

Like writing to inform and document, writing to explore uses denotative language to record how and what you explored and to describe alternatives or proposed solutions. Follow the principles of style that you read about under "Writing to Inform." However, keep in mind that because what you propose or conclude may be tentative, your language will be conditional. Words such as "seem" and "appear" reflect the tentativeness of your findings or proposed solutions.

Case: Occasion for Writing an
Evaluation Report

What Problem Must The Writer Solve?

Suzanne Eckert, a college senior, has been working as a writing consultant in her college's writing center for the last three years. Although a faculty member advises the center, student consultants operate and staff the center: they schedule advising sessions to help peers as they draft papers for courses, train new writing center consultants, and advertise their service to the college community.

Although the center has been operating for seven years, the consultants have not kept consistent records about their clientele—the students. Because there are no reliable records about student use, it is uncertain how well the center is achieving its goal of helping students at all academic levels with their assigned writing.

Eckert's operator for assessing the center is a questionnaire that gathers information about who uses the center, when, how, and why. Based on the results of her questionnaire and her recent participation in a conference on peer tutoring, Eckert writes a report to the faculty advisor.

> Represent the problem Eckert is solving.

How Does the Evaluation Report Solve the Problem?

Eckert writes a report that aims primarily to explore current use of the center and to persuade the faculty advisor and members of the writing center to take certain actions to help the center achieve its goal. To achieve her primary purpose, she writes to document what she did to investigate the situation and to inform about what she found out—the information about who does and does not use the center. Based on this new information, she instructs readers to take certain actions.

She follows the conventions of a formal report because she is writing to the faculty advisor. Title Page, her Letter of Transmittal, Table of Contents, and Abstract orient her reader to the context of the problem she has explored, how she explored it, what she found, and what she recommends.

She follows a five-part strategy (Figures 12-3 through 12-8) for arranging sections of information. She

- States the problem she explored.
- Describes how she explored the problem.
- Discusses the specific results of her exploration.
- Summarizes her general conclusions.
- Recommends courses of action.

> Reread the sections of Eckert's report, and list the kinds of paragraph patterns she uses in each section. Justify the strategy she uses to sequence these sections for her readers.

AN EVALUATION OF STUDENTS' USE OF THE BEAVER COLLEGE
WRITING CENTER

Prepared for
Dr. Peggy Maki
Faculty Advisor, Beaver College Writing Center

by
Suzanne Eckert
Writing for Careers
Beaver College

April 23, 1985

Figure 12-3   Cover page. (Entire report reprinted by permission from Suzanne Eckert.)

WRITING TO PERSUADE

General Features

Focus

When you write reports that aim primarily to persuade or when you write proposals, you focus on the "you"—your reader's values, perspectives, beliefs, needs—to motivate your reader to accept or support what you are recommending or proposing.

Content

The content of proposals or persuasive reports can range from facts, statistics, or other verifiable information, to expressions of values, beliefs, or opinions. To

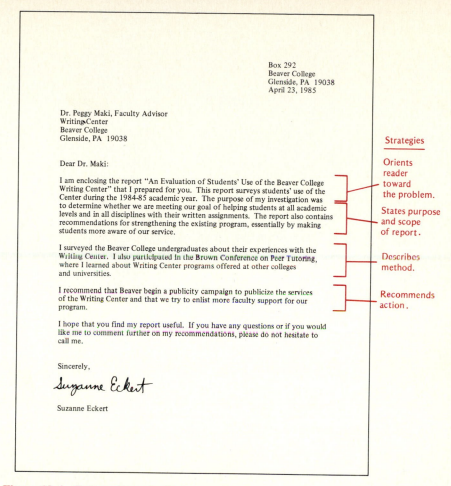

Figure 12-4   Letter of transmittal.

motivate readers to act or respond, you can rely primarily on an appeal to logic. But your proposal can also contain appeals based on emotions and ethos. (Review the "Content" section under "Writing to Persuade" in Chapter 6.)

Strategies for Arrangement

You may write proposals in letter or memo formats. If you use these formats, follow the strategies we described in Chapter 6 under "Writing to Persuade."

When you write a formal proposal, you may begin with an abstract or an executive summary that briefly summarizes a problem or establishes a need and explains how and why the subject of your proposal will solve the problem or fulfill a need. Following the abstract or summary is an introduction that orients your readers to the content and design of the proposal by describing a problem or establishing a need and guiding readers to the sub-topics, such as features of your

CONTENTS

i

Figure 12-5   Table of contents.

product, you will discuss in the proposal. To develop body paragraphs or sections in a proposal, you can use any of the patterns we discussed in Chapter 3 under Strategy Eight: ''Ask What You Have to *Do* in Your Writing.'' To decide what strategies to use, consider your reader's situation and point of view. If you are writing a solicited proposal, you know that your reader is already receptive to your plan or idea. In that case, you ordinarily describe the problem your proposal is

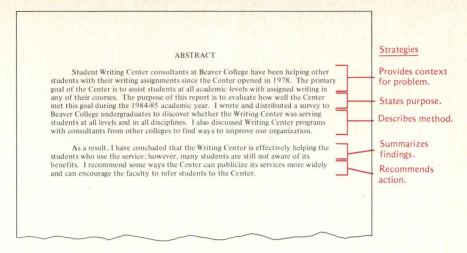

ABSTRACT

Student Writing Center consultants at Beaver College have been helping other students with their writing assignments since the Center opened in 1978. The primary goal of the Center is to assist students at all academic levels with assigned writing in any of their courses. The purpose of this report is to evaluate how well the Center met this goal during the 1984-85 academic year. I wrote and distributed a survey to Beaver College undergraduates to discover whether the Writing Center was serving students at all levels and in all disciplines. I also discussed Writing Center programs with consultants from other colleges to find ways to improve our organization.

As a result, I have concluded that the Writing Center is effectively helping the students who use the service; however, many students are still not aware of its benefits. I recommend some ways the Center can publicize its services more widely and can encourage the faculty to refer students to the Center.

Strategies

Provides context for problem.

States purpose.

Describes method.

Summarizes findings.

Recommends action.

Figure 12-6 Abstract.

designed to solve and show how your plan, product, or solution will solve your reader's problem. However, keep in mind that although your reader may be receptive, your reader may be reviewing proposals from your competitors. Knowing what your competitors will say can help you decide how to arrange information in your proposal. (Review ''Strategies for Arrangement'' under ''Writing to Persuade'' in Chapter 6.) You may write a conclusion restating the advantages or reasons for the reader to support or buy what you are proposing or recommending.

If possible, use graphic elements to persuade readers to buy, support, or accept what you are proposing. For example, if you are selling a mechanism, a diagram of it would help readers understand what it looks like or how it works. (Refer to Chapter 5 to review graphic elements.)

Vocabulary and Style

When you write to persuade, your words can range from connotative to denotative, depending on the kinds of appeals you want to make. The vocabulary should help the reader conclude that the proposal makes a reasonable request. Finally, word choice can range from highly technical to non-technical. (Follow the guidelines for using abbreviations under ''Writing to Inform.'')

Case: Occasion for Writing an Unsolicited Memo Proposal

What Problem Must the Writer Solve?

Johanna I. Jones is a system administrator at McNeil Consumer Products Company. She administers a software system (PICS) that McNeil bought to file pro-

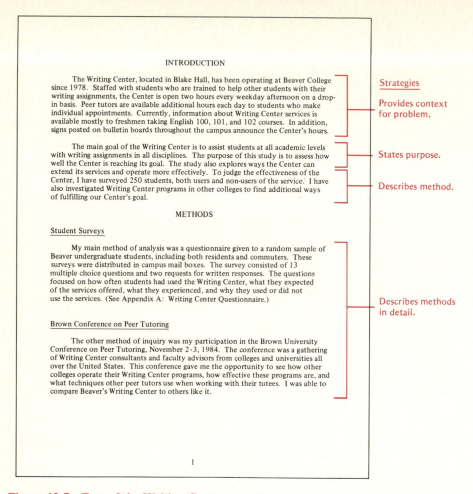

Figure 12-7 Text of the Writing Center report.

duction and inventory control data. Her job requires that she train new employees how to use, maintain, and revise the system when the users request changes in it.

At present, all departments of the company use this system, but because the system was not designed specifically for McNeil, users are constantly requesting that Jones change the program. To revise the program, her programmers must modify the PICS source code and then update the PICS documentation (users' manuals) to keep up with these modifications.

Because the processes of modifying and updating are time-consuming, Jones believes that the documentation should be entered onto her organization's word processing diskettes. That way, it would be easier to make all the revisions that users keep requesting. One of her programmers has already developed a format that makes it possible to enter the PICS onto McNeil's word processing system.

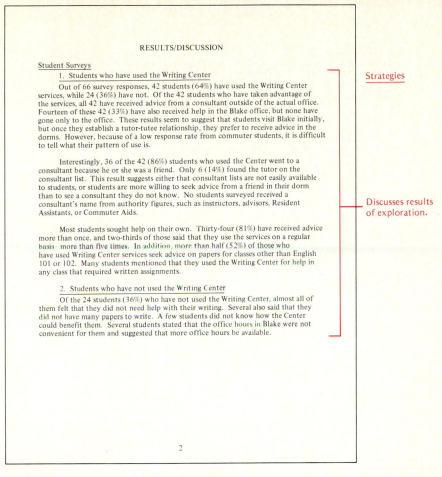

RESULTS/DISCUSSION

Student Surveys

1. Students who have used the Writing Center

Strategies

Out of 66 survey responses, 42 students (64%) have used the Writing Center services, while 24 (36%) have not. Of the 42 students who have taken advantage of the services, all 42 have received advice from a consultant outside of the actual office. Fourteen of these 42 (33%) have also received help in the Blake office, but none have gone only to the office. These results seem to suggest that students visit Blake initially, but once they establish a tutor-tutee relationship, they prefer to receive advice in the dorms. However, because of a low response rate from commuter students, it is difficult to tell what their pattern of use is.

Interestingly, 36 of the 42 (86%) students who used the Center went to a consultant because he or she was a friend. Only 6 (14%) found the tutor on the consultant list. This result suggests either that consultant lists are not easily available to students, or students are more willing to seek advice from a friend in their dorm than to see a consultant they do not know. No students surveyed received a consultant's name from authority figures, such as instructors, advisors, Resident Assistants, or Commuter Aids.

Discusses results of exploration.

Most students sought help on their own. Thirty-four (81%) have received advice more than once, and two-thirds of those said that they use the services on a regular basis more than five times. In addition, more than half (52%) of those who have used Writing Center services seek advice on papers for classes other than English 101 or 102. Many students mentioned that they used the Writing Center for help in any class that required written assignments.

2. Students who have not used the Writing Center

Of the 24 students (36%) who have not used the Writing Center, almost all of them felt that they did not need help with their writing. Several also said that they did not have many papers to write. A few students did not know how the Center could benefit them. Several students stated that the office hours in Blake were not convenient for them and suggested that more office hours be available.

2

Figure 12-7   (Cont.)

Experience has shown her that management will not automatically support projects unless it sees that an employee has investigated all options for solving a problem. Therefore, Jones investigates alternative ways to convert the system: (1) hire two temporary, part-time employees to convert the documentation; (2) have a temporary employee continue to revise the original documentation and add pages on an "as-needed" basis; (3) send the diskettes to an outside service to make the conversion; (4) or use existing personnel to convert the documentation.

If her planning manager supports the project, he will have to present it to his division head, who, in turn, will be responsible for allocating money from the division budget for this project. Jones knows that management will be concerned about the cost of such a project. She also knows that her planning manager's goal is to respond to users' requests as quickly as possible so that information can be

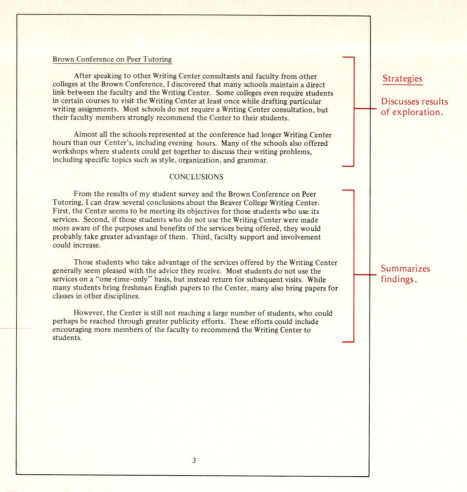

Brown Conference on Peer Tutoring

After speaking to other Writing Center consultants and faculty from other colleges at the Brown Conference, I discovered that many schools maintain a direct link between the faculty and the Writing Center. Some colleges even require students in certain courses to visit the Writing Center at least once while drafting particular writing assignments. Most schools do not require a Writing Center consultation, but their faculty members strongly recommend the Center to their students.

Almost all the schools represented at the conference had longer Writing Center hours than our Center's, including evening hours. Many of the schools also offered workshops where students could get together to discuss their writing problems, including specific topics such as style, organization, and grammar.

CONCLUSIONS

From the results of my student survey and the Brown Conference on Peer Tutoring, I can draw several conclusions about the Beaver College Writing Center. First, the Center seems to be meeting its objectives for those students who use its services. Second, if those students who do not use the Writing Center were made more aware of the purposes and benefits of the services being offered, they would probably take greater advantage of them. Third, faculty support and involvement could increase.

Those students who take advantage of the services offered by the Writing Center generally seem pleased with the advice they receive. Most students do not use the services on a "one-time-only" basis, but instead return for subsequent visits. While many students bring freshman English papers to the Center, many also bring papers for classes in other disciplines.

However, the Center is still not reaching a large number of students, who could perhaps be reached through greater publicity efforts. These efforts could include encouraging more members of the faculty to recommend the Writing Center to students.

Strategies

Discusses results of exploration.

Summarizes findings.

3

Figure 12-7 (Cont.)

filed without delay. Therefore, the criterion of time is also important. She decides that her criteria should be the following: cost and time (turn-around time, time invested by the company, and completion date). Together these criteria are important to all levels of management that will be involved in deciding whether to support the project.

> What restriction does Jones face as manager of the PICS? What does she see as possible operators?

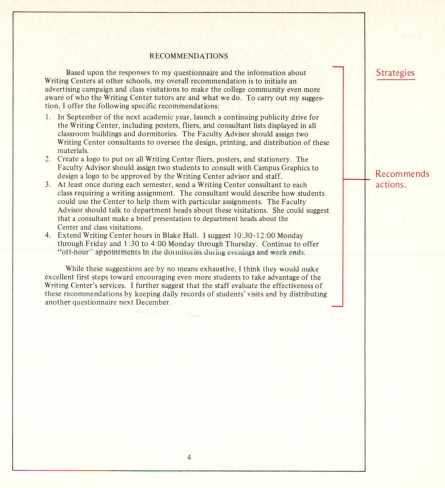

RECOMMENDATIONS

Based upon the responses to my questionnaire and the information about Writing Centers at other schools, my overall recommendation is to initiate an advertising campaign and class visitations to make the college community even more aware of who the Writing Center tutors are and what we do. To carry out my suggestion, I offer the following specific recommendations:

1. In September of the next academic year, launch a continuing publicity drive for the Writing Center, including posters, fliers, and consultant lists displayed in all classroom buildings and dormitories. The Faculty Advisor should assign two Writing Center consultants to oversee the design, printing, and distribution of these materials.
2. Create a logo to put on all Writing Center fliers, posters, and stationery. The Faculty Advisor should assign two students to consult with Campus Graphics to design a logo to be approved by the Writing Center advisor and staff.
3. At least once during each semester, send a Writing Center consultant to each class requiring a writing assignment. The consultant would describe how students could use the Center to help them with particular assignments. The Faculty Advisor should talk to department heads about these visitations. She could suggest that a consultant make a brief presentation to department heads about the Center and class visitations.
4. Extend Writing Center hours in Blake Hall. I suggest 10:30-12:00 Monday through Friday and 1:30 to 4:00 Monday through Thursday. Continue to offer "off-hour" appointments in the dormitories during evenings and week ends.

While these suggestions are by no means exhaustive, I think they would make excellent first steps toward encouraging even more students to take advantage of the Writing Center's services. I further suggest that the staff evaluate the effectiveness of these recommendations by keeping daily records of students' visits and by distributing another questionnaire next December.

Strategies

Recommends actions.

4

Figure 12-7   (Cont.)

How Does the Unsolicited Memo Proposal Solve the Problem?

Having explored these criteria, Jones writes an unsolicited memo proposal to her manager (Figure 12-9), following her organization's prescribed format for memo proposals. She writes to persuade management to hire two part-time employees to make the conversion. To achieve this primary aim, she also writes to inform readers about the present situation, to explore alternative ways of making the conversion, and to instruct readers to take steps to implement the project.

She follows her organization's standard format for a memo proposal. She begins with a "Purpose" section that states what she is proposing, why, and how the project will work. Her "Background" section provides relevant information

APPENDIX A

WRITING CENTER QUESTIONNAIRE

5

Figure 12-8 Appendix.

about the project to readers who may not know its history. Her ''Alternatives'' section lists the options for resolving the problem, and her ''Comparisons'' section explores the criteria for choosing an option. After exploring each alternative in a table, she writes a ''Recommendation'' section stating her claims about the alter-

WRITING CENTER QUESTIONNAIRE

DIRECTIONS: The purpose of this questionnaire is to discover how students are using the Writing Center. Your responses will help the staff determine if we need to make any changes in our program. This questionnaire takes only a few minutes to fill out, but your answers will give us valuable information. Please write a check (✓) next to each appropriate answer. Space is provided at the end for any further comments you would like to make.

Please return this form to Suzanne Eckert, Heinz 226N or Box 292, no later than FRIDAY, APRIL 3. Thank you for your help.

1. ＿Freshman   ＿Sophomore   ＿Junior   ＿Senior

2. Major ＿＿＿＿＿＿＿＿＿＿＿＿＿＿＿＿＿＿＿＿＿

3. ＿Resident   ＿Commuter

4. How many times during this academic year have you visited the Writing Center in Blake Hall?
   ＿0   ＿1   ＿2-4   ＿5 or more

5. How many times have you received advice from a Writing Center consultant somewhere other than Blake Hall?
   ＿0   ＿1   ＿2-4   ＿5 or more

6. How were you referred to a Writing Center consultant?
   ＿Friend   ＿Instructor   ＿Advisor   ＿RA/CA   ＿Consultant list
   ＿Writing Center Open House   ＿Other, please specify

7. Do you feel the consultant helped you with your writing?
   ＿Not at all   ＿Somewhat   ＿A great deal

8. Do you prefer to consult with someone that you
   ＿Already know   ＿Do not know   ＿No preference

9. What aspects of the writing process do you expect the Writing Center to help you with? (You may check more than one.)
   ＿Developing ideas   ＿Puting ideas into clear form
   ＿Revising drafts   ＿Correcting grammar & spelling
   ＿Getting a good grade   ＿Other＿＿＿＿＿＿＿＿＿＿

10. Which of these aspects did the consultant actually help you with? (You may check more than one.)
    ＿Developing ideas   ＿Putting ideas into clear form
    ＿Revising drafts   ＿Correcting grammar & spelling
    ＿Proofreading   ＿Typing
    ＿Getting a good grade   ＿None＿Other＿＿＿＿＿＿＿

6

Figure 12-8   (Cont.)

natives she explored. She concludes her proposal by placing the project into a context of time, "Next Steps," and writes to instruct readers how to implement the project.

Her "Attachments" (we have included only one page of this section of her

11. What were your reasons for seeking help from a consultant?
    __ Instructor's suggestion   __Advisor's suggestion
    __ Decided I needed help   __Wanted a better grade
    __ Required for course   __Other_____

12. For which courses did you bring in writing assignments to the Center?
    __ Freshman English (EN 100, 101, 102)   __Other English
    __ Natural Sciences   __Social Sciences
    __ Humanities   __Other_____

13. If you have never conferred with a Writing Center consultant, why not? (You may
    check more than one.)
    __ I don't usually need help with my writing.
    __ I didn't have to write any papers.
    __ I don't know what the Writing Center will do for me.
    __ I don't know any of the consultants.
    __ I don't like to ask for help.
    __ I don't know where the Writing Center is.
    __ I can't find a consultant when I need one.
    __ Other_____

Answer numbers 14 and 15 on the reverse side:

14. Please make any comments on your experiences with the Writing Center that you
    would like us to know about.

15. Please list any suggestions for improving the Center.

7

Figure 12-8   (Cont.)

proposal) provide supplementary information. Attachment A, ''Option 1,'' is a
more detailed analysis of the alternative she recommends. Its purpose is to provide
additional information for readers who may want to challenge how she arrived at
her decision to recommend the first alternative.

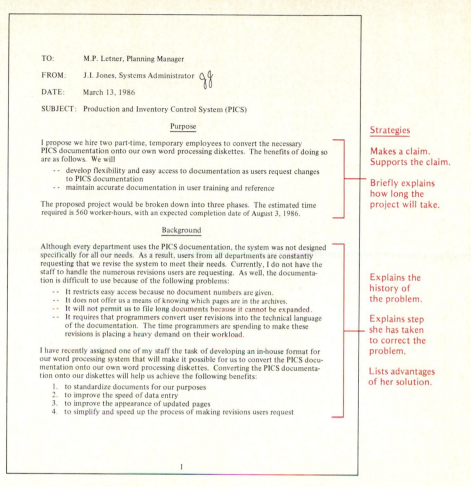

TO: M.P. Letner, Planning Manager

FROM: J.I. Jones, Systems Administrator

DATE: March 13, 1986

SUBJECT: Production and Inventory Control System (PICS)

Purpose

I propose we hire two part-time, temporary employees to convert the necessary PICS documentation onto our own word processing diskettes. The benefits of doing so are as follows. We will

-- develop flexibility and easy access to documentation as users request changes to PICS documentation
-- maintain accurate documentation in user training and reference

The proposed project would be broken down into three phases. The estimated time required is 560 worker-hours, with an expected completion date of August 3, 1986.

Background

Although every department uses the PICS documentation, the system was not designed specifically for all our needs. As a result, users from all departments are constantly requesting that we revise the system to meet their needs. Currently, I do not have the staff to handle the numerous revisions users are requesting. As well, the documentation is difficult to use because of the following problems:

-- It restricts easy access because no document numbers are given.
-- It does not offer us a means of knowing which pages are in the archives.
-- It will not permit us to file long documents because it cannot be expanded.
-- It requires that programmers convert user revisions into the technical language of the documentation. The time programmers are spending to make these revisions is placing a heavy demand on their workload.

I have recently assigned one of my staff the task of developing an in-house format for our word processing system that will make it possible for us to convert the PICS documentation onto our own word processing diskettes. Converting the PICS documentation onto our diskettes will help us achieve the following benefits:

1. to standardize documents for our purposes
2. to improve the speed of data entry
3. to improve the appearance of updated pages
4. to simplify and speed up the process of making revisions users request

1

Strategies

Makes a claim.
Supports the claim.

Briefly explains how long the project will take.

Explains the history of the problem.

Explains step she has taken to correct the problem.

Lists advantages of her solution.

Figure 12-9   Unsolicited memo proposal. (Written with the assistance of Johanna Jones. Used by permission from McNeil Consumer Products Company, Pennsylvania.)

What kinds of patterns of arrangement does Jones use in each section of her proposal? Look at her attachment A. Discuss the kinds of supplemental information she uses in this attachment to substantiate the claims she makes about Option 1 in the body of the proposal.

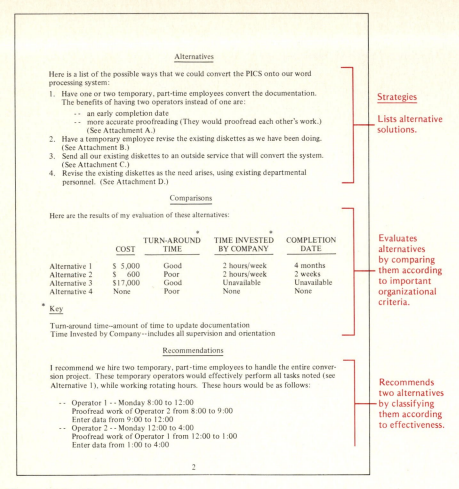

Figure 12-9   (Cont.)

Case: Occasion for Writing a Solicited Proposal

What Problem Must the Writer Solve?

In its local newspaper, a township announces a "Request for Proposal" for plans to develop the township's sewer system because of projected increases in population by the year 2000. In response to this "Request for Proposal," a group of engineers at Lawdry, Inc., an engineering firm, submits a proposal to the township, attempting to sell Lawdry's plan to develop a new sewer system. The goal of the proposal is to sell the system; the writers' initial state consists of all the information they have obtained about the township. A restriction that may prohibit Lawdry from getting the job is cost: Lawdry does not know what other competitors

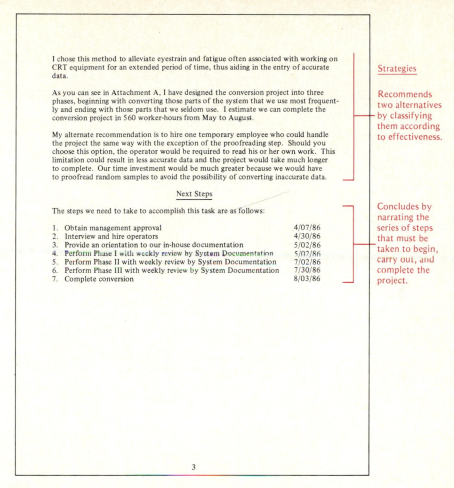

I chose this method to alleviate eyestrain and fatigue often associated with working on CRT equipment for an extended period of time, thus aiding in the entry of accurate data.

As you can see in Attachment A, I have designed the conversion project into three phases, beginning with converting those parts of the system that we use most frequently and ending with those parts that we seldom use. I estimate we can complete the conversion project in 560 worker-hours from May to August.

My alternate recommendation is to hire one temporary employee who could handle the project the same way with the exception of the proofreading step. Should you choose this option, the operator would be required to read his or her own work. This limitation could result in less accurate data and the project would take much longer to complete. Our time investment would be much greater because we would have to proofread random samples to avoid the possibility of converting inaccurate data.

Strategies

Recommends two alternatives by classifying them according to effectiveness.

Next Steps

The steps we need to take to accomplish this task are as follows:

1. Obtain management approval   4/07/86
2. Interview and hire operators   4/30/86
3. Provide an orientation to our in-house documentation   5/02/86
4. Perform Phase I with weekly review by System Documentation   5/02/86
5. Perform Phase II with weekly review by System Documentation   7/02/86
6. Perform Phase III with weekly review by System Documentation   7/30/86
7. Complete conversion   8/03/86

Concludes by narrating the series of steps that must be taken to begin, carry out, and complete the project.

3

Figure 12-9 (Cont.)

are charging to construct similar systems. The operators for solving the problem are the claims that Lawdry can make about constructing an effective system. By explaining their plan, the engineers hope to persuade the township that Lawdry's fee is worth the township's investment.

How Does the Solicited Proposal Solve the Problem?

The purpose of the proposal is to persuade members of the township council to hire Lawdry, Inc., to construct the new sewer system (Figure 12-10). To achieve this primary purpose, writers of the proposal also write to inform, to explore, and to instruct. They write to inform the township council what they know about the township to demonstrate their understanding of the problem. They write to explore the effects of population increase on the present sewer facilities and to project how

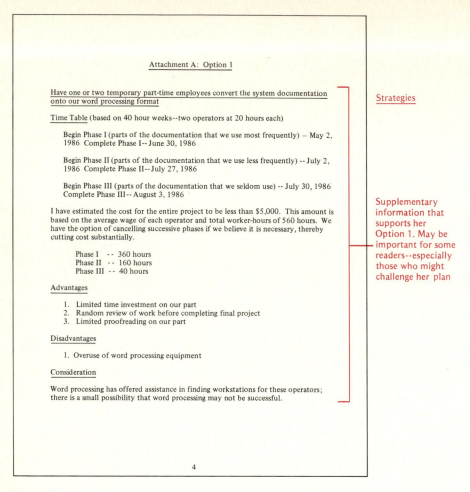

Figure 12-9   (Cont.)

developing a new system will affect the environment. Finally, they write to describe how they will construct a system that will serve the population and suite the conditions of the environment.

    Figure 12-10 is the table of contents to Lawdry's proposal, which lists the topics the engineering firm covers. The writers use a formal proposal format. First, they describe the problem the township is facing in the "Forward" to demonstrate that they understand the problem. They then summarize their plan for a sewage collection system in the "Scope of Plan" to introduce readers to Lawdry's solution to the problem. The body of the proposal (From "Population" to "Construction Cost Estimates") moves from an exploration of the present and future conditions to a description of the proposed facilities the writers believe will solve the township's problems. The "Conclusions and Recommendations" section restates the problem and outlines how Lawdry, Inc., will develop a comprehensive sewer plan.

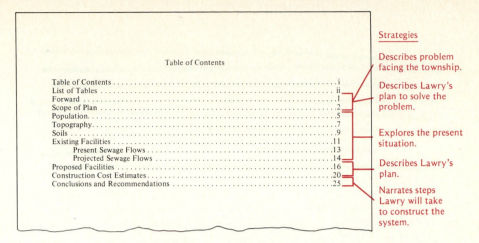

Strategies

Describes problem facing the township.

Describes Lawry's plan to solve the problem.

Explores the present situation.

Describes Lawry's plan.

Narrates steps Lawry will take to construct the system.

Figure 12-10   Table of contents in a solicited proposal for a sewer collection system.

How do you think the sections of this formal proposal help the township decide which proposal to select from all the competing engineering firms that also submitted proposals?

In this chapter you have seen some representative occasions when writers in organizations compose reports and proposals. To write the documents you just read, writers first had to think about the kind of organizational problem they had to solve either within their own organization or in terms of another organization. In your own writing on the job, you will find that the time you spend analyzing an organizational problem will help you in two ways:

1   To determine the purpose or purposes of your reports and proposals
2   To determine the strategy you should use in these documents to sequence information for your readers

1. What problems have you observed in an on-campus or off-campus organization that are preventing that organization from meeting its goals or objectives? List as many problems as you can think of. From this list, select a problem that is significant to the organization and that you are capable of investigating. Analyze the problem according to the components of a problem: the goal, the initial state, the restrictions, and operators. What kind of a document would you write—a report or a proposal—to solve this problem? What kinds of information would you need to investigate to write this report or proposal?

2. Take a look at your school's proposal format for requesting an independent study. Discuss the rationale behind its required format. Explain the kinds of information your readers are requesting from students. Why are your readers, department members, or committee members, asking for this kind of information? How does this kind of information help readers decide to accept or reject an independent study?

3. Collect as many reports and proposals as you can and bring them to class. As a taxpayer, you may have received county reports; as a stockholder, you may have received annual reports; as a member of an organization on campus or off campus, you may have received other kinds of reports. Or an organization you are a member of may have written or received a proposal. As you read over these documents, answer the following questions about each one:

    1. What organizational problem does the document solve?
    2. What are the primary and secondary purposes of the document?
    3. What is the focus in the document?
    4. What strategy has the writer used to sequence paragraph or section patterns for readers?
    5. Why do you think the writer used this particular strategy?
    6. What kind of language did the writer use? Why?
    7. What kind of graphic elements, if any, did the writer use? Why?

CHAPTER

13

WRITING REPORTS
AND PROPOSALS

PART 1: STRATEGIES FOR
GETTING STARTED

What distinguishes the writing of reports and proposals from the writing of other documents is the amount of time it takes writers to research an issue or problem— days, weeks, months, even years. Because writing reports and proposals involves research, writers manage the process of composing these documents by developing a work plan. A work plan is a schedule of tasks and sub-tasks that helps writers achieve the goal of finishing a report or proposal. These tasks include gathering and recording information; planning, drafting, revising and editing reports and proposals; and designing a final document.

In this chapter we will show you the strategies report and proposal writers follow to accomplish these tasks. Specifically, in Part 1, we discuss strategies for getting started—gathering and recording information. In Part 2, we discuss strategies for planning, drafting, revising and editing; and in Part 3, we discuss strategies for designing a final document. When you write a report or proposal, refer to this chapter to help you develop a work plan. Or use the chapter as a ready reference while you compose either document.

Gathering Information

Once you understand the problem you have to solve in a report or proposal, you need to determine the kinds of information that will help you solve that problem. Here, again, the problem-solving model is useful: it helps you think about the kinds of information you need. Having defined the *goal* of your report or proposal, ask yourself the following questions:

Goal:	What do I want my research to accomplish?
Initial State:	What do I already know about the problem? What do I still need to find out?
Operators:	What steps do I need to take to locate or generate the information I need?
Restrictions:	What might prevent me from locating or generating the information I need?

To gather sources for your report or proposal, you will engage in primary and secondary research. *Primary research* includes what you observe on the job, what you gather from organizational records, and what you gather from interviewing or surveying people. Primary research is first-hand research. *Secondary research* includes what you gather from published sources, such as books, periodicals, reference works, and journals. Reports and proposals written in organizations often depend more on primary research than on secondary research.

Primary research

Information that you gather from observations

The information you record when you investigate an accident, inspect equipment, or review in-house records is an example of primary research. The organizational activities that you participate in provide one source of information for reports and proposals. Usually, you record your observations in a notebook or log so that you accurately document what you observe.

Information that you gather from organizational documents

Organizational records are yet another source of information. These are useful when you want to reconstruct the sequence of events leading up to a situation or problem, or when you want to measure changes in methods, practices, or behaviors. Here is a list of some of the organizational documents you might need to investigate:

Letters
Memos
Reports
Proposals
Organizational forms
Minutes of meetings
Health forms
Employee payroll documents
Accounts receivable or payable
Inventory sheets
Sales records
Attendance records

These resources may be filed in computer storage and retrieval systems. As a report or proposal writer, you may have to search through these resources to summarize information, such as trends in hiring practices. Recall in Chapter 12 that the accountant had to go through diesel repair receipts to summarize the costs of diesel breakdowns.

Information that you gather from questionnaires

Your own observations may not always provide you with enough information. You may also need to survey others' knowledge, experience, or patterns of thought and behavior. If you need to measure a large sample of people's attitudes, reactions, beliefs, habits, behaviors, actions, or preferences, then you will need to use a questionnaire. A questionnaire asks respondents from a representative sample of a population to record their responses to a series of questions or statements. Your tally of responses to these questions or statements will enable you to make inferences about the large population this sample represents.

You can administer these questionnaires during an interview (see the next section), or you can mail them. The advantage of mailing questionnaires is that you can survey more people and include a greater geographical distribution. The disadvantages are that many people do not respond to mailings (a 50 percent response rate is considered a very good response rate); some people may not answer all the questions; and others may misinterpret a question. Respondents who wonder what a question is asking do not have the opportunity to ask for clarification.

Once you have decided how you will sample, you need to determine the size of your sample. In some situations you may be able to measure 100 percent of a population. For example, you could question all the students in a class you are taking. In most situations, however, you will need to survey a large population, such as all students attending your school. Because you usually cannot survey all members of a population, you will survey a representative sample of them. In determining the sample population, you want to be aware of any biases that might exist in your selection process. For example, if you want to survey residents' attitudes toward a community problem and you use a resident telephone directory, your sample would exclude those who have unlisted telephone numbers and those without telephones. Yet those people's responses would be important for a survey that aimed to include all economic sectors of the community.

Two common sampling approaches you can use are called random sampling and stratified random sampling.

1   In *random sampling* you select from the larger population a sample of predetermined size. When you use this approach, members of subgroups within that population have an equal chance of being selected as respondents. For example, if you wanted to survey students' reactions to an issue at your school, you could select every tenth name from a list of all the students. That way members of all the subgroups (freshmen, sophomores, juniors, and seniors; part- and full-time students; graduate and undergraduate students; college age and continuing education students) have an equal chance of being chosen to respond. A word of caution, however: attempt to avoid a biased sample. If you want to survey the entire student population, but the list you use fails to include certain subgroups, such as part-time students, your survey would be biased.

2   In *stratified random sampling* you first classify members of your sample into proportional subgroups and then ask every *nth* member of each subgroup to fill out a questionnaire. You might want to survey freshman reactions to a campus issue, then sophomore, junior, and senior reactions. Or you might want to survey residents' attitudes toward a community problem according to their income level.

The following guidelines will help you formulate questions and organize a questionnaire.

Guidelines for choosing questions

The following list surveys two kinds of questions you can ask in a questionnaire: closed-ended and open-ended. To avoid asking questions that do not contribute to your purpose (as many questionnaires do), ask yourself how you will use the information you obtain from a question.

Closed-ended questions ask people to select from a predetermined number of responses. Some of the most common types of closed-ended questions are described in the following paragraphs.

Likert Scale questions offer respondents a scale of responses to choose from. This scale allows a respondent to take an extreme position or a position within the extremes. Here is an example of a representative Likert scale question which gives a respondent a range of choices:

> *Should smoking be prohibited on airplanes?*
> ☐   *Strongly agree*
> ☐   *Agree*
> ☐   *Undecided*
> ☐   *Disagree*
> ☐   *Strongly disagree*

In this type of question, you will want to limit the range of responses to only the ones *you* are interested in measuring. A disadvantage of this type of question is that it does not accurately measure the intensity of responses. Intensity is difficult to measure. For example, all respondents do not necessarily react to an issue with the same intensity of agreeing or disagreeing.

Yes-no or *true-false* questions are other types of closed-ended questions. A yes-no question is:

> *Have you ever tried X's brand of tomato soup?*
> ☐   *Yes*
> ☐   *No*

Multiple-choice questions are also closed-ended questions because they, too, limit the kinds of responses. A preference question is an example of a multiple-choice question:

> *Which of these sizes would you buy?*
> ☐   *6 ounces (oz.)*
> ☐   *12 oz.*
> ☐   *18 oz.*

Rank-order questions require that a respondent use numbers to indicate preference, evaluations, or priorities. In the following question, the respondent has to order responses according to degree of importance (with 1 least important and 4 most important):

> *At the next committee meeting, which topics do you*
> *think we should discuss? Rank-order your*
> *responses from 1 to 4:*
> *Length of vacation* _____
> *Salarly increase* _____
> *Medical benefits* _____
> *Policy on sick leave* _____

Of course, the writer must explain how the rank order works. Does 1 to 10 mean from most important to least important or vice versa?

    Closed-ended questions are easy to tally because the range of responses is predictable. However, these questions may be inadequate because you may not have thought to include other equally valid responses. Notice the limited number of responses a researcher gives respondents in the following question:

> *What do you believe are the major causes of*
> *Americans' dissatisfaction with our President?*
> ☐   *President's foreign policy*
> ☐   *President's economic policy*
> ☐   *President's position on nuclear disarmament*

    Open-ended questions ask respondents to express their reactions in their own words. In these questions, a researcher leaves sufficient space for respondents to record their individual answers. Open-ended questions are more difficult to write and tally than closed-ended questions because you must categorize the diverse responses after all the questionnaires have been returned. The advantage of these questions is that respondents may record reactions, attitudes, or beliefs that you would not have thought to measure. What kinds of responses could you expect from the following open-ended questions:

> •   How do you feel about permitting smoking on
>   airplanes?
> •   In what ways could this course be improved?

Guidelines for sequencing and developing effective questions

Whether you are using open-ended or closed-ended questions, here are some guidelines for sequencing and developing effective questions.

1   Try to begin with a "snare question," a question that your respondents will be motivated to answer.

2   Attempt to sequence questions from simple-to-answer to difficult-to-answer. Beginning with difficult questions usually discourages respondents from continuing. As repondents move from one section or kind of question to another, consider introducing each section by explaining the purpose of that section and instructing respondents to fill out each section. For example, you might change from a closed-ended to an open-ended section. Specify the kinds of open-ended responses you want—one sentence, two sentences, or a brief paragraph.

3   Use vocabulary that is appropriate for your respondents' age, occupation, level of knowledge, or experience. For example, as a patient entering a hospital, would you know what "acute-care" means in the following question on a hospital admission form?

> Have you ever been treated in an acute care
> hospital?

4   Focus a question so that the respondent is not tempted to give or check off more than one response to a question. Some respondents might want to check off more than one response in the following question:

> Of our three kinds of tablets, which one do
> you take when you have the common cold?
>   —X-tol I?
>   —X-tol II?
>   —X-tol III?

5   Ask brief questions to speed up the reading and responding time. Generally, respondents become annoyed or lose interest in a questionnaire when they have to wade through lengthy questions or text.

6   Ask questions that respondents can answer "on the spot." Most respondents become annoyed with questions that require them to do any extra work, such as rummaging through household records.

7   Use positive sentences whenever possible because they are generally easier to comprehend. Respondents often misinterpret negative sentences such as this one:

> Check one of the following responses: The college should not permit alchohol in the dorms.
> - ☐ Yes
> - ☐ No

> What are the possible misinterpretations of that negative question?

8   Restrict recall time. When you ask respondents to recall information, try not to tax respondents' memories about actions in the distant past. Try to limit questions to the recent past. In asking respondents how often they have used a product, specify a time: within the last week, within the last two weeks, and so on.

9   Use "skip questions" to move respondents through a questionnaire. "Skip questions" tell respondents to jump to another section of questions according to how they respond to a particular question. A skip question follows:

> If you answer yes to this question, skip to question 10.

Avoid writing the following kinds of questions:

1   *Double-barreled* questions that ask two questions at one time. For example, what difficulty would a respondent have answering this question?

> What do you think of our product and our marketing strategy?

2   *Response-set* questions that are worded in such a way that a respondent or a group of respondents continually replies with the same answer to

every question. After a while, respondents no longer think about their responses; they simply continue to reply with their patterned response.

3 *Biased* questions that condition respondents' answers. For example, in the following question, notice how the writer has prompted respondents to answer with a "Yes":

> Don't you think the company's vacation policy is absurd?

4 *Threatening* questions that raise personal or religious issues. If it is necessary to ask these kinds of questions, build toward them in your questionnaire. You can lead up to them by first asking less threatening questions or by surrounding them with less threatening questions.

5 *Duplicate* questions that seek the same information, unless your purpose in repeating is to check whether respondents are answering consistently. To check the respondents' consistency in replying, reword the question each time.

> Read Eckert's questionnaire in Chapter 12, Figure 12-8. As you read this questionnaire, identify the kinds of questions she asked.

Guidelines for organizing and designing the questionnaire

You need to develop a strategy for introducing your text and arranging your questions. Also, you need to design your questionnaire so that it is visually appealing. No one wants to fill out a cluttered-looking questionnaire. Introduce your respondents to the questionnaire in either a cover letter or a spoken introduction. A good introduction accomplishes three aims: to inform, instruct, and persuade.

You inform by identifying yourself, explaining the purpose of your questionnaire, and explaining the types of questions. You instruct by telling people how to fill out the questionnaire and when, where, and how you would like to have it returned. If you are mailing a questionnaire and want it returned by mail, include a self-addressed envelope to motivate respondents to return it. In other cases, you may want respondents to return questionnaires to a central location. If that is the case, specify that location.

Finally, you write to persuade readers, your respondents, to fill out the questionnaire. Usually, the best way to persuade your respondents is to explain how their answers will help you achieve your purpose or how the information you gain from them will benefit them. You may also offer to share your results with them if they are interested. It is also possible to persuade readers by appealing to their egos by saying, "You have been chosen...." Some writers include a gift to persuade respondents to fill out the questionnaire; others may promise one when they have received the completed questionnaire. Understanding your respondents' level of motivation should help you determine what is the most appropriate way to motivate them. Thank respondents for filling out a questionnaire.

Follow the principles of document design we discussed in Chapter 5 to make your questionnaire visually appealing in its layout. In particular, use headings, short copy blocks, and highlighting techniques. Provide respondents with enough space to check off responses so that you know what box or line they checked off. Also, provide enough space for written responses. If you include graphic elements, follow the principles of graphic design we discuss in Chapter 5.

Information that you gather from interviews

Personal or telephone interviews are still another type of primary research. They are appropriate when you have a small population to sample, such as department heads in a small organization. The advantages of interviewing are as follows: you are more likely to get the kinds of information you want because you are speaking directly to the interviewees. You can make judgments about interviewees' responses based on their gestures and facial expression, as well as on their words. You can clarify uncertainties interviewees have about your questions. You can also ask "probe questions," questions that allow you to follow up on a reply; and you have the opportunity to redirect an interview if that redirection helps you get the kinds of information you want. The disadvantage of an interview is that you, the interviewer, may bias an interviewee's replies through your facial expressions or tone of voice.

To develop questions for an interview, follow the guidelines we suggested for formulating questions for a questionnaire. To prepare for a personal interview, make sure you write down the questions ahead of time and then memorize them or work inconspicuously from notes. That way you will have a plan for asking questions, and you will maintain eye contact while you ask questions.

Here are some guidelines to follow when you conduct a personal or telephone interview:

1 Call or write to the interviewee to set up an appointment for the interview. At that time, tell the interviewee what the purpose of your interview will be and why the interviewee will be an important source of information for the kind of problem you are trying to solve. Also, explain how long the interview will take. Base your time estimate on how long you think you will need to ask your questions (so that you avoid an unnecessary follow-up interview) and on how much time you think or know your interviewee can spare. If you want to tape the interviewee's responses, ask for permission.

2 Carefully prepare your questions so that all of them are relevant to your purpose. You don't want to waste your interviewee's time with irrelevant questions. To avoid asking irrelevant questions, ask someone else to review your questionnaire and ask yourself how each of your questions achieves your goal. Organize your questions in an order that enables you to build on what you have already asked an interviewee or to follow up on a certain response. You should anticipate the kinds of responses you will hear and be prepared to redirect a question or ask further questions to get the kinds of information you want.

3 When you begin the interview, state your purpose for interviewing and explain what kinds of questions you will be asking.

4 Jot down your interviewee's responses exactly as the interviewee states them or paraphrase them accurately.

5 If you do not record or tape responses during the interview, make sure you write down the content of the interview immediately after it takes place.

6 Thank the interviewee. To show your gratitude, you might offer to share the finished document that will include this person's information.

Secondary research

Secondary research takes place in libraries and other repositories of information where you investigate such published writings as books, journals, and newspapers. These sources bring you the results of other writers' investigations.

Writers use secondary sources to support claims and verify observations made in their reports and proposals. Referring to reliable secondary sources helps make your research credible and convincing. You can also cite secondary sources to refute competing claims. Which specific secondary sources you choose for a given report will depend on what your readers regard as reliable information in a particular field. The nature of these resources will also depend on your readers' expertise in a given subject. Many readers, such as scholars, will respect only publications which have gone through a rigorous review process. Readers in various fields often value information in their professional and trade journals.

Once you identify the problem you need to research and the general kinds of sources you want to investigate first, you can begin your secondary research. You can locate useful sources two primary ways: by conducting a manual search in the card catalog and through various bibliographies, indexes, and directories or by initiating a computer search using appropriate data bases. As you become versed in a particular field of work, you will learn which resources people in your field rely on.

Conducting a manual search

You can use the flowchart in Figure 13-1 to help you locate sources in a library. The reference sources listed on the right help you locate the books, articles, and data you need.

Some unusually comprehensive lists of reference works for report and pro-

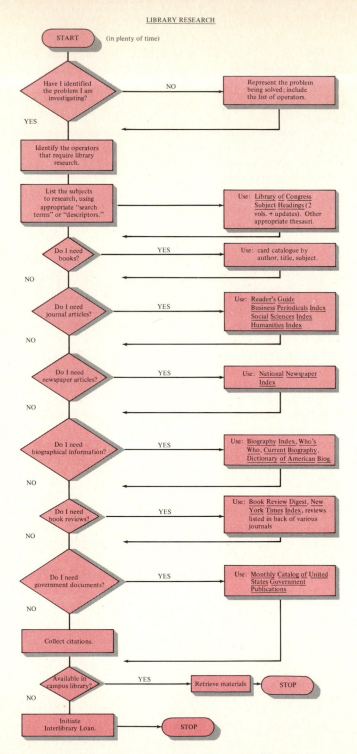

Figure 13-1   A strategy for library research. (Prepared with the assistance of Suzanne Kinard, Reference Librarian, Eugenia Atwood Library, Beaver College.)

posal writers in business, industry, and government appear in *The Research and Report Handbook* by Ruth Moyer, Eleanour Stevens, and Ralph Switzer. Their guides to government publications are particularly useful. There are few substitutes, however, for a good reference librarian.

Conducting a computer search

An on-line computer search uses an automated retrieval system to locate citations on a particular topic. Various data bases lead you to journal and newspaper articles, conference proceedings, dissertations, and books. Before conducting a computer search, however, you need to find out which data bases your library or place of work subscribes to. The table in Appendix C lists many of the data bases that are currently available.

Computer searches take less time than manual searches and usually offer you a greater quantity of citations from more diverse publications. However, you need to allow thirty minutes to an hour to outline a search strategy and fill out necessary forms. Results of on-line searches can be available immediately on your computer screen. Off-line searches, which are less expensive, are printed out and mailed to you. They take about a week for delivery.

You will need to find out how searches are arranged on your campus or at your workplace. However, before you decide to engage in a computer search, decide whether it is more beneficial for your particular project than a manual search. Use the chart in Figure 13-2 to help you decide.

RECORDING INFORMATION

Once you have located sources you think are useful, you need to survey them quickly. You want to find out whether you want to use an entire book or article or

---

WHEN ARE COMPUTER SEARCHES ADVISABLE?

- When you are writing a report or proposal that requires a comprehensive survey of literature.

- When you need the most current research in a given field. The information stored in data bases is more up-to-date than citations in printed indexes and abstracts.

- When a topic is difficult or impossible to search manually. For example, some topics contain two or more concepts:
  - . . . The use of SAT scores in predicting the G. P. A.
    - or
  - . . . The effect of U.S. interest rates on foreign exchange rates
    - or
  - . . . The effect of a presidential election on inflationary expectations.

Figure 13-2   Criteria for computer searches. (Source: Eugenia Atwood Library, Beaver College.)

SOME PUBLIC TV STATIONS LET SPONSORS PITCH THEIR PRODUCTS

By Ronald Alsop
Staff Reporter of THE WALL STREET JOURNAL

This spring, General Foods Corp. will invest something less than $2 million to sponsor a 10-part TV series called "The Sporting Life." Messages for such products as sugar-free Jell-O and Cool Whip topping will be broadcast, and the company will plug the program and its brands with a coupon promotion in Sunday newspapers.

Sounds like marketing as usual, except for the fact that the series will air on public television stations. "This is the first time a variety of consumer brands have pooled their marketing dollars to underwrite a public TV series," says William Shaw, promotion director at General Foods. "We believe the program will give consumers additional incentive to buy our brands because we'll contribute a quarter to public broadcasting for each proof-of-purchase we receive."

As General Foods has discovered, once pure public TV stations are edging ever closer to accepting paid commercial advertising. Some stations experimented briefly with advertising a few years ago, but government regulators decided against such a drastic change. Instead, the rules on corporate messages were liberalized so that program supporters could tell more about themselves and even flash a picture of their products. The Public Broadcasting Service calls it "enhanced underwriting," but some revenue-hungry stations are testing the limits and allowing what smacks of soft-sell ads.

The more liberal underwriting credits, which began appearing last year, have caused rifts in the public broadcasting system. State-funded stations are especially uneasy because they fear a loss of government backing if it appears that they are running commercials. Some stations consider the General Foods underwriting unseemly and are reluctant to run "The Sporting Life" even though they like the series of athlete profiles. Says Charles Vaughan, president of WCET in Cincinnati: "Clipping proof-of-purchase seals may be good for the local PTA, but it really isn't appropriate for PBS."

So far, the new policy is attracting mostly sponsors who already had their eye on public television and its audience of well-educated, affluent viewers. In fact, the American Gas Association, which was persuaded to underwrite the "Nature" series last fall, considers PBS "a pretty good advertising bargain," according to spokesman John W. Clark. The group of natural gas distributors will spend about $750,000 of its $20 million national ad budget for underwriting this year and calculates that the cost to reach 1,000 households through public TV is about $3.50. That compares with about $5 to reach 1,000 homes on a commercial channel.

Some aggressive stations have begun calling on ad agencies and consumer product companies to let them know underwriter messages no longer need to be so short and sweet. "We're able to go after a whole new group of companies that are more into product marketing." says Christopher Ridley, marketing manager at WGBH in Boston. In the past, PBS tended to attract giant companies like Mobil Corp. that were looking for an image boost with consumers.

Figure 13-3   The original newspaper article. (Source: *The Wall Street Journal*, Jan. 24, 1985, p. 33. Used by permission from Dow Jones & Company.)

only certain sections. You also need to decide what sort of notes to take. Will you search for and record isolated pieces of information, or will you need to summarize an entire article, chapter, or book?

The *Wall Street Journal* article in Figure 13-3 is the kind of source you might use to research a marketing report. Read the article to get a sense of what it says.

If the underwriting rules hadn't been changed, WGBH isn't sure it ever would have convinced a W.R. Grace & Co. division to help fund a gardening series and feature its Peter's Professional Plant Food in the credit. "W.R. Grace felt strongly that the product had to be shown because people might recognize the package but not the name," Mr. Ridley says.

Ad agencies are watching public TV more closely these days, but they still complain of too many restrictions. Superlatives generally are banned, and comparative claims can't be made about a competitor's products. Consumers can't be shown using products, although "generic employees" such as an unidentified lab scientist or factory worker are usually acceptable. Ford Motor Co., underwriter of "Washington Week in Review," pleaded for permission to show its cars cruising down the highway during its credit, but the station insisted that they remain parked. "We unsuccessfully argued that a car's natural environment is in motion," says Doug McClure, Ford's advertising director.

Ford might have had more luck at another station. The degree of permissiveness varies greatly. The Nebraska Educational Television Network still allows only 10-second messages, while New Jersey Network allots some underwriters 30 seconds and even interrupts programs for sponsors' messages. "We think it's beneficial to viewers as well as underwriters. It's hard to sit still all the way through some of these hard-hitting documentaries," says Hendrix Niemann, general manger of New Jersey Network.

On his network, a store called the Carpet Factory displays samples of floor coverings, Johnson & Johnson bills itself as "the world leader in health care" and Warner-Lambert Co. shows a table top cluttered with such brands as Sinutab and Listerine. Carteret Savings & Loan Association in Morristown, N.J., even managed to use one of its 30-second ads from commercial TV after editing out lines about low interest rates for mortgages and car loans. The ad showed former Olympics decathlon champion Bob Mathias jogging through New Jersey and noted that Carteret has 90 offices.

Most stations claim they have received virtually no viewer complaints about expanded underwriter credits. In fact, says Vincent Saele, president of WYES in New Orleans, "Some viewers told us they would rather see some ads than have programs interrupted constantly so the local station can beg for money."

Figure 13-3   (Cont.)

Then read the following sections of this chapter to see the different ways you might take notes from this article or summarize it.

Taking Notes

Consider this scenario. A researcher in a marketing firm is asked to investigate the advisability of advertising on public television stations. One of his sources is the

Wall Street Journal article, "Some Public TV Stations Let Sponsors Pitch Their Products," which you just read in Figure 13-3. The researcher reads this article primarily to find leads for other sources of information, including names of people or organizations he might want to call on. As a result, his note-taking aims to retrieve only the information he needs.

His notes look like this:

Opportunities for advertising on public broadcasting stations do exist—some stations refer to these ads as "*enhanced underwriting*." The following stations have accepted these ads:

WGBH Boston (Chas. Ridley, marketing
    manager)
Nebraska Ed. Tel. Network
New Jersey Network
WYES New Orleans (Vincent Saele,
    president)

The following companies have purchased advertising time:

General Foods
American Gas Association (John W. Clark,
    spokesperson)
Peter's Professional Plant Food
Ford Motor Company
Johnson & Johnson
Warner-Lambert Company
Local N.J. firms: Carpet Factory, Carteret
    S&L Association

Once the researcher has listed his leads, he can follow up on them by interviewing and writing inquiries and consulting other library materials. For example, he can think about locating profiles of the companies that advertise on public stations, or about consulting public records of the stations' budgets and operations.

If you were researching attitudes toward advertising on public stations, how useful would the *Wall Street Journal* article be? For example, what notes might you take if you wanted to find out about:

Viewers' attitudes
The stations' attitudes
The advertisers' attitudes?

How might you follow up on these leads?

Writing a Summary

Selective note-taking is only one useful way to record information. Writing a more complete summary of what you have read is another. The amount and kind of recording you do depends on your purpose. For example, you might need to collect information about a certain topic over a long period of time. In that case, you will want to write fairly extensive notes. Most likely, a full summary that represents a miniature version of the article or book will be more useful. Sometimes you are asked to summarize articles or other long pieces of information for a supervisor or for your co-authors, if you are preparing a report collaboratively. Other occasions exist as well.

To prepare a full summary, you will, of course, take more complete and detailed notes. One writer's notes on the *Wall Street Journal* article, for example, looked like this:

—many pub. tv stations accept commercial advertising
—some stations advertised last yr as experiment
—gov regs have been revised so that companies could provide more infor-mative messages and pictures of products, but no hard-sell ads
—called ''more liberal underwriting,'' ''*enhanced underwriting*''

—too much advertising could cause station to lose
  gov backing
—some stations find GF ads unacceptable
—Chas. Vaughan of WCET says ads not
  "appropriate"
—Am Gas Association underwrote "Nature" series
      —thought ads a "bargain": $3.50 per 1000
        households vs $5.00/1000
      —also good "image boost"
—C. Ridley, mrkt mgr WGBH Boston, invites
  advertisers
—Peters Prof Plant Food funded gardening
  program.
      —showed product in message
—Ad agencies find too many restrictions on ads
      —Banned are
            superlatives
            comparative claims
            showing consumers using products
—Ford Motor Co. sponsors "Washington Week in
  Review"
—Neb Ed Tel Ntwk allows 10 sec. messages
—NJ Ntwk = 30 secs., programs can be
  interrupted
      —Hendrix Niemann, gen'l mgr
      —Advertisers: Carpet Factory, Johnson &
        Johnson, Warner-Lambert Co., Carteret
        S&L
      —No viewer complaints
      —Vincent Saele, pres WYES, New Orleans:
        "Some viewers told us they would rather
        see some ads than have programs
        interrupted constantly so the local station
        can beg for money."

From these notes, the writer wrote a rough draft of the summary:

Opportunities for commercial advertising on public
television stations exist, but the amount and kind is specified by government regulations. Some stations, such as
WGBH (Boston), Nebraska Educational Network, New Jersey
Network, and WYES (New Orleans), welcome advertisers, while
others reject it. Stations often refer to advertising as
"enhanced underwriting." Yet even some of the stations
that accept advertising prohibit ''hard-sell'' ads. Some
agencies find the prohibitions too restrictive. For example,
ads must avoid superlatives, comparative claims, and pictures
of consumers using products. However, other agencies see two
advantages in advertising on public stations. First, the ads
reach a select audience that is highly educated and affluent.
Second, ads cost $1.50 less per 1000 households than on com-
mercial stations. Satisfied corporate advertisers include:
General Foods, Ford Motor Company, Johnson & Johnson, and
Warner-Lambert Company.

The writer read his summary paragraph aloud. He then revised it in the following way to organize the information more clearly and to correct troublesome
sentences, word choices, and typographical errors:

Many public television stations and advertisers welcome
commercial advertising on public broadcasting networks, but
the amount and kind of commercials are specified by government regulations. Some stations, such as WGBH (Boston),
Nebraska Educational Network, New Jersey Network, and WYES
(New Orleans) accept advertising (often referred to as
"enhanced underwriting"), although other stations have
rejected it. The stations that accept advertising follow
government guidelines prohibiting "hard-sell" ads. For
example, ads must avoid superlatives, comparative claims,

```
and pictures of consumers using the advertised products.

Some agencies find these prohibitions too restrictive. Des-

pite these restrictions, other firms cite two advantages of

advertising on public stations. First, the ads reach a

highly educated and affluent audience. Second, ads cost $1.50

less per 1000 households than those on commercial stations.

Corporate advertisers include the following: General Foods,

Ford Motor Company, Johnson & Johnson, and Warner-Lambert

Company.
```

Paraphrasing and Quoting

Whether you are summarizing or taking some other form of notes, you need to surround exact transcriptions of sections, sentences, and phrases from documents with quotation marks. When writing a full summary or taking selective notes, you should avoid relying on verbatim transcriptions. Instead, learn to quote selectively and depend primarily on paraphrasing.

> Look back at the last draft of the writer's summary. Why do you think the writer quoted *enhanced underwriting* directly from the article? Do you think anything important would have been lost if he left out that phrase?

The second quoted phrase, "hard-sell," is one the summary writer chose to quote. Since that hyphenated word appears in common usage, you might argue that the summary writer did not have to quote it. However, by doing so, he has called attention to the fact that *he* isn't characterizing the prohibited commercials as "hard-sell" ads. Rather, he is indicating that *the author* of the *Wall Street Journal* article characterized them that way. Thus the summary writer is simply delivering someone else's characterization to his readers. Why do you think this summary writer chose to make that distinction in this case?

To paraphrase effectively, practice reading large sections of a piece of writing—for example, a long paragraph or several short ones. Then without looking at the original copy, write down the gist of what the writer said. Compare your version with the original and change whatever you must to make your paraphrase more accurate. Another way to avoid quoting too much, intentionally or unintentionally, is to write down brief fragments of information rather than whole sentences. When you bring these fragments together in connected writing, you are likely to find yourself constructing your own sentences, rather than echoing the ones you read. You still need to check your notes against the original document to make sure that you did not inadvertantly play back the author's words.

PART 2: STRATEGIES FOR PLANNING, DRAFTING, REVISING, AND EDITING
Developing an Overall Plan

Once you have researched all or most of the information you think you need to solve the problem your report or proposal sets out to solve, you can begin thinking about how to arrange it. Some organizations provide guidelines for submitting reports or proposals. These guidelines often include a format writers can follow. Organizations, or departments within them, that routinely produce particular kinds of reports are the ones most likely to develop such formats.

For example, an engineering firm that conducts most of its business by writing sales proposals to customers usually develops a standard format for those proposals. Similarly, schools requiring routine observation reports on their faculty usually develop a format for observers to record their observations. Other organizations provide such general guidelines as ''Proposals written for superiors can be no longer than two pages.'' Some organizations require one-page proposals to all internal readers.

Because the format and final plan for organizing a report or proposal depends on its purpose, readers, and context, no one can supply all the plans that do or can exist. In Chapter 12 you saw how various writers constructed their reports and proposals to meet their readers' needs. No one plan would have suited all of them.

With that statement in mind, you can look at the report and proposal outlines on the next few pages. Use these strategies for arrangement as suggestions to stimulate your thinking about how to organize your own report or proposal.

Designing Reports and Proposals for Readers

In general, reports and proposals are designed to give readers an overview of the entire contents first, the general proposition next, the discussion in the middle, and the specific supporting information last. Results of a survey and raw data, for example, are placed in appendixes after the recommendations or conclusions.

Reports begin with a general overview and end with specific, supporting documentation for another reason: reports have multiple readers who have different reasons for reading. For example, the senior members of an organization often read reports to stay informed about the projects their organization is taking on and the status of various divisions within the organization. Such readers use reports essentially to monitor the organizations for which they have executive responsibility. Executive readers also scan reports for information that enables them to make decisions. These readers rely on the abstract, or summary, of the report to give them an overview of its contents. Such readers, however, are unlikely to examine all the details, such as the data in the appendixes.

On the other hand, the technical staff has other responsibilities. Instead of making or reviewing decisions, members of this staff are responsible for checking the data to see if they were properly researched and accurately calculated. These readers are likely to pay less attention to the discussion sections and turn quickly to the appendixes.

Strategies for organizing specific reports

To help your readers find their way through a report or proposal, you will customarily divide it into several parts, each with a descriptive heading. You saw, for example, the ways writers divided and arrranged information in the reports you surveyed in the previous chapter. You can borrow or, better yet, adapt the following report strategies to suit your purposes and readers.

A consulting report

Consulting reports are written by independent consultants or consulting firms to evaluate some aspect of an organization and to recommend improvements. These reports can help members of an organization understand why some phase of an operation isn't working. These reports can also outline ways an organization can plan and implement new goals or operations. The aspect of the organization that consultants investigate varies. It can be, for example, a manufacturing process, a method of managing a company, the procedures for maintaining financial records, or the means of marketing or delivering goods or services.

Sometimes consulting reports simply document what investigators discovered, while other reports also recommend ways to correct a reported problem. Some consultants' reports double as a sales proposal for a firm's services. In that case, the closing recommendations of the report would include hiring the services of the consulting firm. Such reports would include a section stressing the benefits to be gained by employing the particular firm.

One useful strategy for organizing a consulting report is to:

1 Describe the background of the study
2 State its objectives and scope
3 Describe the procedures followed during the investigation
4 Summarize the findings
5 Summarize the recommendations
6 Enumerate the benefits of following the recommendations

Some consulting reports need not describe the history and background of the study because they are understood by the readers and writers. In that case, a better strategy would be to write a briefer report, such as the following one:

1 State the objectives of the study
2 Describe the procedures followed during the investigation
3 Summarize the findings

4   Summarize the recommendations
5   Enumerate the benefits of following the recommendations

A monitoring report

Monitoring reports make evaluations. These reports record investigations carried out by an authorized agent or agency, who determines whether an organization is following established guidelines, laws, criteria, or objectives. For example, teams from state agencies regularly investigate hospital procedures and report their findings to the licensing agency. Monitoring reports can also be written internally, that is, by one member or department within an organization for other readers in that organization. For instance, a comptroller may require an accountant to investigate why the costs of a construction site have increased beyond the budgeted amount.

Monitoring reports vary greatly in scope and length. Some routine monitoring reports can be organized in the following way:

1   State the purpose of the investigation
2   Classify and describe the areas evaluated
3   Summarize the findings and recommendations for each area

Some monitoring reports also include the methods used to investigate the problem.

A feasibility report

Feasibility studies explore several alternative solutions to a problem. Many feasibility studies also recommend which of the alternatives to adopt by matching each one against clearly stated criteria. Rather than focusing on past procedures, these reports explore future courses of action. Feasibility reports can require writers to do both first-hand primary research and library research.

In some cases, writers need to summarize the reasons for making the study at the beginning of the report, show the procedures used to explore the problem, and then list the recommendation. Such feasibility reports can be organized like this:

1   State purpose of study or the problem to be solved
2   List and describe the alternatives
3   List the criteria
4   Evaluate each alternative according to the criteria
5   Recommend one of the alternatives (optional)

Sometimes readers want to know the recommendations first. With these recommendations in mind, readers will then review the process by which the writers made their decisions. In such cases, feasibility reports can take the following form:

1   Recommend a solution
2   Describe the background
3   List and describe the alternatives

4   Evaluate each alternative according to the criteria
5   Recommend an alternative
6   List the steps needed to implement the recommendation

Strategies for organizing specific proposals

Proposals make requests. These documents are designed to motivate someone in an organization to make a decision that will enable the request to be carried out. Exactly how proposals are arranged will depend on how typical or unusual they are in a particular organization, what the relationship between the reader and writer is, and whether the proposal was solicited or unsolicited by the recipient. Grant awarding agencies, such as the National Institutes for Health or the National Endowment for the Humanities, usually provide forms that writers strictly follow. The examples of proposals described below will give you some idea of the way proposal formats vary with the circumstances under which they are written.

An academic research proposal

Academic proposals make two primary kinds of requests. One is permission to carry on a particular kind of study. Undergraduates, for example, petition departments to grant credit for completing an independent study project. The other request tries to persuade an institution or funding agency to award a grant to conduct a particular study. Graduate students and faculty members frequently write this kind of proposal.

Since institutions and agencies that fund higher education assume that students and scholars will make such requests, proposal writers don't need to persuade the organization about the value of granting such requests. The value is assumed. Instead, these writers need to focus on convincing readers that a particular study is worthwhile and that the writer is competent to carry it out. In an academic proposal the writer needs to:

1   State the question or problem to be explored
2   Explain why finding an answer or solution is important
3   Describe the research methods, including the sources to be consulted
4   Outline the schedule for completing each phase of the project
5   State the researcher's qualifications (may be optional for some independent studies)

A request for improving a product or procedure

Many proposals, especially internal ones, suggest ways in which an organization can improve some phase of its operations. These requests are often made by employees who observe a problem they want to make management aware of. You will see an example of this kind of proposal in Chapter 15. In that case study, a parent makes a proposal to an elementary school principal to suggest an improvement in the school.

Such proposals can take many forms. Often, though, it's best to put the request first so that the readers know immediately what decision they're being asked to make. The following outline shows how to request an improvement:

1 State exactly what you are requesting
2 Describe the background of your request (What led you to make it?)
3 Enumerate and describe the possible solutions
4 Evaluate each one against the criteria
5 Recommend the best solution
6 Enumerate the steps to carry out the solution

A sales proposal for a product or service

Some proposals are written to initiate the sale of a product or service. Writers of such a proposal need to show their readers the benefits of purchasing the product or service from the writer's firm, usually by highlighting how effectively their offer will suit the customer's needs.

Sales proposals can vary in scope and length, depending on the kind of product or service being offered and the complexity of the project. A comprehensive proposal can contain sections in which you:

1 Summarize the project
2 Describe the background of the problem
3 Define the scope of the plan and its objectives
4 Describe the methodology
5 Estimate the time for completion
6 Evaluate the plan
7 Itemize the cost
8 Document the qualifications of the firm and personnel assigned to the project

If the proposal is for a technologically complex product, such as computer hardware, the writers need to define the scope and plan in careful detail. Their customers will want to know, for example, the results of reliability and quality control tests, the terms of installation and repair, and the amount of training provided to the employees who will use the equipment. In the scope and plan section of such a sales proposal, you need to:

1 Describe the product
2 Describe optional or additional equipment
3 List the features and benefits of the product
4 Describe the following support services
      Deliverable items and services
      Production items
      Spares
      Quality control

Reliability
Support equipment
Related services
Training

5 Describe the appropriate facilities for operating and storing the equipment

Revising and Editing Reports and Proposals

After you have refined your test draft, making sure you have achieved your primary and secondary purposes for readers, follow the review steps you have read about:

First Review
Read for Purpose and Appropriateness
Second Review
Read for Arrangement and Cohesion

Because reports and proposals can be long, it is especially important that you write a descriptive outline, sketch a branching outline, or write a conventional outline. Those strategies will force you to look closely at your strategies for arranging sections of information. We also suggest that you use a reader or readers to comment on your draft. Use the Reader Reviews at the end of this chapter.

Third Review
Read for Sentences and Language
Fourth Review
Read for Accuracy

As part of the fourth review, we suggest that you make a checklist of items similar to those listed under ''Fourth Review: Read for Accuracy, Strategy One: Check the Accuracy of Information'' in Chapter 4. Along with those items, check figure numbers and textual references in figures throughout your text. Readers become easily disgruntled when they cannot find the figure you are referring them to.

PART 3: STRATEGIES FOR DESIGNING A FINAL DOCUMENT

Satisfied with the content and style of their reports and proposals, writers finally design those documents. As you have already seen in Chapter 12, reports and proposals may be written in a letter or memo format or in a formal report or proposal format. Because you know how to format letters and memos (as discussed in Chapter 7), we will now describe some of the conventional formats you may find in your organization for setting up a formal report or proposal.

The following list describes the conventional parts of a formal report or proposal and their function for readers. You may use some or all of these parts in a report or proposal. Some reports and proposals may follow a different order or may use different terms to label the parts of these documents. Both the purpose of the report and readers' expectations of the kind of information in these documents determine what parts a writer includes. As a report or proposal writer, you will need to understand the kinds of information you should include in each segment of these prescribed formats.

Conventional Parts of Formal Reports and Proposals

The conventional parts of a formal report or proposal are as follows:

1 *Front matter*, consisting of the following parts:
   - Title page
   - Letter of Transmittal
   - Table of Contents
   - List of Tables and Figures
   - Abstract
2 *Body of the report or proposal*, consisting of the following parts:
   - Introduction
   - Major and subheadings
   - Conclusions
   - Recommendations
3 *End matter*, consisting of the following parts:
   - Appendixes or Attachments
   - References or Works Cited

The following list describes the conventional parts of a report or proposal and their functions. To familiarize yourself with the parts, refer to Eckert's evaluation report in Chapter 12 (Figures 12-3 to 12-8).

PARTS OF A FORMAL REPORT OR PROPOSAL	FUNCTIONS OF THE PARTS
FRONT MATTER	
Title Page—includes the title of the document, the name of the writer and the writer's position, the date the writer submits the document, the name of the person within an organization who will read the report and that reader's position, or the name of the organization that will receive the report. Generally, center the	Gives the reader an understanding of the focus of the report.

PARTS OF A FORMAL REPORT OR PROPOSAL	FUNCTIONS OF THE PARTS

FRONT MATTER

title approximately one-third down from the top of the page. Some organizations may use preprinted cover pages or binders which include an organization's logo. Develop a brief, yet specific title, avoiding noun strings, lengthy prepositional phrases, or stereotypic expressions. Avoid such titles as ''The Impact of Future Ramifications on Our Potential to Cope with The Central Issues on Our Policy Agenda.'' Instead, condense the title, naming the issue, problem, or action you will discuss in the document, such as ''Evaluation of Our Present Merit Policy.'' (See Figure 12-3.)

Letter of Transmittal—occurs either as a separate letter accompanying the document or as a page or pages of the document after the title page (see Figure 12-4.)

Places document in a context for the reader, flags the problem or issue the document solves, and may state recommendations.

Table of Contents—lists major headings and subheadings in the document. The table of contents in Eckert's report lists major and subheadings (Figure 12-5). In reports or proposals that contain technical information, such as in Figure 13-4, writers usually use Arabic numerals to number main and minor headings. Pages in a table of contents are numbered with lowercase Roman numerals.

Helps readers predict content and select information that may be of immediate interest.

List of Tables or Figures—shows the page number of important graphics included in the report or proposal. Number pages in a list of tables with lower case Roman numerals. Figure 13-5 illustrates a list of figures.

Helps readers locate graphics which complement or supplement text. Some readers initially depend on the graphics rather than on text to survey information.

Abstract—condenses the entire report or proposal in one page or paragraph (two pages at the most). There are two kinds of abstracts that you may write: a *descriptive*

Presents readers with an overview of the report or proposal. Help readers decide if the document is

PARTS OF A FORMAL REPORT OR PROPOSAL	FUNCTIONS OF THE PARTS

FRONT MATTER

abstract or an *informative abstract*. In a descriptive abstract you say what your document *does* without saying what you

worth reading or disseminating to others in an organization.

TABLE OF CONTENTS

i

Figure 13-4 Example of a table of contents. (By permission from Dee McCormac, Pacer Systems, Inc., Pennsylvania.)

PARTS OF A FORMAL REPORT OR PROPOSAL	FUNCTIONS OF THE PARTS

FRONT MATTER

conclude or recommend. Think of the abstract as an elaborated table of contents to a document. You might say, for example, ''This report examines the effects of a shorter work week'' or ''This report investigates optional sites for building our fourth plant.'' In an informative abstract, you tell readers what the document *says*, including what you conclude and recommend. You describe the conditions that gave rise to the problem you investigated, state the problem, discuss how you solved the problem, what you found, and what you recommend. This kind of abstract is a condensed version of the report or proposal. You always write the abstract after you have written the entire document. The easiest way to sequence information in your abstract is to look back at the headings you used in your

---

LIST OF FIGURES

Figure 13-5 Example of a list of figures. (By permission from Dee McCornac, Pacer Systems, Inc.)

| PARTS OF A FORMAL REPORT OR PROPOSAL | FUNCTIONS OF THE PARTS |

FRONT MATTER

document. Eckert's abstract, Figure 12-6, is an example of an informative abstract. Number the abstract page either with Roman or Arabic numerals. These numbers are centered at the bottom of the page. (For more information on pagination, see the section on formatting pages in this chapter.)

BODY OF THE REPORT OR PROPOSAL

Major headings and subheadings—itemize the main and subordinate topics in a document. Use grammatically parallel headings, asking appropriate questions readers would ask, or providing the kinds

Help readers scan a document to preview its structure and anticipate the contents of each section.

5.2.2 Annual employee evaluations

Annual employee evaluations are considered inadequate by some and sufficient by many. Proponents of an annual appraisal state that, if held more frequently, formal appraisals tend to become a mechanical, worthless procedure. However, the appraisal process should be on-going and continuous (Henderson, 1976). Henderson feels that the traditional completion of an appraisal form will continue to be an annual event. Pacer, with its employee input form and the structure of the work units, appears to be justified in using an annual review.

5.2.3 Salary adjustment at the annual review

Pay and performance go hand-in-hand. As Belcher stated in his article on "Pay and Performance," paying employees on the basis of their performance is the way to obtain performance motivation in organizations. Not only does this approach make sense intuitively but it also has a solid theoretical base (Belcher, 1980). The problem is not tieing performance to pay but whether or not to do the two at the same time. Moskal pointed out that Dr. Levinson believes there should be no taboo against discussing salary in conjunction with year-end performance assessments. If a subordinate has been kept informed of significant incidents throughout the course of the year, then the impact on his or her salary adjustment should not come as a surprise (Moskal, 1982). The other argument is that the performance appraisal session should be separate from the dollar award session. The reason given for separating the two is that, when they are given together, the employee hears nothing except how much more he will get in his pocket (Berg, 1976:288). Anyone given an appraisal in conjunction with a salary review can sympathize with that statement. A recommended approach for Pacer will be addressed in Section Six.

Figure 13-6   Example of in-text documentation. (By permission from Dee McCornac, Pacer Systems, Inc.)

PARTS OF A FORMAL REPORT OR PROPOSAL	FUNCTIONS OF THE PARTS

BODY OF THE REPORT OR PROPOSAL

of topics readers would expect or want to know about. (See section on formatting pages for examples of how to arrange headings on a page. See also Figure 12-7.)

END MATTER

Appendixes or Attachments—consist of supplementary information which supports findings, observations, or conclusions in the report. Examples of appendixes are letters, contracts, organizational records or data, sample questionnaires or interviews, results of questionnaires or interviews, or photographs. Sometimes an appendix contains a *Glossary*, a list of terms used in the report and their definitions. Label appendixes by letter: A, B, C, and so forth. Also title them to describe their contents. Eckert included her questionnaire in an appendix to her report (Figure 12-8).

Document your observations, conclusions, or findings.

References or Works Cited—alphabetically list primary and secondary resources you

Acknowledge sources and authorities that appear in the

References

Belcher, D. W. 1980. Pay and performance. Compensation Review. 3(2): 23–25.

Berg, J. G. 1976. Managing compensation. Amacon, New York.

Brinkerhopp, D. W. & Kanter, R. M. 1980. Appraising the performance appraisal. Sloan Management Review. 77(78): 36.

Bushardt, S. C. & Schnake, M. E. 1981. Employee evaluation: Measure performance, not attitude. Management World. 8(12): 41–42.

Friedman, B. A. & Mann, R. W. 1981. Employee assessment methods assessed. Personnel. 16: 69.

Henderson, R. I. 1976. Compensation management. Reston Publishing Company, Inc., Virginia.

Figure 13-7   Example of references page. (By permission from Dee McCornac, Pacer Systems, Inc.)

PARTS OF A FORMAL REPORT OR PROPOSAL	FUNCTIONS OF THE PARTS

END MATTER

consulted in writing a document. Many organizations now follow the American Psychological Association's (APA) format for referring to authorities within the text of a document (see Figure 13-6) and for listing references (see Figure 13-7). Note that references in the text include the writer's last name, followed by the date of publication and page. Resources in the "References" page are listed alphabetically with the author's last name first. If you need to find out about other conventional documentation styles, such as the Modern Language Association (MLA) style, refer to a handbook.

document and that were helpful in your research. Also help readers locate information they might want to verify or look into further.

Formatting Pages

In general, here are the guidelines for margins, pagination, and sequencing of major and subheadings.

Margin spacing and pagination

The following dimensions are usually used on a page of text:

Top margin:	1 to $1\frac{1}{4}$ inches
Left margin:	1 inch
Bottom margin:	1 to $1\frac{1}{2}$ inches
Right margin:	1 inch

Usually position page numbers 1 inch above the bottom line, beginning with Arabic numerals on the first page of the body of the text.

Major headings and subheadings

Headings correspond to the list of headings in the Table of Contents. On a page they are usually located as follows:

Major headings are centered on the page. They may be underlined if they appear in a combination of upper and lower case or they may appear in capital letters.

Subheadings are placed at the left-hand margin and are underlined.

Sub-subheadings under subheadings are indented five spaces under the sub-heading and are underlined. The sequence of headings on a page looks like this:

MAJOR HEADING

<u>Subheading</u>

　　<u>Sub-heading</u>

Proofreading

Follow the strategies we recommend for the fourth review step: Read for Accuracy. After a final proofreading, often with the help of others whose "fresh eyes" usually catch what yours might not, the document is ready for its readers.

Checklist for Formal Reports
Content

1   Have I included accurate and comprehensive information to achieve the purpose of this report?
2   Have I checked the accuracy of my information?

Strategies for arrangement

1   Have I condensed my report in a descriptive or informative abstract? Does the descriptive abstract tell what the report *does*? Does the informative abstract tell readers what the report *says*? (Refer to pages 309–310 in this chapter.)
2   Does my introductory section provide readers with a context for understanding the problem, a statement of the problem, and a statement of how the report will unfold?
3   Have I reviewed the strategies for arranging sections to make sure that these strategies are appropriate for my readers and their use of the report? Have I written a descriptive outline or drawn a branching outline to take an objective look at how I sequenced sections for my readers?
4   Have I used cohesive devices—including headings and subheadings—to guide my reader through the information from sentence to sentence and section to section?
5   Have I drawn logical conclusions based on my discussion in the report?
6   Are my recommendations based on what I concluded?

Vocabulary and Style

1   Have I unpacked weighty sentences?
2   Have I varied my sentence structures to achieve the emphasis I want and to avoid repetitive sentence structures?

3   Do my word choices consistently convey the relationship I want to establish with my reader?
4   Do my word choices project the image of myself and my organization that I want to project?
5   Have I avoided biased language?
6   Have I used fresh language?

Conventions of the language

1   Have I followed the conventions of spelling, punctuation, and grammar?

Layout

1   Have I applied the principles of effective document design? (See "Checklist" at the end of Chapter 5.)

Format

1   Have I followed one of the following formats for a report?
    ☐   Letter?
    ☐   Memo?
    ☐   Formal report format?
    ☐   Other organizational format?

Checklist for Formal Proposals

Content

1   Have I included accurate and comprehensive information to persuade my readers to accept or support what I am proposing?
2   Have I checked the accuracy of my information?

Strategies for arrangement

1   Have I condensed my proposal in an informative abstract which explains the problem that my proposal intends to solve and, generally, how what I propose will solve that problem?
2   Does my introductory section provide readers with a context for understanding the problem, a statement of the problem, and how the proposal will solve the problem?
3   Have I reviewed the strategies for arranging sections of the proposal to lead my readers to accept what I am proposing? Have I written a descriptive outline or drawn a branching outline to take an objective look at how I have sequenced sections for my readers?

4 Have I used cohesive devices—including headings and subheadings—to guide my readers through the information from sentence to sentence and section to section?

5 Have I drawn logical conclusions based on my discussion in the proposal?

6 Are my recommendations based on what I conclude? Have I lead my readers to accept these recommendations, as well?

Vocabulary and Style

1 Have I unpacked weighty sentences?

2 Have I varied my sentence structures to achieve the emphasis I want and to avoid repetitious sentence structures?

3 Do my word choices consistently convey the relationship I want to establish with my reader?

4 Do my word choices project the image of myself and my organization that I want to project?

5 Have I avoided biased language?

6 Have I used fresh language?

Conventions of the language

1 Have I followed the conventions of spelling, punctuation, and grammar?

Layout

1 Have I applied the principles of effective document design? (See "Checklist" at the end of Chapter 5.)

Format

1 Have I followed one of the formats for a proposal?
- ☐ Memo?
- ☐ Letter?
- ☐ Formal proposal format?
- ☐ Other organizational format?

REVISING REPORTS OR PROPOSALS FOR A SPOKEN PRESENTATION: A CHECKLIST

You may have to make a spoken presentation of your report or proposal to listeners either within or outside your organization, such as prospective customers or clients. You may have to present your sales proposal to an organization that has solicited proposals from other firms like yours. How you sell your product during a spoken presentation may be just what it takes to persuade the potential customer to buy your product or service. In-house, you might have to present progress reports or strategy reports to decision makers to gain their support for your work. To be compelling, spoken presentations can't simply mimic the outline of the report they're drawn from. Speakers need to significantly revise written reports to emphasize only the key points of interest to their audience.

The following checklist will help you prepare for these kinds of presentations.

Purpose

What is (are) the purpose(s) of this spoken presentation?

- ☐ To inform?
- ☐ To document?
- ☐ To explore?
- ☐ To persuade?
- ☐ Other?

Listeners

Who are my listeners? Are they members of my organization or outsiders? What is their level of understanding of this problem or issue? What is their motivation for listening?

- ☐ Asked to attend?
- ☐ Required to attend?
- ☐ Volunteered to attend?
- ☐ Called for the presentation themselves?
- ☐ Concerned about resolving a problem?
- ☐ Scheduled to meet for progress reports?

What use will they make of my report or proposal?

- ☐ Explore a problem with me?
- ☐ Learn about the recent developments of a problem?
- ☐ Learn what I have discovered as a result of research?
- ☐ Learn what I have concluded as a result of research?
- ☐ Make a decision based on what I say?
- ☐ Understand the status of a project?
- ☐ Other?

What kind of relationship do I want to establish with my listeners?

- ☐ Formal?
- ☐ Informal?
- ☐ Other?

What preconceptions do they have about me?

- ☐ See me as an authority within my organization?
- ☐ See me as an expert in my field?
- ☐ Other?

Strategies for Arrangement

- ☐ What kinds of information should I present and in what order?
- ☐ What transitional words will I use to move from one major point to the next?
- ☐ How will I open my presentation?
- ☐ What strategies for arrangement will I use to sequence information for my listeners? (Review strategies for arrangement for various reports and proposals in Chapter 12.)
- ☐ How will the arrangement of my spoken presentation differ from the written report or proposal?
- ☐ How will I close my presentation?
  - ☐ State my conclusions?
  - ☐ State my recommendations?
  - ☐ Restate how my conclusions and recommendations solve a problem?
  - ☐ Urge listeners to take immediate action to solve a problem?
  - ☐ Warn listeners of consequences if they choose not to heed the conclusions or recommendations I state?
  - ☐ Other?

Format

Where will I be speaking? What format should I use for this location?

- ☐ Read the presentation?
- ☐ Memorize the presentation?
- ☐ Speak from notes?
- ☐ Speak from visual media
- ☐ Incorporate a question-and-answer period?
- ☐ Other?

How long should I speak?

- [ ] How much time is available?
- [ ] How long can I expect listeners to want to pay attention?
- [ ] How long should I allow for questions?
- [ ] Should I invite questions during or after my presentation?

How will I pace my presentation so that I speak neither too quickly nor too slowly?

Audiovisual Media

What kinds of audiovisual media should I use to achieve my purpose? What is the advantage of using one or more of these media?

- [ ] Graphics such as diagrams, charts, and tables (see Chapter 5)?
- [ ] Model?
- [ ] The product itself?
- [ ] Other?

What media should I use to I achieve my purpose and make it possible for all listeners to hear or see audiovisual media?

1 Visual media:

- [ ] Slide projector?
- [ ] Overhead projector?
- [ ] Chalkboard, clothboard?
- [ ] Flipchart?
- [ ] Hand-out?

2 Audiovisual media:

- [ ] Videotape?
- [ ] Videodisk?
- [ ] Film or motion picture?
- [ ] Tape recorder?
- [ ] Record?
- [ ] Other?

1. In Chapter 12 you isolated a problem that you could handle in a report or proposal. Now go through the tasks and strategies we outlined in this chapter and write that report or proposal. Before you start, develop a work plan, listing the tasks you have to do and your target dates to do them. Include in your work plan what you have to do (interview, develop and send out a questionnaire, research primary and secondary resources, etc.) and when you plan to do these tasks. Also, include in your work plan dates for planning, drafting, having a peer review a test draft, revising and editing, designing a final document, presenting your report or proposal (if you have to give a spoken presentation), and handing in your final copy.

   At the end of the projects and exercises you will find Reader and Writer Reviews which your instructor may ask you and a peer to fill out.

2. Select an organizational issue that you are interested in and develop a preliminary bibliography for that issue. What kinds of information will you want to search for, and where will you search for it?

3. Select an article on an organizational issue you are interested in. Summarize that article in a memo to your instructor. Include a copy of the article with your summary.

4. Develop a questionnaire about an organizational issue that is appropriate for employees or peers to respond to. Distribute that questionnaire; summarize the results in a memo to your instructor.

5. Research impending legislation at the local, state, or federal level and explore the effects this legislation will have. In a report to an appropriate reader or readers (e.g., community residents) explore the effects, come to a conclusion about the positive or negative effects, and recommend whether you think the legislation should be passed.

6. If you have the opportunity to assist someone in a profession, such as to assist a congressperson, write a memo report to your peers explaining the kinds of responsibilities you carried out or the kinds of responsibilities that a professional carries out. Keep a log of your observations.

7. Write an investigative report of a company you might want to apply to. Investigate the overall status of the company and the particular aspects of the company that would be useful for you (and other potential applicants with your background) to know before interviewing for a position in that company. Pose the question you want your investigation to answer and develop a research strategy.

8. If you have had a management course, write a profile of a chief executive officer (CEO) which answers this question:

   (a) According to Peters and Watterman, authors of *In Search of Excellence*, ". . . . it appears that the real role of the chief executive is to manage the *values* of the organization" (26). Does this observation apply to the CEO you researched?

WRITER AND READER REVIEWS
Writer Review of a Test Draft of a Report

Problem or issue

1   What is the question this report sets out to answer or the main problem it sets out to solve?

Readers and purpose

1   Who are my readers? What do I know about their interest in and motivation for reading this report? (Recall the "Checklist of Questions Writers Need to Ask" in Chapter 1.)
2   How do I think my readers will answer my question or solve the problem before reading my report? How do I want my readers to answer my question or solve the problem after reading my report?
3   What are my purposes for writing this report? (To inform, to document, to instruct, to explore, to persuade?)

Strategies for arrangement

1   Trace the strategies for arrangement that you have used in this test draft by filling out the following descriptive outline:

Section 1 or Paragraph 1

What does it do (e.g., identifies the problem or issue, raises a question about an issue)?
What does it say (e.g., "Sales over the last quarter have fallen by 20%")?

Section 2 or Paragraph 2

What does it do?
What does it say?

Section 3 or Paragraph 3

What does it do?
What does it say?

Section 4 or Paragraph 4

What does it do?
What does it say?
(Continue using the outline if you have more sections or paragraphs.)

Readers' response

1 How do I think my readers will respond to the strategies for arrangement I have used?
2 What information should I add, delete, or rearrange to ensure that my readers will respond the way I want them to?
3 What sections or paragraphs should I add, delete, or rearrange to ensure that my readers will respond the way I want them to?

Graphic elements

1 If I have used graphic elements in this test draft, why did I use them and how did I integrate them into or along with the text?

WRITER AND READER REVIEWS
Reader Review of a Test Draft of a Report
Problem or issue

1 What is the question this report sets out to answer or the main problem it sets out to solve?

Readers and purpose

1 Who are the readers? What do you know about their interest in and motivation for reading this report? (Recall the ''Checklist of Questions Writers Need to Ask'' in Chapter 1.)
2 How do you think the readers will answer the question or solve the problem before reading the report?
3 What is the writer's purpose or purposes in writing this report? (To inform, to document, to instruct, to explore, to persuade?)

Strategies for arrangement

1 Trace the strategies for arrangement that the writer has used in this test draft by filling out the following descriptive outline:

Section 1 or Paragraph 1

What does it do (e.g., identifies the problem or issue, raises a question about an issue)?
What does it say (e.g., "Sales over the last quarter have fallen by 20%")?

Section 2 or Paragraph 2

What does it do?
What does it say?

Section 3 or Paragraph 3

What does it do?
What does it say?

Section 4 or Paragraph 4

What does it do?
What does it say?
(Continue using the outline if the writer has more sections or paragraphs.)

Readers' response

1 How do you think the readers will answer the question or solve the problem after reading this report?
2 What information should the writer add, delete, or rearrange to ensure that readers will respond the way the writer wants them to?
3 What sections or paragraphs should the writer add, delete, or rearrange to ensure that readers will respond the way the writer wants them to?

Graphic elements

1 If the writer used graphic elements in this test draft, why do you think the writer used them and how did the writer integrate them into or along

with text? Do you think it is necessary to use graphic elements? Why or why not?

WRITER AND READER REVIEWS

Writer Review of a Test Draft of a Proposal

Problem or need

1 What is the problem this proposal sets out to solve or the need that it establishes?

Readers and purposes

1 Who are my readers? What do I know about their interest in and motivation for reading this report? (Recall the "Checklist of Questions Writers Need to Ask" in Chapter 1.)

Strategies for arrangement

1 Trace the strategies for arrangement that you used in this test draft by filling out the following descriptive outline:

Section 1 or Paragraph 1

What does it do (e.g., identifies the problem or establishes a need)?
What does it say (e.g., "Because population growth is expected to double by 1999, the township must consider alternative ways of disposing of waste")?

Section 2 or Paragraph 2

What does it do?
What does it say?

Section 3 or Paragraph 3

What does it do?
What does it say?

Section 4 or Paragraph 4

What does it do?
What does it say?
(Continue using the outline if you have more sections or paragraphs.)

Readers' response

1 How do I think my readers will respond to what I have proposed after reading my proposal?
2 What kinds of appeals have I used to persuade my readers to respond to my proposal? What are examples of these appeals?
3 What information should I add, delete, or rearrange to ensure that readers will respond the way I want them to?
4 What sections or paragraphs should I add, delete, or rearrange to ensure that readers will respond the way I want them to?
5 If I think my readers might be initially against the plan I am proposing, what have I done to encourage them to be more receptive?

Graphic elements

1 If I have used graphic elements in this test draft, why did I use them and how did I integrate them into or along with the text?

WRITER AND READER REVIEWS
Reader Review of a Test Draft of a Proposal

Problem or need

1 What is the problem this proposal sets out to solve or the need that it establishes?

Readers and purpose

1 Who are the readers? What do you know about their interest in and motivation for reading this report? (Recall the ''Checklist of Questions Writers Need to Ask'' in Chapter 1.)
2 How do you think the readers will solve the problem or respond to the need before reading the proposal?

3　Besides the primary purpose of persuading, what are the writer's secondary purposes? (To inform, to document, to instruct, to explore?)

Strategies for arrangement

1　Trace the strategies for arrangement that the writer used in this test draft by filling out the following descriptive outline:

Section 1 or Paragraph 1

What does it do (e.g., identifies the problem or establishes a need)?
What does it say (e.g., "Because population growth is expected to double by 1999, the township must consider alternative ways of disposing of waste")?

Section 2 or Paragraph 2

What does it do?
What does it say?

Section 3 or Paragraph 3

What does it do?
What does it say?

Section 4 or Paragraph 4

What does it do?
What does it say?
(Continue using the outline if the writer has more sections or paragraphs.)

Readers' response

1　Now that you have read the test draft, how do you think the readers will respond to what the writer has proposed?
2　What kinds of appeals has the writer used to persuade the readers to respond to the proposal? What are examples of these appeals?
3　What information should the writer add, delete, or rearrange to ensure that readers will respond the way the writer wants them to?

4   What sections or paragraphs should the writer add, delete, or rearrange
    to ensure that readers will respond the way the writer wants them to?
5   If you think the readers might be initially against the plan being proposed,
    what has the writer done to encourage them to be more receptive?

Graphic elements

1   If the writer used graphic elements in this test draft, why do you think
    the writer used them and how did the writer integrate them into or along
    with text? Do you think it is necessary to use graphic elements? Why or
    why not?

CHAPTER
14

A WRITER AT WORK: A CASE STUDY OF COMPOSING A PROPOSAL

PART 1: IDENTIFYING THE PROBLEM

Mimi Seyfert, a part-time continuing education student, was given a class assignment to write a proposal that would cause a change in an organization she was familiar with. Seyfert worked on campus several hours a week, but she had no access to business or corporate organizations. However, she did have a child enrolled in an elementary school, and she was a board member of that school's Organization of Parents and Teachers (OPT). She had been thinking of several ideas for changes she would like to see in the school.

Specifically, Seyfert wanted to convince the principal to change his mind about closing the student-run school store. She believed that with the help of an OPT board committee, she could effect this change in spite of the principal's initial opposition. If she handled this proposal well, Seyfert believed that she could develop a good working relationship with the principal. If she did, she could depend on that relationship to help her enact some of her other ideas.

What follows is a representation of how Mimi Seyfert put her proposal together from her initial thinking to her finished document.

Background

In previous years about eighteen fifth graders were chosen to work in the Franklin Elementary School Store. The store was open three mornings a week before classes started and three afternoons after school. The inventory included various school supplies that students needed to purchase. These supplies included notebooks, pencils, pens, art supplies such as posterboards, and music supplies such as clarinet reeds and violin strings. The store also stocked sweatshirts and T-shirts with the school logo.

Although the children operated the store themselves, serving as sales clerks and accountants, the school secretary was responsible for overseeing them. She also had to verify that the amount of cash in the cash box and the amount recorded on the inventory sheet corresponded. The secretary found that the cash box contents and the inventory sheet didn't always tally. She told the principal. He became concerned that the children were learning poor business practices. He also believed that as long as the children knew that their record keeping was inaccurate and that no one was watching them as they worked, some might be tempted to help themselves to the supplies. In addition, the principal didn't want the school secretary or any other member of the school staff to take on the responsibility of monitoring the children as they worked. Doing so would take away time from the other responsibilities school personnel were being paid to do. For these reasons, the principal decided not to reopen the school store in September.

PART 2: GETTING STARTED

Representing the Problem

Seyfert represented the problem she was working on in the following way:

WHAT IS MY GOAL?
　　To persuade the principal to reopen the school store.
WHERE AM I NOW?
　　The principal announced that the school store would no longer operate.
WHAT WILL I DO TO MEET MY GOAL?
　　Write a proposal to convince the principal to reopen the school store.
　　To write the proposal, I will need to:
　　　1 Investigate the reasons the school store wasn't operating successfully
　　　2 Survey other schools for information about their school stores
　　　3 Enlist support among parents for reopening the store
　　　4 Develop operating procedures (1) that fifth graders can follow with little difficulty and (2) that will teach good business practices
　　　5 Develop an educational rationale for maintaining the store

WHAT MIGHT RESTRICT ME FROM MEETING MY GOAL?

1   Not enough time. School has just opened and the store should be operating by the first week in October.

2   Not enough help from others. Will teachers and other parents help with researching and writing the proposal?

Anticipating the Reader's Point of View

After writing down what she had to do to meet her goal, Seyfert then thought about how her proposal reader, the school principal, would be likely to respond to her suggestion. She realized that if she hoped to change the principal's mind, she would first need to understand his thinking.

First, she thought about the principal's *knowledge* of the issue:

> Let's see, George Haley already knows the school store is closed. What he doesn't yet know, though, is how everyone else—the parents, the teachers, and the students—feels about his decision to close the school store. This is new information to him. Besides supplying Haley with this new information, I will also need to counter the negative information the secretary has given him about the poor operating procedures. I will need to let him know *how* the store can work better.

Seyfert also thought about what the principal's *motivation* would be for reading her proposal. She surmised that his motivation would be guided mostly by his previous negative experiences with the school store:

> Haley might regard my proposal as another bothersome distraction from something more important that he has to do. After all, he's working under deadlines, too. Why should he pay attention to my proposal after he's already made up his mind? I have to assume that Haley doesn't want to spend more time on this issue, so I will have to compose a proposal that is both brief and convincing from his point of view. He has to be able to determine in just a couple of minutes that the store is valuable to the children and that it can operate with little or no inconvenience to him or the staff.
>
> Just *saying* how much the parents would like to see the store reopened isn't enough. I'll need to *show* him what the advantages of reopening the store are. I can get other parents and interested teachers to help me brainstorm a list of advantages. That way others will have an investment in this project too. Also I think I'll have a better chance of motivating Haley to accept my proposal if I smooth the way first by casually mentioning to him that some of the children and parents are disappointed that the store has been closed.

Finally, Seyfert thought about the *use* George Haley would make of her proposal:

Well, at worst, he'll toss it in the waste paper basket. But I really don't think he will because it's to his advantage to maintain good relationships with the parents. In the past he's listened to parents' concerns. But he probably won't be the only one making use of my proposal. He'll probably show our suggestions for reorganizing the store to the school secretary since she'll have to be involved in some way. That means I'll have to think about how to involve her in the procedures. Also, I'll have to represent her in a positive way in this proposal. I doubt Haley will have to show this report to any one else in the school district since he has authority over this issue in his building. He may keep the report on file, though, as a reference. And he may duplicate the operating procedures for the secretary and others to refer to.

Developing a Work Plan

To help her break down the process of writing the proposal into smaller steps and to estimate how much time she could allow for each step, Seyfert sketched a work plan (Figure 14-1). She came up with a week-by-week schedule. She tried to space the various steps to allow herself enough time to introduce the idea of reopening the school store to members of the school community. She wanted them to feel they had been consulted along the way. She also wanted to allow herself enough time to draft and revise her proposal, especially considering that she was working part-time and taking other courses while working on this project.

As Seyfert thought about what she had to do, she realized that writing a proposal involves writing more documents than just the proposal itself. She needed to compose several memos and announcements to parents and teachers to gather information and keep them posted. She would also have to develop a survey to find out what other schools were doing. In addition, her professor, like a supervisor at work, required her to turn in a progress report.

Seyfert discovered that reports and proposals are like icebergs. The finished document is like the peak of ice that rises above the water's surface. Readers, like travelers on ships, see only that peak. However, a pyramid of papers lies beneath the surface. Writers like Mimi Seyfert need to figure out how to allow enough time for drafting not only the final proposal, but also the pyramid of memos and letters that precede the final copy. A work plan helps a writer coordinate all that writing and reach the surface.

PART 3: GATHERING INFORMATION

Interviews, Meetings, and Observations

To develop her proposal, Seyfert needed to understand the school store's previous operations thoroughly. She was aware of its general operations since she helped

Work Plan - 3 Weeks

1st week
- bring up issue of school store at
  OPT board meeting
- find volunteers
  to contribute ideas / draw up proposal
- talk to Haley
- find out what last yr's problems were
- Write summary of these problems
- call meeting of volunteers / send memo

2nd week
- meet w/ volunteers / brainstorm solutions
- plan proposal
- talk / write to teachers
- do telephone survey of other schools
- draft proposal
- write progress report
- show draft to volunteers

3rd Week
- peer review of draft in class
- revised proposal / conf. w/ inst.
- type + proofread proposal / get help
- give proposal to Haley

Figure 14-1   Seyfert's first work plan.
This plan helped the writer anticipate and sequence the work of writing her proposal by her deadline. Compare this work plan with the one she revised three weeks later (Figure 14-6).

set up the store and purchase its inventory last year. She had also observed the children at work, which enabled her to draw some conclusions about their attitudes toward their jobs and ability to follow the procedures that had been outlined for them. However, Seyfert knew that she needed to rely on more than a few random observations. She also needed to match those observations against the secretary's perceptions and the information in last year's account books.

Seyfert decided to talk to the secretary, Mrs. Creighton, and look at the books before proceeding. But even before she talked to the secretary, she jotted down notes on her own observations about the school store (Figure 14-2). That way she could later compare them to the secretary's account. She also wrote down the questions she wanted to ask the secretary (Figure 14-3).

After interviewing the secretary, Seyfert understood the difficulties of being responsible for the school store. She noted to herself that the new procedures should make little or no demands on Mrs. Creighton.

Seyfert then wrote a memo summarizing the information she found. She sent this memo to the parents who volunteered to help reopen the store at the OPT board meeting. Seyfert sent this memo to those parents before they met to brainstorm ideas for reorganizing the store and writing the proposal.

She wrote this memo for two main reasons. First, she wanted everyone involved to have accurate information about past procedures. She also wanted the memo to serve as a springboard for the parents' thinking before they attended the meeting. Seyfert found that when people come to meetings prepared with some ideas, they can accomplish more in a shorter time.

Seyfert's memo appears in Figure 14-4. It represents an important part of her process of gathering and communicating information. When you read her final

Problems/Observations
- not enough $ in cash box
- accountants seemed to have trouble following inventory sheet
- students seemed bored
- " " crowded--space too small for 3 children
- children attached little importance to job
  - no reward at end of year

Figure 14-2 Seyfert's notes.
The writer wrote down her observations about the problems children encountered while working in the school store. She incorporated these notes into the memo she later sent to parents on her committee. (See Figure 14-4.)

ask the secretary :

1) How much time she can spend on
   school store business M, W, F —
2) If she, or anyone taught children
   how to use adding machine
3) If she'd be willing to simply
   get the cash box from the
   safe + put it back each time
4) If she sees any advantages in
   having a school store
5) Does she have any suggestions
   about how store should be run??

Figure 14-3   Interview questions.
Seyfert jotted down the questions she wanted to ask the school secretary about the school store. The writer wrote them to make sure she came away with all the information she needed. Would you ask other questions in this case? What do you think the value of asking numbers 4 and 5 might be?

proposal, notice how she made use of this preliminary writing even though the memo itself never surfaces in the proposal she eventually gave to the principal.

```
                                September 15, 1985


TO:    School Store Advisory Committee
FROM:  Mimi Seyfert, Chairwoman
RE:    Brainstorming Session 9/19/85


First of all, thank you for volunteering to help find a way

to reopen the school store.  We will meet in the Conference

Room at 9:30 A.M. on Thursday, September 19.
```

To help you understand the operational problems of the school
store, I wrote and attached a summary of the store's procedures, problems, and possible causes of those problems. I've
added my suggestions for possible solutions. I think our
discussion will go better if we have this information in front
of us.

The most important part of the attached information sheet is
the section called ''Possible Solutions--Your Thoughts.''
Please think about possible solutions so we can become a
thriving business once more. If our stock doesn't go up on
Wall Street, at least our children can feel a sense of pride
and responsibility in learning how to run the store.

<u>SEE</u> <u>YOU</u> <u>ON</u> <u>THURSDAY</u>, SEPTEMBER <u>19</u> <u>AT</u> <u>9:30</u> <u>A.M.</u>

INFORMATION SHEET ON FRANKLIN ELEMENTARY SCHOOL STORE

Summary of Start-up Procedures: Eighteen fifth graders chosen as store workers.
Principal assigned 3 students to each shift, Monday, Wednesday, or Friday A.M. or P.M.
Principal chose manager and assistant manager; met with them to tell them their responsibility was to let the parent coordinator know when stock is low.

Summary of Operating Procedures: Workers on each shift ask school secretary for cash box with $5.00 change and for key to store.
They unlock the store.
One worker (the ''accountant'') sits at desk with inventory sheet and adding machine.
Two other workers (''sales clerks'') serve customers.
Sales clerks tell accountant what has been sold and gives him or her the customers' money.
Accountant marks sale on inventory sheet and gives change to sales clerk.
Accountant totals inventory sheet before closing.
Accountant counts money in cash box and takes it and the inventory sheet to the school secretary.
Secretary checks cash box. She should find $5.00 more in cash box than inventory sheet indicates has been sold.

The Problem: Money in the cash box and inventory sheet do not tally. The secretary tells the principal, who is worried about having students (1) learn bad business practices, (2) do inaccurate calculations, and (3) possibly walk off with supplies.

Possible Causes of the Problem: Crowded inventory sheets. (Accountant's eye must skim the front and back of a single-spaced $8\frac{1}{2} \times 11$ inch sheet to find item being purchased.)
Too much inventory to keep track of at once.
Space too small for three workers. (Store occupies a closet.)
No instruction given on use of adding machine.
Boredom sets in as year progresses.
Not enough prestige assigned to job.
No reward or recognition at end of year.

Conclusion: The principal is convinced that the only possible solution is a completely parent-supervised operation.

POSSIBLE SOLUTIONS

MY THOUGHTS: *Assign two workers (sales clerks) per shift.
*Eliminate accountant.
*Meet with students to explain and rehearse operating procedures and use of adding machine.
*Give sales clerks responsibility for entire transaction:
(1) Give customer merchandise
(2) Write up sales slip
(3) Take money and give change
(4) Put sales slip in cash box
(5) Total sales slips and cash box receipts
*Send letters of selection to students:
"Congratulations, you have been selected . . . "
*Open store two days a week.
*Choose students whose strength is math.
*Plan reward for end of year: ice cream party???

YOUR THOUGHTS:

Figure 14-4   Seyfert's memo to the parents who volunteered to help her reopen the school store.

Surveys and Questionnaires

Besides gathering information about the Franklin Elementary School Store, Seyfert also wanted to find out whether other schools had similar operations. If so, she wanted to understand them and present this information to the parents on her committee. She decided the fastest way to gather this information was by telephoning other schools.

Seyfert drafted and typed a list of questions she thought would give her the information she needed (Figure 14-5). She made copies of this list so that she could easily fill in the answers others gave her over the phone. Having readable and organized copies of these responses would help her by facilitating the job of tallying and evaluating the responses. It would also provide her with readable information she could show to others, such as the parent volunteers, or which she could include in the appendix of her finished proposal. Seyfert realized that demonstrating to others that she proceeded in a systematic way would lend authority to her arguments and make her proposal more convincing.

She looked up the names and phone numbers of fourteen public and private elementary schools in her area. When she called each one, she identified herself and her reason for calling. She then asked to speak to the person who could give her the information she needed. Sometimes she had to call back or wait for someone to return her call.

PART 4: EVALUATING PROGRESS
Assessing the Information

Seyfert had four sources of information to assess: the results of the telephone survey you just saw, her notes from her interview with the school secretary, her notes from reviewing last year's account books, and her notes from the meeting with the parents on her OPT committee. The question on her mind was, "Do I have enough information and workable strategies to begin writing this proposal, or should I consult other sources?"

Her meeting with the parent volunteers was useful. They agreed on what needed to be changed, and they came up with a new set of procedures. Some of these included Seyfert's original ideas, such as eliminating the accountant and putting two rather than three students on each shift. They disagreed with her, however, on the hours of operation; they preferred to keep the store open three days a week as it had been last year. They also elected to install a new crew of students at midyear to keep boredom from setting in. The group applauded the idea of writing letters of congratulations to the selected students and rewarding them at the end of the year.

When the meeting ended, Seyfert reviewed the notes she took and filled in some details she didn't take down during the meeting. She wanted to write down all the information she needed while it was still fresh in her mind. These notes formed the preliminary writing for the section entitled "The New System," which you will see later in the draft of her proposal (Figure 14-11).

SURVEY OF ELEMENTARY SCHOOL STORES

Name of School _____

Location _____

Person I Spoke to _____ Position _____

1.　Does your school operate a school store?
　　If yes,

2.　Who is in charge?
　　What are the specific responsibilities?

3.　What role, if any, do students have in running the store?

4.　When is it open?

5.　What does the inventory include?

6.　What are the benefits of operating a school store?

Figure 14-5　A telephone survey.
Explain why you think these questions would or would not be useful if they were mailed
to the respondents.

　　You have already seen how Seyfert made use of the notes she took during
her talk with the secretary when she wrote the memo to the OPT committee (Figure
14-4). After her meeting with those parents, she concluded that she didn't need
any more information from the secretary. However, she decided that the next time
she saw the principal, she would mention that her committee had worked out a
plan for running the store without the secretary's services.

Only the survey results troubled her. Of the fourteen schools she called, only five had school stores. Four of those were run by employees of the school. The one school store that did use student help was open only three times during the school year: at the beginning of each semester and right before the winter holiday, when stock included gifts that the children could purchase for their families and friends. These were not results to rest any claims on.

Seyfert considered calling more schools, figuring she'd probably find some more with stores. But as she was typing a draft of the progress report her professor required, something happened. As she wrote the words "I plan to call more schools" and looked at those words sitting on the page, she recognized the futility of carrying out that plan. Finding even two or three more schools with stores would hardly compel the principal to believe that operating a school store was essential.

Instead, she realized that she could use this seemingly negative information in a positive way. She could say that she found that only a few schools had discovered the convenience of operating a store on site. Furthermore, not one of them was regularly offering students the opportunity to develop the personal skills and responsibility that running a school store could provide. She could say that keeping the school store open would be a unique feature of Franklin Elementary School, one that the principal could point to with pride.

Having made that decision about the information she had generated, Seyfert listed other things she would need to do before she could draft her proposal. This list (Figure 14-6) was incorporated into the progress report she submitted to her instructor.

I need to:
  — find 6 volunteers + 2 or 3 substitutes
        to supervise the school store
  — Write letter to 5th grade teachers
        asking for the names of
        12 students
  — Make appointment w/inst. at
        about wrtg. draft
  — Write "publicity" to parents + students

Figure 14-6   Revision of Seyfert's original work plan.
Seyfert wrote this list during the third week of her project, when she realized she needed more time than she anticipated to complete her proposal. She incorporated this list into the progress report she turned in to her instructor.

Evaluating the Work Plan

Before Seyfert wrote the final draft of that memo, however, she evaluated her progress by checking what she had done and what she still needed to do against her original work plan. She discovered that she needed more time than she origi-

---

MEMORANDUM

TO: Dr. Maki

FROM: Mimi Seyfert

DATE: October 9, 1985

RE: Progress Report on Proposal to Reopen School Store

Specific Problem

I am proposing to reopen the Franklin Elementary School Store by the end of this month. Due to bookkeeping errors and problems supervising the students who ran the store, the principal decided not to reopen it this September. Closing the store means that fifth graders who were not chosen to be on the student government or the safety patrol will have no special area of responsibility in their last year of elementary school.

Reasons and Benefits of Solving This Problem

As last year's School Store Chairwoman—appointed by OPT (Organization of Parents and Teachers)—I feel responsible for the store's demise. The group of parents and teachers that I represent supports the presence of a school store for several reasons: (1) it is a convenience for the children who use it; (2) it is a convenience for their parents, especially those who work and have less time for shopping trips to purchase art, music, and other supplies children regularly need; (3) it offers an activity that teaches responsibility and builds the confidence of the children who run the store. OPT believes that providing such opportunities is important because graduating fifth graders will transfer to a middle school where they are expected to take on new responsibilities. We believe Franklin Elementary has a responsibility to prepare its students for the middle school experience.

Possible Solutions

When I told the principal I was disappointed about his decision to close the school store, he replied, "Submit a proposal to reopen it." That is exactly what I am doing.

Operators

I have taken the following steps so far:
    (1) Met with OPT and recruited volunteers to help me think through our proposal.
    (2) Researched what last year's problems were.
    (3) Brainstormed a new set of operating procedures with the volunteers.
    (4) Taken a telephone survey of other schools to find out if they had stores.

Figure 14-7   Seyfert's progress report to her instructor. (Used by permission from Mimi Seyfert.)

nally anticipated. Why? First, she decided that her finished proposal should include a list of the names of parents who volunteered to assist the children on each shift. Doing so, she figured, would be more likely to convince the principal that the revised operating procedures were ready to go into effect. However, she would need more time to recruit these parents. Seyfert included her new target dates in her progress report (Figure 14-7).

Future Plans and Timetable

I have found my original workplan and timetable too optimistic. I tried to complete this project ahead of your due date so that we could begin operating the store by the first week in October. I now see that it's better to take an extra two or three weeks. It's better to have the school open later in the fall than not at all. I still need to:

(1) Find six volunteers and two or three substitutes to supervise the school store (by 10/25).
(2) Write letters to the fifth grade teachers asking them to recommend 12 students to work in the store during the first half of the year (by 10/14).
(3) Set up a conference with you to discuss the draft I'm writing (by 10/14).
(4) Set up peer review of draft (by 10/14).
(5) Write "publicity" letter to parents and students for possible inclusion in the appendix of the proposal (by 10/25).
(6) Revise draft (by 10/25).
(7) Give Haley finished proposal (by 10/27).

I had considered redoing my telephone survey since the results were not favorable, but I have decided against that idea. I think my argument can rest on how useful the store is to FES. When I have my conference with you, I would like to discuss what documents, if any, I should include in an appendix.

Figure 14-7 (Cont.)

PART 5: WRITING AND REVISING DRAFTS

Testing Ways to Organize Information

When Seyfert sat down to write a draft of her proposal, she had already accumulated many documents that would be useful to her. Her various memos, summaries, brainstormings, lists, and surveys provided her with the preliminary writing for her draft. In other words, she didn't sit down with a blank page and just a few notes to refer to, as a letter writer might. Instead, she had most of the content of her report in hand. Her major job was figuring out how to organize the information in a clear and rhetorically effective way.

She looked back on her class notes to see whether any of the patterns for organizing a proposal that her instructor suggested would be appropriate for her use. Most of them were too formal to suit the circumstances of her proposal to the principal. Yet she found one pattern that she could use with a little modification. This pattern describes what to do in each section of the proposal:

1   Give the background of the problem
2   State the objectives and scope of the proposal
3   Explain the procedures used to research it
4   Summarize the findings
5   Summarize the recommendations
6   State the benefits of accepting the recommendations

Seyfert decided that the first two sections were irrelevant since the principal was aware that the store was closed and Seyfert and others wanted it opened. She further decided that whatever brief background and objectives statements she needed to make could appear in her memo of transmittal. She realized that she would need to summarize her findings about why the store did not succeed last year and her recommendations for reorganizing it. Seyfert thought about making a side-by-side comparison of the old system and the new one. She also thought that ending with the benefits of reopening the store was an excellent strategy.

Taking her lead from the proposal pattern she found, she then listed what she needed to *do* in her proposal. She came up with the following list:

1   Make request
2   State rationale for keeping the store
3   List criteria for changes
4   Give background on problems of operating store

5   Summarize proposed operating procedures
6   Attach names of parent volunteers
7   Convey approval of fifth-grade teachers
8   State benefits to be gained

After Seyfert wrote this list, she realized that it was more useful as a checklist to make sure that she did everything she needed to do to make her appeal effective than as a prediction of her final pattern of organization. Seyfert knew from her previous experiences that sometimes a better plan of organization than her original one came to her while she was writing. She also knew that peer reviewers would give their opinions about how well her pattern of organization succeeded.

Seyfert felt no obligation to use the list she jotted down as a script for writing her draft. That is, she didn't begin composing her draft by writing out her request, the first point on her list, and then drafting each of the eight sections in sequence. Instead she began with something familiar, something she had written about before—a process description of how the store operated last year. Seyfert continued to work her way up and down the list until she wrote all the parts she needed. As she wrote one part, she would decide which would be the most productive section to work on next. For example, as she was writing her description of the old system, her plans for the new one echoed in her head. She wrote them next. She began each new section on a separate piece of paper so that she could rearrange the parts, if she wanted to.

By writing just one section at a time, Seyfert used a divide-and-conquer strategy to get through a first draft. That is, by breaking her proposal into sections and then writing just one section at a time, Seyfert was able to make the job look less ominous. Each time she finished a section, she felt a sense of accomplishment. She could see herself moving toward the end of the draft, step by step.

Reading and Reviewing the Test Draft

Usually before going on to the next part, Seyfert would read over what she had written. She would do this several times with an eye for making changes. The example in Figure 14-8 shows her first revision of a paragraph summarizing the operating procedures used the previous year.

One of the sections Seyfert puzzled over was the conclusion, in which she would state the benefits of accepting her proposal. She knew the last section had to be a strong section, in which the advantages of reopening the school store according to her recommendations would compel the reader. She had to make Mr. Haley see at a glance that her plan was valuable and workable. Since she learned that bulleting information can make it easier to read, she thought she would present the benefits of reopening the store in a list. That way, she figured, the principal

Procedures

Last year, 1982-3, the school store gave 18 children, chosen by their fifth grade teachers, the responsibility of working as clerks in the store. Each clerk worked a ten-minute shift, once a week, either before school or after school. Each shift was a three-student team. Before each shift the team would pick up the cash box from Mrs. Creighton. The students were instructed on the store's operations, and they signed up for shifts at a meeting with the Principal and the School Store Chairperson at the beginning of the school year.

* Add: Two students (clerks) stood at the counter filling orders + taking \$. Another student (bookkeeper) sat at a desk with a sales sheet tracking items sold + w/a cash box making change. At the end of the shift the bookkeeper tallied the sales sheet + the cash box. Five \$ in change remained in the cash box. The additional \$ was kept for a deposit. All the \$ went back to the school safe at the end of the shift.

Figure 14-8   First draft of a paragraph with revisions.
What kind of revisions did Seyfert make in her paragraph? Do you think they were appropriate at this point in the composing process? Why or why not? Would you recommend any other changes at this point or before she gives her proposal to the principal?

could quickly see the reasonableness of her plan. Seyfert wrote the list in Figure 14-9. She didn't make any changes in it after she read it over. Look at Figure 14-9 to see the results of her decision to present the conclusion in the form of a list.

<u>Benefits</u>

- A good example of how a small business works
- More thorough instruction so children will know what is expected of them
- Twelve 5th graders given the chance to have a position with responsiblity
- A convenient spot for school supplies, especially music supplies
- No reponsibility on part of administration for running store
- Each grade will be familiarized with inventory and prices in the store

Figure 14-9   The first draft of the conclusion.
If you reviewed Seyfert's draft, what would you say about her conclusion? What are its strengths? What changes would you recommend? Tell her what you think about the content, the format for presenting it, its visual and verbal clarity, and its persuasiveness. Will the conclusion motivate the principal to act in Seyfert's favor? Why or why not?

Reviewing and Revising a Completed Draft

Knowing when to stop

Seyfert finished writing all the sections she decided her proposal needed. Before she put them aside, she reread them essentially for content. To do so, she kept asking herself, "Have I written everything my reader needs to know here?" As she reread, she also tested her order of presenting that information by asking, "Does it make sense to have this section following that one?" By the time she finished reviewing the whole draft, she found she couldn't see what she had written with fresh eyes.

To help her get a better picture of what she had written, she put her draft aside for a day. When she picked up her draft again, she began a formal review process consisting of two parts. First she wrote a self-analysis of her draft by using the Writer Review form that her instructor gave her. The review form helped her analyze her work in a systematic way. After completing her review, she gave her draft and the questions she had about it to readers for their systematic review (See Chapter 13, pp. 324–327 for Writer and Reader Reviews).

Getting the most from the review process

Analyzing your own draft in a systematic way is actually the first step in the reader review process. Writers can generally gain more insight from what someone else has to say about their writing if they have given it some serious thought first.

Part of the writer's own review process involves writing a descriptive outline of the draft. Interestingly, writing an outline *after* writing a draft can be more useful than writing one before composing the draft. Writing a draft can be like learning to perform ballet or some other complicated dance, without using a mirror. You can learn the right movements, but you can't see how they look to an audience. Reviewing your own draft is like holding up a mirror to what you have done. It allows you to see your work as others will.

When you're ready to give your draft to readers for their review, we suggest that you don't show them your own outline of your draft. If you do, you might influence their reading of your work in progress. The objective of this part of the review procedure is to see what your readers can understand on their own. Then you can compare what you think you said with what your readers think they read.

You can benefit tremendously from this process if you take some time to discuss any differences you find between your outline and your readers'. You may discover that a particular reader was off base at some point, or you may find out that you need to rewrite particular sections of your report. Writing and comparing descriptive outlines gives you a chance to judge how adequately your message is coming across to readers. If your descriptive outlines match each other, your paper most likely says what you think it does. Your outline will also help you write the abstract of your report or proposal.

In addition to writing a descriptive outline, you can help yourself by writing down questions you have about particular parts of a draft. For example, Seyfert asked her readers: "Do you get a clear picture of how the school store should operate this year from my description on page 5?" Questions such as these will help you see what you need to work on.

You can also show these questions to your draft readers to help them focus on the aspects of the draft that you need help with. Posing clear and specific questions that point to a page or paragraph in your paper can elicit particularly useful responses from draft readers, responses you can use as you revise. Such questions also help your readers avoid giving you such general comments as, "This paper doesn't flow." Or "I think you write clearly." Comments like those simply don't help you revise.

Whatever the results of the draft review process are, however, be prepared to make your own decisions about how to proceed next. In this situation, as in others you encounter in your lives, don't feel compelled to take someone else's advice. Instead, consider others' suggestions with an open mind and then decide which ones to follow.

PART 6: WRITING THE FINAL DRAFT

So far you have seen how Seyfert planned, researched, and drafted some sections of her proposal. Next you will see the first connected draft of the proposal. The draft consists of two parts: a transmittal memo to the principal (Figure 14-10) and the body of the proposal (Figure 14-11).

As you read the draft, notice the ways Seyfert made use of her preliminary writing by incorporating it into the memo and proposal. Also think about how the draft could be improved to better suit its readers and its purpose. After you've

MEMORANDUM

TO: Mr. George Haley, Principal, Franklin Elementary

FROM: Mimi Seyfert, Chairwoman, OPT School Store Committee

DATE: October 27, 1985

SUBJECT: OPT Proposal for Reopening the School Store

In the beginning of September, we discussed the possibility of reopening the school store. We offer you the attached proposal in response to your request for specific information about how the store could operate if it were reopened.

A committee of five parents met to research and recommend procedures for operating the store. The procedures we recommend should eliminate the problems we had last year because the new procedures were drawn up to meet the following criteria:

    (1) to ensure accuracy in making and recording cash transactions
    (2) to free Mrs. Creighton from responsibility for checking cash receipts and records
    (3) to reduce the chances that students will become bored or careless as they carry out their responsibilities.

Our proposal explains why the store ran into some problems last year and how we plan to eliminate them this time. The fifth grade teachers are 100% behind this plan and will recommend students to work in the store as soon as you give them the okay.

The OPT Committee, the teachers, and many students hope the school store will become a thriving business this year. The store gives a group of fifth graders who have not been chosen for the Safety Patrol or the student government a chance to learn responsibility and to make an important contribution to their school during their last year here. The store also offers all the children the convenience and fun of purchasing necessary school supplies while attending school. In our research we discovered that Franklin elementary is one of only two schools in this area that offers children these opportunities.

With your approval, we will soon open our doors for business.

Figure 14-10   Seyfert's transmittal memo. (Used by permission from Mimi Seyfert.) Memos like this one introduce a report orproposal to the primary readers.

done that, write a Reader Review of the draft using the Review form in Chapter 13. Compare your review with at least two others written by members of your class. On the basis of those reviews, decide how best to revise Seyfert's draft. Then write another draft, perhaps the final version.

As you revise, imagine that you are in Seyfert's place. You have all the

SUMMARY

We request that the Franklin Elementary School Store be reopened to promote pride and responsibility in fifth grade workers, and to offer fun and a convenient source of supplies for the children. To help the store run more smoothly, we intend

— to get commitments from six mothers to be School Store Aides each year. Each mother would supervise one shift, freeing the school secretary for administration. Six aides would enable the store to be open six shifts: Monday, Wednesday and Friday, in the morning and in the afternoon;

— to have a Chairperson to coordinate operation, make deposits and order supplies; and

— to have an informative meeting for students and aides to explain the operation of the school store.

We would like to operate the store out of the closet opposite the Office as we did last year.

INTRODUCTION:

The school store is closed this year because of problems it caused last year. We are excited about a new plan for its operation that will enable us to open it again and help it to run more smoothly. Children are inquiring about why the store is closed this year. Fifth graders are anxious to be a part of it. Teachers indicate that the school store affords another area of responsibility for those children whose self-esteem is low because they have not been chosen to be safeties or student-government representatives.

A study of the old system of running the store and the new proposed system of running the store helps highlight the problems from last year and the advantages for this year.

1

Figure 14-11 A complete draft of the proposal.

information and explanations of the context of this writing that you need in order to write a final copy.

When you have finished, compare your proposal with others written by members of your class. Then discuss and defend your reasons for writing the final draft as you did.

THE OLD SYSTEM

Last year, 1984-5, the school store gave 18 children, chosen by their fifth grade teachers, the responsibility of working as clerks in the store. The students were instructed on the store's operation, and signed up for shifts at a meeting with the Principal and the School Store Chairperson at the beginning of the school year. Each clerk worked a ten-minute shift, once a week, either before school or after school. Each shift was composed of three students. Before each shift this team would pick up the cash box from the school secretary.

While selling, two students stood at the counter filling orders and taking money. Another student sat at a desk with a sales sheet tracking items sold and with a cash box making change. At the end of the shift, the student in charge of the money tallied the sales sheet and the cash box. Five dollars in various change remained in the cash box for the next shift. The additional money was kept for a deposit. All the money went back to the office at the end of the shift.

Problems with the Old System:

- We found money taken in and inventory sold was not the same. This meant the children were not doing the math correctly. Sometimes the total was off by $4.00. This is a negative experience for them because they know they are doing it wrong.

- We found the school secretary spent too much time with the clerks of the store and their financial problems. She neglected other administrative duties.

- We found instruction on the store's operation was inadequate. For example, in December I found the children did not know how to use the adding machine.

- We found boredom setting in as the year progressed and horseplay going on during shift.

THE NEW SYSTEM

Under our new plans, the school store will give 32 children, chosen by their fifth grade teachers, the responsibility of working as clerks or representatives. School store clerks will be instructed on the store's operation, and will sign up for shifts at a meeting with the Principal, the School Store Chairperson and the Aides just before we open the store. School store representatives will be instructed on their duties and given inventory sheets for distribution at this meeting as well. Each clerk will work a ten-minute shift, once a week, either before or after school on Monday, Wednesday or Friday. Each shift will be a two-student team. Before each shift the team will pick up the cash box from the school secretary.

2

Figure 14-11   (Cont.)

While selling, each clerk will have an inventory sheet on a clipboard. Each clerk will be responsible for taking the customer's order, filling it, checking off the item sold on the inventory sheet, collecting the money and making changes when necessary. In other words, each clerk will be responsible for an entire transaction. This method will make the tallying more accurate. At the end of the shift, the Aide will help the students tally their totals with the money collected in the cash box. Five dollars in various change will remain in the cash box for the next shift. The additional money will be set aside in the office for a deposit. All the money will go back to the office at the end of the shift.

The new system creates a position: school store representative. After safeties and student government representatives have been chosen in the fifth grade, we find much disappointment and loss of self-esteem among those not chosen for one of these special jobs. Therefore, we would like to have as many children work for the school store as possible. With this in mind, we propose a new position of responsibility: the school store representative.

There would be one representative from each fifth grade section (four students altogether) whose job it would be:

- to acquaint his or her section and all sections of one other grade with the school store inventory; and

- to post inventory and price list in these homerooms so children will have a way to find out what is available in the store and the cost of all items.

> For example: Susie is the representative for 5A. She is responsible for acquainting 5A and all sections of first grade about the supplies available in the store. She will post the inventory list, with prices, in the various homerooms.

Advantages of the New System:

- The School Store Aide will help tally the inventory sold and the money taken in. This will result in correct totals. The children will have the positive experience of a good job being done. We will secure the Aides with the help of a flyer taken home by the children. Interested people will contact me by phone. An Aide will work one shift for the school year. For example, Mrs. Smith will be responsible for Monday mornings all year (or get a substitute).

3

Figure 14-11   (Cont.)

— The school secretary will spend little time with the school store people. She will give the cash box to the team at the beginning of each shift. At the end of each shift, she will put money to be deposited in a separate envelope and put the cash box and deposit back in the safe. She will not have to worry about any financial problems. She will carry on her administrative duties instead.

— The instruction on the school store's operation will be very important in the initial meeting. We will introduce items to be sold to the students, as well as the inventory sheet so they can familiarize themselves with them. Each child will have a chance to try the adding machine.

— The workers will all change halfway through the year to give other children a chance to work, and to avoid boredom and horseplay.

— The change at midyear and the new job of school store representative will enable more children to work in the store. More students will have a sense of participation and pride to prepare for their jump to the Middle School the following year.

CONCLUSION

Last year the school store did not operate efficiently and it should not be allowed to continue in its old form. However, the idea for a school store is a good one and well worth saving. The new form for the store solves all the problems of last year, and also improves on other aspects of the store. For example, we can now involve 32 children instead of 18.

The children, the teachers, and the parents can all benefit from the reopening of our store as a source of supplies and school spirit.

In this era of cuts in funds for education, we need all that volunteer effort can offer. The volunteer aides will pick up almost all the work the administration was providing last year. This effort will expose the children to the way a little business works and will be a learning experience as well. There's no learning like learning by doing.

4

Figure 14-11   (Cont.)

SECTION SIX:

STRATEGIES FOR WRITING COLLABORATIVELY

CHAPTER 15

WRITING COLLABORATIVELY

STRATEGIES FOR WRITING COLLABORATIVELY

A manager is asked by her supervisor to write a memo to all division heads requesting them to warn their staffs about using the company's postage meter for personal correspondence. The supervisor has learned that some employees have regarded the meter as a fringe benefit. The manager drafts a letter to persuade the division heads to take up this issue with members of their staffs in a way that will get results without offending those who have not made personal use of the meter. She works on the tone of her own letter, trying to sound firm but not harsh. She shows a draft to her supervisor, who likes it but suggests changing a few words that sound too accusatory. After making the changes, the manager gives her draft to her secretary to type.

A team of employees from a state health agency makes a routine visit to a hospital to determine whether its operations conform with state regulations. Each team member has a list of areas to check and an allotted amount of time to complete the inspection. At the end of the inspection period, all team members submit their observation reports to the group. The group members then discuss their findings. Working together they write a draft of their investigative report, one that synthesizes all of their individual reports. The team leader later revises the draft, circulates it among her team for further comments, incorporates their suggestions, and submits it to the home office.

An engineering firm that bids on government contracts has a deadline by which to write a complex competitive proposal. The marketing manager notifies the proposal manager and technical leader about the decision to bid on this particular contract. With the specifications in hand, the proposal manager and technical leader decide on a proposal concept and present it to a team of reviewers. These reviewers suggest a few changes before the proposal concept is sent on to the core team of writers. The members of this team bring together various kinds of expertise in engineering, production, and management. Together they establish the guidelines for their bid, including the products they will offer, the production schedules they will follow, the personnel to assign to the job, and the estimated costs. Their projections are checked by a review team that makes suggestions before sending the proposal to a team of writers assembled from various departments. This team is led by a proposal coordinator, who assists with the editing and production of the final document. Only when a final review team approves the proposal can it be sent to the potential customer.

THE PRACTICE OF COLLABORATIVE WRITING IN ORGANIZATIONS

Rarely do you see an organizational document with a single authorship. As the three scenarios that open this chapter illustrate, writers in organizations practice various forms of collaborative writing, from simple to complex.

Writers can talk about their ideas with co-workers or supervisors before sitting down to compose or dictate. Before sending out final copies, writers also show drafts of letters, memos, and reports to co-workers or supervisors for their comments. In addition, writers frequently give their drafts to a secretary or word processing pool to type final copies. In fact, this form of collaboration is so typical in organizations that it has generated a convention to go with it: typists type both their own initials and the writer's initials in the lower left-hand corner of the final copy of letters and memos. This custom clearly acknowledges one kind of collaboration.

The forms of collaboration illustrated at the beginning of this chapter are more complex. Report or proposal writing usually brings together managers from several departments, specialists with diverse areas of expertise, members of investigative teams, or employees from various supervisory levels of an organizational hierarchy. Reports produced in technical fields require contributions from such diverse specialists within an organization that a project manager is often hired to coordinate a team of writers and keep their work on schedule.

HOW TO SURVIVE THE COLLABORATIVE WRITING PROCESS

As the examples you just read suggest, collaborative writing requires us to manage two complex processes simultaneously: the process of writing and the process of making decisions with others. Since most, if not all, of the writing you are accustomed to doing in school is authored by only one person, you might wonder how you go about writing with others.

Certainly, working in a group is risky. You might believe that you will surrender some freedom to do what you think is best. You might fear that you will lose some control over your own fate. You might even worry that you will do more work than the others and, worse yet, not receive credit for your good ideas or long hours. These concerns are realistic.

Working with others to reach a single goal also challenges some deeply held beliefs. One of these is that important contributions in all fields are made by rugged individuals working alone.

Yet research shows that a group can produce more solutions—and more creative solutions—to most kinds of problems than any of its individual members can while working alone. The process by which this happens is called *synergy*. This process is so powerful that some researchers, including William Ouchi, author of *Theory Z* (1981), and Thomas J. Peters and Robert H. Waterman, Jr., authors of *In Search of Excellence* (1982), have concluded that organizations that regularly depend on small group problem-solving efforts tend to be more stable and productive than those that do not.

To participate successfully in a group, you will find it helps to understand the dynamics of how groups function. This chapter will introduce you to some useful information about group work. In addition, the readings listed at the end of this book lead you to further, more complete sources of information. Observing groups in action and being an active participant in a group yourself provide two additional and powerful ways to understand groups.

Such first-hand experience prepares you to participate simultaneously as a separate person and a member of a group. Through observation and participation, you can learn how and when to propose your own ideas as well as how to encourage others' suggestions. This process depends on excellent communication skills—speaking, writing, and especially listening skills.

Working on a collaborative writing project in this course can help you in all those ways.

Understanding Collaborative Writing Processes

When people collaborate during most or all of the phases of writing a single document, the process of composing that document will depend on numerous variables. These include how well the people know each other, how well they have worked together in the past, the length and complexity of the document, the importance of the document to individual members and to the organization they work in, the technological assistance available to them, the support they feel they are getting from their organization, the deadline, the number of readers with different interests in the document, the writers' individual work habits, their areas of expertise, and their abilities to work as members of a group. With a list like that, you can see why it is difficult to establish a single, predictable process for collaborative writing.

However, when you write with others, you can count on alternating times when you work together with times when you work alone. You will probably find that you will need to spend time in the beginning of the process to define the problem you are working on, to discuss what the document needs to contain, to develop a presentation strategy, to anticipate difficulties, to establish a work plan, and to get to know one another. Going through these steps can save you time in the long run. Poorly planned documents usually take longer to revise. Problems that occur as the deadline nears can be more frustrating for a group to handle than ones it encounters in the early stages of working together.

To give you some idea of how the process of writing collaboratively can be carried out, we list a sequence of steps some groups actually go through on-the-job (Figure 15-1).

Strategies for Writing Collaboratively

As you prepare to work on a collaborative writing project, you can keep the following strategies for survival in mind.

Strategy One: Allow Time to Get Acquainted

When a group first meets, members are usually more concerned about getting to know each other than with working on the problem at hand. This *circling activity*, as it is sometimes called, might seem like a waste of time, yet it is a necessary part of group development: people need to get acquainted before they can work together. Have members introduce themselves to the group, talk about their understanding of the project they are working on, and exchange phone numbers and class schedules. This last step allows participants to continue working outside of class and to set up convenient meeting times and deadlines.

Strategy Two: Draw out Silent Partners

Groups work better when everyone feels included. Groups also benefit from having a variety of ideas and opinions to consider as they make decisions. For those

AN OVERVIEW OF ONE COLLABORATIVE WRITING PROCESS

1. Brainstorming to discover an overall theme or concept, a presentation strategy, and an outline of the contents

2. Delegating authority

3. Researching and writing in isolation
   (Writers each write an individual version of an entire document or section; or they each work on a different section, which will be pooled with sections written by other group members.)

4. Convening for progress meetings to discuss what has been completed and to establish new responsibilities for the next meeting

5. Writing a test draft

6. Reviewing and revising the test draft:

   - sending drafts to specialists within the organization, such as lawyers, who are not members of the writing group
   - further writing in isolation
   - holding progress meetings to review and revise

7. Writing a complete and nearly final draft

8. Reviewing and editing the nearly final draft

9. Reviewing the draft by a third party, that is, someone who is not a member of the writing group

10. Reviewing the effectiveness of the document design

11. Typing and proofreading

12. Evaluating the effectiveness of document based on the action the readers took

Figure 15-1   A collaborative writing strategy.

reasons, you want to encourage any quiet members of your group to speak up. Sometimes you will need to clear the way for your silent partners by restraining the talkative ones who dominate your discussions. To give everyone a chance, you could say, "You've given us several good ideas, Josh. I wonder what Keith is thinking." Or you could begin your meeting by allowing everyone an equal time to speak before going into a freewheeling discussion.

Strategy Three: Allow and Encourage Disagreements

Especially in the beginning of your project, let people air their opinions, especially if they conflict with one another. Disagreeing while you are defining the problem at hand is useful. Such disagreements provide a way to understand what different group members think the group is trying to accomplish. If you disagree with the prevailing opinion, say so in a nonthreatening, matter-of-fact way. That is, avoid directing negative comments toward your co-workers or their ideas. Instead, simply state your idea as an option. You could say, ''Another way we could do that is by . . . .''

Strategy Four: Avoid Settling on Quick and Easy Answers

The first solution you come up with is not always your best. In fact, it is often wise to let a decision, even a strongly agreed on one, sit for a day or two. Then reconvene and discuss it again. Arriving at a decision quickly can mean that members aren't participating actively. They may either not be paying attention, be letting others think for them, be withholding dissenting views, or be afraid that by questioning the prevailing opinion, they will be admitting ignorance.

Strategy Five: Avoid Looking for the One Right Answer

Except for problems that can be solved by alogrithmic formulas, most problems we encounter have many workable solutions. A group's task, therefore, is not to look for a single right answer, but rather for a solution that is likely to work under the circumstances at hand. Waiting around for the one right answer causes frustration.

Sometimes a search for a single, right answer is a way of delaying the moment of truth when the group must present its decision for the final evaluation. Of course, any problem we try to solve could be solved better if only we had more of something—time, money, intelligence, support, information. You name it. In fact, however, the work of any individual or group cannot go on forever. Therefore, aim to make the best decision you can in the time and under the circumstances you're given.

Strategy Six: Work toward Achieving Consensus

Consensus is the process of agreeing on one solution among many alternatives, by discussing rather than voting. Voting ends discussion; working to achieve consensus encourages it. Voting either openly or secretly tends to cut short the necessary process of discovering subtle or ambiguous differences among the proposed solutions. Voting also tends to create factions whose members form loyalties toward each other rather than toward the group as a whole.

The process of reaching consensus depends on having all members of a group feel that they understand others' points of view. Members can communicate their understanding by matter-of-factly restating what they think the other positions are. While the solution that is finally chosen might not be the first choice of all group members, all participants can agree to support it. If participants believe that a solution is reached fairly in an open discussion, they are more likely to support it.

Strategy Seven: Develop a Work Plan

Once your group decides on an overall plan of action, you need to divide it into a series of tasks and set a deadline for each task. Divide the work fairly among the group members and write down the name of the person taking responsibility for completing each task. Work is usually divided according to group members' expertise or, in workplaces, according to each participant's position within the organization. Some groups are happier when routine jobs, such as typing, proofreading, telephoning, taking notes at meetings, and leading discussions are rotated.

No matter how you divide the work, however, allow plenty of time to implement your plan. Also end each meeting by making sure that all participants understand what they are to accomplish by the next meeting.

Strategy Eight: Appoint a Recorder for Each Meeting

At each group meeting someone needs to take notes during the discussion. That way the group is less likely to lose the ideas it generates. The group also needs to have someone record its final decisions. Sometimes it's useful to have all members write and then read what they understand the decision to be. The group can develop its consensus from these individual statements, and the recorder can write the consensus view that everyone agrees on. It's best for the recorder to write ideas as they are offered on a chalkboard or flipboard for everyone to see.

Because the recorder usually talks less than other members of the group, rotating this job allows equal participation.

Strategy Nine: Keep the Discussion on Track

To keep a project running smoothly, organizations that frequently produce collaboratively written documents can assign a project manager to oversee the writing process. Sometimes the manager is a skilled writer employed specifically to manage writing projects. Sometimes the manager is an administrator working on a particular team of employees from various departments within an organization. Whatever the case, these project managers have the authority to do what they must to keep meetings focused and moving toward the goal at hand.

What can you do in a classroom to keep your discussions on track? Since no one member of your peer group has administrative authority over the others, you can assign responsibility for leading each meeting on a rotating basis. For example, the recorder can double as time keeper. He or she can interrupt the discussion to review what still needs to be done and tell the group how much time is left. The recorder can also silence anyone dominating the discussion. For example, a recorder can say, "I already have a lot of your ideas on paper, Mike. I think Sarah wants to say something now." Be firm about keeping vociferous people under control.

If two or more people begin discussing something irrelevant among themselves, a recorder can ask them what their discussion has to do with the work at hand. Don't be embarrassed about reminding people that your deadline is approaching.

Another strategy for keeping the group on track is to appoint a project manager to see your work through from beginning to end. If possible, appoint someone who has taken management courses. A collaborative writing project gives this student a wonderful chance to put theoretical studies into practice.

Strategy Ten: Be Flexible

No one is perfect. Something usually goes wrong.

GENERATING IDEAS IN A GROUP

If your instructor has not assigned a specific group project for you to work on, the purpose of your first group meeting will be to generate ideas for what to do. If your instructor has assigned a particular project, the purpose of your first meeting will be to represent the problem you are solving and to pool ideas about the overall theme or concept for your project. For example, if your team is writing a computer manual, you will need to decide what kinds of information you want to highlight, what the overall tone of the writing should be, and what the manual should look like. That is, if your readers are not accustomed to using machines, you might suggest taking a humorous approach. You might also suggest emphasizing information about what to do when something goes wrong. Those suggestions contribute toward a decision about an overall concept.

Brainstorming sessions seem to work best when all members think about the issue at hand before the meeting, write their ideas on paper, and bring those papers to the meeting. That way, you can begin each session by having group members read their ideas in turn, as the recorder writes them on a chalkboard or flipboard. After everyone has spoken, you can begin a freewheeling discussion. Often the ideas members hear from their group stimulate still more ideas. Let them flow before you evaluate them.

A. F. Osborn[1] has developed some guidelines for successful brainstorming. The following guidelines have been adapted from his:

1   Rule out personal criticisms that focus on the writer rather than the document. (For example, don't say: "Ronnie, your work is careless." Say instead: "This needs to be proofread before we can turn it in.")

2   Rule out savage or demeaning language. (For example, don't say: "That illustration is terrible." Say instead: "That illustration seems too small to show me all the parts clearly. I think it would be more useful if it were larger. What do you think?")

3   Encourage freewheeling. (For example, don't say: "That's a ridiculous suggestion." Such criticisms restrain freewheeling. Say instead: "What are some other suggestions?")

4   Encourage quantity.

5   Build on suggestions offered by members of the group. Follow up on each other's ideas.

REVIEWING DRAFTS IN A GROUP

Once your group decides on an overall concept or approach to take, all members should compose drafts that interpret that concept in their own way. Do this work by yourselves. Then bring your rough drafts to the next group meeting. When you look over these drafts, you are likely to find a rich assortment of strategies for designing your document and presenting your message to readers. Your job will be to select workable ideas from the various drafts. Don't worry about fine-tuning language, graphics, or layout at this point. Read for ideas.

The following procedure can help you focus your attention on culling ideas as you review each other's drafts:

1   Appoint a recorder who will take notes during your discussion, report on the group's progress at the end of the meeting, and serve as time keeper and task keeper as you move along.

2   Form a circle and pass your draft to the person on your left. Continue passing the drafts around until everyone has looked at all of them.

3   Read each draft you receive, but don't make any changes on it. Instead, write your observations about it on a separate piece of paper. Do you see any differences in what the drafts say? What are the features of various drafts that you would like to incorporate in the final document? Does the group need to research anything or clarify any information before continuing?

4   Give everyone a chance to read their comments about the drafts. Remem-

[1]A. F. Osborn, *Applied Imagination* (Charles Scribner's Sons, New York: 1963).

ber, you are not trying to evaluate drafts to find the best one. Let everyone read before opening a free discussion. If new ideas occur to you while someone is speaking, write them down and suggest them after all participants have read their comments.

5 Discuss your various comments about the drafts as the recorder takes notes. Negotiate your differences until you can reach consensus about what strategies to use in your final document.

6 Decide how to divide the work of writing a test draft among members of the group. Realize that any plans you make at this point should be flexible.

7 Devise a work plan, agree on when to meet next, and restate what each person should accomplish by that time.

8 Review what you accomplished in your meeting. You can also discuss what was easy and what was difficult for you to do as a group.

The illustrations in Figures 15-2, 15-3, and 15-4 show you the various ideas for writing a manual of operating instructions for a microfilm reader that one group of students brought to their group meeting. After you consider them, you can compare them with the final copy in Figure 15-5. Notice how the students incorporated ideas from each other's drafts into their final version.

DESIGNING A FINAL DOCUMENT IN A GROUP

Once all the members of your group have collaborated their efforts to produce a test draft, you will need to review it together. This procedure works best when everyone has a copy of the draft in front of them. The purpose of this review is to decide how to revise the draft. You might be able to make these decisions in one meeting, or you might want to work up still another test draft and review it at another meeting.

The procedures for reviewing your test draft and moving it toward becoming the final document are listed below. They are designed to encourage you to come up with as many ideas as you can.

1 Appoint a recorder to take on the usual tasks.

2 Allow members of the group enough time to read and write comments about the draft on a separate piece of paper. If your test draft is for a set of instructions, see whether each member of the group can actually carry out the instructions and get the desired results.

3 Find the appropriate checklist in this book for writing the kind of document your group is working on, and refer to that list as you review the draft. A checklist appears at the end of Chapters 7, 10, and 13. In some cases, the "Reader Reviews" that appear in Chapters 7, 10, and 13 will be useful for this review step.

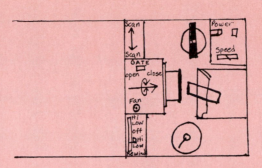

1. Load reel on lower spindle--film should
   be going clockwise.
2. Push power switch to ON position.
   —to prevent film reel from turning,
   move LOW SPEED ADJUST lever
   to SLOW
3. Push GATE switch to OPEN.
4. Feed film through (a) lower set of
   white rollers, (b) set of flat glasses,
   (c) upper set of white rollers,
   (d) blue TAKE UP REEL. (There
   is a slot in this reel for film
   to slide into.)
5. Push GATE switch to CLOSE.

Figure 15-2   First student's test draft.

4   Let all members read their comments on the test draft as the recorder
    writes them down in plain view.
5   When everyone has finished, comment on the reviews, add other sug-
    gestions, and identify what the group appears to believe the strong and
    weak points of the draft are.
6   Try to reach consensus on which features of the test draft should remain

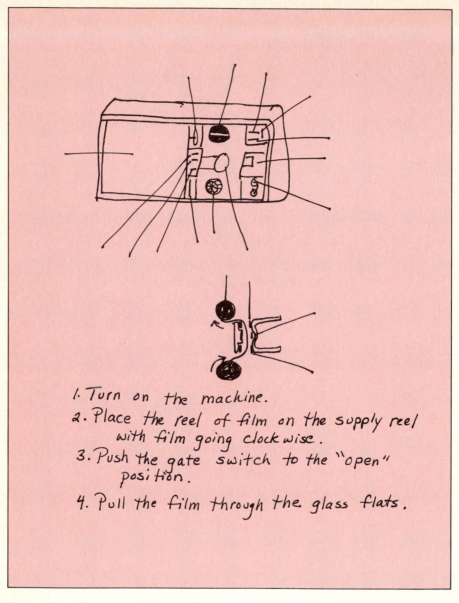

1. Turn on the machine.
2. Place the reel of film on the supply reel with film going clockwise.
3. Push the gate switch to the "open" position.
4. Pull the film through the glass flats.

Figure 15-3   Second student's test draft.

and which should be changed. Decide whether you need to do any further research before making these decisions.

7   Develop a list of what needs to be done next, who will do it, and when it will be done. How close are you to your deadline?

8   Have the recorder read back the decisions you have made during the meeting.

9   Make plans for final formatting and proofreading.

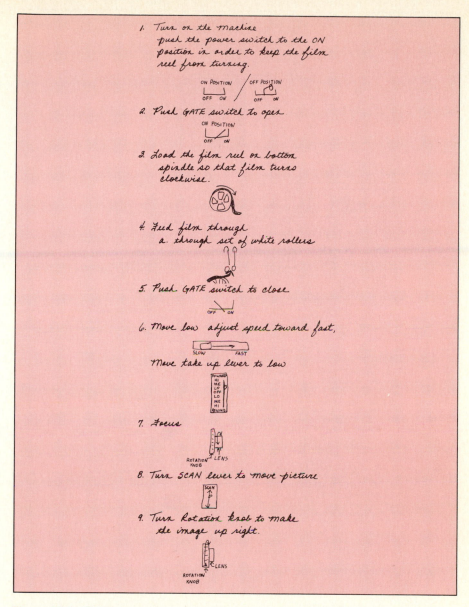

Figure 15-4   Third student's test draft.

In some classes, you might be able to engage a third-party review of your test draft. That review is useful because it gives you an outsider's view of your work. Third-party reviews can follow the same procedures for reviewing a test draft as the ones listed above.

In Figure 15-5, you can see a page from the finished manual of operating instructions that a group of students designed.

INSTRUCTIONS FOR OPERATING
THE MICROFILM READER

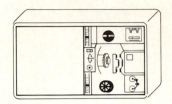

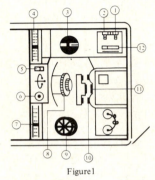

LIST OF FUNCTIONAL PARTS
(Figure 1)

1 Light Intensity Switch
2 Power Switch
3 Take Up Reel
4 Scan Lever
5 Gate Switch
6 Focus Knob
7 Take Up Lever
8 Image Rotation Knob
9 Supply Reel
10 Roller Guides
11 Glass Flats
12 Speed Adjustment Lever

Figure 1

** OPERATING INSTRUCTIONS **

(1) Load SUPPLY REEL (9) of microfilm on lower spindle. Film and reel should turn clockwise.

(2) Set SPEED ADJUSTMENT LEVER (12) to slow speed to prevent film reel from turning while you thread the film.

(3) Push POWER SWITCH (2) to ON position.

(4) Feed film through:

- LOWER ROLLER GUIDES (A)
- SET OF GLASS PLATES (B)
- UPPER ROLLER GUIDES (C)
- TAKE UP REEL (D)

as shown in Figure 2.

Figure 2

note: Slide the end of the film into the slot located on the TAKE UP REEL.

(5) Push GATE SWITCH (5) to "close."

(6) Move SPEED ADJUSTMENT LEVER (12) to "fast."

(7) Move TAKE UP LEVER (7) to "low."

(8) Turn FOCUS KNOB (6) to adjust the picture.

(9) Adjust the LIGHT INTENSITY SWITCH (1) to "high" or "low."

(10) To scan the image from left to right, slide the SCAN LEVER (4).

(11) If the image is not upright, turn the IMAGE ROTATION KNOB (8).

TO REWIND

Once you are finished viewing the microfilm, push the TAKE UP LEVER (7) to "low," "medium," or "high," and the film will rewind.

Figure 15-5   Final draft of the instructions.

PROJECTS AND EXERCISES

1　Working together in a small group, write a brief set of instructions, procedures, or directives for readers to use on your campus or at your place of work. To discover some ideas for your project, first turn to Chapter 9 to review the reasons organizations often need to develop procedural documents. Then think about what people on your campus or at your place of work need to know how to do. Can you write instructions or improve already published instructions on how to use a machine, how to register for or withdraw from courses, how to request travel funds, how to write a trip report, how to charter a campus organization, how to ask a faculty member for a letter of recommendation, or something else? Use the procedures outlined in this chapter as you decide on a project, devise a work plan, divide the labor, and draft and revise your procedural document.

2　Working as a group, substantially revise a set of poorly written instructions that accompany a product. Or write instructions for a product that does not provide them for consumers, but should. Before you decide on a strategy for presenting the instructions to your readers, identify the range of people who might use the product, their range of mechanical expertise, their levels of literacy, and the occasions people might use the product. Your instructor might bring in or suggest some products to use for this assignment.

3　Use the strategies for writing collaboratively described in this chapter to write one of the reports or proposals introduced in Section Five. Look both within each chapter and in the Projects and Exercises section at the end of chapters 12 and 13 for ideas.

4　Follow the procedures outlined on the following pages to write a set of instructions explaining how to disconnect an automobile horn when it gets stuck.

    (*a*)　Read the following article which explains to newspaper readers how they can disconnect the horn in their cars if it becomes stuck. Notice how the introduction, the organization of information, and the attitude of the writer toward the readers are appropriate for a newspaper article.

CARING FOR YOUR CAR

HOW TO STOP A HORN FROM BLOWING WHEN IT'S STUCK

By Ray Hill

You've probably heard it before—a horn that won't stop blowing on some unfortunate motorist's car. It's not a common problem. But it does happen. And if it happens to you, it can be embarrassing and annoying—not to mention loud.

If you know what to do, you can stop a stuck horn from blowing. Here's what you need to know:

When a horn won't stop blowing, the problem is usually caused by one of three things: the horn-ring switch in the steering wheel has remained closed, the horn relay has remained closed, or the horn wire that runs up the steering column has a break in the insulation and is touching bare metal. Probably the more common causes of the three are the relay or horn-ring switch.

The easiest way to stop a horn from blowing is to simply disconnect the horn wire. A wire attaches to the horn (the "Hot"wire), and the ground (which, basically, allows a complete electrical circuit) is where the horn bolts to the metal body of the automobile.

Pulling the horn wire from its connector is easy. Simply locate the horn (or horns, as the case may be), and pull the wire from its connector. Some cars have one horn—in which case you'll have to disconnect only one wire. Many cars have two horns. In this case you'll have to disconnect the wire from each horn.

Sometimes, though, it's difficult to reach the horn because of its location. The horn is generally located at the front of the car in the grill area. But it may defy a clean shot with your hand at the connecting wire. In any case, be sure the engine is off when you are searching for the horn—you don't want to get your fingers caught in any moving parts. Also be sure you don't have any jewelry on your fingers or wrists. And don't wear any clothing that might get snagged on a bolt or other protrusion.

If the horn is not easily accessible, another way to silence it while you collect your wits is to disconnect the negative battery cable. This eliminates the electrical source your horn is using for power.

Of course that means that you'll need a wrench to loosen and remove the battery cables (or pliers, with the spring-type battery-terminal connector). If you carry an adjustable wrench, pliers and a couple of screwdrivers as part of a small emergency tool-kit, you'll have no problem. If not, then you'll have to borrow a wrench or pliers.

The negative battery cable is marked, often with a minus sign or with an abbreviation, such as NEG.

After you have removed the negative battery cable, you can carefully work your hand into the area where the horn is and disconnect the horn wire. After the horn wire

(b) Form a small group with other members of you class and rewrite the information in the article for another audience, another purpose, and in a different format.

(c) Once you have formed groups, your instructor will assign each group an audience and a description of the use they will make of the instructions from columns A and B on the menu on the next page.

is disconnected, replace the negative battery cable and take the car to a garage to have a mechanic trouble-shoot it.

One difficulty with something like this, it's not the easiest problem in the world to trouble-shoot. Sometimes a sticking relay will come unstuck when its electrical power supply is cut off, as it is when you disconnect the battery cable. And after the power is turned on again, the horn may work normally for a while.

Or if the problem is caused by a bare wire that only occasionally rubs against metal, this, too, can be hard to trouble-shoot. The easiest problem to trouble-shoot is when the horn starts blowing as soon as the horn wire is reconnected. In this case the mechanic can find the problem quickly. A horn that sticks intermittently, though, can be a tough nut for the mechanic to crack. You can believe him when he tells you the problem took some time to solve.

From column C, your group will choose a presentation strategy that you decide best suits your readers and the use they will make of the instructions. As you work together, apply what you have learned about designing instructions for readers and about working together to meet goals.

When your group is ready to start, begin with the following steps:

1 Appoint a recorder for your group.
2 Appoint someone to read these instructions out loud and to read the newspaper article aloud.
3 Decide as a group how to write the best instructions you can in the time you are given. Decide which format and what organization and layout would work best for your readers and the use they will make of the instructions. Decide also whether you will include graphic elements.
4 Plan and prepare the drafts and finished instructions. Decide how you will divide the labor, devise a suitable work plan, and meet the deadline you have been given for turning in the manual.

Menu for Exercise 4

A Readers and Type of Document	B Readers' Use of Document	C Presentation Strategy
(1) High school students in a drivers' education class (a classroom hand-out)	(1) To be able to perform the task while looking at the instructions	(1) Narrative
		(2) Step-by-step list
		(3) Step-by-step list with graphics
(2) Owners of a particular make and model of an automobile (a page in an owner's manual)	(2) To be able to explain the task to someone else	(4) Question list
(3) Students in an auto mechanics class (a page in a reference manual)	(3) To be able to explain the instructions in writing on a test	(5) Flowchart
		(6) Other
(4) Women reading a popular self-help magazine aimed at female readers	(4) To be able to perform the task from memory	

SOME GRAB-BAG EXPRESSIONS TO AVOID

AVOID	USE
along the lines of	like
as of this date	today
at the present time	now
at this point in time	now
by means of	with, by
for the purpose of	for
for the reason that	since, because
in accordance with	according to
inasmuch as	to
in order to	to
in a position to	can, may
in the possession of	has, have
in a satisfactory manner	satisfactorily
in view of	like
in the nature of	if
in the event of	if
in connection with	of, in, on
in relation to	toward, to
in the amount of	for
on the basis of	by
on the grounds that	since, because
owing to the fact that	since, because
on the part of	by, among, for
on behalf of	for
prior to	before
subsequent to	after
with a view to	to
with reference to	about (or leave out)
with regard to	about (or leave out)
with the result that	so that

(Adapted by permission from Jefferson D. Bates, *Writing with Precision*, 3d ed., Washington, D.C.: Acropolis Books Ltd., 1983.)

APPENDIX B

GUIDELINES FOR AVOIDING BIASED LANGUAGE

As you write various kinds of documents in this course and in your writing on the job, use the following guidelines to help you avoid using biased language.

BIAS AGAINST MINORITY GROUPS

A minority group is one that differs in some respects from a larger or more dominant population. Minority groups include ethnic, cultural, national, religious, and what are sometimes loosely referred to as racial groups. Discrimination against these groups can manifest itself in many ways in both language and illustration. Some guidelines follow for avoiding bias against minority groups.

For example, when using terms to designate minority groups, try to be sensitive to the preferences of the groups themselves. This suggestion is sometimes difficult to follow, because the acceptability of a term can vary with time and place. The following list indicates terms that are currently acceptable, as well as some that are deprecated or questionable.

Commonly Encountered Minority-Group Designations

aborigine/aboriginal. Widely used to refer to the aboriginal peoples of Australia, although some prefer the term *Australian blacks.* Capitalization depends on whether the term is regarded as a proper name or a descriptive designation.

alien, resident alien. Acceptable when it refers to a non-U.S. citizen.

American. The use of the term *American* to refer to a citizen of the United States is acceptable. *United States citizen* is generally used when it is necessary to emphasize the distinction between a U.S. citizen and a citizen of, say, a South American country or Canada. Immigrant groups that have settled in the United States are described as *American* (as in *Irish-American*).

American of Hispanic background. See *Latin American.*

American policy, American economy. The terms *United States policy* and *United States economy* are preferable. (See also *we/our.*)

Amerind, Amerindian. Not recommended. The term *American Indian* or *Native American* is preferable.

Anglo-American. Not recommended. Use *English-speaking* or *white*, depending on what is meant.

Asian. Widely used to refer to various peoples from the Near and Far East. Acceptable, but be specific if possible (e.g., *Chinese, Japanese*). (See also *oriental.*)

black. Widely accepted. Like *white*, *black* is considered a generic or descriptive term and is therefore usually not capitalized. (Adapted by permission from Marie M. Longyear, Ed., *The McGraw-Hill Style Manual*, New York: McGraw-Hill Co., 1983.)

374

Boricua. Carib word for natives of Puerto Rico. Not recommended as an English-language substitute for *Puerto Rican.*

Chicano, Chicana. Often used by Mexican-American activists instead of *Mexican-American.*

coloured. Has application in South Africa for people of mixed African and other ancestry.

Cosa Nostra. Use *organized crime.*

English. Should be distinguished from *British* and *Briton.* Not everyone in Great Britain is English.

Eskimo. Widely used. However, the term *Innuit* (singular, *Innuk*) is preferred by Arctic and Canadian peoples and is often an acceptable alternative. These terms are sometimes spelled with one *n: Inuit, Inuk.*

ethnic, ethnics. Colloquialism. Usually refers to "new immigrant" nationalities from southern and eastern Europe, but may be applied to any group.

gringo. Colloquialism. Not recommended.

Hebrew. A language. Not acceptable for reference to a person or a religion, except in the context of ancient Israel.

Hispanic (adj.) See *Latin American.*

Hispanic-American. See *Latin American.*

Ibero-American. See *Latin American.*

Indian. The preferred term is *American Indian* or *Native American.* Acceptable when used to refer to an individual from India.

Irish-American, Italian-American, Polish-American, etc. Used in political and sociological writing to refer to people of foreign heritage who have settled in the United States.

Israeli. Citizen of Israel; not all Israelis are Jews.

Jew. Person whose religion or religious background is Jewish.

Latin American. There is wide confusion over what term to use when referring to Spanish- and Portuguese-speaking people in the Western Hemisphere. *Hispanic* is often used instead of *Latin American* in referring to residents of the United States who speak Spanish or are one or two generations removed from Spanish-speaking people from one of the Central American, South American, or Caribbean countries. However, some groups object to the term *Hispanic* on the grounds that it emphasizes a shared European cultural heritage rather than a shared new world cultural heritage. And certainly not all Spanish-speaking people from Central America, South America, or Caribbean countries are of Spanish descent. When possible, be specific.

    Some resent *Latin American,* saying it is insensitive to national differences; some find it inaccurate, since not all people referred to as Latin American speak a Latin-based language. Further, it usually does not include French speakers.

    Again, when possible, be specific. *Central American* or *South American* can also be used. *Latin American* is preferable to *Hispanic-American* (often used for Spanish speakers who have settled in the United States). *Ibero-American* is acceptable, but clumsy; use *Brazilian* instead of *Luso-American.*

Latino. Preferred by some groups to *Hispanic.*

Mafia. Use *organized crime.*

Mexican-American. Acceptable.

Mongoloid, Negroid, Caucasoid. Not recommended. The names from which these terms were derived—*Mongolian, Negro, Caucasian*—are no longer considered valid as terms for designating races. Further, *-oid* has a pejorative connotation.

mulatto. Not recommended. The term is from the Spanish *mulo,* ''mule,'' and is used to refer to a person of mixed ancestry. Use *person of mixed ancestry.*

Muslim, Moslem, Muhammadan. These terms refer to persons whose religion is Islam. *Muslim* is preferred in the United States. *Muhammadan* is not recommended. (Note that the term *Muslim* is not interchangeable with *Arab.*)

Native American. Preferred by some groups to *American Indian.* When this term is used with a lowercase *n,* it can refer to a person born in the United States (sometimes called a *native-born American*).

native peoples. Acceptable.

Negro. Acceptable in the appropriate historical context. Preferred by some groups to *black.*

North American. Acceptable.

oriental. Not recommended. Use *Asian,* or be specific.

Québecois, Quebecker, Quebecer. French speakers in Quebec prefer *Québecois;* English speakers in Quebec prefer *Quebeckers.* (*Quebecer,* occasionally used in the United States, can lead to mispronunciation.)

Scottish, Scots, Scotch. Scottish is the preferred adjective; use *Scots* for the people, *Scotch* for certain products or objects (such as whisky).

Spanish-speaking people. See *Latin American.*

third world. Often used to refer to developing countries, especially those not aligned with either the Soviet Union or the United States. In the United States, also used to refer to minority groups taken as a whole. Not recommended. If the term is used, care should be taken to make sure that the intended meaning is clear from the context in which it appears.

WASP. Colloquialism of limited application. Stands for ''white, Anglo-Saxon Protestant.''

we/our (when referring to the United States). Not recommended.

Gender-related bias

Sometimes called *sexism,* gender-related bias can occur in the form of attitudes and assumptions or as an outgrowth of our language itself, which has long used male terms to represent humankind in general. This discussion covers many of the problems associated with editing to eliminate sexism, whether in one's own writing or another's.

Sexist assumptions

Some authors ascribe maleness to general, non-gender-related terms such as *farmer* or *pioneer.* Consider this example:

> Wave after wave of immigrants arrived from Europe, bringing with them their wives and children.

This sentence implies that ''immigrants'' must be men (since immigrants have wives)—but what were the women and children if not immigrants themselves?

As recently as 1976, a book on the subject of good writing asked:

Who is this elusive creature, the reader? ... He is assailed on every side by forces competing for his time; by newspapers and magazines, by television and radio and stereo, by his wife and children and pets....

The author of this passage might be able to defend the use of *he* as a generic pronoun, but the reference to *his wife* is the giveaway—readers, to this writer, were male.

Stereotypes

Stereotyping ascribes certain characteristics to a group of people as a whole, often inaccurately and emotionally. The sexes are frequently stereotyped, girls being characterized as weak, frivolous, or timid; boys as strong, rational, or brave. Avoid the clichés that further such notions:

> The weaker sex
> Feminine intuition
> All brawn and no brains
> She thinks like a man

Also avoid gender epithets:

> Male nurse
> Lady doctor
> Woman anthropologist

Courtesy titles

Use a courtesy title with both male and female names or with neither:

Avoid: Schmidt and Mrs. Thatcher
Prefer: Helmut Schmidt and Margaret Thatcher
   Or: Mrs. Thatcher and Mr. Schmidt
   Or: Prime Minister Thatcher and Chancellor Schmidt
   Or: Schmidt and Thatcher

Ms. is an acceptable and useful designation in place of Miss or Mrs.

Anthropomorphic sexism

There is a tendency to ascribe dominant characteristics to the male of the species, whether biologically warranted or not:

> a bull seal watches over his harem. [Photo caption]

One might just as well say that the females had hired the bull as their bodyguard.

Sentimental feminine abstractions

Personifications of nature (e.g., ''Mother Earth'') generally do not belong in expository writing.

Avoid: The changing face of nature can never be understood unless her metabolism is also studied.
Prefer: The changing face of nature can never be understood unless its metabolism is also studied.

In nautical jargon, ships—even those with masculine names—are referred to as *she*, but the feminine pronoun should be avoided in other contexts:

Avoid: When the *Speedwell* proved unseaworthy, she was abandoned at Plymouth and the entire company crowded aboard the *Mayflower*.
Prefer: When the *Speedwell* proved unseaworthy, *it* was abandoned at Plymouth. . . .

Do not refer to countries as *she:*

Avoid: Romania had claimed the whole of the Banat as the price of her adherence to the Allied cause in 1916.
Prefer: Romania had claimed the whole of the Banat as the price of *its* adherence to the Allied cause in 1916.

Sexist language

Many people believe that the English language itself does much to shape attitudes and have suggested that the word ''man'' and the male pronouns ''he,'' ''him,'' and ''his'' be replaced in all generic senses. Whether such a radical change in the vernacular can ever be accomplished by willing it so is open to question. But wherever you stand on this issue, you should be aware that many people will assume that gender bias exists in writers who use ''man'' and masculine pronouns to refer to all humans.

Occupational titles

Except in a few firmly entrenched terms like ''actress'' and ''waitress,'' words or suffixes indicating gender are best avoided. Some representative occupational titles follow. A complete directory of job titles can be found in *Dictionary of Occupational Titles*, U.S. Department of Labor, Employment and Training Administration.

AVOID	PREFER
aviatrix	aviator
chairman	chairperson; chair
coed	student
delivery boy or man	deliverer
draftsman	drafter
fireman	fire fighter
foreman	supervisor
houseboy	house cleaner; housekeeper
housewife	homemaker
maid	house cleaner; housekeeper
poetess	poet
policeman; policewoman	police officer
postman	letter carrier; mail carrier
repairman	repairer
salesman	sales representative
sculptress	sculptor
usherette	usher

Avoiding generic male pronouns

Traditionally, male pronouns (he, him, his) have been used in English to represent the generic third person singular: "Everyone will turn in his assignment by Thursday." Avoiding such locutions can be time-consuming but is not as difficult as some people think. The simplest but least graceful way to eliminate a generic male pronoun is to change "he" to "he or she" (or "she or he"), which often leads to a clumsy retinue of "her or him," "his or hers," and "himself or herself." Consider this sentence:

When an adolescent starts to define himself as a person, he does so by separating his likes and dislikes from those of his parents.

Recast in a "he or she" mold, the sentence becomes ludicrous:

Poor: When an adolescent starts to define himself or herself as a person, he or she does so by separating his or her likes and dislikes from those of his or her parents.

Clearly, that won't do. With practice and a little care, however, one can apply some simple corrective methods to create an expository prose style that is neither sexist nor ungainly.

Before applying any of the following suggestions, think a passage through to the end. Otherwise you may find that your solution, which solved the problem so aptly at the start, no longer works at the end of the passage, causing you to go back and start over. And be sure to carry through. If you have changed "he" to "they," don't overlook the verb that needs correcting as well. The following paragraphs suggest several ways of recasting the same original sentence:

Original: When an investor buys common stock, he receives a certificate of ownership indicating the number of shares he purchased and their par value.

1 *Pluralize.* Pluralizing is often the best and easiest choice:

> When investors buy common stock, they receive a certificate of ownership indicating the number of shares they purchased and the par value of the shares.

The "adolescent" example lends itself admirably to this solution:

> When adolescents start to define themselves as persons, they do so by separating their likes and dislikes from those of their parents.

2 *Recast in the passive voice.* Don't be afraid of the passive voice. It need not produce tedious prose.

> When an investor buys common stock, a certificate of ownership is received . . . .

3 *Use "you."* Being informal and immediate, this works well in instructions, directives, and descriptions of processes:

> When you invest in common stock, you receive a certificate of ownership indicating the number of shares you purchased and their par value.

4 *Use "we."* This device also has an informal tone:

> When we invest in common stock, we receive a certificate of ownership indicating the number of shares we purchased . . . .

5 *Use "one."* Although *one* may sound stiff and formal in some contexts, it is often extremely useful:

> When one buys common stock, one receives a certificate of ownership indicating the number of shares purchased . . . .

(Note "one . . . *one*," not "one . . . *he*.")

6 *Use a relative pronoun.* Often overlooked, this construction can solve many wording problems:

An investor who buys common stock receives a certificate of ownership . . . .

7   *Use a participle.* A participle can serve the same function as the *who* construction:

An investor buying common stock receives a certificate of ownership . . . .

8   *Use "she or he" (or "he or she").* As noted above, this is the most obvious
solution, but it can also be the most inelegant and soporific:

Poor: When an investor buys common stock, he or she receives a certificate of
ownership indicating the number of shares he or she purchased and their
par value.

Reserve *he or she* for isolated occurrences.

9   *Recast without pronouns.* It's astonishing how expendable pronouns can be:

An investor in common stock receives a certificate of ownership indicating the number of shares purchased (or *that were* purchased) and their par
value.

10   *Repeat the noun.* Many writers are reluctant to resort to repetition, but the result
is not always inelegant:

When an investor buys common stock, the investor receives a certificate
of ownership . . . .

Overreliance on repetition, of course, can create leaden prose.

11   *Rephrase.* If all other attempts fail, rewrite the sentence. For example:

A certificate of ownership indicating the number of shares purchased and
their par value accompanies every purchase of common stock.

12   *Supply a qualifying statement.* Some writers object to changing generic male
pronouns. There are also subject areas in which the task proves very difficult.
For example, in a discussion of pediatric nursing, it may be expedient to call
the nurse "she" and the infant "he" throughout for clarity. In such instances,
include a statement in the preface or in a footnote calling attention to the fact
that the pronouns were chosen for the sake of convenience and are intended to
be universal.

Several of the foregoing methods can often be combined in what might be called a *mixture solution.*

Original:
By his fourth year, the child's phonological system approximates the model, and he usually corrects the remaining deviations by the time he enters school.

Mixed Solutions:
(1) By the fourth year (*elimination of pronoun*), the child's phonological system approximates the model, and the remaining deviations are usually corrected (*passive voice*) by the time the child (*repetition of noun*) enters school.

(2) Between the ages of three and four (*rephrasing*), the child's phonological system approximates the model, and the child (*repetition of noun*) usually corrects the remaining deviations before entering (*participle*) school.

Other solutions are possible as well. Needless to say, if you are editing someone else's work, the less drastic your revision the better.

BIAS AGAINST DISABLED PEOPLE

Most physically impaired people lead full and useful lives—as teachers, artists, workers, business executives, and parents. They should be fairly represented as integrated members of a larger community.

Discrimination against disabled people is sometimes called *handicapism.* The terms "handicapped person," "disabled person," and "exceptional person" are used interchangeably.

AGE BIAS

Like any other group, elderly people should be represented realistically, showing their diverse human qualities and their value as vital members of their communities.

Discrimination against old people is sometimes referred to as *ageism.*

APPENDIX C

DATA BASES AVAILABLE   October 1985

DATABASE	LABEL	PRODUCER	DESCRIPTION
MEDICINE/PHARMACOLOGY			
AGELINE*	AARP	The American Association of Retired Persons	Information on aging
COMBINED HEALTH INFORMATION DATABASE*	CHID	Combined Health Information Database	Health care
COMPREHENSIVE CORE MEDICAL LIBRARY●	CCML	Several major medical publishers	Full text of medical textbooks and journals
DRUG INFORMATION FULL TEXT●*	DIFT	American Society of Hospital Pharmacists	Full-text information on current and investigational drugs
EMBASE*	EMED	Elsevier Science Publishers	Biomedicine and health
HEALTH AUDIO-VISUAL ONLINE CATALOG	HAVC	Northeastern Ohio Universities	Audiovisual materials in medicine
HEALTH PLANNING AND ADMINISTRATION*	HLTH	National Library of Medicine (NLM)	Health economics, administration and planning
INTERNATIONAL PHARMA-CEUTICAL ABSTRACTS*	IPAB	American Society of Hospital Pharmacists	Pharmaceutical and drug-related information (left-hand truncation available)
IRCS MEDICAL SCIENCE DATABASE●	IRCS	IRCS Medical Science	Full-text biomedical research
MEDICAL/PSYCHOLOGICAL PREVIEWS*	PREV	BRS/Saunders	Current awareness for medical and psychology journals
MEDLINE (AND BACKFILES)*	MESH (MS78) (MS74) (MS70)	National Library of Medicine (NLM)	Medicine, nursing, dentistry (left-hand truncation available)
MEDLINE (CONCATENATED CURRENT & BACKFILES)*	MESZ	National Library of Medicine	Medicine, nursing, dentistry (left-hand truncation available)
NURSING & ALLIED HEALTH LITERATURE*	NAHL	CINAHL Corporation	Nursing and health care
PHYSICAL/APPLIED SCIENCES			
ACS JOURNALS ONLINE●*	CFTX	American Chemical Society	Chemistry, full-text coverage
CA SEARCH (AND BACKFILE)*	CHEM (CHEB)	Chemical Abstracts Service	Chemistry (left-hand truncation available)
COMPENDEX*	COMP	Engineering Information, Inc.	Engineering
HAZARDLINE●*	HZDB	Occupational Health Services, Inc.	Full-text, hazardous substance information
IHS VENDOR INFORMATION●	VEND	Information Handling Services	Vendor product information
INDUSTRY AND INTERNATIONAL STANDARDS	STDS	Information Handling Services	Engineering standards
INDUSTRY STANDARDS AND MILITARY SPECIFICATIONS	ISMS	Information Handling Services	Concatenated industry and military engineering standards
INSPEC (AND BACKFILE)*	INSP (INSB)	Institute of Electrical Engineers, London, England	Engineering, physics, and computer science
KIRK-OTHMER ENCYCLOPEDIA OF CHEMICAL TECHNOLOGY●*	KIRK	John Wiley & Sons, Inc.	Chemical technology, full-text coverage
MATHSCI*	MATH	American Mathematical Society	Mathematics, statistics, and computer science
MILITARY AND FEDERAL SPECIFICATIONS AND STANDARDS	MLSS	Information Handling Services	Military and federal specifications and standards
ONLINE MICROCOMPUTER SOFTWARE GUIDE AND DIRECTORY●	SOFT	Online, Inc.	Microcomputer software information
ROBOTICS INFORMATION*	RBOT	EIC/Intelligence, Inc.	Robotics
VOLUNTARY STANDARDS INFORMATION NETWORK	VSIN	Information Handling Services	Voluntary standards

(Used by permission from BRS Information Technologies.)

DATABASE	LABEL	PRODUCER	DESCRIPTION
LIFE SCIENCES			
AGRICOLA*	CAIN	National Agricultural Library (NAL)	Agriculture
BIOSIS PREVIEWS (AND BACKFILE)*	BIOL (BIOB)	BioSciences Information Service	Biological sciences
BIOSIS (MERGED)	BIOZ	BioSciences Information Services	Biological sciences
MERCK INDEX	MRCK	Merck & Company	Chemicals, drugs and substances of biological importance
POLLUTION ABSTRACTS*	POLL	Cambridge Scientific Abstracts	Pollution
BUSINESS			
ABI/INFORM*	INFO	Data Courier, Inc.	Business
ABSTRACTS OF WORKING PAPERS IN ECONOMICS*	AWPE	Cambridge University Press	Economics
BUSINESS SOFTWARE DATABASE*	BSOF	Data Courier, Inc.	Micro, minicomputer software products
CORPORATE AND INDUSTRY RESEARCH REPORTS ONLINE INDEX	CIRR	JA micropublishing inc.	Company and industry research reports and presentations
HARVARD BUSINESS REVIEW/ONLINE●*	HBRO	John Wiley & Sons, Inc.	Business and management
INDEX TO FROST & SULLIVAN MARKET RESEARCH REPORTS*	FSIS	Frost & Sullivan, Inc.	Market research information
INDUSTRY DATA SOURCES*	HARF	Information Access Co.	Industry Data
IRS PUBLICATIONS●	IRSP	Internal Revenue Service	Full text of IRS tax information publications
MANAGEMENT CONTENTS*	MGMT	Information Access Company	Business
PATDATA*	PATS	BRS	All patents registered through U.S. Patent Office
PREDICASTS ANNUAL REPORTS ABSTRACTS*	PTSA	Predicasts, Inc.	Company-specific business and economic information
PREDICASTS: PROMPT*/F&S INDEX* (CONCATENATED CURRENT* AND BACKFILE*)	PTSP PTSI (PTSL) (PTSB)	Predicasts, Inc.	Business and economics
TRADE AND INDUSTRY INDEX ™	BIZZ	Information Access Company	Developments in major industries
SOCIAL SCIENCES/HUMANITIES			
ABLEDATA	ABLE	National Rehabilitation Information Center	Rehabilitation products for the disabled
ALCOHOL USE/ABUSE*	HAZE	University of Minnesota College of Pharmacy	Alcoholism
ARTS AND HUMANITIES SEARCH*	AHCI	Institute for Scientific Information	Arts and humanities
CATALYST RESOURCES FOR WOMEN	CRFW	Catalyst Library	Current information on women and carrers
DRUGINFO*	DRSC	University of Minnesota College of Pharmacy	Drug abuse
DRUGINFO/ALCOHOL USE-ABUSE*	DRUG	University of Minnesota College of Pharmacy	Drug abuse and alcoholism
FAMILY RESOURCES*	NCFR	National Council on Family Relations	Marriage and family literature
LANGUAGE AND LANGUAGE BEHAVIOR ABSTRACTS*	LLBA	Sociological Abstracts	Language and linguistics
LEGAL RESOURCE INDEX ™	LAWS	Information Access Company	Legal reviews, journals
MENTAL MEASUREMENTS YEARBOOK●*	MMYD	Buros Institute of Mental Measurements	Standardized testing materials
NIMH*	NCMH	National Institute of Mental Health	Mental health and related information
PAIS INTERNATIONAL (PUBLIC AFFAIRS INFORMATION SERVICE)*	PAIS	Public Affairs Information Service	All social sciences
PSYCINFO*	PSYC	American Psychological Association	Psychology (left-hand truncation available)
REHABDATA*	NRIC	National Rehabilitation Center	Rehabilitation literature
RELIGION INDEX*	RELI	American Theological Library Association	Religion
SOCIAL SCISEARCH* (AND BACKFILE*)	SSCI (SSCB)	Institute for Scientific Information	Social science
SOCIAL SCISEARCH (MERGED)	SSCZ	Institute for Scientific Information	Social science
SOCIAL WORK ABSTRACTS	SWAB	National Association of Social Workers	Social work, related fields
SOCIOLOGICAL ABSTRACTS*	SOCA	Sociological Abstracts	Sociology and related disciplines

DATABASE	LABEL	PRODUCER	DESCRIPTION
EDUCATION			
BILINGUAL EDUCATION BIBIOGRAPHIC ABSTRACTS*	BEBA	National Clearinghouse for Bilingual Education	Bilingual/bicultural education
EDUCATIONAL TESTING SERVICE TEST COLLECTION*	ETSF	Educational Testing Service	Educational testing materials
ERIC*	ERIC	National Institute of Education	Education
EXCEPTIONAL CHILD EDUCATION RESOURCES*	ECER	Council for Exceptional Children	Exceptional child education
NATIONAL COLLEGE DATABANK™•*	PETE	Peterson's Guides, Inc.	College and university profiles
ONTARIO EDUCATION RESOURCES INFORMATION DATABASE	ONED	Ontario Ministry of Education	Educational research, reports, and curriculum guidelines
RESOURCE ORGANIZATIONS AND MEETINGS FOR EDUCATORS	ROME	National Center for Research in Vocational Education	Profiles and activities of educational groups
RESOURCES IN COMPUTER EDUCATION	RICE	Northwest Regional Educational Laboratory	Computer applications in education
RESOURCES IN VOCATIONAL EDUCATION	RIVE	National Center for Research in Vocational Education	Vocational education
SCHOOL PRACTICES INFORMATION FILE*	SPIF	BRS	Education programs, practices, and materials
TEXAS EDUCATION COMPUTER COOPERATIVE*	TECC	Texas Education Computer Cooperative	Evaluations of educational software
VOCATIONAL EDUCATION CURRICULUM MATERIALS	VECM	National Center for Research in Vocational Education	Vocational curriculum materials
REFERENCE/MULTIDISCIPLINARY			
ABSTRAX 400*	A400	Information Sources, Ltd.	Abstracts of popular periodical literature
ACADEMIC AMERICAN ENCYCLOPEDIA DATABASE•	AAED	Grolier Electronic Publishing, Inc.	Multi-disciplinary encyclopedia
ACS DIRECTORY OF GRADUATE RESEARCH•*	DGRF	American Chemical Society	University chemistry-related departments and faculty
AMERICAN MEN AND WOMEN OF SCIENCE•*	MWSC	R.R. Bowker	Directory of scientists
ASSOCIATIONS PUBLICATIONS IN PRINT	APIP	R.R. Bowker	Association literature
BOOKS IN PRINT*	BBIP	R.R. Bowker	U.S. books in print
BOOKSINFO*	BOOK	Brodart, Inc.	800,000 books in print
CALIFORNIA UNION LIST OF PERIODICALS*	CULP	California Library Authority for Systems and Services (CLASS)	California periodicals holdings
CROSS*	CROS	BRS	Cross-file searching
DISSERTATION ABSTRACTS ONLINE	DISS	University Microfilms	Multi-disciplinary
FILE*	FILE	BRS	BRS database directory
GPO MONTHLY CATALOG*	GPOM	U.S. Government Printing Office	Government publications
KNOWLEDGE INDUSTRY PUBLICATIONS DATABASE	KIPD	Knowledge Industry Publications, Inc.	Publicly available databases
MAGAZINE INDEX™	MAGS	Information Access Company	General interest magazines
NATIONAL NEWSPAPER INDEX™	NOOZ	Information Access Company	Five major American newspapers
NEWS*	NEWS	BRS	System update file
NTIS*	NTIS	National Technical Information Service	Government reports, all areas
OCLC EASI REFERENCE	OCLC	Online Computer Library Center, Inc.	OCLC Online Union Catalog subset
SPORT DATABASE*	SFDB	Sport Information Resource Centre	Sport, fitness, recreation, sports medicine
SUPERINDEX•*	SUPE	Superindex, Inc.	Science, medicine, technology, and engineering
TERM*	TERM	BRS	Social science thesauri
ULRICH'S INTERNATIONAL*	ULRI	R.R. Bowker	Directory of periodicals
UMI ARTICLE CLEARINGHOUSE*	UMAC	UMI Article Clearinghouse	UMI document delivery information

*These databases are available to library schools via BBS/Instructor.
•These databases are full text.

FOR FURTHER READING

CONTEXTS FOR WORKING AND WRITING IN ORGANIZATIONS

Aldrich, Pearl G. "Adult Writers: Some Reasons for Ineffective Writing on the Job." *College Composition and Communication*, 33 (1982), 284–287.

Bataille, Robert T. "Writing in the World of Work: What Our Graduates Report," *College Composition and Communication*, 33 (1982), 276–280.

Faigley, Lester and Thomas P. Miller. "What We Learn from Writing on the Job," *College English*, 44 (1982), 557–569.

Goswami, Dixie, et al. *Writing in the Professions*, American Institutes for Research, Washington, D.C., 1981.

Odell, Lee and Dixie Goswami. *Writing in Nonacademic Settings*, Guilford Publications, Inc., New York, 1986.

Terkel, Studs. *Working*, Avon, New York, 1975.

PROBLEM-SOLVING

Flower, Linda. *Problem-Solving Strategies for Writing*, 2d ed., Harcourt Brace Jovanovich, New York, 1985.

Hayes, John R. *The Complete Problem Solver*, The Franklin Institute Press, Philadelphia, 1981. [See also "Collaborative Working and Writing"]

PROCESSES
Overviews of Composing

Cooper, Charles R. and Lee Odell. *Research on Composing: Points of Departure*. National Council of Teachers of English, Urbana, Ill., 1978.

Flower, Linda S. and John R. Hayes. "The Dynamics of Composing: Making Plans and Juggling Constraints," in Lee W. Gregg and Erwin R. Steinberg (eds.), *Cognitive Processes in Writing*, Lawrence Erlbaum Associates, Hillsdale, N.J., 1980, pp. 31–50.

Flower, Linda S. and John R. Hayes. "Problem-Solving Strategies and the Writing Process," *College English*, 39 (1977), 449–461.

Hairston, Maxine. "The Winds of Change: Thomas Kuhn and the Revolution in the Teaching of Writing," *College Composition and Communication*, 33 (1982), 76–88.

Halpern Jeanne W. "Teaching the Processes of Business Writing," in Jeanne W. Halpern (ed.), *Teaching Business Writing: Approaches, Plans, Pedagogy, Research*, American Business Communication Association, University of Illinois at Urbana-Champaign, 1983, pp. 21–36.

Hayes, John R. and Linda S. Flower. "Identifying the Organization of Writing Processes," in Lee W. Gregg and Erwin R. Steinberg (eds.), *Cognitive Processes in Writing*, Lawrence Erlbaum Associates, Hillsdale, N.J., 1980, pp. 3–30.

Murray, Donald M. *Write to Learn*, Holt, Rinehart & Winston, New York, 1984.

Selzer, Jack. "Exploring Options in Composing," *College Composition and Communication*, 35 (1984), 276–284.

Young, Richard E. "Concepts of Art and the Teaching of Writing," in James J. Murphy (ed.) *The Rhetorical Tradition and Modern Writing*, The Modern Language Association of America, New York, 1982, pp. 130–141.

Young, Richard E. et al. *Rhetoric: Discovery and Change*, Harcourt, Brace World, New York, 1970.

Revision

Flower, Linda. "Writer-Based Prose: A Cognitive Basis for Problems in Writing," *College English*, 41 (1979), 19–37.

Flower, Linda S., et al. *Revising Functional Documents: The Scenario Principle*, Document Design Project, Technical Report No. 10, American Institutes for Research, Washington, D.C., 1980.

Lanham, Richard A. *Revising Business Prose*, Charles Scribner's Sons, New York, 1981.

Sommers, Nancy. "Revision Strategies of Student Writers and Experienced Adult Writers," *College Composition and Communication*, 31 (1980), 378–388.

Style and Cohesion

Bates, Jefferson D. *Writing with Precision*, 3d ed., Acropolis Books, Washington, D.C.: 1983.

Halliday, M. A. K. and Ruqaiya Hasan. *Cohesion in English*, Longman, London, 1976.

Markels, Robin Bell. *A New Perspective on Cohesion in Expository Paragraphs*, Southern Illinois University Press, Carbondale and Edwardsville, Ill., 1984.

Strunk, William and E. B. White. *The Elements of Style*, 3d ed., Macmillan, New York, 1979.

Sudol, Ronald A. (ed.), *Revising: New Essays for Teachers of Writing*, National Council of Teachers of English, Urbana, Ill., 1982.

Williams, Joseph M. *Style: Ten Lessons in Clarity and Grace*, 2d ed., Scott, Foresman and Company, Glenview, Ill., 1985.

Zinsser, William. *On Writing Well: An Informal Guide to Writing Non-Fiction*, 2d ed., Harper & Row, New York, 1980.

Dictation

Gould, John D. "Experiments on Composing Letters: Some Facts, Some Myths, and Some Observations," Lee W. Gregg and Erwin Steinberg (eds.), *Cognitive Processes in Writing*, Lawrence Erlbaum Associates, Hillsdale, N.J., 1980, pp. 97–127.

Gould, John D. "How Experts Dictate," *Journal of Experimental Psychology: Human Perception and Performance*, 4 (1978), 648–661.

Computers and Composing

Halpern, Jeanne W. and Sarah Liggett. *Computers and Composing: How the New Technologies Are Changing Writing*, Carbondale and Edwardsville: Southern Illinois University Press, 1984.

SPECIAL ISSUES
Document Design

Felker, Daniel B. (ed.), *Document Design: A Review of the Relevant Research*, American
Institute for Research, Washington, D.C., 1980.
Felker, Daniel B., et al. *Guidelines for Document Designers* (pamphlet), American Institute
for Research, Washington, D.C., November 1981.
Jonassen, David H. *The Technology of Text: Principles for Structuring, Designing, and
Displaying Text*, Educational Technology Publications, Englewood Cliffs, N.J.,
1982.
Simply Stated (formerly called *Fine Print*, 1980), American Institutes for Research, Wash-
ington, D.C.

Writing Reports and Proposals

Holtz, H. and T. Schmidt. *The Winning Proposal: How to Write It*, McGraw-Hill, N.Y.,
1981.
Iacone, Salvatore J. *Modern Business Report Writing*, Macmillan, New York, 1985.
Lewis, Phillip V. and William H. Baker. *Business Report Writing*, 2d ed., Grid Publishing,
Columbus, Ohio, 1983.
Mathes, J.C. and Dwight Stevenson. *Designing Technical Reports: Writing for Audiences
in Organizations*, Bobbs Merrill, Indianapolis, 1976.
Stewart, Rodney D. and Ann L. Stewart. *Proposal Preparation*, A Wiley-Interscience Pub-
lication, John Wiley & Sons, New York, 1984.

Writing Questionnaires

Babbie, Earl. *The Practice of Social Research*, 3d ed., Wadsworth Publishing, Belmont,
Calif., 1983.
Sudman, Seymour and Norman M. Bradborn. *Asking Questions*, Jossey-Bass, San Fran-
cisco, 1982.

Writing Abstracts

Cremmins, Edwards T. *The Art of Abstracting*, ISI Press, Philadelphia, 1982.
Guinn, Dorothy Margaret, ''Composing an Abstract: A Practical Heuristic,'' *College Composition and Communication*, 30 (1979), 380–383.

Making Spoken Presentations

Applbaum, Ronald L. and Karl W. E. Anatol. *Effective Oral Communication for Business
and the Professions*, Science Research Associates, Chicago, 1982.
Kroll, Barry M. and Roberta J. Vann (eds.). *Exploring Speaking-Writing Relationships:
Connections and Contrasts*, National Council of Teachers of English, Urbana, Ill.,
1981.

Developing Arguments

Corbett, Edward P. J. *Classical Rhetoric for the Modern Student*, 2d ed., Oxford University Press, New York, 1971.

Flower, Linda S. "Teaching a Rhetorical Case," in Jeanne W. Halpern (ed.), *Teaching Business Writing: Approaches, Plans, Pedagogy, Research*, American Business Communication Association, University of Illinois at Urbana-Champaign, 1983, pp. 115–128.

Hairston, Maxine. *A Contemporary Rhetoric*, 3d ed., Houghton Mifflin Co., Boston, 1982.

Kinneavy, James L. *A Theory of Discourse*, Prentice Hall, Englewood Cliffs, N.J., 1971; rpt. W. W. Norton, 1980.

Lunsford, Andrea A. "Aristotelian vs. Rogerian Argument: A Reassessment," *College Composition and Communication*, 30 (1979), 146–151.

Selzer, Jack. "Emphasizing Rhetorical Principles in Business Writing," in Jeanne W. Halpern (ed.), *Teaching Business Writing: Approaches, Plans, Pedagogy, Research*, American Business Communication Association, University of Illinois at Urbana-Champaign, 1983, pp. 3–20.

Toulmin, Stephen. *Uses of Argument*, Cambridge University Press, New York, 1958.

Toulmin, Stephen, Richard Rieke, and Allen Janik. *An Introduction to Reasoning*, Macmillan, New York, 1979.

COLLABORATIVE WORKING AND WRITING

Bruffee, Kenneth A. *A Short Course in Writing*, 2d ed., Winthrop, Cambridge, Mass., 1980, pp. 103–134.

Elbow, Peter. *Writing Without Teachers*, Oxford University Press, New York, 1973.

Janis, Irving L. "Groupthink," *Psychology Today*, November 1971, p. 43 ff.

Myers, Michele Tolela and Gail E. Myers. *Managing by Communication: An Organizational Approach*, McGraw-Hill, New York, 1982.

Osborn, A. F. *Applied Imagination*, Charles Scribner's Sons, New York, 1963.

Ouchi, William. *Theory Z: How American Business Can Meet the Japanese Challenge*, Addison-Wesley, Reading, Mass., 1981.

Peters, Thomas J. and Robert H. Waterman, Jr. *In Search of Excellence: Lessons from America's Best-Run Companies*, Harper & Row, New York, 1982.

Schmuck, Richard A., et al. *Handbook of Organizational Development*, National Press Books, Palo Alto, 1972.

Schmuck, Richard A. and Patricia A. Schmuck. *Group Processes in the Classroom*, 2d ed., University of Oregon, Eugene, 1975.

HANDBOOKS

Brusaw, Charles T., et al. *Handbook of Business Writing*, 2d ed., St. Martin's Press, New York, 1982.

Brusaw, Charles T., et al. *Handbook of Technical Writing*, St. Martin's Press, New York, 1982.

Moyer, Ruth, et al. *The Research and Report Handbook for Business, Industry, and Government*, Student ed., John Wiley & Sons, New York, 1981.

INDEX

Memos:
  checklist for, 171
  closing for, 161–162
  definition of, 114
  drafting, 153–162
    examples of, 50–53, 161
  editing, 162–163, 185
    example of, 333
  format for, examples of, 169–170
  for gathering and communicating
      information, example of, 336
  getting started, 149–152
  kinds of: directive, examples of, 199, 214,
      217, 220
    documentary, 126–127
      example of, 127
    goodwill, 118–119
      example of, 119
    inquiry, example of, 180
    instructional, 130–132
      examples of, 133, 153
    periodic report, 257–258
      example of, 258
    progress, 129–130
      example of, 130
    response (reply), example of, 180
    transmittal, 346
      example of, 347
    unsolicited proposal, 267–275
      example of, 275
  openings for, 155–157
  parts of, examples of, 169, 170
  problems solved by, 115
  proofreading, 170
  purposes of, 116–117
  revising, 162–163
Methods, section of report, 266
  example of, 268
Minutes of monthly meeting, 260
  example of, 261
Models:
  as heuristic for writing, 42, 149–150
  for problem-solving (see Problem-solving)
Modified block format, 163
  example of, 166
Monitoring reports, 302

Narration:
  as heuristic for writing, 44
  as strategy for arrangements (see
      Arrangement, strategies for)
Notes in instructions, 196

Notetaking, 294–296
  from interview, 337
    use of, example of, 334
  from observations, example of, 333
  from survey, 337
  (See also Interviews; Questionnaires;
      Telephone survey)
Numbering graphic elements, 104–105
Numbers:
  accuracy of, 75
  and cohesion, 64
  as highlighting technique, 85, 89, 168
    example of, 89
  in parts of correspondence, 163, 168
  as strategy for arrangement, 131, 196, 202

Operators in defining a problem, definition of,
    25
Oral reports (see Spoken presentations)
Organization:
  definition of, 5
  of a document (see Arrangement)
Organization chart, example of, 94
Organizational records, 282–283
Organizational setting for writing, 5
Organizational writing:
  definition of, 5
  general features of, 13–15
  kinds and purposes of, 12
Osborn, A. F., 363
Ouchi, William, 357
Outlines:
  branching, 60–61, 305
  conventional, 61, 305
  descriptive, 59–60, 150, 305, 345–346
  expanded, 153
    example of, 158
  as strategy for revising documents, 59–61,
      305–306
    example of, 60

Pagination of proposal or report, 307–312
Paraphrasing, 299–300
Persuasion, 132–142
  emotional appeal, 135
  ethical appeal, 135
  logical appeal, 134
  Rogerian strategy, 136
Peters, Thomas J., 357
Photographs, 91–92
  example of, 31